Principles of Accounting
Study Guide and Selected Readings
Second Edition

Principles of Accounting

Study Guide and Selected Readings

Second Edition

Belverd E. Needles, Jr.
DePaul University

Edward H. Julius
California Lutheran College

Houghton Mifflin Company   **Boston**
Dallas   Geneva, Illinois   Hopewell, New Jersey   Palo Alto

Cover photograph by Dave Wade

Printed in the U.S.A.

Library of Congress Catalog Card Number 83–80989

ISBN: 0-395-34332-I

ABCDEFGHIJ-M-89876543

Contents

To The Student

This self-study guide is designed to help you improve your performance in your first accounting course. You should use it in your study of *Principles of Accounting*, Second Edition, by Needles, Anderson, and Caldwell.

Reviewing the Chapter

This section of each chapter summarizes in a concise but thorough manner the essential points related to the chapter's learning objectives. All key terms are covered in this section or in the Testing Your Knowledge section.

Testing Your Knowledge

Each chapter contains a matching quiz of key terms, a completion exercise, true-false questions, and multiple-choice questions to test your understanding of the learning objectives and vocabulary of the chapter. Every second chapter includes a crossword puzzle to test your knowledge of key terms.

Applying Your Knowledge

An important goal in learning accounting is the ability to work exercises and problems. In this section of each chapter, you can test your ability to make two or three of the most important applications in the chapter.

Readings

Most chapters include one or two current readings to provide you with a broader understanding of the accounting profession, careers in all fields of accounting, and current issues in areas such as inflation accounting, international accounting, and the conceptual framework of the Financial Accounting Standards Board.

Specimen Financial Statements

The complete annual financial report for The Coca-Cola Company is reproduced for your reference throughout the course. This financial report contains the financial statements and all related notes and other financial information made available to the company's stockholders and others interested in Coca-Cola's financial performance and status.

Review of Financial Accounting Theory

Because it is sometimes difficult in the first accounting course to see where all the parts fit in, an overview of accounting theory is presented as a separate section at the end of the study guide.

The study guide concludes with answers to all questions, exercises, problems, and crossword puzzles.

B.E.N.
E.H.J.

Chapter Reviews,
Questions,
and
Readings

Chapter One

Accounting in Business and Society

Reviewing the Chapter

1. Making a decision involves (a) setting a goal, (b) considering alternatives, (c) making the actual decision, (d) taking action, and (e) using feedback to evaluate the results. Accounting assists in planning, control, and evaluation by providing useful financial information to the decision maker. **Planning** involves setting a course of action. **Control** is the process of comparing actual operations with planned operations. And **evaluation** is the process of studying the decision system to improve it.

2. **Accounting** is an information system that measures, processes, and communicates financial information. **Bookkeeping**, a small but important aspect of accounting, is the mechanical and repetitive record-keeping process. A distinction is usually made between **management accounting**, which focuses on information for internal users, and **financial accounting**, which involves the preparation, reporting, analysis, and interpretation of accounting information in reports for external users.

3. The **computer** is an electronic tool that rapidly collects, organizes, and communicates vast amounts of information. The computer does not take the place of the accountant. However, the accountant must understand how it operates since it is an integral part of the accounting information system.

4. A **management information system (MIS)** is an information network that takes in all major functions of a business, called subsystems. The accounting information system is the financial hub of the management information system.

5. There are basically three groups that use accounting information: management, financially interested outsiders, and government and citizen groups with an indirect financial interest in the business.

   a. For a business to survive, **management** must make a satisfactory profit to hold investor capital (called **profitability**) and must keep sufficient funds on hand to pay debts as they fall due (called **liquidity**). The company will have other goals, such as improving its products and expanding operations. It is management that directs the company toward these goals by making decisions.

   b. Most businesses publish financial statements that report the profitability and financial position of the company. Potential investors use these financial statements to assess the strength or weakness of the company. Financial statements are also examined by potential creditors to determine the company's ability to repay a loan.

c. Society as a whole, through its government and citizen groups, also makes use of financial information. Society's interest is represented by taxing authorities, regulatory agencies, economic planners, and citizen groups.

6. The accounting profession can be divided into four broad fields: management accounting, public accounting, government and other nonprofit accounting, and accounting education.

7. An accountant employed by a business is said to be in **management accounting**. Though decision making is the function of management, the management accountant must first provide relevant data and then help management make the best decision. Specific activities of management accountants include general accounting, cost accounting, budgeting, tax accounting, information systems design, and internal auditing.

8. **Public accounting** is a profession that has gained the same stature as law and medicine. **Certified public accountants (CPAs)** are accountants licensed by the state. To become a licensed CPA, one must pass the uniform CPA exam and meet educational and experience requirements. CPAs perform a number of services, most of which are classified as auditing, tax services, management advisory services, or small business services.

a. An auditor is a public accountant brought in to give an independent professional opinion as to whether a company's financial statements fairly show its financial position and operating results. **Auditing**, or the attest function, makes it possible for users to depend on the statements as a basis for their decisions. The auditor must, of course, gather together sufficient evidence before he or she can give an opinion.

b. Public accountants perform **tax services** by preparing tax returns, making sure of compliance with tax laws, and bringing tax considerations into the decision-making process.

c. **Management advisory services** consist of any recommendations that the public accountant can make to improve a company's operations.

d. Many CPA firms offer **small business services**. In this area they provide such services as setting up an accounting system and preparing financial statements.

9. Nonprofit accounting is practiced by thousands of accountants in various capacities. Here, accountants are concerned, not with profitability, but with the proper and efficient use of public resources. For example, government accountants prepare financial reports and audit tax returns for many agencies, such as the Federal Bureau of Investigation, the Internal Revenue Service, the General Accounting Office, the Securities and Exchange Commission, the Interstate Commerce Commission, and the Federal Communications Commission. Hospitals, colleges, foundations, and other nonprofit organizations also employ accountants. When accountants are hired to judge the impact of government and other human service programs, they are doing **social accounting**. These programs deal with such concerns as welfare, housing, education, and pollution.

10. Accounting instructors are needed in both secondary schools and colleges. In either setting they need to meet certain educational qualifications.

11. The three basic forms of business organization are sole proprietorships, partnerships, and corporations. Accountants recognize each form as an economic unit separate from its owners.

a. A **sole proprietorship** is a business owned and managed by one person. The owner receives all profits, absorbs all losses, and is personally liable for all debts of the business.

b. A **partnership** is a business owned and managed by two or more persons. The owners divide profits and losses according to a predetermined ratio, and each is personally liable for all debts of the business.

c. A **corporation** is a business owned by

stockholders but managed by a board of directors. Each stockholder is liable only to the extent of his or her investment, and ownership can be transferred without affecting operations.

12. **Accounting theory** provides the reasoning behind and framework for **accounting practice. Generally accepted accounting principles (GAAP)** are the set of guidelines and procedures that constitute acceptable accounting practice at a given point in time. The set of GAAP changes continually as business conditions change and practices improve.

13. The **American Institute of Certified Public Accountants (AICPA)** is the professional association of CPAs. It was instrumental in developing GAAP, mainly through the Accounting Principles Board (APB), from 1959 to 1973.

14. In 1973, the **Financial Accounting Standards Board (FASB)** succeeded the Accounting Principles Board as the authoritative body in the development of GAAP. This group is separate from the AICPA and issues Statements of Financial Accounting Standards.

15. The **Securities and Exchange Commission (SEC)** is an agency of the federal government. It has the legal power to set and enforce accounting practice for companies that are required to report to it. Generally, these are companies whose securities are traded by the general public.

16. The **Internal Revenue Service (IRS)** enforces and interprets the set of rules that govern the assessment and collection of federal income taxes.

17. The **Government Accounting Standards Board (GASB)** was established in 1983 and is responsible for issuing accounting standards for state and local governments.

18. International accounting organizations include the International Accounting Standards Committee (IASC) and the International Federation of Accountants (IFAC), which was formed in 1977.

19. There are other organizations of accountants besides the AICPA. The National Association of Accountants (NAA) was organized to deal with cost and managerial accounting, the Financial Executives Institute (FEI) is interested primarily in financial accounting, and the American Accounting Association (AAA) is concerned chiefly with accounting education and accounting theory.

Testing Your Knowledge

Matching

Match each term with its definition by writing the appropriate letter in the blank.

M   1. Accounting
C   2. Bookkeeping
Q   3. Computer
H   4. Management information system
L   5. Management
D   6. Financial statements
G   7. Management accounting
O   8. Public accounting
P   9. Nonprofit accounting
N   10. Certified public accountant
I   11. Auditing
K   12. Sole proprietorship
B   13. Partnership
F   14. Corporation
E   15. Generally accepted accounting principles
A   16. AICPA
J   17. FASB

a. The professional organization of CPAs
b. A business owned and managed by two or more persons
c. The repetitive record-keeping process
d. Periodic reports on the profitability and financial position of a company
e. The guidelines that define acceptable accounting practice at a given point in time
f. A business owned by stockholders but managed by a board of directors
g. The branch of accounting concerned with providing managers with financial information needed to make decisions
h. The information network that links a company's functions together
i. Examining a company to express an opinion about its financial statements
j. The authoritative body that currently establishes accounting principles
k. A business owned and managed by one person
l. A company's decision makers
m. An information system that measures, processes, and communicates economic information
n. An expert accountant licensed by the state
o. The branch of accounting that deals with auditing, taxes, and management advisory services
p. Accounting for hospitals, colleges, and government
q. An electronic tool that rapidly processes information

Completion

Use the lines provided to complete each item.

1. The accounting profession encompasses four broad fields. List them.

Management acctg
Public acctg.
Non profit acctg.
Acctg Education

2. What five steps should be followed in making a decision?

Set a goal
Consider alternatives
Select alternative
Take action
Evaluate - feedback

3. Briefly distinguish between bookkeeping and accounting.

Bookkeeping - small repetitive record keeping part; Acctg. - information system that measures, processes & communicates financial info.

4. List the three areas of specialization in public accounting.

Auditing
Tax preparing - services
Mgnt. advisory

5. What three broad groups use accounting information?

Mgnt.
financially interested outsiders - direct
Govt. + citizen groups - indirect

6. What two objectives must be met for a company to survive?

Profitability
Liquity

True-False

Circle T if the statement is true, F if it is false.

T F 1. Bookkeeping is only one aspect of accounting.

T **F** 2. A corporation is managed directly by its stockholders.

T **F** 3. Internal auditing is a service provided by public accounting.

T **F** 4. An auditor expresses his or her opinion as to whether a company is a good investment.

T F 5. Generally accepted accounting principles are not like laws of math and science; they are guidelines which define correct accounting practice at the time.

T F 6. An accountant provides information to management, which then makes decisions.

T F 7. The financial reports that direct management's attention to problem areas are examples of control information.

T **F** 8. The attest function has to do with the work of a cost accountant.

T **F** 9. The FASB is a branch of the IRS.

T F 10. A management information system deals with other activities of a business besides accounting.

T **F** 11. Accounting practice has changed very little in recent years.

T F 12. A sole proprietor is personally liable for all debts of a business.

T F 13. Generally, a partner risks more than just the amount of his or her investment.

T F 14. Liquidity refers to the ability to pay debts when they fall due.

Multiple-Choice

Circle the letter of the best answer.

1. Which of the following is *not* a facet of management accounting?
   a. Budgeting
   b. Public accounting
   c. Information systems design
   d. Cost accounting

2. Companies whose stock is publicly traded must file financial statements with the
   a. FASB.
   b. APB.
   c. SEC.
   d. AICPA.

3. Generally accepted accounting principles
   a. have eliminated all the weaknesses in accounting practice.
   b. are accounting rules formulated by the NAA.
   c. are sound in theory, but rarely used in practice.
   d. are changing continually.

4. The current authoritative body dictating accounting practice is the
   a. FASB.
   b. APB.
   c. SEC.
   d. AICPA.

5. One characteristic of a corporation is
   a. unlimited liability of its owners.
   b. the ease with which ownership is transferred.
   c. ownership by the board of directors.
   d. dissolution upon the death of an owner.

6. Which of the following groups uses accounting information primarily to help protect the public?
   a. Taxing authorities
   b. The American Accounting Association
   c. Regulatory agencies
   d. Internal auditors

7. In a partnership,
   a. profits are always divided equally among partners.
   b. management consists of the board of directors.
   c. no partner is liable for more than a proportion of the company's debts.
   d. dissolution results when any partner leaves the partnership.

8. The principal purpose of an audit by a CPA is to
   a. express an opinion on the fairness of a company's financial statements.
   b. detect fraud by a company's employees.
   c. prepare the company's financial statements.
   d. assure investors that the company will be profitable in the future.

Applying Your Knowledge

Exercise

1. Lindlay Steel Company always publishes annual financial statements. This year, however, it has suffered a huge loss and is trying to keep this fact a secret by refusing anyone access to its financial statements. Why might each of the following nevertheless insist upon seeing Lindlay's statements?
   a. Potential investors in Lindlay
   b. The Securities and Exchange Commission
   c. A bank that is considering a loan request by Lindlay
   d. Present stockholders of Lindlay
   e. Lindlay's management

The Accounting Profession in the 1980s

The AICPA president takes a worldwide perspective in viewing the likely challenges and opportunities for the profession.

When as accountants we attempt to peer into the future, we tend to forget that we do not operate in a vacuum. We sometimes fail to recognize that we are an integral part of a highly complex business world and that trends in our society, both nationally and internationally, can have a profound effect on the future of our profession.

Thus, before examining what faces the profession in the next decade, let me review the developments in society which appear to have a bearing on our future. These developments, while interdependent, can be classified and described in many different ways. Those identified are mentioned without attempting to be precise or exhaustive or to place them in any order of importance. Broadly stated, they are four in number.

The first is the explosion in the volume of information available to all levels of the population. Television, communication satellites and computers have had a tremendous effect on what we know about all of our institutions and have facilitated the growth of giant multinational corporations.

Perhaps because "familiarity breeds contempt," our greater knowledge has resulted in a considerable breakdown in trust in most of our institutions and a general cynicism about the level of integrity in all segments of our society. This has led to demands for accountability in all walks of life.

A second development has been the increase in mobility made possible by jet air travel. This has contributed to the growth in information, the alteration of family and religious patterns and the ability of corporations to operate on a global scale.

A third matter of significance has been the emergence of a widespread concern about the quality of life. This has manifested itself in a broad range of expensive social welfare and environmental protection programs adopted by governments at all levels. These have contributed heavily to massive governmental deficits and chronic inflation that ironically threaten to reduce our economic standard of living and make governmental wards of us all. The demand for a bet-

Source: Article by Wallace E. Olson. Reprinted from the July 1979 issue of *The Journal of Accountancy.* Copyright © 1979 by the American Institute of Certified Public Accountants, Inc.

ter life is, no doubt, due in part to the information explosion.

An important aspect of the concerns about the quality of life has been the demand for a better distribution of wealth. The struggle to determine the appropriate shares for labor, investors, managers, government and less developed countries poses an enormous challenge to accounting and accountants.

A fourth phenomenon of our times is the growth of huge corporate entities with multinational operations. As previously indicated, the increases in mobility, communications and information have helped break down national barriers and open international markets on a far broader scale. This, in turn, has placed strains on the international monetary system and has made our economic and business lives more interdependent internationally than ever before.

What I have briefly described is a mosaic of social, technological and economic developments that have greatly accelerated the rate of change in the fabric of our society. It is this rapid change and the growing complexity of all aspects of our social and business lives that promise to place heavy demands on our profession in the years to come. More effective accounting and accountability are imperative if business and government are to cope successfully with the complex problems they face today and will be confronted with in the years ahead. We have a vital role to play in that process and should not miss the opportunity to contribute our talents and expertise. In doing so, we must be prepared to undergo changes within our own profession to assure that the responsibilities we assume are fully met. The balance of this presentation is devoted to speculation about the nature of these changes.

Expansion of Role

I have indicated that I expect our role and range of services to expand substantially in the future. It is difficult to be specific other than to point out where this is already happening. There are substantial pressures for auditors to assume some degree of responsibility for reviewing and reporting on an increasing amount of information which is not part of financial statements but is included in published annual reports. Representations about social actions, systems of internal accounting control, projections of future operations, compliance with codes of conduct and the effects of inflation on capital and earnings are examples of the types of supplemental information and disclosures that we are being asked to review and report on.

It is reasonable to expect that the demands for greater accountability on the part of both profit and nonprofit entities will result in a greater volume of such disclosure requirements. Users of such information will want some assurance from independent auditors that the information is properly reported.

We have also witnessed a substantial expansion in the management consulting services provided to business and government by our profession. Because business transactions are becoming far more sophisticated and complex, we can expect the growth in both the volume and diversity of our consulting services to continue. The need for the application of our analytical skills and expertise to areas other than auditing financial statements and taxation is likely to be so great as to override any concerns that rendering nonaudit services to audit clients poses a risk of impairment of audit independence.

Perhaps more controversial is the prediction that we will become involved in helping governments bring their spending programs under control. Although professionals from other nations may not agree that legislators and governmental officials will seek or permit the participation of public practitioners in governmental affairs, our experience in the United States indicates otherwise.

There is an increasing awareness in our government that the economic statistics on which national policy decisions are based are derived from the financial statements of business. This accounts for the recent attention being devoted to our performance and the calls for governmental regulation of our profession.

A natural outgrowth of this attention is a recognition of our ability to objectively analyze and make sense out of complex data. As experts in financial measurement, we can provide valuable assistance in measuring the costs and benefits of governmental programs. Such analyses are vital if the politicians are to make informed decisions about which programs should be reduced or eliminated to achieve balanced budgets.

This role as objective analyst will not evolve immediately because it is likely that governments must reach the brink of bankruptcy before it becomes good politics to curtail spending. However, I believe the experience of New York City will ultimately be shared by other governmental units. In addition, we are already experiencing a grass roots movement against big government and excessive spending. This is requiring a painful reexamination of where and how cuts can be made.

I am not suggesting that we will necessarily become politicians, but I do expect that we will become valued advisers to legislators and governmental officials if we have the courage and will to do so. In my view, this is an opportunity to be of service that we should embrace even though I recognize that it involves accompanying risks.

In summary, I believe that the current trends all point to a continuing expansion in our role and in the volume and range of the services provided by our profession. To meet the demands of this expansion we must take steps to modify our organizational structure and entrance requirements to accommodate a wider range of disciplines. At the same time, we must improve our standards and performance and effectively regulate ourselves to maintain the quality of our work.

Organizational Structure and Education

If, in an expanded role, we are to deal with matters in the future that tend to be highly subjective, we will find it necessary to draw representatives of other disciplines into our ranks. The increased bodies of knowledge required will also make it difficult for a single individual to maintain competence in all areas of practice and will result in greater specialization within the profession.

The profession's organizations will find it difficult to deal with the question of whether they should formally accredit and recognize specialists. If they do so, it will raise questions about whether a qualified accountant is competent to provide the whole range of services.

If we come to accept the concept of being a multidiscipline-based profession with formal specialization, it will have a substantial impact on the entrance and education requirements. Entrance examinations would have to cover a broader range of subjects but at less depth than at present. Additional examinations in greater depth and each in a single body of knowledge would be administered for formal accreditation of specialization.

Pre-entry education curriculums might have to cover more subjects to prepare students for a broader coverage in the profession's entrance examinations. Others, however, foresee a different approach because they believe that it is not practicable to broaden the curriculum. In their opinions, specialists should be drawn from other disciplines and undergo a concentrated conversion course in the discipline of accounting.

While I concur that specialists must be brought into the profession, I believe that general practitioners will nevertheless require training in a wider range of subjects. Perhaps the solution lies in a longer period of pre-entry education. In the U.S. we have urged that five-year programs be adopted to permit the expanded curriculum which we believe is necessary to become a qualified accountant.

In any event, it seems clear that it will be imperative for all accountants to attend continuing education courses to maintain their competence and keep informed of new developments. It is unlikely that we can maintain high levels of performance by depending solely on an entrance examination and subsequently acquired experience. For this reason, I believe that mandatory continuing education will ultimately be universally adopted.

The profession's organizational structure must also find a way to cope with the existing divisive pressures and those that are likely to occur in the future. The great disparity in the size and resources of accounting firms ranging from local to international firms already creates substantial tensions, and these are likely to be intensified by the step-up in competition that I foresee as a result of the repeal of restrictions on advertising and solicitation. Such self-imposed restrictions are being increasingly challenged as being self-serving and contrary to the interests of consumers.

Another source of friction is the adoption of accounting standards applicable to large publicly traded companies that are either irrelevant or too costly to apply to the small privately held clients of the local practitioner. The profession will ultimately recognize that the smaller private companies must be exempted from some of the financial reporting requirements applicable to publicly traded companies. Based on our experience in the U.S., this will not be easy to accomplish because many will regard such a step as a two-tier system of first- and second-class standards.

Finally, the organizational structure must provide for a better means of self-regulation, which will be discussed later.

Accommodating specialization, multidisciplines, the interests of small, medium-sized and large firms, the need for accounting standards tailored to the type of client and a more effective system of self-regulation—all under a single umbrella organization—will present a formidable challenge to the ingenuity and skill of the profession's leaders. Time will reveal whether this can be achieved or whether the profession will ultimately divide into two or more groups. In my view, we ought to do everything possible to remain a unified profession and should take appropriate steps to alleviate the internal pressures I have been describing.

Technical Standards

I have indicated that I expect the traditional services to receive continuing attention in the future because the demands for improved and more reliable financial reporting will increase. Despite the concern about information overload, we can expect that financial reports will become more voluminous and complex than they are now.

High on the list of priorities is the attempt to eliminate distortions caused by inflation. Even though data about current values and amounts expressed in units of general purchasing power will be reported as supplemental information, I do not believe this will be particularly effective. Neither will it be feasible to quickly and radically depart from historical costs in the primary financial statements. After many false starts, I believe that we will gradually change the valuation methods to some form of current cost applied to certain of the items in the basic financial statements. Perhaps all that will be done will be to revise the accounting for fixed assets and inventories.

While this limited approach may offend the sensitivities of our technical experts, there is substantial evidence that the users of financial statements neither comprehend nor find useful some of our more esoteric notions such as unrealized holding gains, gearing adjustments or measurement in units of general purchasing power.

Other developments that are foreshadowed in financial reporting are disclosures on a host of subjects. These include the makeup and compensation of management and boards of directors, relationships with independent auditors and legal counsel, contingencies and deficiencies in systems of internal control. Also included are compliance with social and environmental requirements and corporate codes of conduct, forecasts of operating data and some form of management report to accompany financial statements.

Because of the sheer volume and complexity of the information to be reported, it seems inevitable that the traditional format of financial statements and reports will have to be reconsidered. I have suggested that a new format be devised to group information along natural lines of interest to users, primarily for predictive purposes. Information is at present scattered throughout financial reports and is difficult to work with.

If such an approach was adopted, the need for a closed articulation system of reporting would be reduced and the traditional financial statements could be greatly condensed but retained as a transitional measure.

Another matter that requires attention is the need to speed up the process of harmonizing accounting and auditing standards internationally and facilitating practice across national borders. The International Accounting Standards Committee and the International Federation of Accountants are making good progress but we must find a way to ensure compliance with the standards being established. I am aware of the barriers of national sovereignty that exist. But somehow they must be surmounted or accounting could well become an impediment rather than an aid to the increasing volume of international trade. The organizations involved don't have much time left to act because other groups such as the United Nations are beginning to take action in this area out of concern about control of the activities of multinational corporations.

The profession will also be forced to reexamine its audit techniques in a search to make audits more effective in detecting irregularities. The rash of spectacular audit failures in past years and the revelations about illegal acts on the part of corporate managements have raised loud cries that auditors should be responsible to detect all material management frauds. Obviously we must do better if we are to retain our credibility. There should be greater emphasis on interrogation methods, increased use of computers to perform audit procedures and more frequent application of statistical sampling techniques. I am sure there are also new techniques that should be devised to make audits more effective.

In summary, much remains to be done in the area of financial accounting and reporting and auditing standards. Those who yearn for a return to the days of less standards and responsibilities are apt to be disappointed. All the signs point in the opposite direction.

Regulation

Another major area of concern in the years ahead will be the need to devise an effective system of self-regulation. The heavy criticism arising from major business failures has caught the attention of government in several countries, particularly in the U.S. The natural inclination of legislators is to impose additional forms of governmental regulation.

In the U.S., we have been striving to avoid more governmental regulation on the grounds that as professionals we can regulate ourselves more effectively. Whether there is more governmental involvement or not, I expect that improved enforcement of compliance with technical standards and finding a means of sanctioning accounting firms as entities as well as disciplining individuals will be expected of the profession.

Accomplishing these goals is no easy task. Such questions as what should be done when civil liability litigation is involved as well as how compliance with technical standards can be effectively monitored must be considered. In the U.S., the American Insti-

tute of CPAs has established a division for membership by accounting firms with requirements to comply with quality control standards and submit to a peer review every three years. Overseeing the activities of the division is a public oversight board comprised of five prominent individuals from outside the profession. While peer reviews may not currently be an acceptable approach in other countries, as demands for better regulation increase some equally effective system of monitoring the quality of practice will have to be devised. Clearly, the profession must be seen to be taking effective action when audit failures occur and it is established that standards of due care were not met.

Redress through litigation for civil damages may be viewed by some as ample protection of the public but in today's environment the profession is also expected to take all reasonable precautions to provide an additional measure of insurance against audit failures. Those who hope for relief from legal liability are not being realistic. We can expect more regulation, not less, and being held to higher standards of responsibility in the years ahead.

Conclusion

The profession is on the threshold of a period of great opportunity and challenge. Most of the trends of our times point toward a continuing escalation in the demands for accountability in all segments of our society. As impartial auditors and analyzers, we are in a unique position to help restore confidence in our institutions and aid governments to regain their financial health.

This is a role that goes well beyond that of the present. To fill it we will have to exercise the courage to accept greater responsibilities that involve making judgments that are substantially more subjective than those in the past. Some may wish to shrink from assuming such risks. If we do, we will have lost an opportunity to make a vital contribution and to greatly enhance the stature of our profession in the process.

To meet the challenge, we will have to take advantage of every ounce of our ingenuity to solve the perplexing problems we are already encountering. It will require strong leadership to improve what we are already doing at the same time that we are blazing a new trail to an expanded role. We will have to improve our standards as well as our performance and devise an effective means of assuring that we deserve to remain self-regulated. We will need to find ways to absorb the skills of other disciplines into the profession to broaden our competence. Above all, we will need unity and cooperation to succeed.

Chapter Two

Accounting as an Information System

Reviewing the Chapter

1. To make an accounting measurement, the accountant must answer the following basic questions:
   a. What is to be measured?
   b. When should the measurement occur?
   c. What value should be placed on the measurement?
   d. How is the measurement to be classified?

2. Accounting is concerned with measuring transactions of specific business entities in terms of money.
   a. For accounting purposes, a business is treated as a **separate entity** distinct from its owners, creditors, and customers.
   b. **Business transactions** are economic events that affect the financial position of a business. Business transactions may involve an exchange of value (for example, sales, borrowings, and purchases) or a nonexchange (for example, the physical wear and tear on machinery, and losses due to fire or theft).
   c. All business transactions are recorded in terms of money. This is called the **money measure** concept. In the United States, the basic unit of money measure is dollars.

3. Every transaction affects a firm's financial position. Financial position is shown by a balance sheet, so called because the two sides or parts of the balance sheet must always equal each other. In a sense, the balance sheet presents two ways of viewing the same business: the left side shows the assets (resources) of the business, whereas the right side shows who provided the assets. Providers consist of owners (listed under "owner's equity") and creditors (represented by the listing of "liabilities"). Therefore, it is logical that the total dollar amount of assets must equal the total dollar amount of liabilities and owner's equity. This is the **balance sheet equation**, also known as the accounting equation. It is formally stated as

   $$\text{assets} = \text{liabilities} + \text{owner's equity}$$

   Other correct forms are

   $$\text{assets} - \text{liabilities} = \text{owner's equity}$$
   $$\text{assets} - \text{owner's equity} = \text{liabilities}$$

4. **Assets** are the economic resources of a business. Examples of assets are cash, accounts receivable, inventory, buildings, equipment, patents, and copyrights.

5. **Liabilities** are debts of the business. Examples of liabilities are money borrowed from banks, amounts owed to creditors for goods bought on credit, and taxes owed to the government.

6. **Owner's equity** represents resources invested by the owner. **Equity** is described by the FASB as "the residual interest in assets after deducting the liabilities."[1]

7. Every transaction changes the balance sheet in some way. In practice, companies do not prepare a new balance sheet after each transaction. However, it is important for the accounting student to understand the exact effect of each transaction on the parts of the balance sheet.

8. Although every transaction changes the balance sheet, the balance sheet equation always remains in balance. In other words, dollar amounts may change, but assets must always equal liabilities plus owner's equity.

9. Accountants communicate their information through **financial statements**. The four principal statements are the income statement, statement of owner's equity, balance sheet, and statement of changes in financial position.

10. The **income statement**, whose components are revenues and expenses, is perhaps the most important financial statement. Its purpose is to measure the business's success or failure in earning an income over a given period of time.

11. The **statement of owner's equity** relates the income statement to the balance sheet by showing how the owner's capital changed during the period. The owner's capital at the beginning of the period is the first item on the statement. Because net income belongs to the owner, it is added to beginning capital, as are any additional investments made by the owner during the period. Finally, any withdrawals by the owner during the period are subtracted, as is a net loss, to arrive at the owner's capital at the end of the period. This ending figure is then transferred to the owner's capital account in the balance sheet.

12. The **balance sheet** shows the **financial position** of a business on a certain date. The resources used in the business are called **assets**, debts of the business are called **liabilities**, and the owner's financial interest in the business is called **owner's equity**.

13. The **statement of changes in financial position** shows much information that is not present in the balance sheet or income statement. This statement discloses all of the business's important financing and investing activities during the accounting period. Financing activities might include obtaining cash through an owner's investment or through the sale of equipment. Investing activities might include the purchase of a building or land.

14. Every financial statement has a three-line heading. The first line gives the name of the company. The second line gives the name of the statement. The third line gives the relevant dates (the date of the balance sheet or the period of time covered by the other three statements).

---

[1] *Statement of Financial Accounting Concepts*, "Elements of Financial Statements of Business Enterprises" (Stamford, Conn.: Financial Accounting Standards Board, 1980), par. 43.

Testing Your Knowledge

Matching

Match each term with its definition by writing the appropriate letter in the blank.

h 1. Financial statements

m 2. Balance sheet

b 3. Income statement

k 4. Statement of owner's equity

f 5. Statement of changes in financial position

c 6. Separate entity

L 7. Business transaction

i 8. Money measure

a 9. Asset

g 10. Liability

j 11. Owner's equity

e 12. Balance sheet equation

d 13. Withdrawals

a. An economic resource of a business
b. The statement that shows a company's profit or loss over a certain period of time
c. The accounting concept that treats a business as distinct from its owners, creditors, and customers
d. Assets taken from the business by the owner for personal use
e. Assets = liabilities + owner's equity
f. The statement that shows the sources and uses of funds during the period
g. A debt of a business
h. The accountant's principal means of communication
i. The standard that all business transactions should be recorded in terms of dollars
j. The owner's economic interest in a company
k. The statement that shows the changes in the owner's capital account during the period
l. An economic event that affects a company's financial position
m. The statement that shows the financial position of a company on a certain date

Completion

Use the lines provided to complete each item.

1. List the four principal financial statements and state briefly the purpose of each.

Statement	Purpose
a. Income statement	a. shows success or failure (profit or loss) over period of time
b. Statement of OE	b. changes in owner's capital over period
c. balance sheet	c. shows financial position of co. at point in time
d. Statement of changes in financial position	d. shows sources + uses of funds during period

2. On the lines that follow, insert the correct heading for the annual income statement of Alpha Company on June 30, 19xx.

Alpha Company
Income Statement
For the year ending June 30, 19xx

3. Show two acceptable forms of the balance sheet equation.

$A = L + OE$

$OE = A - L$

True-False

Circle T if the statement is true, F if it is false.

(T) F 1. The balance sheet shows the financial position of an economic entity as of a specific date.

T (F) 2. The major sections of a balance sheet are assets, liabilities, owner's equity, revenues, and expenses.

(T) F 3. The income statement is generally considered to be the most important financial statement.

(T) F 4. A business should be understood as an entity that is separate and distinct from its owners, customers, and creditors.

(T) F 5. A business transaction does not always involve an exchange of money.

T (F) 6. One form of the balance sheet equation is assets + liabilities = owner's equity.

T (F) 7. Transactions involving revenue and expenses will in some cases throw the balance sheet equation out of balance.

(T) F 8. Revenues have the effect of increasing owner's equity.

(T) F 9. The payment of a liability will decrease both Cash and Accounts Payable.

T (F) 10. Collection of an account receivable will increase both Cash and Accounts Receivable.

(T) F 11. In practice, a balance sheet is not prepared after each transaction.

T (F) 12. The existence of Accounts Receivable on the balance sheet indicates that the company has one or more creditors.

(T) F 13. When expenses exceed revenues, a company suffers a net loss.

T (F) 14. The measurement stage of accounting involves preparation of the financial statements.

T (F) 15. Withdrawals appear as a deduction in the income statement.

Multiple-Choice

Circle the letter of the best answer.

1. Which is _not_ a proper form of the balance sheet equation?
   a. Assets – liabilities = owner's equity
   b. Assets = liabilities + owner's equity
   c. Assets – owner's equity = liabilities
   (d.) Assets + liabilities = owner's equity

2. Which of the following is _not_ a major account heading in the balance sheet or income statement?
   (a.) Accounts Receivable
   b. Owner's Equity
   c. Liabilities
   d. Revenues

3. The net income figure appears in all of the following statements _except_
   a. the statement of changes in financial position.
   b. the income statement.
   c. the statement of owner's equity.
   (d.) the balance sheet.

4. Which of the following statements does _not_ involve a distinct period of time?
   a. Income statement
   (b.) Balance sheet
   c. Statement of changes in financial position
   d. Statement of owner's equity

5. The purchase of an asset for cash will
   a. increase total assets and increase total owner's equity.
   b. increase total assets and increase total liabilities.
   c. increase total assets and decrease total liabilities.
   d. have no effect on total assets, liabilities, and owner's equity.

6. Payment of a liability will
   a. decrease total liabilities and decrease total owner's equity.
   b. decrease total assets and increase total owner's equity.
   c. decrease total assets and decrease total liabilities.
   d. have no effect on total assets, liabilities, and owner's equity.

7. Which of the following would *not* appear on the balance sheet?
   a. Wages Expense
   b. Robert Katz, Capital
   c. Notes Receivable
   d. Wages Payable

8. Collection on an account receivable will
   a. increase total assets and increase total owner's equity.
   b. have no effect on total assets, but will increase total owner's equity.
   c. decrease both total assets and total liabilities.
   d. have no effect on total assets, liabilities, and owner's equity.

Applying Your Knowledge

Exercises

1. Randi Company had assets of $100,000 and liabilities of $70,000 at the beginning of the year. During the year assets decreased by $15,000 and owner's equity increased by $20,000. What is the amount of liabilities at year-end? $ 35,000

2. Following are the accounts of Acme TV Repair Company as of December 31, 19xx.

Accounts Payable	$ 1,300
Accounts Receivable	1,500
Building	10,000
Cash	?
Land	1,000
Roger Sands, Capital	17,500
Equipment	850
Truck	4,500

Using this information, prepare a balance sheet *in good form*. (You must derive the dollar amount for Cash.)

3. Following are the transactions for the Sanet Painting Company for the first month of operations.
   a. Pat Sanet invested $20,000 cash into the newly formed business.
   b. Purchased paint supplies and equipment for $650 cash.
   c. Purchased a company truck on credit for $5,200.
   d. Received $525 for painting a house.
   e. Paid one-half of the amount due on the truck previously purchased.
   f. Billed a customer $150 for painting his garage.
   g. Paid $250 for one month's rental of the office.
   h. Received full payment from the customer whose garage was painted (transaction f).
   i. Sold a company ladder for $20. The buyer said he would pay next month.
   j. Pat Sanet withdrew $1,000 from the business for personal use.

In the table that appears below, show the effect of each transaction on the balance sheet accounts by putting the dollar amount, along with a plus or minus, under the proper account. Determine the balance in each account at month's end. As an example, transaction a has already been recorded.

Trans-action	Assets				Liabilities	Owner's Equity
	Cash	Accounts Receivable	Supplies and Equipment	Trucks	Accounts Payable	Pat Sanet, Capital
a	+$20,000					+$20,000
b	− 650		+650			
c				+5200	+5200	
d	+ 525					+ 525
e	− 2600				− 2600	
f		+ 150				+ 150
g	− 250					−250
h	+ 150	− 150				
i		+ 20	− 20			
j	−1000					−1000
Balance at end of month	16,175	+20	+630	+5200	+2600	19,425

5850

22025

2600

22025

Crossword Puzzle
For Chapters 1 and 2

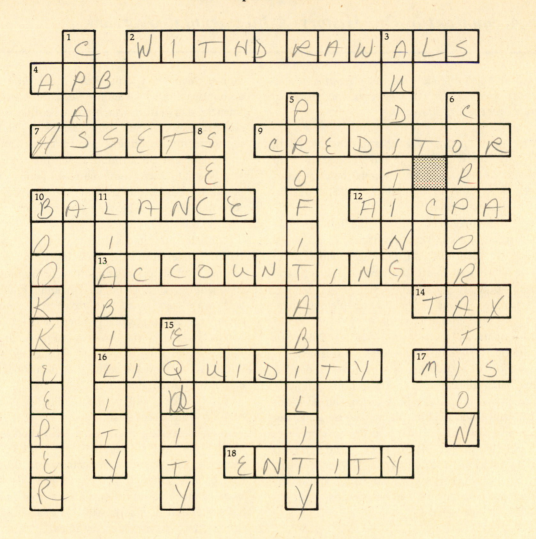

ACROSS

2. Statement of owner's equity component
4. Former principle-setting body
7. Resources of a company
9. One to whom another is indebted
10. _____ sheet
12. Professional organization of accountants
13. The language of business
14. Branch of public accounting
16. Measure of debt-paying ability
17. Data-generating network
18. Separate _____ concept

DOWN

1. Professional accountants
3. Branch of public accounting
5. Measure of business performance
6. Form of business organization
8. Regulatory agency of publicly-held corporations
10. Recorder of business transactions
11. Debt of a company
15. Ownership in a company

The Accountant in Our History: A Bicentennial Overview

The accounting profession has made significant contributions to the industrial and economic growth of America over the last 200 years.

Exactly when the first accountant came to North America is a matter of dispute and adroit scholarship. If we wish to believe a recent popular description of the crew accompanying Columbus on the famous discovery voyage, consider this:

"There were forty men. . . aboard the flotilla, including a surgeon and the royal controller of accounts, sent along to keep tabs on Columbus's swindle sheet when he started to figure the cost of the gold and spices he would accumulate."

This passage perhaps serves as a suitable note to introduce this brief commentary on the role and impact of accountants and accounting over the 200 years since the Declaration of Independence was issued.

The subject of accounting as we know it today has become much advanced in application and emphasis over the past two centuries in America. Our review of its significance will begin with its uses by leaders in the colonies. We will consider also the developments of the early industrial period of the U.S. through 1880 and then focus on the era of the CPA movement, 1890 to 1930. Finally, we will study the World War II period and conclude with an observation about the 1970s and the years ahead.

The Colonial Period

Our Founding Fathers made good use of the rudiments of what today is a highly specialized professional pursuit. In setting out the uses of accounting or "bookkeeping methodiz'd" as it was known, consider the lifestyle of the times. In 1776 almost all (95 percent) of the estimated 2½ to 3 million American settlers lived on farms. The population hugged the seacoast and waterways in order to expedite the transportation and trade needed to sustain its relationship with the Eurocentric world. Accounting was based as much on barter as on cash, which was in short supply and of unstable value. Payments came in the form of rum, beef, butter and other forms of commodity

Source: Article by Gary John Previts. Reprinted from the July 1976 issue of *The Journal of Accountancy.* Copyright ©1976 by the American Institute of Certified Public Accountants, Inc.

money. Merchants kept their records in a series of accounting books beginning with the wastebook (a financial diary) from which journal entries were made and the ledger posted. Apprenticeship in an accounting house or "compting house" of a merchant was the common form of learning about financial records. Mostly young men from well-to-do families were apprenticed thus before being set into business. Annual reporting was only beginning to achieve acceptance and was not of the statement type we know today.

From time to time accountants have encountered historical tales about the documentation supplied by George Washington in support of his supposedly extravagant expense accounts. Benjamin Franklin also is known to have relied on his expense account to pay for his gay and occasionally libertine court life while conducting ministerial business in France. Perhaps we think this deflating to our past revolutionary heroes, but in fact many other such incidents involving leaders of the revolution indicate that some patriots achieved personal success and political influence because of their savvy in "accompts."

Foremost among these was John Hancock who inherited the business fortune of his uncle, Thomas Hancock, the Boston merchant prince. John might have been less blessed had it not been that "Thomas knew as much about his own affairs from an accounting standpoint as was possible in mercantile capitalism . . . [but] John was . . . swamped."[1]

George Taylor, who signed the July Fourth document as a representative of Pennsylvania, came to America as an indentured servant bound to the owner of an iron works. He was sent to work as a furnace coaler but it was thought that he was too weak for the job. Because he had a better education than most youths of those days, he was given a job in the business office handling transactions and accounts. Indeed, Taylor had an accountant's flair for opportunity, for, when the owner of the works died, Taylor married the widow and became owner of the works.

Perhaps the wealthiest of the signers, Charles Carroll of Carrollton (because at least three other Charles Carrolls were prominent in Maryland at the time, he signed himself "of Carrollton") is known for both his longevity—he survived until 1832, the last of the

1. W. T. Baxter, *The House of Hancock* (Cambridge, Mass.: Harvard University Press, 1945), p. 22.

signers to succumb—and for his keeping "meticulous books."

Thomas Jefferson also maintained extensive financial records, as was customary for plantation owners—including an entry in his account books for July 4, 1776, noting a purchase of two items and a donation to charity.

Another signer, Robert Morris, was instrumental in aiding the cause by providing the means of financing for the new Congress. Morris, later acting as superintendent of finance, administered the funds for Congress and, with the backing of Haym Salomon, is noted to have "introduced system into financial accounting" related to the new government. Salomon, called the "Good Samaritan of the Revolution," lent over $200,000 to the United States. He died at the age of 45, and the loan was apparently not repaid.

Henry Laurens, president of the Continental Congress in 1777 and a signer of the Treaty of Paris, used accounts to maintain a record of his personal financial affairs with the state government of South Carolina during the 1770s; and in 1780, his neatly drawn "Statement of Account with the United States," dated January 20, indicates the customary importance placed on such records in early government transactions.

America's New Industrialism

Through the 1790s and early 1800s several hundred business incorporations took place. As the turmoil of the American Revolution and the War of 1812 were replaced by a stable political environment, Americans set out to restore their trade and expand their holdings of new lands west of the Allegheny Mountains. Technical inventions and their labor saving efficiency tended to reduce costs and as turnpikes, canals and then railroads appeared, new markets were opened for goods which, in turn, induced specialized manufactures and early forms of mass production. Industry and commerce became rooted in the midst of a predominantly rural society. By the 1840s the first modern textbook on accounting was written by Thomas Jones, an accountant and commercial teacher in New York City. Jones focused on the statements of accounting as the outcome of the double entry system and relegated the accounts themselves to a support role. He, along with other pioneer educators, such as S. S. Packard, instructed those seeking to learn the mysteries of what was now being called "scientific bookkeeping" by some and the "science of accounts" by others. Packard was a leader in commercial education for nearly half a century, from the 1840s to the years preceding the passage of CPA legislation. As a proprietor of a Bryant and Stratton Business College —universities were not disposed to include commercial subjects in their curriculums—Packard was one of many who trained young persons to go forth into the new adventures of corporate business.

One such young man, later called "a bloodless . . . bookkeeper" by a wildcat oilman he had visited, was trained in the points of scientific accounting at Folsom's Business College in Cleveland in 1855. When a group of money men from Cleveland sent the prim 21-year-old bookkeeper, John D. Rockefeller, off to assess the prospects for the commercial future of oil in Pennsylvania, a chapter of American history was begun.

In the decade before the War Between the States, over a dozen public accountants were listed in the New York City directory and by 1895 there were nearly 150.

Perhaps no better idea of the popular image of accounts could be obtained than by reading a short piece appearing in *Harper's Weekly* on January 3, 1857:

"We are a nation of shopkeepers, and none the worse for that . . . It is very important, then, for us to sustain a good commercial name; and to do this, we must take care that the debit does not overbalance the credit account in our ledger. If we allow too large a margin for our expenses we shall be sure, whatever may be the profits of dry good and hardware, to fall short in the final account with our creditors or our conscience."

Although America's early philosophers may have shunned the commercial life, some of them were not averse to using the tools of the accountant in their private lives. Henry Thoreau, for example, found that a simple system of accounting helped him achieve a spartan and self-reliant life at Walden Pond in the mid-1800s. It was necessary, he wrote, that an account of stock be "taken from time to time, to know how you stand." He added: "It is a labor to task the faculties of a man—such problems of profit and loss, of interest, of tare and tret, and gauging of all kinds in it, as demand a universal knowledge."

Some scholars have noted discrepancies in Thoreau's accounts despite their apparent meticulousness. Author Charles Anderson, for example, observes of Thoreau's summary of food expenses ("Yes, I did eat $8.74, all told") that "it is probably not a coincidence that this figure tallies with one claimed as a possible food budget . . . in the *Young Housekeeper* (Boston, 1838)." Also, it is noted that "pecunary outgoes" of $61.99¾ were erroneously totaled as $60.99¾ in Thoreau's original working manuscript. But Thoreau has the good sense, early in pages of his book *Walden*, to issue this disclaimer: "My accounts, which I can swear to have kept faithful, I have, indeed, never got audited, still less accepted, still less paid and settled."

In contrast to Thoreau's relaxed approach to justifying his account records, businessmen of his period were becoming more sophisticated in their application of accounting to industrial operations. During the 1850s, Paul Garner notes in his history of cost accounting, industrialism was beginning to have an impact on the character of account keeping. For the first time, many authors began to consider accounts related to factory and production costs. John Fleming's *Bookkeeping by Double Entry* published in Pittsburgh in 1854 included several changes to reflect cost accounting considerations. Fleming changed the name of the merchandise trading account to "factory account" and also attempted to determine the appropriate treatment for factory buildings. Whether these adjustments truly reflected a general need for cost system information because of the many iron and steel mills near Pittsburgh can only be speculated.

The post Civil War steel boom developed in response to the demands of the westward drive of the railroads. At that time, As Ernest Reckitt, an early CPA leader, later recalled, a businessman named Andrew Carnegie "was one of the first pioneers in the introduction of cost accounting, maintaining a considerable staff in his cost department and [attributing] his great financial success to his knowledge of his costs in the steel industry."

The public's familiarity with keeping accounts, as suggested in the popular columns of *Harper's Weekly* and as used in the financial tool kits of Rockefeller and Carnegie, indicates that accounting was becoming one of the skills needed for small business and in commerce and the home. All this was before the most significant episode of all—the "professionalization" movement which took shape at the close of the century, beginning with the passage of the first CPA law in New York in April 1896.

Enter the CPA

When the first CPA candidates gathered for the first examination in Buffalo and in New York on December 15 and 16, 1896, they were probably unaware of the many thousands who would follow in their footsteps. Within a year the New York State Society of CPAs had been formed, with 24 members. These first few probably also could not have predicted that by 1947, a half century later, this society would number over 5,000 and that today it would have over 20,000 members.

For this reason, we focus on the emergence of the CPA as the central point of development for the accounting profession. The CPA movement, which spread throughout the country during the quarter century after the New York law, laid the foundation for increasing the competence of accountants through education, testing and experience. Financial statements and the ratios evolving therefrom were becoming the essence of the economic and business decisions made throughout a society which for the first time found a majority of the population in cities facing the urban realities of industrialization. As the center of the world capital market shifted from London to New York, the United States became a capital exporting nation. In 1928, E. H. H. Simmons, president of the New York Stock Exchange, noted:

"Since the war . . . not only has the United States become an international lender instead of borrower, but the comparative shortage of capital in this country has been turned into a surplus."

The characteristics of the corporations using capital had also changed as the CPA era developed. Corporations were rapidly merging so that by the turn of the century ownership and management of major business enterprises were separated, necessitating financial reporting of a dimension and frequency not envisioned in the proprietary years of closely owned and managed corporations.

By 1917, having survived a clash with Congress on the matter of federal licensure of accountants, members of the national CPA organization cooperated with government agencies to prepare a document—*Uniform Accounts*—which, when released, received wide circulation and is acknowledged as the first attempt to present a set of national standards for accounting practice. The 1929 revision of these early rules and the rules themselves, however, were all too little and too late to play a role in the "casino-like" atmosphere which pervaded trading in the stock markets of the 1920s.

The catastrophe which followed throttled the capital markets and nearly crippled the economy. While earlier attempts to make inroads into the secrecy and "private ledgers" associated with large concerns had been made by leaders in the profession, not until the Securities Act of 1933 and 1934 was there sufficient legal leverage for the CPA to make progress in identifying the form and content of financial statements and the principles underlying them. For while the controversy over the need for and effectiveness of the Securities Acts continues, there is no denying that these laws reflected a potent political response which established the dimensions of action for the next generation of accountants—including the pressure for more frequent, more consistent and more detailed presentation and analysis of corporation accounts and business activity.

Early Professional Leaders

Among the early CPAs were a significant number who gave of their time not only for the benefit of professional self-interest but also in service to their country and their communities. During World War I accountants served in several key positions. R. H. Montgomery, an early author, teacher and founding partner of the firm now known as Coopers & Lybrand, worked under Bernard Baruch at the War Industries Board, accepting a field rank commission. Joseph Sterrett, of Price Waterhouse & Co., was decorated for his service on the Dawes Commission, the agency charged with settling the problems of Germany's reparation payments. L. W. Blyth, of Ernst & Ernst, responded to the request of Newton D. Baker, secretary of war, and took on the task of establishing the accounting system for the Ordnance Department.

In their own communities, early accounting leaders were instrumental in moving accounting education from the level of proprietary commercial education into universities. Arthur Andersen, James Marwick, S. Roger Mitchell, Allen R. Smart, Arthur Young and other CPAs were prominent in supporting the successful development of the School of Commerce at Northwestern University in 1908. They were preceded by a group of New Yorkers led by Charles Waldo Haskins, co-founder of the firm of Haskins & Sells, who acted as a formative influence in establishing the School of Commerce, Accounts and Finance at New York University, which opened October 1, 1900. Haskins also served as the first dean.

If these contributions seem modest, it must be remembered that they represent only a few examples and do not take account of the many significant roles and activities of the other prominent professional leaders of the time, such as Charles E. Sprague, Arthur Lowes Dickinson and Henry Rand Hatfield, each of whom contributed significantly to professional education and practice in the first decades of this century. These men and 32 others have been accorded the honor of membership in the Accounting Hall of Fame, which was established in 1950 at the Ohio State University.

During the early 1900s, as people drew closer together to live and work in cities, comprehensive municipal accounting systems were developed, including the necessary budgetary accounts. Under the leadership of accounting educators, such as Frederick Cleveland and Lloyd Morey, new systems were effectively put to use early in the century. Popular contact with accounting was not limited, however, to such distant although important matters as municipal finance. The levying of a federal income tax before World War I caused individuals, as well as businesses, to seek advice on how their taxes might legitimately be minimized. As a result, there was an increasing focus on how earnings were to be measured. The average person's perplexity with this subject might best be represented by this poem written at the turn of the century by a leading American poet:

> Never ask of money spent
> Where the spender thinks it went
> Nobody was ever meant
> To remember or invent
> What he did with every cent.
>
> Robert Frost
> "The Hardship of Accounting"

We also find that American speech was absorbing accountants' parlance. By the 1920s, it was common practice to evaluate a losing business as "in the red" and a profitable one as "in the black."

Aiding the War Effort

George O. May, the practitioner's counterpart to Professor William A. Paton during the classical years of formative CPA accounting theory, noted the significance of accounting during the World War II years as follows:

"The importance of the part played by accounting in our economy of today requires no demonstration. We see daily how rules of accounting become in effect rules of law. Within wide areas value is recognized as being dependent upon income; the measurement of income is an accounting process. . . ."

With these words, May acknowledged what had been heralded by DR Scott a decade earlier. Scott held that our society, indeed our culture, depends on financial data for its operation, maintenance and continued prosperity. Accounting makes the difference between economic communication and economic chaos.

The World War II effort again drew important talent from every rank of the young profession. Paul Grady headed the Navy's cost inspection service under Admiral Baldwin. Arthur Carter assisted Secretary of War Robert P. Patterson, becoming a major general in charge of fiscal matters for Army Service Forces. When the federal government undertook to plan its accounting, auditing and financial reporting functions through the Hoover Commission efforts of the late 1940s and early 1950s, again CPAs worked on key task forces.

J. Harold Stewart, a partner of Arthur Young & Company, for example, headed the second Hoover Commission's Budget and Accounting Task Force in 1953.

CPAs grew in number rapidly after World War II. At only 9,000 in 1945, AICPA membership rolls spurted to 38,000 in 1960, 74,000 a decade later, and now exceed 120,000. As early as 1933, A. A. Berle, Jr., in an article entitled "Public Interest in Accounting," wrote: "It becomes plain that accounting is rapidly ceasing to be in any sense of the word a private matter."

Actually, the stock market crash of 1929, following a spate of public criticism of the "easy" financial practices and reporting that had become rife in industry, was a major factor in spurring required audits of listed companies and therefore growth of accounting as a profession. In his book *Main Street and Wall Street*, Harvard Professor William Z. Ripley cited "the docility of corporate shareholders permitting themselves to be honey-fuggled." George O. May, in response to Ripley's criticism of then current reporting practices, said, "The time has come when auditors should assume larger responsibilities, and their position [should] be more clearly defined."

In 1932, the New York Stock Exchange required listed companies to agree that their financial statements would bear the certificate of accountants "qualified under the laws of some state or country." That same year AICPA President John B. Forbes named May chairman of a special new committee on accounting principles. In the wake of Institute efforts to achieve voluntary action to deal with some of the problems, Congress passed the Securities Acts of 1933 and 1934.

Arthur H. Carter, then president of the New York State Society of CPAs, had recommended before Congress that financial statements should be examined by an independent auditor who should express his opinion on their fairness. Carter said it would be impractical for a government agency to perform such examinations. The 1933 act contained an audit provision, but it wasn't until after the 1934 act created the Securities and Exchange Commission that machinery was set up for audits by independent public accountants. Carman G. Blough, CPA, was appointed the first chief accountant of the SEC.

As John L. Carey, former administrative vice president of the Institute, wrote in the *Journal* in September 1969: "The influence of the SEC on accounting and auditing standards and practice was tremendous. Without doubt the securities acts strengthened the position of independent auditors in insisting that clients follow sound principles and make adequate disclosures. The commission's requirements also greatly increased the volume of auditing engagements. And it must be conceded that the SEC's goad prodded the profession to make improvements both in accounting and auditing that otherwise might have taken longer to achieve."

The Countdown of History

Since the 1930s, the business world has become more complex, and the role of the accountant has necessarily expanded. Taking a bicentennial perspective, over the past 200 years more than 90 percent of the population has left the farm to work in the big city. Since 1876, American private foreign investment has increased tenfold; in the past 30 years, the United States has supplied more than half of the industrial world's need for capital. And the CPA must now venture into this intricate world of multinational decision making made even more complicated by political action and foreign regulations. For this reason the typical accountant today is better educated than his predecessors so he can help clear the financial fog that can surround statements. Over the past two decades whether required by law or not, most CPAs have had a baccalaureate degree in accounting.

CPAs now serve in increasing numbers as chief executive officers and chief financial officers in business and industry. Since World War II many CPAs have held important posts in the Cabinet, at the World Bank and on the New York Stock Exchange. Most recently, a CPA, L. William Seidman, was appointed by President Ford as a special personal adviser. A CPA, Kenneth S. Axelson, is also engaged in assisting the mayor of New York, himself a CPA, to develop a sound plan for the city's finances.

The accountant can look back at the profession's history and how it has complemented the growth of industry and the economy and realize that the assembly line could hardly run without a balance sheet and an income statement to back it up. We have entered an age of "popular political accountancy" in which our idiom has become the password. To paraphrase Paul A. Samuelson, "The bottom line—that's what it's about."

Chapter Three

The Double-Entry System

Reviewing the Chapter

1. Before recording a business transaction, the accountant must determine three things:
   a. When the transaction occurred (the **recognition problem**)
   b. What value should be placed on the transaction (the **valuation problem**)
   c. How the components of the transaction should be categorized (the **classification problem**)

2. A sale is recognized (entered in the accounting records) when the title to merchandise passes from the supplier to the purchaser, regardless of when payment is made or received.

3. **Cost**, or the dollar value of any item involved in a business transaction, is recorded at its original cost (also called historical cost). Generally, any change in value after the transaction is not reflected in the accounting records.

4. Every business transaction is classified by means of records called **accounts**. Each asset, liability, owner's equity, revenue, and expense has a separate account.

5. All of a company's accounts are contained in a book or file called the **ledger**. Each account appears on a separate page, and the accounts generally are in the following order: assets, liabilities, owner's equity, revenues, and expenses. A listing of the accounts with their respective account numbers, called a **chart of accounts**, is presented at the beginning of the ledger for easy reference.

6. Although the accounts used by companies will vary, there are some that are common to most businesses. Some typical assets are Cash, Accounts Receivable, Notes Receivable, Prepaid Expenses, Land, Buildings, and Equipment. Some typical liabilities are Accounts Payable, Notes Payable, and Bonds Payable.

7. The owner's capital account (an owner's equity account) represents the owner's investment in the company at any point in time. If William Marshall were an owner, the name of the account would be William Marshall, Capital. If there is more than one owner, a separate capital account must be kept for each.

8. The owner's withdrawals account (also an owner's equity account) records amounts withdrawn from the business for personal living expenses, in anticipation of earning a profit. If Paula Post were an owner, her withdrawals account would be called Paula Post, Withdrawals, or Paula Post, Drawing. As with the capital account, there must be a separate withdrawals account for each owner.

9. A separate account is also kept for each

type of revenue and expense. The exact revenue and expense accounts used will vary depending on the kind of business and its operations. Revenues cause an increase in owner's equity. Expenses cause a decrease.

10. The **double-entry system** of accounting requires that for each transaction there must be one or more accounts debited and one or more accounts credited, and that total debits must equal total credits.

11. An account in its simplest form, a **T account**, has three parts:
   a. A title that expresses the name of the asset, liability, owner's equity, revenue, or expense
   b. A left side, which is called the **debit** side
   c. A right side, which is called the **credit** side

12. At the end of an accounting period **account balances** are calculated in order to prepare the financial statements. If using T accounts, there are three steps to follow in determining these account balances:
   a. Foot (add up) the debit entries. The **footing** (total) should be made in small numbers beneath the last entry.
   b. Foot the credit entries.
   c. Subtract the smaller total from the larger. A debit balance exists when total debits exceed total credits; a credit balance exists when the opposite is the case.

13. To determine which accounts are debited and which are credited in a given transaction, one uses the following rules:
   a. Increases in assets are debited.
   b. Decreases in assets are credited.
   c. Increases in liabilities and owner's equity are credited.
   d. Decreases in liabilities and owner's equity are debited.
   e. Revenues increase owner's equity, and are therefore credited.
   f. Expenses decrease owner's equity and are therefore debited.

14. To record a transaction, one must (a) obtain a description of the transaction, (b) determine which accounts are involved and what type each is (for example, asset or revenue), (c) determine which accounts are increased and which are decreased, and (d) apply the rules stated in 13a-f.

15. As transactions occur, they are recorded initially and chronologically in a book called the **journal**. The **general journal** is the simplest and most flexible type of journal. Each transaction **journalized** (recorded) in the general journal contains (a) the date, (b) the account names, (c) the dollar amounts debited and credited, (d) an explanation, and (e) the account numbers, if posted. A line should be skipped after each **journal entry**, and more than one debit or credit may be entered for a single transaction (called a **compound entry**).

16. Each day's journal entries must be posted to the ledger accounts. **Posting** is a transferring process that results in an updated balance for each account. The dates and amounts are transferred, and new account balances are figured. The Post. Ref. columns must be used for cross-referencing between the journal and ledger. When more increases than decreases have been recorded for an account (the usual case), then its balance (debit or credit) is referred to as its **normal balance**. For example, assets have a normal debit balance.

17. Periodically the accountant must double-check the equality of the debits and credits in the accounts. This is formally done by means of a **trial balance**.

18. If the trial balance does not balance, one or more of several possible errors have been made in the journal, ledger, or trial balance. The accountant must then locate the errors to put the trial balance in balance. It is important to know, however, that it is possible to make errors that would not cause the trial balance to be out of balance (that is, errors that would not be detected through the trial balance).

19. To summarize, proper accounting procedure requires that certain steps be followed (additional steps will be introduced in subsequent chapters):
   a. Journalize transactions as they occur
   b. Post the journal entries to the ledger accounts when convenient
   c. Prepare a trial balance periodically to test the equality of debit and credit balances.

Testing Your Knowledge

Matching

Match each term with its definition by writing the appropriate letter in the blank.

_k_ 1. Original (historical) cost
_f_ 2. Account
_q_ 3. Debit
_o_ 4. Credit
_b_ 5. Account balance
_g_ 6. Ledger
_a_ 7. Posting
_m_ 8. Prepaid expenses
_l_ 9. Accounts Payable
_d_ 10. Chris Roberts, Capital
_j_ 11. Chris Roberts, Withdrawals
_r_ 12. Double-entry bookkeeping
_e_ 13. Trial balance
_n_ 14. Journal
_p_ 15. Post. Ref.
_h_ 16. Footing
_c_ 17. Compound entry
_i_ 18. Unearned revenue

a. Transferring data from the journal to the ledger
b. The amount in an account at a given point in time
c. An entry with more than one debit or credit
d. An account that represents an owner's equity in a company
e. A procedure for checking the equality of debits and credits in the ledger accounts
f. A record that occupies a page of the ledger
g. The book that contains all of a company's accounts
h. Adding up
i. A liability arising when payment is received prior to the performance of services
j. An account that represents amounts taken out of a business for personal expenses
k. The proper valuation to place on a business transaction
l. Amounts owed to others
m. Amounts paid in advance for goods or services
n. The book of original entry
o. The right side of a ledger account
p. The column in the journal and ledger that provides for cross-referencing between the two
q. The left side of a ledger account
r. The method that requires both a debit and a credit for each transaction

Completion

Use the lines provided to complete each item.

1. Proper accounting procedure requires that certain steps be followed, from the initial recording of information to the preparation of statements. List the steps.

   Journalize transactions
   Post journal entries to ledger
   Prepare trial balance

2. Given the following journal entry, indicate which part of the entry applies to each measurement problem listed.

   July 14 Cash   150
             Accounts Receivable   150
               Collection on account

   a. _Recognition problem_   _July 14_
   b. _Valuation problem_   _150_
   c. _Classification problem_   _Cash 150_
      _A/R 150_

3. Describe a transaction that will require a debit to one asset and a credit to another asset.

Payment of A/R account

4. Describe a transaction that will require a debit to a liability and a credit to an asset.

Payment of A/P account

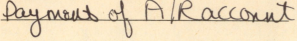

True-False

Circle T if the statement is true, F if it is false.

T **(F)** 1. A sale should be recorded only on the date of payment.

(T) F 2. Historical cost is another term for original cost.

(T) F 3. There must be a separate account for each asset, liability, owner's equity, revenue, and expense.

T **(F)** 4. The credit side of an account implies something favorable.

T **(F)** 5. For a given account, total debits must always equal total credits.

T **(F)** 6. Management can quickly determine cash on hand by referring to the journal.

(T) F 7. The number and titles of accounts will vary among businesses.

T **(F)** 8. Promissory Note is an example of an account title.

(T) F 9. Prepaid expenses are classified as assets.

(T) F 10. Increases in liabilities require credits.

T **(F)** 11. In all journal entries, at least one account must be increased, and another decreased.

T **(F)** 12. Failure to post an entire entry would be disclosed by the trial balance.

T **(F)** 13. Journal entries are made after they are entered into the ledger accounts.

(T) F 14. In the journal, all liabilities and owner's equity accounts must be indented.

(T) **(F)** 15. A debit is never indented in the journal.

(T) F 16. Posting refers to transferring data from the journal to the ledger.

(T) F 17. The reference column of a journal or ledger should be empty until after posting.

Multiple-Choice

Circle the letter of the best answer.

1. Which of the following is *not* considered in initially recording a business transaction?
   a. Classification
   b. Recognition
   c. Summarization
   d. Valuation

2. When a liability is paid, which of the following is true?
   a. Total assets and total liabilities remain the same
   b. Total assets and total owner's equity decrease.
   c. Total assets decrease by the same amount that total liabilities increase.
   d. Total assets and total liabilities decrease.

3. Which of the following is *not* true about a proper journal entry?
   a. All credits are indented.
   b. All debits are listed before the first credit.
   c. An explanation is needed for each debit and each credit.
   d. A debit is never indented, even if a liability or owner's equity account is involved.

4. When an entry is posted, what is the last step to be taken?
   a. The explanation must be transferred.
   b. The account number is placed in the reference column of the ledger.

c. The journal page number is placed in the reference column of the journal.
d. The account number is placed in the reference column of the journal.

5. Which of the following errors will probably be disclosed by the preparation of a trial balance?
   a. Failure to post an entire journal entry.
   b. Failure to record an entry in the journal.
   c. Failure to post part of a journal entry.
   d. Posting the debit of a journal entry as a credit, and the credit as a debit.

6. When cash is received in payment of an account receivable, which of the following is true?
   a. Total assets increase.
   b. Total assets remain the same.
   c. Total assets decrease.
   d. Total assets and total owner's equity increase.

7. Which of the following is increased by debits?
   a. Ronald Harper, Withdrawals
   b. Unearned Revenue
   c. Bonds Payable
   d. Ronald Harper, Capital

8. Which of the following accounts is an asset?
   a. Unearned Revenue
   b. Prepaid Rent
   c. Ann Jefferson, Capital
   d. Fees Earned

9. Which of the following accounts is a liability?
   a. Interest Payable
   b. Interest Expense
   c. Interest Receivable
   d. Interest Earned

Applying Your Knowledge

Exercises

1. Following are all the transactions of Pinnacle Printing Company for the month of May. For each transaction, provide *in good form* the journal entry required. Use the journal provided on the following page.

May 2 Joe Romano formed the Pinnacle Printing Company by investing $28,000 cash.
   3 Rented part of a building for $300 per month. Paid three months' rent in advance.
   5 Purchased a small printing press for $10,000 and photographic equipment for $3,000 from Irvin Press, Inc. Paid $2,000 and agreed to pay the remainder as soon as possible.
   8 Hired a pressman, agreeing to pay him $200 per week.
   9 Received $1,200 from Doherty's Department Store as an advance for brochures to be printed.
   11 Purchased paper for $800 from Pulp Supply Company. Issued Pulp a promissory note for the entire amount.
   14 Completed a $500 printing job for Sullivan Shoes. Sullivan paid for half, agreeing to pay the remainder next week.
   14 Paid the pressman his weekly salary.

   15 Paid Irvin Press, Inc., $1,000 of the amount owed for the May 5 transaction.
   18 Received remainder due from Sullivan Shoes for the May 14 transaction.
   20 Mr. Romano withdrew $700 from the business for his personal living expenses.
   24 Received an electric bill of $45. Payment will be made in a few days.
   30 Paid the electric bill.

2. Following are three balance sheet accounts, selected at random from Holding Company's ledger. For each, determine the account balance.

Accounts Receivable	
2,000	1,000
750	
bal. 1,750	

Accounts Payable	
1,200	4,200
2,000	
bal.	1,000

Cash	
15,000	1,000
4,000	1,200
	2,200
bal. 14,600	

a. Accounts Receivable has a (debit) or credit) balance of $ _1750_ .
b. Accounts Payable has a (debit or credit) balance of $ _1000_ .
c. Cash has a (debit or credit) balance of $ _14,600_ .

		General Journal		
Date		Description	Debit	Credit
May	2	Cash	28,000	
		Joe Romano, Capital		28,000
		To record the owner's original investment		
	3	Prepaid rent (3 mos.)	900	
		Cash		900
		Rent space in building - 3 mos. advance		
	5	Equipment	13,000	
		Cash		2000
		A/P		11,000
		Bought printing press + photographic equip. from		
		Irvin Press ($2000 cash, remainder credit)		
	8	Salary expense No entry	200	
		Joe Romano, Capital		200
		Hired pressman @ $200/wk		
	9	Cash Revenue	1200	
		Unearned Revenue		1200
		Advance pymt for brochures to be printed		
	11	Supplies	800	
		N/P		800
		Paper from Pulp Supply Co.		
	14	Cash	250	
		A/R	250	
		Revenues Capital		500
		Printing job for Sullivan Shoes		
	14	Salaries expense	200	
		Cash		
		Pressman wkly salary		
	15	A/P	1000	
		Cash		1000
		Paid Irvin press $1000 for Mays purchase		
	18	Cash	250	
		A/R		250
		Remainder of May 14 from Sullivan Shoes		
	20	Joe Romano, W/D	700	
		Cash		700
		Living expenses		
	24	Util expense	45	
		A/P		45
		Elec Bill		
	30	A/P	45	
		Cash - pd elec. bill		45

3. Following are two journal entries. Post both entries to the ledger accounts provided. Only those accounts needed have been provided, and previous postings have been omitted to simplify the exercise.

		General Journal			Page 7
Date		Description	Post. Ref.	Debit	Credit
Apr.	3	Cash	11	1,000	
		Revenue from Services	41		1,000
		Received payment from Malden Company for services			
	5	Accounts Payable	21	300	
		Cash	11		300
		Paid Douglas Supply Company for supplies purchased on March 31 on credit			

Cash   Account No. 11

Date		Item	Post. Ref.	Debit	Credit	Balance Debit	Balance Credit
Apr	3		7	1000		1000	
	5		7		300	700	300

Accounts Payable   Account No. 21

Date		Item	Post. Ref.	Debit	Credit	Balance Debit	Balance Credit
Apr	5		7	300		300	

Revenue from Services   Account No. 41

Date		Item	Post. Ref.	Debit	Credit	Balance Debit	Balance Credit
Apr	3		7		1000		1000

You Can Call It Earnings . . . You Can Call It Income, Or . . .

The titles used in the annual report often depend upon the whims of the financial vice president.

Terminology used in financial statements varies widely and is sometimes confusing and outdated. For example, the Coca-Cola Company changed in 1978 from Statement of *Profit and Loss* to Statement of *Income*. The controller of the company was asked, "Why did you not use the suggested Statement of Earnings?" His reply was that the president and board chairman still preferred to use the title Profit and Loss Statement. They were persuaded, however, to make the change to Income Statement for two reasons. First, the term Profit and Loss was antiquated and, second, they desired to move into the mainstream. As a result, the company selected the title Income Statement because it is currently used by most firms.

Conversations and interviews with the management of a number of the 600 companies surveyed in *Accounting Trends and Techniques* indicate that the terminology used often depends upon the whim of financial vice president. Such was the case when the Exxon Corporation changed in 1979 from Statement of Financial Position to Balance Sheet. The chief financial officer felt that "balance sheet" sounds better and accordingly, used his influence to change the title of the statement. The problem is magnified by the use of out-dated terminology in high school and college-level textbooks. All disciplines, including accounting, use textbooks that are inconsistent and often use incorrect financial accounting terminology.

A cursory inspection of textbooks in use illustrates the problem. For example, *A Survey of Basic Accounting* by Salmonson, et al. states:

Stockholder's equity is the term given to the owners' interest in a corporation. The terms *shareowners' equity, capital, proprietorship,* or *net worth* are used in statements of financial position as synonyms for stockholders' equity.[1]

Pyle, White and Larson state in the 1978 edition of *Fundamental Accounting Principles*:

The terms owner equity, proprietorship, net worth, and capital are often used synonymously. All four indicate the equity, in the assets, of the owner or owners of a business.[2]

Finance and management textbooks are notorious for their use of incorrect and outdated terminology. One of the most common graduate textbooks in finance, *Financial Management and Policy* by Van Horne, has the terms net worth and capital surplus throughout the text.[3] Many current management textbooks use terminology that existed in the 1950s. Probably the worst offender of all is the U.S. Small Business Administration. One of the books in the Small Business Management Series uses such terms as profit and loss statement, surplus, and reserve.[4]

It is obvious that a problem exists. Many executives as well as academicians appear to be chained to the past. A senior partner of Ernst and Whinney comments:

The prevailing reason for not changing is the status quo phenomenon plus that fact that many executives were schooled at a time when the out-of-date terms were in use. Even though the terminology used in their financial statements may be confusing and archaic, we can only suggest changes to our clients. The problem needs to be brought to corporate management's attention through academic journals and professional seminars.

In general, corporate financial management as well as CPA firms state that they are not concerned so much with terminology. Their main concern, which is a valid one, is making money for the company. We will examine why changes occur in accounting terminology as well as determine the extent to which preparers of financial statements appear to be interested in current accounting practice.

Source: Article by Ray G. Jones, Jr. Reprinted from the May 1982 issue of *Management Accounting.* Copyright ©1982 by the National Association of Accountants.

1. R. F. Salmonson, Roger H. Hermanson, and James Don Edwards, *A Survey of Basic Accounting*, Richard D. Irwin, Inc., Homewood, Ill., 1973, pp. 34–35.

2. William W. Pyle, John A. White, and Kermit D. Larson, *Fundamental Accounting Principles,* 8th ed., Richard D. Irwin, Inc., Homewood, Ill., 1978, p. 85.

3. James C. Van Horne, *Financial Management and Policy*, 5th ed., Prentice-Hall, Inc., Englewood Cliffs, N.J., 1980, p. 355.

4. Jack Zwick, *A Handbook of Small Business Finance*, Small Business Management Series No. 15, Small Business Administration, Washington, D.C., 1975, pp. 7–13.

Evolution of Standardized Financial Statements

In 1917, the Federal Reserve Board and the Federal Trade Commission became aware of the many variations in the way that financial statements were prepared and submitted to banks for the purpose of obtaining credit. Recognizing a need to standardize financial statements, they asked the American Institute of Accountants (AICPA since 1957) to prepare a statement of standard procedures. After its approval by the Institute and the Federal Trade Commission, the Federal Reserve endorsed the standardized procedures. They were first published in the April 1917 issue of the Federal Reserve Bulletin. In the same year they were revised and published in a pamphlet called *Uniform Accounting*. In 1918 the pamphlet was reprinted as *Approved Methods for the Preparation of Balance-Sheet Statements*.[5]

In 1936, the AICPA revised an earlier edition and published *Examination of Financial Statements by Independent Public Accountants*. The preface to the 1936 revision states:

Developments of accounting practice during recent years have been in the direction of increased emphasis on accounting principles and consistency... The suggestions contained in this bulletin are intended to apply to examinations by independent public accountants of financial statements prepared for credit purposes or for annual reports to stockholders.[6]

In the publication, the Federal Trade Commission and Federal Reserve Board recommended that nonoperating or extraordinary charges or credits be listed under Other Income or Charges. The term Net Income for the Period was eliminated and called Net Profit for the Period. By so doing, the intent was to make the Profit and Loss Statement more consistent.

From their beginning in 1920 and 1936, respectively, the Committee on Terminology and the Committee on Accounting Procedure of the American Institute of CPAs have done a great deal to standardize accounting terminology and procedure. In 1941, the Committee on Terminology suggested a general discontinuance of the use of the term *surplus* in corporate accounting and substituted in owners' equity a term which emphasizes the difference between legal capital, capital in excess of legal capital, and undivided profits. The proposal was approved "as an objective" by the Committee on Accounting Procedure in 1949. Another recommendation made in 1948 by the Committee on Terminology was to limit the use of the term *reserve*. Such a change was recommended because the term was being used with varying and somewhat conflicting meanings. Between November 1940 and October 1949, eight of the Accounting Research Bulletins issued by the Committee on Accounting Procedure were developed by the Committee on Terminology.[7]

In October 1970, the American Institute of CPAs issued APB Statement No. 4. The title of the statement is "Basic Concepts and Accounting Principles Underlying Financial Statements of Business Enterprises." In general, the AICPA would like to increase the usefulness of accounting standards by advancing the written expression of financial accounting principles. In particular, APB Statement No. 4 has two broad goals. The first is to provide a basis for enhanced understanding of the broad fundamentals of financial accounting. The second is to provide a step toward development of a more consistent and comprehensive structure of financial accounting. APB Statement No. 4 does not change, supersede or interpret Accounting Research Bulletins or opinions of the Accounting Principles Board that are currently in effect. The Statement, however, does modify some of the definitions of technical accounting terms in the Accounting Terminology Bulletins, which are considered useful guides to financial accounting terminology. Some suggested terminology changes are Statement of Earnings and Statement of Financial Position. These are to be used in place of the older terms, Income Statement and Balance Sheet.[8]

Terminology in Use Today

Assets, Liabilities, and Owners' Equity The titles used for financial statements in 1970 and 1980 are shown in Table 1. The data suggest that companies are slow to change the titles of the two major financial statements. There do appear to be some interesting changes taking place, however, which we will discuss.

Usage of the title, Statement of Financial Condition, has declined from about 4% in 1970 to less than 2% in 1980. In fact, the number using this title continued to drop throughout the decade of the seventies. The

5. Eldon S. Hendriksen, *Accounting Theory*, 3rd ed., Richard D. Irwin, Inc., Homewood, Ill., 1977, p. 56.
6. American Institute of Accountants, *Examination of Financial Statements by Independent Public Accountants*, New York, January 1936.

7. AICPA, *Accounting Terminology Bulletin No. 1*, "Review and Resume (of the eight original terminology bulletins)," New York, August 1953.
8. AICPA, *Statement of the Accounting Principles Board No. 4*, "Basic Concepts and Accounting Procedures Underlying Financial Statements of Business Enterprises," New York, October 1970.

use of the title, Statement of Financial Position, declined in the last decade reaching a low in 1979. In that year only 43 companies of the 600 tracked by the AICPA used the title. However, two companies, Dun & Bradstreet and General Foods, changed to Statement of Financial Position in 1980. Dun & Bradstreet stated that the Statement of Financial Position ties in better with the Statement of Changes in Financial Position. General Foods stated that it changed to Statement of Financial Position because it is a more descriptive title.

In general, the financial officers and accounting directors who were interviewed said that although they have no aversion to changing from Balance Sheet to Statement of Financial Position, they feel no pressing need to change at this time, and they believe their stockholders would accept either title.

Earnings Use of the term, Income Statement, declined 2% between 1970 and 1980. The term reached a peak in popularity in 1974 when 386 of 600 companies surveyed by the AICPA reported Statement of

Income in their annual report to the stockholders. This decline is not a major change, yet it does reflect a gradual change in the meaning of the terminology used to identify the statement.

The number of companies that used the title, Earnings Statement, was about the same for both the 1970 and 1980 periods. The use of the title appears to have reached its low point in 1975 when the annual reports of only 163 firms contained it.

Although the Statement of Operations shows a gain for the period, its use appears to increase whenever companies report a loss. Interviews with company executives revealed a preference for the title, Income Statement, which is reflected in Table 1. Yet a large number of the executives believe the meaning of the titles is changing. John A. Hagan, vice president and controller of R.J. Reynolds Industries, Inc. notes:

Earnings is a better description of what the financial statement is trying to show. Income is somewhat more synonymous with revenue. For over 30 years our firm has used the title Statement of Earnings.

Table 1
Titles Used for Financial Statements, 1970 and 1980

	1970		1980	
	Number	%	Number	%
Assets, liabilities, and owner's equity				
Balance Sheet	518	86.3	544	90.7
Statement of Financial Position	57	9.5	45	7.5
Statement of Financial Condition	25	4.2	11	1.8
	600	100.0	600	100.0
Earnings				
Statement of Income	380	63.3	367	61.2
Statement of Earnings	178	29.7	175	29.2
Statement of Operations	37	6.2	56	9.3
Other	5	.8	2	.3
	600	100.0	600	100.0
Changes in financial position				
Statement of Changes in Financial Position	—	—	599	99.8
Statement of Source and Application of Funds	472	78.7	1	0.2
Changes in Working Capital	50	8.3	—	—
Funds Statement	29	4.8	—	—
Other	22	3.7	—	—
No statement	27	4.5	—	—
	600	100.0	600	100.0

Source: *Accounting Trends and Techniques*—1971 and 1981.

The use of "Income Statement" seems to imply the overall income of the company while "Earnings Statement" is used to emphasize the earnings of the firm. Internal consistency of the statement is less than desired. One still sees the use of *gross profit* or *profit margin* as well as *income before taxes* even in the statement of earnings of some companies.

Changes in Financial Position The response to the use of Statement of Changes in Financial Position is overwhelming. It went from zero percent in 1970 to 99.8% in 1980. Only one firm, which shall remain anonymous, used the old title of Statement of Source and Application of Funds. Of course, APB Opinion No. 19, "Reporting Changes in Financial Position," issued in 1971 by the AICPA was instrumental in the phenomenal compliance with this title.

Other Accounting Terms

Table 2 shows some captions used in financial statements. Most of the surveyed companies show a preference for the title Stockholders' Equity. The term Net Worth, which is incorrect, is used in isolated cases only. The move is definitely away from all other titles except for Common Stockholders'/Shareholders' Equity. A SEC requirement for a change in the presentation of preferred stock, which is subject to mandatory redemption, became effective for the fiscal period ending September 15, 1979. As a result of this change, such preferred issues are displayed separately from common stockholders' equity.

Additional Paid-in Captial is gaining in usage. It increased by over 12% in the 1970s while the next used caption, Captial in Excess of Par or Stated Value, increased by only 5%. There is a continuing trend away from the use of the term *surplus*. In 1970, a total of 58 companies used surplus to describe additional capital and only 26 used the term in 1980. The use of the term surplus has long been discouraged by the AICPA Committee on Terminology. AICPA feels that the word surplus is unsuitable in the equity section of the position statement because its public connotation is something over and above what is necessary.

The use of the term Retained Earnings has increased from 77% in 1970 to 83.5% in 1980. Only three firms in 1980 used the term *earned surplus*. This term is becoming obsolete largely due to Accounting Terminology Bulletin No. 1, which recommends that earned surplus be replaced by terms which indicate source, i.e., retained income, retained earnings, etc.

The use of the term "reserve" declined dramatically during the seventies. In 1970, 35% of the 600 firms used the word reserve in 372 presentations. By 1980

less than 15% of the firms used the word in only 113 presentations. Because of the different meanings attached to the term reserve, the AICPA in Accounting Terminology Bulletin No. 1 recommended its use be restricted. The term reserve when used to describe an appropriation of retained earnings is considered acceptable, although its use also continues to decline.

Battle over the Balance Sheet

The most interesting development is in the Statement of Assets, Liabilities, and Owners' Equity. There appears to be some misunderstanding concerning the titles Balance Sheet and Statement of Financial Position. Some practitioners as well as academicians believe there is a difference implied in the use of the two statements. However, Paragraph 11 of APB Statement No. 4 states that a Balance Sheet or Statement of Financial Position presents three major categories: Assets, Liabilities, and Owners' Equity. Thus, the two statements contain identical information according to APB Statement No. 4. Paragraph 10 of APB Statement No. 4 divides the process of reporting the economic activities of a firm into two basic types: financial position, which relates to a point in time, and changes in financial position, which relate to a period of time.

Even though the slowest area to change is the title of the Assets, Liabilities, and Owners' Equity Statement, a ray of hope is appearing. Accounting textbooks are beginning to recognize the more descriptive terminology for this statement. Meigs and Meigs state:

Alternative titles for the balance sheet include statement of financial position and statement of financial condition. Although "balance sheet" may not be a very descriptive term, it continues to be the most widely used, perhaps because of customs and habits.[9]

Kieso and Weygandt state:

Use of the term "statement of financial position" has declined although it is conceptually more appealing."[10]

Welsch, Zlatkovich, and Harrison make one of the stronger cases against use of "balance sheet":

A balance sheet presents the assets, liabilities, and owners' equity of an enterprise, at a specific date,

9. Walter B. Meigs and Robert F. Meigs, *Accounting: The Basis for Business Decisions*, 5th ed., McGraw-Hill Book Company, New York, 1981, p. 102.
10. Donald E. Kieso and Jerry D. Weygandt, *Intermediate Accounting*, 2nd ed., John Wiley & Sons, Inc., Santa Barbara, Calif., 1977, p. 158.

Table 2
Terminology Used in Financial Statements, 1970 and 1980

	1970		1980	
	Number	%	Number	%
Owner's equity				
Stockholders', Shareholders', or Shareowners' Equity	514	85.6	492	82.0
Stockholders' or Shareholders' Investment	43	7.2	32	5.3
Common Stockholders'/Shareholders' Equity	–	–	46	7.7
Other or no title	43	7.2	30	5.0
	600	100.0	600	100.0
Additional capital				
Additional Paid-in Capital	195	32.5	265	44.2
Capital in Excess of Par or Stated Value	133	22.2	165	27.5
Capital Surplus	129	21.5	62	10.3
Paid-in Surplus	28	4.6	13	2.1
Other captions	30	5.0	13	2.1
No additional capital account	85	14.2	77	12.8
	600	100.0	595	100.0
Earnings retained for use in the business				
Retained Earnings	463	77.2	501	83.5
Earnings with Additional Words	57	9.5	54	9.0
Income with Additional Words	32	5.3	24	4.0
Earned Surplus	32	5.3	3	0.5
Companies with Deficits	15	2.5	18	3.0
Other	1	0.2	–	–
	600	100.0	600	100.0
Presentation of reserve				
In assets only	63	10.5	48	8.0
In assets and liabilities	38	6.3	11	1.8
In liabilities only	108	18.0	33	5.5
In neither assets nor liabilities	391	65.2	508	84.7
	600	100.0	600	100.0
Total Presentations of Reserve	372		113	

Source: *Accounting Trends and Techniques*—1971 and 1981.

measured in conformity with generally accepted accounting principles. Because it is a presentation of the current financial position of an entity, it is often referred to as the statement of financial position. The designation balance sheet was adopted during the period when accounting first evolved; it refers to the fact that it balances in terms of the fundamental accounting model: Assets = Liabilities + Owners' Equity. It is unfortunate that this nondescriptive designation continues to be widely used today. Because of wide usage, we use it in this text, although reluctantly. Titles such as "Statement of Financial Position" or "Statement of Assets, Liabilities, and Owners' Equity" are to be preferred.[11]

Current accounting textbooks place very little emphasis on the terminology used for the Earnings Statement. A typical comment is as follows:

11. Glenn A. Welsch, Charles T. Zlatkovich, and Walter T. Harrison, Jr., *Intermediate Accounting*, 5th ed., Richard D. Irwin, Inc., Homewood, Ill., 1979, p. 134.

Alternative titles for the income statement include *earnings statement, statement of operations,* and *profit and loss statement.* However, *income statement* is by far the most popular title for this important financial statement.

Although such a statement is true, use of the title Income Statement has begun to decline. This decline may be due to the fact that earnings per share is almost universally used. Another factor is that most managerial finance textbooks have Earnings Before Interest and Taxes analysis in financial leverage since the 1950s. Finally, APB Statement No. 4 may be having some effect. Paragraph 149 states that all the profit-directed activities of an enterprise that comprise the revenue-earning process may be called the *earning process.*

The rapid change to the title Statement of Changes in Financial Position was caused by a number of factors. First, it was a relatively new statement at the time APB Opinion No. 19 was issued. Second, the change was widely and readily accepted because the number of firms which began to use the title in 1971 was 526 out of the 600 in the survey. Finally, the title is a very descriptive one. In fact, some authorities believe that the use of this statement led to less emphasis of the Earnings Statement and emphasis on the Assets, Liabilities, and Owners' Equity Statement.

Defliese, Johnson and Macleod give one of the better terminology descriptions for the caption Stockholders' Equity. They state:

Accountants now prefer the terms "stockholders' equity," "capital," or "net assets" over the term "net worth," which was widely used at one time. Net worth has the disadvantage of suggesting present realizable value. Since the assets shown in most balance sheets prepared in accordance with generally accepted accounting principles are a mixture of known values (cash), estimates of current values (receivables), and unexpired and unamortized historical costs (inventories, fixed assets, and intangible assets), the owners' equity or excess of assets over liabilities as reflected by the accounts would only coincidentally approximate the present worth of a business.[12]

Almost all of the accounting textbooks today discourage the use of the term reserve. More and more, the texts are emphasizing the use of retained earnings rather than earned surplus. The use of the term additional paid-in capital is now showing up in some texts. For example, Kieso and Weygandt use it throughout the text while Welsch, et al. note that capital in excess of par or stated value is sometimes called additional paid-in capital. All of these are encouraging developments in the standardization of accounting terminology and should speed the process of uniform accounting procedure.

Toward Standardization?

The terminology used in financial statements has changed considerably in the decade of the seventies. A trend toward the use of more meaningful terminology such as Statement of Changes in Financial Position, Additional Paid-in Capital, and Retained Earnings is evident. The use of older terms such as Net Worth and Earned Surplus in financial statements has almost been discontinued.

The two areas which are changing the slowest are the titles of the two major financial statements. There is some indication, however, that the use of titles for the major statements is beginning to change. Managers and accountants are becoming aware of the need for better terminology in financial statements. This awareness is evident in the helpful descriptions used in recently published financial statements and in the attention given this subject by professional groups, periodicals and textbooks. It is clear that the ideas advanced in the terminology bulletins have had a positive effect. Perhaps someday all terminology in financial reports will be consistent and reflect current accounting practice. From the earliest years of accounting the trend has been moving toward standardization. The sooner this is accomplished, the more efficient accountancy will be for the preparers as well as the users of statements.

12. Philip L. Defliese, Kenneth P. Johnson, and Roderick K. Macleod, *Montgomery's Auditing,* 9th ed., John Wiley & Sons, Inc., New York, 1975.

Chapter Four

Business Income and Adjusting Entries

Reviewing the Chapter

1. Earning a **profit** is an important goal of most businesses. A major function of accounting is to measure and report the success or failure of a company in achieving this goal. This is done by means of an income statement.

2. **Net income** is the net increase in owner's equity resulting from the operations of the company. Net income results when revenues exceed expenses, and a net loss results when expenses exceed revenues.

3. **Revenues** are the price of goods sold and services rendered during a specific period of time. Examples of revenues are Sales (the account used when merchandise is sold), Commissions Earned, and Advertising Fees Earned.

4. **Expenses** are the costs of goods and services used in the process of gaining revenues. Examples of expenses are Telephone Expense, Wages Expense, and Advertising Expense.

5. Revenue and expense accounts are sometimes referred to as **nominal accounts** because they are temporary in nature. Their purpose is to record revenues and expenses during a certain accounting period. At the end of that period, their totals are transferred to the owner's capital account, leaving zero balances to begin the next accounting period.

6. Balance sheet accounts are sometimes referred to as **real accounts** because their balances can extend past the end of an accounting period. They are *not* set back to zero.

7. The **periodicity** assumption (the solution to the **accounting period problem**) states that although measurements of net income for short periods of time are approximate, they are nevertheless useful to statement users. Income statement comparison is made possible through accounting periods of equal length. A **fiscal year** covers any twelve-month accounting period used by a company. Many companies use a fiscal year that corresponds to the calendar year, which is a twelve-month period that ends on December 31.

8. Under the **going-concern** assumption (the solution to the **continuity problem**), the accountant assumes that the business will continue to operate indefinitely, unless there is evidence to the contrary.

9. When the **cash basis of accounting** is used, revenues are recorded when cash is received, and expenses are recorded when cash is paid. This method, however, can lead to distortion of net income for the period.

10. According to the **matching rule**, revenues should be recorded in the period(s) when

they are actually earned, and expenses should be recorded in the period(s) when they are incurred. The timing of cash payments or receipts is irrelevant. **Accrual accounting** consists of all techniques used to apply the matching rule.

11. A problem arises when revenues or expenses apply to more than one accounting period. The problem is solved by making **adjusting entries** at the end of the accounting period. Adjusting entries allocate to the current period the revenues and expenses that apply to the current period, deferring the remainder to future periods. A **deferral** is the postponement of the recognition of an expense already paid or of a revenue already received [see 12(a) and (b) below]. An **accrual** is the recognition of an expense or revenue that has arisen but has not yet been recorded [see 12(c) and (d) below].

12. Adjusting entries are required to accomplish several things:
    a. To divide recorded costs (such as the cost of machinery or prepaid rent) among two or more accounting periods
    b. To divide recorded revenues (such as commissions collected in advance) among two or more accounting periods
    c. To record unrecorded revenues (such as commissions earned but not yet billed to customers)
    d. To record unrecorded expenses (such as wages earned by employees after the last payday in an accounting period)

13. When an expenditure is made that will benefit more than just the current period, the initial debit is usually made to an asset account instead of to an expense account. Then, at the end of the accounting period, the amount that has been used up is transferred from the asset account to an expense account.
    a. **Prepaid expenses** like Prepaid Rent and Prepaid Insurance are debited when they are paid for in advance.
    b. An account for supplies such as Office Supplies is debited when supplies are purchased. At the end of the accounting period, an inventory of supplies is taken. The difference between supplies available for use during the period and ending inventory is the amount used up during the period.
    c. A long-lived asset such as a building, trucks, or office furniture is debited to an asset account when purchased. At the end of each accounting period, an adjusting entry must be made to transfer a part of the original cost of each long-lived asset to an expense account. The amount transferred or allocated is called **depreciation**.
    d. The **Accumulated Depreciation** account is called a **contra account** because on the balance sheet it is subtracted from its associated asset account. Thus proper balance sheet presentation will show the original cost, the accumulated depreciation as of the balance sheet date, and the undepreciated balance.

14. In making the adjusting entry to record depreciation, Depreciation Expense is debited and Accumulated Depreciation is credited.

15. Sometimes payment is received for goods before they are delivered or for services before they are rendered. In such cases a liability account such as **Unearned Revenues** or Unearned Fees would appear on the balance sheet. This account is a liability because it represents revenues that still must be earned.

16. Often at the end of an accounting period, expenses have been incurred but not recorded in the accounts because cash has not yet been paid. An adjusting entry must be made to record these **accrued (accumulated) expenses**. For example, interest on a loan may have accrued that does not have to be paid until the next period. A debit to Interest Expense and a credit to Interest Payable will record the current period's interest for the income statement. This entry will also record the liability for the balance sheet.

17. Similarly, revenues have often been earned but not recorded because no payment has been received. An adjusting entry must be made to record these **accrued revenues**. For example, interest that has been earned may not be received until the next period. A debit must be made to Interest Receivable and a credit to Interest Earned.

18. After all the adjusting entries have been posted to the ledger accounts and new account balances have been computed, an **adjusted trial balance** should be prepared. If it is in balance, the adjusted trial balance is then used to prepare the financial statements.

19. Adjusting entries are made mainly so that financial statements will be useful and will meet accounting standards. Adjusting entries offer a means of using accrual accounting to prepare financial statements that may be compared between periods and are relevant to users. Adjusting entries often involve estimates, but the estimates should be supported by objective evidence.

20. Errors that are discovered in the journal or ledger must be corrected. Depending on the kind of error, correction is made by drawing a line through the incorrect data or by preparing a correcting entry. In no case should the error be erased.

Testing Your Knowledge

Matching

Match each term with its definition by writing the appropriate letter in the blank.

i 1. Net income

d 2. Revenues

n 3. Expenses

r 4. Expired cost

c 5. Unexpired cost

q 6. Nominal accounts

f 7. Real accounts

k 8. Fiscal year

e 9. Going-concern assumption

o 10. Cash basis of accounting

a 11. Accrual accounting

h 12. Matching rule

m 13. Adjusting entry

p 14. Depreciation expense

l 15. Accumulated depreciation

j 16. Contra account

b 17. Unearned revenue

g 18. Adjusted trial balance

t 19. Deferral

s 20. Accrual

a. All techniques used to apply the matching rule

b. A liability that represents an obligation to deliver goods or render services

c. That portion of an asset that has not yet been charged as an expense

d. A general term for the price of goods sold or services rendered

e. The assumption that a business will continue indefinitely

f. Accounts whose balances extend beyond the end of a period

g. A method of determining whether accounts are still in balance

h. The idea that revenues are recorded when earned and that expenses are recorded when incurred

i. The amount by which revenues exceed expenses

j. An account that is subtracted from an associated account

k. Any twelve-month accounting period used by a company

l. An example of a contra account to plant assets

m. An end-of-period allocation of revenues and expenses relevant to that period

n. The cost of doing business

o. Recording revenues and expenses when payment is received or made

p. The expired cost of a plant asset for a particular accounting period

q. Accounts that begin each period with zero balances

r. A descriptive term for expense

s. Recognition of an expense or revenue that has arisen but has not yet been recorded

t. Postponement of the recognition of an expense already paid or of a revenue already received

Completion

Use the lines provided to complete each item.

1. Briefly summarize the four situations requiring adjusting entries.

Divide recorded costs among 2+ periods
Divide recorded revenues among 2+ periods
Record unrecorded revenues
Record unrecorded expenses

2. Briefly explain the matching rule.

Revenues should be recorded when they are earned, & expenses when incurred

3. Define depreciation as the term is used in accounting.

The amt. transferred to an expense acct. from an asset acct. at end of period

4. Distinguish between prepaid expenses and unearned revenues.

Prepaid expense - liability paid for in advance = asset until used. Un. Rev. - assets paid for in advance = liab. until earned

True-False

Circle T if the statement is true, F if it is false.

T F 1. Accumulated Depreciation is a real account, whereas Depreciation Expense is a nominal account.

T F 2. Expired costs can be found in the income statement.

T **F** 3. A calendar year refers to any twelve-month period.

T F 4. The cash basis of accounting often violates the matching rule.

T **F** 5. Under the accrual basis of accounting, the timing of cash payments is vital for recording revenues and expenses.

T F 6. Adjusting entries must be made immediately after the financial statements are prepared.

T F 7. Prepaid Insurance represents an unexpired cost.

T **F** 8. Office Supplies Expense must be debited for the amount in ending inventory of office supplies.

T **F** 9. Since Accumulated Depreciation appears on the asset side of the balance sheet, it will have a debit balance.

T F 10. As a machine is depreciated, its accumulated depreciation increases and its unexpired cost decreases.

T **F** 11. Unearned Revenues is a contra account to Earned Revenues in the income statement.

T F 12. When an expense has accrued but payment has not yet been made, a debit is needed for the expense and a credit for Prepaid Expenses.

T F 13. The adjusted trial balance is the same as the trial balance, except as modified by adjusting entries.

T **F** 14. If one has made a sale for which the money has not yet been received, one would debit Unearned Revenues and credit Earned Revenues.

T F 15. The original cost of a long-lived asset should appear on the balance sheet even after depreciation has been recorded.

T F 16. When a journal entry has been posted to the wrong account in the ledger, it is necessary to prepare another journal entry to correct the error.

T F 17. Adjusting entries help make financial statements comparable from one period to the next.

Multiple-Choice

Circle the letter of the best answer.

1. Which of the following is an example of a nominal account?
   a. Prepaid Rent
   b. Unearned Revenues
   c. Wages Expense
   d. Accumulated Depreciation, Building

2. Depreciation does *not* apply to
   a. trucks.
   b. office supplies.
   c. machinery.
   d. office equipment.

3. An account called Unearned Fees is used when there are
   a. recorded costs that must be divided among periods.
   b. recorded revenues that must be divided among periods.
   c. unrecorded expenses that must be recorded.
   d. unrecorded revenues that must be recorded.

4. Depreciation best applies to
   a. recorded costs that must be divided among periods.
   b. recorded revenues that must be divided among periods.
   c. unrecorded expenses that must be recorded.
   d. unrecorded revenues that must be recorded.

5. Which of the following will *not* appear in the adjusted trial balance?
   a. Prepaid Insurance
   b. Unearned Management Fees
   c. Net Income
   d. Depreciation Expense

6. An adjusting entry made to record accrued interest on a note receivable due next year would consist of
   a. a debit to Cash and a credit to Interest Income.
   b. a debit to Cash and a credit to Interest Receivable.
   c. a debit to Interest Expense and a credit to Interest Payable.
   d. a debit to Interest Receivable and a credit to Interest Earned.

7. The periodicity assumption recognizes that
   a. net income for a short period of time is an estimate.
   b. a business is assumed to continue indefinitely.
   c. revenues should be recorded in the period earned.
   d. a twelve-month accounting period must be used.

8. Prepaid Rent is
   a. an expense.
   b. a contra account.
   c. a liability.
   d. an asset.

Applying Your Knowledge

Exercises

1. On January 1, 19x1, Gotham Bus Company began its business by buying a new bus for $24,000. One-eighth of the cost of the bus is depreciated each year. Complete *in good form* the balance sheet as of December 31, 19x3.

Gotham Bus Company
Balance Sheet
December 31, 19x3

Assets

Cash		$5,000
Accounts Receivable		3,000
Company Vehicles	24,000	
Less Accum. Depr.	9,000	
		15,000
Total Assets		23,000

2. For each set of facts, provide the dollar amount that would be recorded.
   a. The cost of supplies at the beginning of the period was $510. During the period, supplies that cost $800 were purchased. At the end of the period, supplies that cost $340 remained. Supplies Expense should be recorded for $ 970
   b. The company signed a lease for $14,000 on July 1, 19x1, to cover the four-year period beginning July 1, 19x1. How much Rent Expense should they record on December 31, 19x1? $ 1750
   c. The company was paid $600 in advance for services to be performed. By the end of the period, only one-fourth of it had been earned. How much of the $600 will appear as Unearned Revenues on the balance sheet? $ 450

3. Following is the trial balance for the Darby Company.

Darby Company
Trial Balance
December 31, 19x1

	Debit	Credit
Cash	$ 77,300	
Notes Receivable	5,000	
Prepaid Advertising	8,000	
Prepaid Insurance	1,000	
Supplies	500	
Office Equipment	9,000	
Buildings	90,000	
Accumulated Depreciation, Buildings		$ 6,000
Notes Payable		1,500
Unearned Revenues		2,800
Alice Darby, Capital		100,000
Alice Darby, Withdrawals	13,000	
Revenues from Services		212,000
Wages Expense	118,500	
	$322,300	$322,300

The facts that follow are based on this trial balance. For each item, make the adjusting entry in the journal provided on the next page. Keep in mind that Darby Company operates on a calendar year.
   a. Cost of supplies on hand, based on physical count, is $375.
   b. Wages of $2,500 for the five-day work week ($500 per day) are paid and recorded every Friday. December 31 falls on a Thursday.
   c. Services amounting to $600 were rendered during 19x1 for customers who had paid in advance.
   d. Five percent of the cost of the building is taken as depreciation for 19x1.
   e. One-quarter of the prepaid advertising expired during 19x1.

f. All of the insurance shown on the trial balance was paid for on July 1, 19x1, and covers the two-year period beginning July 1, 19x1.

g. Work performed for customers which has not been billed or recorded amounts to $2,200.

h. Accrued interest on the note payable amounts to $52. This interest will be paid when the note matures.

	Date		Description	Debit	Credit
			General Journal		
a	12	31	Supplies Expense	125	
			Supplies		125
b		31	Wages ~~Payable~~ Expense	2000	
			Wages ~~Expense~~ Payable		2000
c		31	Unearned Revenue	600	
			Earned Revenue		600
d		31	Depreciation Expense, Building	4,500	
			Accumulated Depreciation, Buildings		4500
e		31	Advertising expense	2000	
			Prepaid Advertising		2000
f		31	Insurance Expense	250	
			Prepaid Insurance		250
g		31	Fees receivable	2200	
			Fees earned		2200
h		31	Interest ~~Pay~~ Expense	52	
			Interest Payable		52

Crossword Puzzle
For Chapters 3 and 4

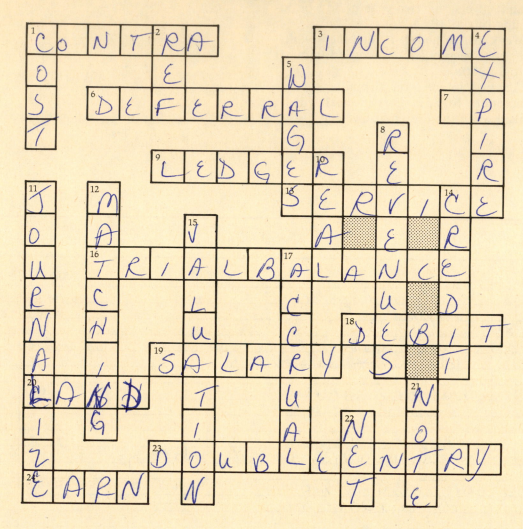

ACROSS

1. An account subtracted from another
3. See 22-Down
6. Postponement of a revenue or expense
7. Journal column title
9. Where the accounts are kept
13. A source of revenues
16. Test of debit and credit equality (2 words)
18. Left side of journal or ledger
19. Monthly- or yearly-rate compensation
20. One asset not subject to depreciation
23. _____ bookkeeping (hyphenated)
24. Realize (revenues)

DOWN

1. Historical _____ principle
2. Post. _____ column
4. Become an expense
5. Hourly- or piecework-rate compensation
8. Income statement item
10. Opposite of nominal
11. Record transactions
12. Rule applied through accrual accounting
14. Right side of journal or ledger
15. Assignment of a dollar amount to
17. Recognition of unrecorded revenues or expenses
21. Written promise to pay
22. With 3-Across, the term accountants use in referring to *profit*

The World According To GAAP

Accountants are beginning to worry that their smaller clients are being unfairly penalized by disclosure overkill.

No one said it was easy for General Motors or IBM to remain always in compliance with the voluminous Generally Accepted Accounting Principles. But what the accounting profession is beginning to realize is that it's even tougher for small businessmen to live with GAAP. "When the FASB develops standards, they're probably developed with larger companies in mind," says Harvey Moskowitz, Seidman & Seidman's national director of accounting. "Sometimes the standards they develop are too costly and complicated for smaller businesses."

Stanley Scott, chairman of the American Institute of Certified Public Accountant's new Special Committee to Study Accounting Standards Overload, agrees. "There's a strong feeling that a lot of the standards emanating from the standards setters do not really have an applicability to small or privately held companies," he says.

Small businessmen also agree:

☐ Privately held Dierckx Equipment Corp. (annual sales: $25 million) does a lot of leasing as part of its equipment business. GAAP requires that those leases be capitalized, and that has placed Dierckx in the middle of a catch-22 with the banks. If it doesn't capitalize its leases, it's not in compliance with GAAP, and the bank may not like that. If it does capitalize leases, its leverage ratio looks a lot worse, and the banks may not like that. Not only does this GAAP requirement endanger Dierckx' credit rating, but the cost of complying with that *one* requirement is $7,500 annually. Says Financial Vice President Ray Romano: "It's just a paper entry. It's immaterial. But it adds a lot of bookkeeping time. Our auditors must spend at least three days just going through the lease transactions, and without that requirement that wouldn't be necessary."

☐ New Brunswick Scientific Co., Inc. (annual sales: $16 million) has two accountants and a small bookkeeping staff. Keeping up with the slew of GAAP requirements has become a significant time problem.

Source: Article by Jay Gissen. Reprinted from the June 8, 1981 issue of *Forbes Magazine* by permission.

Controller Steve Rothstein finds GAAP burdensome and costly. "It's impossible to keep up with it all," he says.

☐ AW Computer Systems, Inc. (annual sales: $3 million) has a staff of 22 people. Before it went public last year, an accountant used to come in once or twice a year and a bookkeeper handled the ledger. Now it spends $70,000 annually for public reporting. The annual report has 12 footnotes covering 7 full pages. Says Controller Brad Smith: "It's a terrible burden. There's an awful lot of disclosure and I'm not really too sure that it's all that informative to the readers of the statements. What's going on here?"

Now some accounting firms are exploring the possibility of creating a sort of "little GAAP" for small companies. That might disturb statement users like bankers and investors, but there need be no significant information loss if little GAAP were intelligently designed, the firms argue.

Numbers Game

This may be easier said than done, however. Take the obvious task of defining "small," for instance. The logical source for such a definition, the FASB, doesn't have one. Inflation might make any dollar cutoff meaningless in a short time, it feels. A split between publicly held and privately owned companies wouldn't do the trick either. After all, some private companies are huge and some public ones are tiny.

Then there is the thorny question of which disclosure requirements to drop. Although most accounting firms agree that some disclosure requirements are too severe for small businesses, they differ widely as to which ones are painful enough to alter. When it comes to measurement principles—the rules for reporting that affect the bottom-line performance of a company—the disagreements are strong. Says Seidman's Moskowitz; "Only chaos could result from using different measurement principles for small and large companies, because users would be thoroughly confused. It would certainly raise credibility questions about the financial statements."

Proponents of alternate measurement standards for small companies claim that such confusion could be avoided if the alternative principles were sanctioned by the standards setters and limited to a well-defined group. "There are some of us in the profession that feel we should at least take a good look at whether we can develop alternative measurement principles," says Charles Chazen, a partner at Laventhol & Horwath. "Not all clients are quite the size of GM."

Certainly for clients smaller than GM, many principles seem nearly useless. Take, for example, FASB Statement 13, Accounting for Leases, issued in 1976. Capitalizing a lease changes the net income of a company, but to small companies with few leased items that don't normally need the accounting manpower to do the test procedure, FASB 13 is an unnecessary complication. Says New Brunswick Scientific Controller Rothstein: "Things like lease capitalization are impossible for a small firm to administer with a small staff. It's putting a tremendous strain on us just to keep current with the regulations."

"On one hand, if I leave his figures in and take exception in GAAP in a footnote, he gets all upset and says, 'What do you mean I'm not reporting correctly?'" says Terry Most, a partner at Most & Horowitz, a small Madison Avenue firm whose largest client has annual sales of $15 million. "But if I make all the changes, he won't even recognize his own numbers. I'd have to spend a few hours explaining and a few hours to do all the new calculations. We might have just doubled his accounting fee."

That doesn't sit well with the small-business owner who only uses his statements as part of the formality to get a loan from the bank. The bank doesn't necessarily care to see GAAP statements—in many cases, it would be satisfied with a representative alternative—but pressure within the industry and GAAP's "golden rule" reputation can make the bank balk when it's not applied.

Some other FASB statements that often come into question include compensated absences and capitalization of interest costs which many practitioners feel are accounted for generally anyway. Says Most: "An expense is an expense and I accrue it. But if you go to a small businessman and tell him that his bookkeeper has to track compensated absences, he says, 'the hell with you.'"

What's more, there have been many complaints that auditing procedures as a whole have been designed for larger companies that have fairly extensive segregation of accounting duties. The AICPA is aware of the problem and is looking at ways to fix it. Says Dan Guy, director of auditing research: "You can't apply a large-client audit approach in a small-business setting. It doesn't work." Still, that large-client approach *is* applied in many cases—whether it works well or not.

Although these difficulties have been an issue for several years, until now the AICPA and FASB have been addressing them at a glacial pace. Finally, last year, the AICPA offered two categories of membership, one for public company practitioners and one for private ones. A step. The FASB also admitted that it just isn't necessary for private companies to report earnings per share. Another step. And supplemental current value accounting is only required for the top 1,500 or so public companies. Progress.

"We're trying to understand the problems and their underlying causes better," says Glen Hildebrand, the FASB's assistant director of research and technical activities, "but we've reached no conclusions." Clearly, the AICPA and FASB are going to have to reach some conclusions soon. Says Laventhol & Horwath partner Edward O'Grady: "It would be unrealistic for both of those bodies to ignore it. It's going to happen because it's got to."

Chapter Five

Completing the Accounting Cycle

Reviewing the Chapter

1. The steps in the **accounting system** (also called the **accounting cycle**) are as follows:
   a. The transactions are analyzed from the source documents.
   b. The transactions are recorded in the journal.
   c. The journal entries are posted to the ledger.
   d. The accounts are adjusted at the end of the period with the aid of a work sheet.
   e. Financial statements are prepared from the work sheet.
   f. The nominal accounts are closed to conclude the current accounting period and to prepare for the new accounting period.

2. Accountants use **working papers** to help organize their work and to provide evidence in support of the financial statements. The **work sheet** is one such working paper. It lessens the chance of overlooking an adjustment. It acts as a check on the arithmetical accuracy of the accounts. And it aids in preparing financial statements. The work sheet is never published but is a useful tool to the accountant.

3. The five steps in the preparation of the work sheet are as follows:
   a. Enter the account balances (debit or credit) into the Trial Balance columns, and total the columns.
   b. Enter the adjustments into the Adjustments columns and total the columns. A letter identifies the debit and credit for each adjustment and may act as a key to a brief explanation at the bottom of the work sheet.
   c. Enter into the Adjusted Trial Balance columns (by means of **crossfooting**) the account balances as adjusted, and total the columns.
   d. Extend (transfer) the account balances from the Adjusted Trial Balance to either the Income Statement column or the Balance Sheet column, depending on which type of account is involved.
   e. Total the Income Statement and Balance Sheet columns. Then enter the net income or loss in the Income Statement and Balance Sheet columns (one will be a debit, the other a credit) as a balancing figure. Finally, recompute the column totals.

4. Once the work sheet is completed, it can be used to (a) prepare the financial statements, (b) record the adjusting entries in the journal, and (c) record the closing entries in the journal, thus preparing the records for the new period.

5. **Closing entries** (also called **clearing entries**) serve two purposes. First, they tranfer net income or loss to the owner's capital ac-

count. Second, they reduce revenue and expense accounts to zero so that these accounts may begin accumulating net income for the next accounting period. There are four closing entries, as follows:

a. Revenue accounts are closed. A compound entry debits each revenue account for the amount required to give it a zero balance and credits **Income Summary** for the revenue total. The Income Summary account exists only during closing entries and does not appear in the work sheet or in the financial statements.

b. Expense accounts are closed. A compound entry credits each expense account for the amount required to give it a zero balance and debits Income Summary for the expense total.

c. The Income Summary account is closed. After revenue and expense accounts have been closed, the Income Summary account will have either a debit balance or a credit balance. A credit balance indicates net income. A debit balance indicates a net loss. If a credit balance exists, then Income Summary must be debited for the amount required to give it a zero balance. The owner's capital account is credited for the same amount. The reverse is done when Income Summary has a debit balance.

d. The withdrawals account is closed. The owner's withdrawals account is credited for the amount required to give it a zero balance. The owner's capital account is debited for the same amount.

6. After posting the closing entries to the ledger, a **post-closing trial balance** must be prepared to verify again the equality of the debits and credits in the accounts. Only balance sheet accounts appear because all income statement accounts have zero balances at this point.

7. At the end of each accounting period, the accountant makes adjusting entries to record accrued revenues and expenses. Many of the adjusting entries are followed in the next period by the receipt or payment of cash. Thus it would become necessary in the next period to make a special entry dividing amounts between the two periods. To avoid this inconvenience, the accountant can make **reversing entries** (dated the beginning of the new period). Reversing entries, though not required, allow the bookkeeper to simply make the routine bookkeeping entry when cash finally changes hands. Not all adjusting entries may be reversed. In the system we will use, only adjustments for accruals may be reversed. Deferrals may not.

Testing Your Knowledge

Matching

Match each term with its definition by writing the appropriate letter in the blank.

d ___ 1. Accounting cycle
g ___ 2. Working papers
i ___ 3. Work sheet
b ___ 4. Foot
h ___ 5. Crossfooting
f ___ 6. Reversing entry
c ___ 7. Closing entries
a ___ 8. Income summary
e ___ 9. Post-closing trial balance

a. An account used only during closing entries
b. Add a column
c. The means of transferring net income or loss to the owner's capital account
d. The sequence from transaction analysis to closing entries
e. A final proof that the accounts are in balance
f. The opposite of an adjusting entry, journalized to facilitate routine bookkeeping entries
g. Documents that help accountants organize their work
h. Adding from left to right
i. A working paper that facilitates the preparation of financial statements

Completion

Use the lines provided to complete each item.

1. What four accounts or kinds of accounts are closed out each accounting period?

   Revenue

   Expenses

   Withdrawals

   Income Summary

2. List the five columnar headings of a work sheet in their proper order.

   Trial Balance

   Adjustments

   Adjusted Trial Balance

   Income Statement

   Balance Sheet

3. In general, what accounts will appear in the post-closing trial balance? What accounts will not appear?

   Assets, Capital, Liabilities;

   Expenses, Revenues

4. The six steps in the accounting cycle are presented here in the wrong order. Place the numbers 1 through 6 in the spaces provided to indicate the correct order.

   3 The journal entries are posted to the ledger.

   6 The nominal accounts are closed.

   1 The transactions are analyzed from the source documents.

   4 The accounts are adjusted, usually with the aid of a work sheet.

   2 The transactions are recorded in the journal.

   5 Financial statements are prepared from the work sheet.

True-False

Circle T if the statement is true, F if it is false.

(T) F 1. The work sheet is prepared before the formal adjusting entries have been made in the journal.

(T) F 2. Preparation of a work sheet helps reduce the possibility of overlooking an adjustment.

T (F) 3. Total debits will differ from total credits in the Balance Sheet column by the amount of the net income or loss.

(T) F 4. The statement of owner's equity is prepared after the formal income statement, but before the formal balance sheet.

T (F) 5. The Income Summary account can be found in the statement of owner's equity.

T (F) 6. Closing entries convert real and nominal accounts to zero balances.

T (F) 7. When revenue accounts are closed, the Income Summary account will be credited.

T F 8. The owner's withdrawals account is closed to the owner's capital account.

T F 9. When the Income Summary account is closed, it always requires a debit.

T (F) 10. The post-closing trial balance will include the owner's withdrawals account.

T (F) 11. The work sheet is published with the balance sheet and income statement as a supplementary statement.

T (F) 12. A key letter is needed in the Adjusted Trial Balance column of a work sheet to show whether it is extended to the Balance Sheet column or to the Income Statement column.

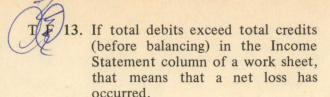 T F 13. If total debits exceed total credits (before balancing) in the Income Statement column of a work sheet, that means that a net loss has occurred.

Multiple-Choice

Circle the letter of the best answer.

1. Which account will appear in the post-closing trial balance?
   a. Interest Earned
   b. Income Summary
   c. Richard Weber, Capital
   d. Richard Weber, Withdrawals

2. Which of the following is true?
   a. Closing entries are prepared before formal adjusting entries.
   b. The work sheet is prepared after the post-closing trial balance.
   c. Formal adjusting entries are prepared before the work sheet.
   d. The financial statements are prepared before closing entries.

3. Which of the following accounts would normally have a debit balance?
   a. Accumulated Depreciation, Machinery
   b. Notes Payable
   c. Marion Valdez, Withdrawals
   d. Accounting Fees Earned

4. If total debits exceed total credits (before balancing) in the Balance Sheet column of a work sheet,
   a. a net income has occurred.
   b. a net loss has occurred.
   c. a mistake has definitely been made.
   d. no conclusion can be drawn until the closing entries have been made.

5. Which of the following accounts would *not* be involved in closing entries?
   a. Unearned Commissions
   b. Larry Weiss, Capital
   c. Telephone Expense
   d. Larry Weiss, Withdrawals

6. When a net loss has occurred,
   a. all expense accounts are closed with debits.
   b. the Income Summary account is closed with a credit.
   c. the owner's withdrawals account is closed with a debit.
   d. all revenue accounts are closed with credits.

7. Which of the following is *not* an objective of closing entries?
   a. To transfer net income or loss into the owner's Capital account
   b. To produce zero balances in all nominal accounts
   c. To update the revenue and expense accounts
   d. To be able to measure net income for the following period

8. Reversing entries
   a. are dated as of the end of the period.
   b. are the opposite of adjusting entries.
   c. may be made for depreciation previously recorded.
   d. are the opposite of closing entries.

Applying Your Knowledge

Exercises

1. Following are the accounts of a work sheet's Adjusted Trial Balance for the month of July. In the journal provided, write the necessary closing entries. All accounts have normal balances.

Accounts Receivable	$2,000	Utilities Expense	150
Accounts Payable	1,000	Eleanor Barrett, Capital	3,000
Cash	3,500	Eleanor Barrett, Withdrawals	2,500
Rent Expense	500		
Revenues from Services	4,700		
Telephone Expense	50		

General Journal

Date		Description	Debit	Credit
		Revenues from Services	4,700	
		Income Summary		4,700
		To close revenue accts		
		Income Summary	700	
		Rent Expense		500
		Telephone Expense		50
		Utilities Expense		150
		To close expense accts.		
		Eleanor Barrett, Capital	2500	
		Eleanor Barrett, W/D		2500
		To close W/D accts.		
		Income Summary	4000	
		Eleanor Barrett, Capital		4000
		To close income Summary		

2. Using the information from Exercise 1, complete the following statement of owner's equity.

Barrett's Fix-It Shop
Statement of Owner's Equity
For the Month Ended July 31, 19xx

Eleanor Barrett, Capital 7/1/xx	3000
Add: Net Income	4000
Subtotal	7000
Less: Eleanor Barrett, w/d	2500
Eleanor Barrett, Capital 7/31/xx	4500

3. The following items *a* through *f* provide the information needed to make adjustments for Steve's Outdoor Maintenance Service as of December 31, 19xx. Complete the entire work sheet using this information. Remember to use key letters for each adjustment.

 a. On December 31, there is $200 of unexpired rent on the storage garage.

 b. Depreciation taken on the lawn equipment during the period amounts to $1,500.

 c. An inventory of lawn supplies shows $100 remaining on December 31.

 d. Accrued wages on December 31 amount to $280.

 e. Grass-cutting fees earned but as yet uncollected amount to $50.

 f. Of the $300 landscaping fees paid for in advance, $120 had been earned by December 31.

Steve's Outdoor Maintenance Service
Work Sheet
For the Year Ended December 31, 19xx

Account Name	Trial Balance		Adjustments		Adjusted Trial Balance		Income Statement		Balance Sheet	
	Debit	Credit	Debit	Credit	Debit	Credit	Debit	Credit	Debit	Credit
Cash	2,560				2,560				2,560	
Accounts Receivable	880		e. 50		930				930	
Prepaid Rent	750			a. 550	200				200	
Lawn Supplies	250			c. 150	100				100	
Lawn Equipment	10,000				10,000				10,000	
Accum. Deprec., Lawn Equip.		2,000		b. 1,500		3,500				3,500
Accounts Payable		630				630				630
Unearned Landscaping Fees		300	f. 120			180				180
Steve Charles, Capital		6,000				6,000				6,000
Steve Charles, Withdrawals	6,050				6,050				6,050	
Grass Cutting Fees		15,000		e. 50		15,050		15,050		
Wages Expense	3,300		d. 280		3,580		3,580			
Gasoline Expense	140				140		140			
	23,930	23,930								
Rent Expense			a. 550		550		550			
Depreciation Expense			b. 1,500		1,500		1,500			
Lawn Supplies Expense			c. 150		150		150			
Landscaping Fees Earned				f. 120		120		120		
Wages Payable				d. 280		280				280
			2,650	2,650	25,760	25,760	5,920	15,170	19,840	13,510
Net Income							9,250			9,250
							15,170	15,170	19,840	19,840

4. On December 1, Bowman Company borrowed $20,000 from a bank on a note for 90 days at 12 percent (annual) interest. Assuming that interest is not included in the face amount, prepare the following journal entries:

a. December 1 entry to record the note
b. December 31 entry to record accrued interest
c. December 31 entry to close interest
d. January 1 reversing entry
e. March 1 entry to record payment of note plus interest.

			General Journal		
Date			Description	Debit	Credit
12	1		Cash	20,000	
			N P		20,000
	31		Interest Expense	200	
			Accrued Interest Payable		200
	31		Income Summary	200	
			Interest expense		200
			To close Interest Expense		
1	1		Interest Payable	200	
			Interest Expense		200
			To reverse adjusting entry		
3	1		N P	20,000	
			Interest Expense	600	
			Cash		20,600
			Repayment of note + interest		

Chapter Six

Accounting for Merchandising Operations

Reviewing the Chapter

1. A merchandising firm is a wholesaler or retailer that buys and sells goods (merchandise) in finished form. Such a firm uses the same basic accounting methods as a service company. However, merchandising requires some additional accounts and concepts and results in a more complicated income statement. Accounting for a merchandising firm is also different from that for a manufacturing firm.

2. The income of a merchandising firm is computed as follows:

   Revenues from sales (net sales)
   – Cost of goods sold
   ──────────────────────────────
   = **Gross margin from sales**
   – Operating expenses
   ──────────────────────────────
   = **Net income**

   a. Revenues from sales (net sales) consist of gross proceeds from the sale of merchandise (**gross sales**) less sales returns and allowances and sales discounts.
   b. **Cost of goods sold** is the amount that the merchandising company originally paid for the goods that it sold during a given period. If, for example, a merchandising firm sells for $100 a radio that cost the company $70, then revenues from sales are $100, cost of goods sold is $70, and gross margin

   from sales is $30. This $30 gross margin helps pay for **operating expenses** (all expenses other than cost of goods sold). What is left after subtracting operating expenses represents net income or net loss (if operating expenses are greater than gross margin). Preparing an income statement in this way provides useful information to management, which is continually trying to improve net income.

3. When a cash sale is made, Cash is debited and Sales is credited for the amount of the sale. When a credit sale is made, Accounts Receivable is debited and Sales is credited (at the point of sale, it is not known if the customer will pay within the discount period or will return some goods). Generally, a sale is recorded when the goods are delivered and title passes to the customer, regardless of when payment is made.

4. When a cash customer returns goods for a refund, **Sales Returns and Allowances** is debited and Cash is credited. For a credit customer, Sales Returns and Allowances is debited and Accounts Receivable is credited. The Sales Returns and Allowances account is debited instead of the Sales account to provide management with data about dissatisfied customers. In the income statement it is a contra account to Gross Sales.

5. When goods are sold on credit, terms will vary as to when payment must be made. For instance, n/30 means that full payment is due within 30 days after the invoice date, and n/10 eom means that full payment is due 10 days after the end of the month.

6. Often a customer is given a discount for early payment, and the merchandiser records a sales discount. Terms of **2/10, n/30**, for example, mean that a 2 percent discount will be given if payment is made within 10 days of the invoice date. Otherwise, the net amount is due within 30 days.

7. **Sales discounts** are recorded when payment is received within the discount period. Cash and Sales Discounts are debited; Accounts Receivable is credited. Sales Discounts is a contra account to Gross Sales in the income statement.

8. The accountant calculates the cost of goods sold as follows:

   Beginning inventory (at cost)
   + Net purchases (see item 9)

   = Cost of goods available for sale
   − **Ending inventory** (at cost)

   = Cost of goods sold

9. Net purchases is calculated as follows:

   (Gross) purchases
   − Purchases returns and allowances
   − Purchases discounts

   = Subtotal
   + Freight in

   = Net purchases

10. **Merchandise inventory** appears as an asset in the balance sheet and includes all salable goods owned by the company no matter where the goods are located. Goods in transit to which a company has acquired title are included in ending inventory. However, goods that the company has formally sold are not included, even if the company has not yet delivered them. To simplify inventory taking, which usually takes place on the last day of the fiscal year, many companies end their fiscal year during the slow season.

11. There are two ways of determining inventory.
    a. The **perpetual inventory method** is used when it is necessary to keep a record of the cost of each inventory item when it is purchased and when it is sold.
    b. The **periodic inventory method** is used when it is unnecessary or impractical to keep track of the cost of each item. Under this method, the company instead waits until the end of the accounting period to **take a physical inventory**. This physical count figure is then multiplied by a derived cost-per-unit figure (explained in Chapter 11) to arrive at the cost of ending inventory.

12. The ending inventory of one period is the beginning inventory of the next period. The beginning inventory is removed from the inventory account, and the ending inventory is entered into the inventory account by means of closing entries.

13. Under the periodic inventory method, all purchases of merchandise are debited to the **Purchases** account and credited to Cash or Accounts Payable. The purpose of the Purchases account is to accumulate the cost of merchandise purchased for resale during the period.

14. If goods are returned to a supplier, the merchandiser debits Cash or Accounts Payable and credits **Purchases Returns and Allowances**. Purchases Returns and Allowances is a contra account to Purchases in the income statement.

15. Often a merchandising company is offered a discount if it pays within a given number of days. It may select either the gross method or the net method of recording the transaction.
    a. Under the gross method, the purchase is initially recorded at the gross purchase price. If the company makes payment within the discount period, it debits Accounts Payable, credits **Purchases Discounts**, and credits Cash.

b. Under the net method, the purchase is recorded at first at the net purchase price (that is, the gross purchase price less the purchase discount offered). If the company does *not* make payment within the discount period, it debits Accounts Payable, debits Discounts Lost, and credits Cash. However, if payment *is* made within the discount period, no discount account is recorded.

16. When a merchandising firm pays for transportation costs on goods purchased, it debits **Freight In** (or **Transportation In**) and credits Cash. A merchandiser in Chicago, for instance, must pay the freight in from Boston if the terms specify FOB Boston or **FOB shipping point**. However, the supplier in Boston pays if the terms are FOB Chicago or **FOB destination**. Freight out is a cost of selling (not buying) merchandise, and should not be confused with freight in.

17. Inventory loss results from theft and spoilage, and is automatically included in the cost of goods sold under the periodic inventory method.

18. Operating expenses consist of selling expenses and general and administrative expenses. Selling expenses are for advertising, salespeople's salaries, sales office expenses, freight out, and all other expenses directly related to the sales effort. General and administrative expenses are all expenses not directly related to the manufacturing or sales effort. Examples are general office expenses and executive salaries.

19. Under a periodic inventory system, the objectives of dealing with inventory at the end of the period are to (a) remove the beginning balance from the Merchandise Inventory account, (b) enter the ending balance into the Merchandise Inventory account, and (c) enter these two amounts into the Income Summary account. These objectives are met by applying either the adjusting entry method or the closing entry method. Though different in form, both methods credit Merchandise Inventory and debit Income Summary for the beginning balance and debit Merchandise Inventory and credit Income Summary for the ending balance.

20. Preparation of a merchandiser's work sheet depends on whether the adjusting entry method or closing entry method is being used. Under either method, the Adjusted Trial Balance column may be eliminated if only a few adjustments are necessary. In addition, many income statement accounts appear in the merchandiser's work sheet that do not appear in the service company's work sheet. Merchandise Inventory, however, must receive special treatment.
a. Under the adjusting entry method, Merchandise Inventory is debited for ending inventory and credited for beginning inventory in the adjustments column. The corresponding credit and debit are to Income Summary.
b. Under the closing entry method, Merchandise Inventory bypasses the adjustments column. Instead, beginning inventory appears as a debit in the Income Statement column. Ending inventory appears as a credit in the Income Statement column and as a debit in the Balance Sheet column.

21. The formal adjusting and closing entries for a merchandiser are similar to those for a service company, with the following exceptions.
a. Under the adjusting entry method, merchandise inventory is handled through adjusting entries, and all nominal accounts are closed in the normal manner.
b. Under the closing entry method, Beginning Inventory, Sales Returns and Allowances, Sales Discounts, Purchases, Freight In, and Freight Out are closed in the same entry that closes expenses. Purchases Returns and Allowances and Purchases Discounts are closed, and Ending Inventory is debited (to record the new balance), in the same entry that closes revenues.

Testing Your Knowledge

Matching

Match each term with its definition by writing the appropriate letter in the blank.

_c_ 1. Merchandiser

_h_ 2. Cost of goods sold

_j_ 3. Gross margin from sales

_e_ 4. Operating expenses

_l_ 5. Sales Returns and Allowances

_k_ 6. Sales Discounts

_b_ 7. Discounts Lost

_g_ 8. Purchases

_i_ 9. Cost of goods available for sale

_d_ 10. Perpetual inventory method

_m_ 11. Periodic inventory method

_o_ 12. Physical inventory

_a_ 13. Freight in

_f_ 14. FOB (free on board)

_p_ 15. Purchases Returns and Allowances

_n_ 16. Purchases Discounts

a. Transportation cost for goods purchased
b. Under the net method of handling discounts, the account used by the buyer when it does not pay for goods early
c. A buyer and seller of goods that are in finished form
d. A system whereby continuous cost records are maintained for merchandise
e. All expenses except for cost of goods sold
f. The point after which the buyer must bear the transportation cost
g. The account used to accumulate the cost of goods bought during the period
h. What a merchandising company paid for the goods that it sold during the period
i. Beginning inventory plus net cost of purchases
j. Revenue from sales minus cost of goods sold
k. The account used by the seller when the buyer pays for goods early under the terms of the sales agreement
l. The account used by the seller when the buyer returns goods
m. A system whereby continuous cost records are *not* maintained for merchandise
n. The account used by the buyer when it pays for goods early under the terms of the sales agreement
o. A count of merchandise on hand
p. The account used by the buyer when it returns goods

Completion

Use the lines provided to complete each item.

1. List the five parts of a merchandiser's condensed income statement in their proper order. Use mathematical signs to indicate their relationship.

Revenues from sales
− Cost of goods sold
= Gross margin from sales
− Operating expenses
= Net Income

2. List the items in the condensed cost of goods sold section of an income statement. Use mathematical signs to indicate their relationship.

Beginning inventory (cost)
+ Net purchases & allowances
= Cost of goods avail. for sale
− Ending inventory (cost)
= Cost of goods sold

3. Using mathematical signs, write the sequence of items involved in figuring net purchases.

Gross purchases
− Purch. returns + allowances
− Purch. discounts
= Subtotal
+ Freight In
= Net purchases

4. Using mathematical signs, write the sequence of items involved in figuring revenues from sales (net sales).

Gross sales
− Sales returns + allow
− Sales Discounts
= Net sales

5. Explain briefly how merchandise inventory is handled in the accounts at the end of the period under the adjusting entry method.

Beg. inv. cred. to merch.
inv. + deb. to income sum.
End inv. debit to merch inv
+ credit to inc. sum.

True-False

Circle T if the statement is true, F if it is false.

T (F) 1. Failure to include a warehouse's merchandise in ending inventory will result in an overstated net income.

T (F) 2. Terms of n/10 eom mean that payment must be made 10 days before the end of the month.

(T) F 3. An overstated beginning inventory will result in an overstated cost of goods sold.

T (F) 4. A low-volume car dealer is more likely to use the periodic inventory method than the perpetual inventory method.

(T) F 5. FOB destination means that the seller is bearing the transportation cost.

(T) F 6. The difference between the adjusting entry method and the closing entry method mainly concerns the treatment of merchandise inventory.

(T) F 7. Sales Discounts is a contra account to Gross Sales.

(T) F 8. Ending inventory appears in both the balance sheet and the income statement.

(T) F 9. Cost of goods available for sale minus cost of goods sold equals ending inventory.

(T) F 10. The perpetual inventory method requires more detailed record keeping than does the periodic method.

(T) F 11. The beginning inventory of a period is the same as the ending inventory of the previous period.

T (F) 12. Purchases Returns and Allowances is closed with a credit.

T (F) 13. Sales Returns and Allowances normally has a credit balance.

T (F) 14. A cash purchase of office supplies that are meant to be used in the day-to-day operation of a business requires a debit to Purchases and a credit to Cash.

(T) F 15. Cost of goods sold will not appear in the income statement of a company that provides services only.

(T) F 16. If gross margin from sales is not enough to cover operating expenses, then a net loss has occurred.

T (F) 17. Under a periodic inventory system, as soon as a sale is made, the cost of the goods sold must be recorded and the inventory account must be decreased.

Multiple-Choice

Circle the letter of the best answer.

1. Burns buys $600 of merchandise from Allen, with terms of 2/10, n/30. Burns immediately returns $100 of goods, and pays for the remainder eight days after purchase. Assuming the gross method of handling discounts, Burns's entry on the date of payment would include a
   a. debit to Accounts Payable for $600.
   b. debit to Sales Discounts for $12.
   c. credit to Purchases Returns and Allowances for $100.
   d. credit to Purchases Discounts for $10.

2. Which of the following normally has a credit balance?
   a. Sales Discounts
   b. Merchandise Inventory
   c. Purchases Returns and Allowances
   d. Freight In

3. If an item of ending inventory is counted twice, then
   a. net income will be understated.
   b. beginning inventory for the next period will be understated.
   c. cost of goods available for sale will be overstated.
   d. cost of goods sold will be understated.

4. On the work sheet, assuming the adjusting entry method, ending inventory will appear on the
   a. debit side of the Income Statement column.
   b. credit side of the Income Statement column.
   c. debit side of the Balance Sheet column.
   d. credit side of the Balance Sheet column.

5. Which of the following is irrelevant in computing cost of goods sold?
   a. Freight In
   b. Freight Out
   c. Merchandise Inventory, beginning
   d. Merchandise Inventory, ending

6. A company purchases $100 of goods on credit with terms of 2/10, n/30. If it initially records the purchase net of the discount available and subsequently pays within the discount period, its journal entry would include a
   a. debit to Purchases Discounts for $2.
   b. credit to Purchases Discounts for $2.
   c. credit to Cash for $100.
   d. debit to Accounts Payable for $98.

7. Which of the following is credited when closed?
   a. Purchases Returns and Allowances
   b. Sales
   c. Beginning inventory
   d. None of the above

Applying Your Knowledge

Exercises

1. Following are the May transactions of Apex Merchandising Corporation. For each transaction, prepare the journal entry in the journal provided. Assume that the periodic inventory method is being used, as well as the gross method of handling purchases discounts.

May 1 Purchased merchandise for $500 on credit, terms 2/10, n/60.

     3 Sold merchandise for $500 on credit, terms 2/10, 1/20, n/30.

     4 Paid $42 for freight charges relating to a merchandise purchase of April.

     5 Purchased office supplies for $100, on credit.

     6 Returned $20 of the May 5 office supplies, for credit.

     7 Returned $50 of merchandise purchased on May 1, for credit.

     9 Sold merchandise for $225, on credit, terms 2/10, 1/15, n/30.

    10 Paid for the merchandise purchased on May 1, less the return and any discount.

    14 The customer of May 9 returned $25 of merchandise, for credit.

    22 The customer of May 9 paid for the merchandise, less the return and any discount.

    26 The customer of May 3 paid for the merchandise.

General Journal

Date	Description	Debit	Credit
May 1	Purchases	500	
	A/P		500
	2/10, N/60		
3	A/R	500	
	Sales		500
	2/10, 1/20, N/30		
4	Freight in	42	
	Cash		42
	From april		
5	Office Supplies	100	
	A/P		100
6	A/P	20	
	Office Supplies		20
	Return for credit purch of 5/5		
7	A/P	50	
	Purchases return + allow.		50
	Return of 5/1 purch.		
9	A/R	225	
	Sales		225
	2/10, 1/15, N/30		
10	A/P	450	
	Cash		441
	Purchase Discounts		9
	Pymt. of 5/1 purchase (less return on 5/7)		
14	Sales return + allow	25	
	A/R		25
	Return of goods sold 5/9		
	Cash	198	
	Sales discounts	2	
	A/R		200
	Pymt of goods sold 5/9		
30	Cash	500	
	A/R		500
	Pymt of goods sold 5/3		

2. Following are the accounts and data needed to prepare the 19xx closing entries for Jefferson Merchandising Company. In the journal provided, prepare Jefferson's closing entries. Assume the closing entry method of handling merchandise inventory.

Advertising Expense	$ 5,000
Arthur Jefferson, Capital	15,000
Arthur Jefferson, Withdrawals	12,000
Freight In	2,000
Freight Out	4,000
Merchandise Inventory (Jan. 1)	10,000
Merchandise Inventory (Dec. 31)	8,000
Purchases	50,000
Purchases Discounts	500
Purchases Returns and Allowances	500
Rent Expense	3,000
Sales	100,000
Sales Discounts	300
Sales Returns and Allowances	200
Wages Expense	7,000

General Journal

Date	Description	Debit	Credit
Dec 31	Income Summary	81,600	
	Advertising Expense		5000
	Freight In		2000
	Merchandise Inv. 1/1		10,000
	Sales Discounts		300
	Sales Rets. & Allow.		200
	Rent Expense		3000
	Purchases		50,000
	Wages Expense		7000
	Freight Out		4000
31	Merchandise Inv. 12/31	8000	
	Sales	100,000	
	Purch. Discounts	500	
	Purch. Rets. & Allow	500	
	Income Summary		109,000
31	Income Summary	27,500	
	A. Jefferson, Cap.		27,500
31	A. J. W/D	12,000	
	A. J. Cap		12,000

3. Using the information from Exercise 2, prepare a partial income statement showing just the computation of gross margin on sales.

Jefferson Merchandising Company
Income Statement
For the Year 19xx

Gross Sales	100,000		100,000
Less Sales Ret & Allow		200	
Less Sales Discounts		300	500
Net Sales			99,500
C/O/S			
Merch. Inv. 1/1		10,000	10,000
Purchases	50,000	50,000	
Less: Purch. Ret. & Allow	500		
Less Purch Discounts	500	49,000	
	49,000		49,000
Add Freight In	2,000	51,000	51,000
Cost Goods Avail Sales	51,000	61,000	
Less Merch Inv. 12/31		8,000	
C/O/S			53,000
Gross margin on Sales			46,500

4. The work sheet for Mammoth Mart has been started, as shown on the next page. Use the following information to complete the work sheet (remember to key the adjustments). Assume the closing entry method of handling merchandise inventory. You will notice that the Adjusted Trial Balance column has been provided, even though it is not absolutely necessary.
   a. Expired rent, $250
   b. Accrued salaries, $500
   c. Depreciation on equipment, $375
   d. Ending merchandise inventory, $620

Mammoth Mart
Work Sheet
For the Month Ended March 31, 19xx

Account Name	Trial Balance Debit	Trial Balance Credit	Adjustments Debit	Adjustments Credit	Adjusted Trial Balance Debit	Adjusted Trial Balance Credit	Income Statement Debit	Income Statement Credit	Balance Sheet Debit	Balance Sheet Credit
Cash	1,000				1000				1000	
Accounts Receivable	700				700				700	
Merchandise Inventory	400		(a) 1650	(d) 400	4700	400	400	1650	1650	
Prepaid Rent	750			(c) 250	500				500	
Equipment	4,200				4200				4200	
Accounts Payable		900				900				900
Marion Valdez, Capital		4,200				4200		400		4200
Sales		9,800				9800		9800		
Sales Discounts	300				300		300			
Purchases	3,700				3700		3700			
Purchases Returns and Allowances		150				150		150		
Freight In	400				400		400			
Salaries Expense	3,000		(b) 500		3500		3500			
Advertising Expense	600				600		600			
	15,050	15,050								
Rent Expense			250		250		250			
Salaries Payable				(b) 500		500				500
Accum. Dep. Equip.				(c) 375		375				375
Deprec. Exp. Equip.			(c) 375		375		375			
Merch. Inventory			1125	1125	13925	16225	9525	10570	7020	5975
Net Income			3125	3125			1045			1045
							10570	10570	7020	7020

Crossword Puzzle
For Chapters 5 and 6

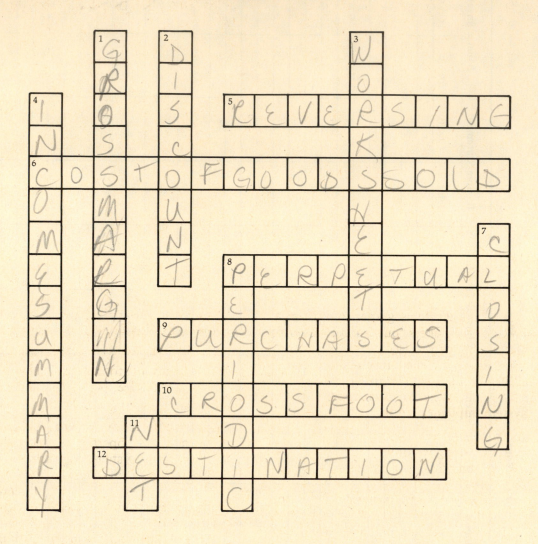

ACROSS

5. Entry opposite of adjusting
6. Inventory-related expense (4 words)
8. Method of accounting for inventory
9. Inventory-acquisition account
10. Add or subtract horizontally
12. FOB _____

DOWN

1. Income statement subtotal (2 words)
2. Reward for paying early
3. Aids to financial statement preparation (2 words)
4. Account used when clearing the accounts (2 words)
7. Clearing the accounts
8. Method of accounting for inventory
11. 2/10, _____/30

Chapter Seven

Accounting Systems and Special-Purpose Journals

Reviewing the Chapter

1. Accounting systems gather data from all parts of a business, put them into useful form, and communicate the results to management. The installation of an accounting system occurs in three phases: **system investigation, system design**, and **system implementation.**

2. In designing an accounting system, the systems designer must adhere to four general principles of systems design, as follows:
   a. The **cost/benefit principle** states that the benefits derived from the accounting system must match or exceed its cost.
   b. The **control principle** states that the accounting system must contain the safeguards necessary to protect assets and make sure data is reliable.
   c. The **compatibility principle** states that the accounting system must be workable for the organization and its people.
   d. The **flexibility principle** states that the accounting system should be able to accommodate changes (as in volume of transactions) in the business.

3. **Data processing** involves gathering information, organizing it in useful form, and communicating the results to decision makers. There are several types of data processing systems, many of which will be described in the following paragraphs.

4. A **computer data processing** system is made up of four basic elements: hardware, software, personnel, and configuration.

5. Computer **hardware** is all the equipment needed to operate a computer data processing system. It basically includes input media and devices, processing and memory units, and output media and devices. Some input devices are optical scanners, card readers, tape readers, and console typewriters. Some output devices are printers and card punches. Remote terminals are used for both input and output. The computer program is executed by the **central processor**, which consists of a **control unit**, an **arithmetic/logic unit**, and **storage** (memory) **units**. Data that are not in the actual process of being manipulated are kept available to the central processor on **secondary, or auxiliary, storage**.

6. Computer **software** is the programs that make it possible to use the hardware. A computer **program** is a sequence of instructions to the computer, and is written in one of several computer languages.

7. The key personnel in a computer system are the **systems analyst** (who designs the data processing system), the **programmer** (who writes the programs), and the **computer operator** (who runs the computer).

8. **Batch processing** is the processing of one job at a time, whereas **on-line processing** allows several jobs to be processed at once by means of remote terminals and random access of information.

9. Companies using **manual data processing** (keeping hand-written accounting records) record an entry in one or more journals. A company can record all of its transactions in the general journal only. However, companies with a large number of transactions also use **special-purpose journals** to save time, effort, and money.

10. Most business transactions fall into one of four types, and are recorded in one of four special-purpose journals, as follows:
    a. Sales of merchandise on credit are recorded in the **sales journal**.
    b. Purchases of merchandise on credit are recorded in the **purchases journal**.
    c. Receipts of cash are recorded in the **cash receipts journal**.
    d. Disbursements of cash are recorded in the **cash payments journal**.

11. The sales journal has four main time-saving features. (a) Each entry requires only one line. (b) Account names need not be written out, since frequently occurring accounts are used as column headings. (c) An explanation is not needed. (d) Only total sales for the month are posted to the sales account, not each individual sale. The same time-saving principles apply to other special-purpose journals.

12. Most companies that sell to customers on credit keep an accounts receivable record for each customer. In this way the company can determine how much a given customer owes at any time. All customer accounts are filed alphabetically in the Accounts Receivable **subsidiary ledger**.

13. The general ledger, however, contains an Accounts Receivable **controlling account**. The controlling account is updated at the end of each month and keeps a running total of *all* accounts receivable. Its balance should equal the sum of all the accounts in the accounts receivable subsidiary ledger.

14. Most companies also use an Accounts Payable controlling account and subsidiary ledger, which function much like the Accounts Receivable controlling account and subsidiary ledger.

15. Transactions that cannot be recorded in a special-purpose journal, such as the purchase of office equipment on credit (assuming a single-column purchases journal), are recorded in the general journal. Closing entries and adjusting entries are also made in the general journal. Postings are made at the end of each day, and in the case of Accounts Receivable and Accounts Payable, postings are made to both the controlling and subsidiary accounts.

16. Special-purpose journals of businesses may be slightly different from those used in the textbook, because the types of transactions may vary. The main point of special-purpose journals is that they should take care of the kinds of transactions a company commonly encounters.

Testing Your Knowledge

Matching

Match each term with its definition by writing the appropriate letter in the blank.

_F_ 1. Data processing

_B_ 2. Special-purpose journal

_L_ 3. Subsidiary ledger

_J_ 4. Subsidiary account

_N_ 5. Controlling account

_D_ 6. Schedule of accounts receivable or accounts payable

_C_ 7. Hardware

_H_ 8. Software

_I_ 9. Systems analyst

_M_ 10. Programmer

_E_ 11. Computer operator

_K_ 12. Batch processing

_G_ 13. On-line processing

_A_ 14. Program

a. A sequence of instructions to the computer

b. Any journal except for the general journal

c. The equipment used in a computer data processing system

d. A formal listing of customers or creditors

e. A person who runs a computer

f. Gathering, organizing, and communicating information

g. The running of several computer jobs simultaneously by means of remote terminals

h. Computer programs, instructions, and routines

i. A person who designs computer systems

j. The record of a customer or creditor in a subsidiary ledger

k. The running of one computer job at a time

l. Where the customer or creditor accounts are kept

m. A person who writes computer instructions

n. Any general ledger account that has a related subsidiary ledger

Completion

Use the lines provided to complete each item.

1. List the four major special-purpose journals, with the type of transaction that should be recorded in each.

Special-Purpose Journal	Type of Transaction
Sales	Sales on Credit
Purchases	Purchases on Credit
Cash Receipts	all cash receipts
Cash Payments	all cash payments

2. Briefly explain why totals in the Other Accounts columns of special-purpose journals should not be posted at the end of the month.

Individual amounts to these accts. are posted daily.

3. Differentiate between controlling and subsidiary accounts.

A controlling acct. is in general ledger - subsidiaries are individual accts

4. List the four general principles of systems design, and briefly describe the significance of each.

a. *cost/benefit - benefit of system must ≥ than cost*

b. *control - must contain safeguards & protect assets*

c. *compatability - must be compatible w/personnel*

d. *flexibility - must be able to accomodate change*

5. The four basic elements of a computer data processing system are

Hardware
Software
Personnel
Configuration

6. In which journal would some accounts be "double-posted," and what does the double-posting signify?

Genl journal - AP or A/R from to controlling & subsidiary accts.

True-False

Circle T if the statement is true, F if it is false.

(T) F **1.** All transactions can be recorded in the general journal, but use of special-purpose journals will probably save time.

T (F) **2.** The purchase of office equipment on credit should be recorded in the purchases journal (assume a single-column journal).

T (F) **3.** Posting to subsidiary accounts should be done at the end of the month.

T (F) **4.** At the end of each month, the column totals in the general journal should be posted to the general ledger.

(T) F **5.** The adjustment for depreciation should be recorded in the general journal.

T (F) **6.** A check is placed in the Post. Ref. column of the sales journal to show that the entry has been posted to the accounts payable subsidiary ledger.

T (F) **7.** A company with 25 sales recorded in the sales journal in a single month should have 25 postings to the sales account.

T (F) **8.** Cash sales should be recorded in the sales journal.

(T) F **9.** The Accounts Receivable and Accounts Payable controlling accounts should not have updated daily balances.

(T) F **10.** In the cash payments journal, Accounts Payable is on the debit side.

(T) F **11.** Accounts receivable in the general journal are posted to both the controlling and the subsidiary account.

T (F) **12.** After a schedule of accounts payable is prepared, its total is compared with the controlling account's balance.

T (F) **13.** The central processor is an important part of a computer's software.

(T) F **14.** The arithmetic/logic unit is part of the central processor.

Circle the letter of the best answer.

1. When the total of the sales journal is posted at the end of the month, there will be a
   a. debit to Cash and a credit to Sales.
   b. debit to Accounts Receivable and a credit to Sales.
   c. debit to Sales only.
   d. debit to Accounts Payable and a credit to Sales.

2. Which statement is *not* true about the Accounts Receivable subsidiary accounts?
   a. Each is a record of a credit customer.
   b. They receive daily postings from the special journals.
   c. A check is placed in the Posting Reference column of the subsidiary account after each posting.
   d. Their balances are used to prepare a schedule of accounts receivable.

3. If our customer returns goods and receives a cash refund, which journal should we use?
   a. Sales journal
   b. Cash receipts journal
   c. Cash payments journal
   d. General journal

4. If our customer returns goods for credit, we should record the transaction in the
   a. sales journal.
   b. cash receipts journal.
   c. cash payments journal.
   d. general journal.

5. Accounts Receivable has no involvement at any time with the
   a. sales journal.
   b. cash receipts journal.
   c. cash payments journal.
   d. general journal.

6. Which statement is *not* true about the Accounts Payable controlling account?
   a. It receives daily postings from the special-purpose journals.
   b. It is found in the general ledger.
   c. Its balance at the end of the month should equal the total in the schedule of accounts payable.
   d. It has an account number.

7. Purchases Discounts would most likely occupy a column in the
   a. sales journal.
   b. purchases journal.
   c. cash receipts journal.
   d. cash payments journal.

8. Purchases has no involvement at any time with
   a. the purchases journal.
   b. the cash receipts journal.
   c. the cash payments journal.
   d. any of the above.

9. Being able to accommodate changes in a business is a description of the
   a. control principle.
   b. compatibility principle.
   c. flexibility principle.
   d. cost/benefit principle.

Applying Your Knowledge

Exercises

1. In the spaces provided, indicate the symbol of the journal that should be used by Targum Appliance Store.

   S = Sales journal
   P = Purchases journal (single-column)
   CR = Cash receipts journal
   CP = Cash payments journal
   J = General journal

   J a. Goods which had been purchased by Targum on credit are returned.

   CR b. Goods which had been purchased by Targum for cash are returned for a cash refund.

   P c. Toasters are purchased on credit by Targum.

   CP d. The same toasters are paid for.

   S e. A blender is sold on credit.

   CP f. The electric bill is paid.

   J g. Adjusting entries are made.

   J h. Office furniture is purchased by Targum on credit.

   J i. Closing entries are made.

   CP j. Targum pays for half of the office furniture.

   CR k. A customer pays a bill and receives a discount.

2. Enter the following transactions of Riley Company into the cash receipts journal provided. Complete the Post. Ref. column as though the entries had been posted daily. Also, make the proper posting notations in the journal as though the end-of-month postings had been made. Accounts Receivable is account no. 114, Sales is account no. 411, Sales Discounts is account no. 412, and Cash is account no. 111.

   Feb. 3 Received payment of $500 less a 2 percent discount from Frank Simpson for merchandise previously purchased on credit.

   9 Sold equipment (account no. 135) for $8,000 cash.

   14 Miriam Riley (capital account no. 311) invested $10,000 more into the business.

   23 Stanley Hall paid Riley Company $150 for merchandise he had purchased on credit.

   28 Cash sales for the month totaled $25,000.

Cash Receipts Journal

Date	Account Credited	Post. Ref.	Other Accts.	Accts. Receiv.	Sales	Sales Disc.	Cash
Feb 3	Frank Simpson	✓		500		10	490
9	Sales Equipment	135✓	8,000		8,000		8,000
14	Miriam Riley, Capital	311✓	10,000				10,000
23	Stanley Hall	✓		150			150
28	Sales	✓			25,000		25,000
			18,000	650	25,000	10	43,640
			✓	(114)	(411)	(412)	(111)

3. A page from a special-purpose journal is
provided below.

| Date | Ck. no. | Payee | Other Account Debited | Post. Ref. | Debits | | Credits | |
					Other Accounts	Accounts Payable	Purchases Discounts	Cash
May 1	114	Vincennes Supply Co.		✓		800	16	784
7	115	Jeppson Bus. Equip.	Office Equipment	167	2000			2000
13	116	Daily World	Advertising Expense	512	350			350
19	117	Olsen Motors		✓		420		420
					2350	1220	16	3554
					(315)	(211)	(413)	(111)

In the spaces provided, please answer the following questions about this journal.

a. What type of journal is this? _C P_

b. What error was made in the preparation of this journal? _Other accts._
should have a ✓, not a # under it

c. Provide an explanation for the four transactions.

May 1 _Paid Vincennes Supply less purchase Discount_

May 7 _Bought Office Equipment for cash_

May 13 _Paid for newspaper advertising_

May 19 _Paid Olsen Motors for purchase on credit_

d. Explain the following:

The checks in the Post. Ref. column _Posted to Individual A/P subsidiary ledgers (daily)_

The numbers 167 and 512 in the Post. Ref. column _Posted to those acct #s daily_

The numbers below the column totals _Posted to those accts at EOM._

Chapter Eight

Internal Control and Merchandising Transactions

Reviewing the Chapter

1. A business establishes a system of **internal control** to (a) safeguard its assets, (b) check the accuracy and reliability of its accounting data, (c) promote operational efficiency, and (d) encourage adherence to prescribed managerial policies. The first two functions, which are referred to as **internal accounting controls**, may include a system of authorization and approval, as well as the separation of duties. The last two functions, which are referred to as **internal administrative controls**, may include employee training programs, performance reports, quality control systems, statistical studies, time and motion studies, and safety campaigns.

2. To be effective, a system of internal control should consist of (a) separation of duties, (b) a sound accounting system, (c) sound personnel policies, (d) reliable personnel, and (e) regular internal review. **Bonding** an employee (an example of good internal control) means insuring the company against theft by that individual.

3. Accounting controls over merchandising transactions help prevent losses from theft or fraud, and help assure accurate accounting records. Administrative controls over merchandising transactions should help to keep inventory levels balanced, to keep enough cash on hand to make early payments for purchases discounts, and to avoid credit losses.

4. Several procedures should be followed to achieve effective internal control over sales and the exchange of cash.

5. Cash received by mail should be handled by two or more employees. Cash received by sales over the counter should be controlled through the use of cash registers and prenumbered sales tickets. At the end of each day, Cash is debited for cash receipts, and Sales is credited for the amount on the cash register tape. If the two amounts do not agree, **Cash Over or Short** is debited when there is a shortage and credited when there is an overage.

6. All cash payments for purchases should be made by check. However, before employees pay cash, they should get authorization in the form of certain signed documents. The system of authorization and the documents used will differ among companies, but the most common documents are described below.
   a. A **purchase requisition** is completed by a department requesting that the company purchase something for the department.
   b. A **purchase order** is completed by the department responsible for the com-

pany's purchasing activities, and it is sent to the vendor.

   c. An **invoice** is the bill sent to the buyer from the vendor.

   d. A **receiving report** is completed by the receiving department, and contains information about the quantity and condition of goods received.

   e. A **check authorization** is a document showing that the purchase order, purchase requisition, receiving report, and invoice are in agreement, and that payment is therefore approved.

   f. When payment is approved, a **check** is issued to the vendor for the amount of the invoice, less the appropriate discount. Remittance advice should be attached to the check, describing the articles being paid for.

7. When a company opens a bank account, the official designated to sign the checks must also sign a **signature card**. The bank keeps the signature card as a record of the company's authorized signature.

8. On receiving a check, the vendor compares its amount with the related invoice and then deposits the check in the bank. The vendor should keep the **deposit ticket**, which lists the cash and currency deposited, as proof of deposit.

9. If the bank has honored the check, it returns the canceled check with the buyer's monthly **bank statement**. The bank statement shows the bank balance at the beginning of the month, all additions and deductions during the month, and the balance at the end of the month.

10. A bank statement's end-of-month balance will rarely agree with the balance in the company's books for that date. Thus the accountant must prepare a **bank reconciliation** to account for this difference and to locate any errors made by the bank or the company. The bank reconciliation begins with the "balance per books" and "balance per bank statement" figures as of the bank statement date. Each figure is adjusted by certain additions and deductions, resulting in two "adjusted cash balance" figures, which should agree. The "balance per books" figure is adjusted by information that the bank knew at the

bank statement date but the company did not. The "balance per bank statement" figure is adjusted by information that the company knew at the bank statement date but the bank did not. Examples of adjustments follow.

   a. **Outstanding checks** are a deduction from the balance per bank statement.

   b. **Deposits in transit** are an addition to the balance per bank statement.

   c. **Service charges** by the bank appear on the bank statement, and are a deduction from the balance per books.

   d. A customer's **NSF (not sufficient funds) check** is deducted from the balance per books.

   e. **Miscellaneous charges** are deducted from the balance per books. **Miscellaneous credits** are added to the balance per books.

   f. **Interest earned** on a checking account is added to the balance per books.

11. After the bank reconciliation has been prepared, adjusting entries must be made so that the accounting records will reflect the new information supplied by the bank statement.

12. Though it is good practice for a company to pay by check, it is often not practical for items of small value. For items like postage, a few inexpensive supplies, and taxi fare, many firms use a **petty cash fund**. One of the best ways to operate a petty cash fund is by the **imprest system**. Under this system, when the fund is started, Petty Cash is debited, and Cash is credited. When payment is made from the fund, the fund's custodian should prepare a **petty cash voucher** showing the date, amount, and purpose of the expenditure. The petty cash fund is replenished periodically and at the end of the accounting period. In each case, all of the expenditures since the fund was last replenished are debited, and Cash is credited. Discrepencies are recorded as Cash Over or Short.

13. The goal of a **voucher system** is to keep maximum control over cash expenditures. Accordingly, each transaction requires the written approval of key individuals. This procedure leaves a trail of written

evidence called an **audit trail** or voucher trail. There are five steps in the operation of a voucher system, as follows:

a. Preparing the **voucher** (written authorization for an expenditure) for each liability incurred.

b. Recording the voucher in the **voucher register**.

c. Paying the voucher as it comes up in the unpaid voucher file by drawing either a check or a **voucher check** and recording it in the **check register**.

d. Posting the voucher and check registers. This process is very similar to posting the purchases and cash payments journals, except that Vouchers Payable takes the place of Accounts Payable.

e. Preparing a schedule of unpaid vouchers from the unpaid voucher file.

Testing Your Knowledge

Matching

Match each term with its definition by writing the appropriate letter in the blank.

F   1. Internal control

D   2. Internal accounting controls

N   3. Internal administrative controls

J   4. Purchase requisition

H   5. Purchase order

B   6. Receiving report

L   7. Check authorization

K   8. Bank reconciliation

O   9. Outstanding check

A   10. NSF check

G   11. Petty cash fund

M   12. Petty cash voucher

E   13. Voucher register

C   14. Check register

I   15. Schedule of unpaid vouchers

a. A bad check

b. A description of goods received by a company

c. A record of vouchers that have been paid

d. The part of internal control that refers to the accounting records

e. The journal that contains a record of each approved voucher

f. A system designed to safeguard assets, promote operational efficiency, encourage adherence to managerial policies, and help achieve accounting accuracy

g. Cash set aside to pay for items of small value

h. An order for goods that is sent to the vendor

i. A listing of debts

j. A document requesting the purchasing department to order certain items

k. An accounting for the difference between book balance and bank balance at a particular date

l. A document that authorizes payment

m. A record of an expenditure from petty cash

n. That part of internal control that refers to the management of operations

o. A check that has been issued, but has not yet been presented to the bank for payment

Completion

Use the lines provided to complete each item.

1. What are the four objectives of internal accounting control?

Safeguard assets
check accuracy + reliability
 of acctg data
promote operational efficiency
Adherence to prescribed
 Managerial policies

2. List five characteristics of a system of internal control that help make it effective.

Separation of duties
Sound acctg system
Sound personnel policies
Reliable personnel
Regular Internal review

3. What four documents should be in agreement before payment is made?

Purchase requisition
Purchase order
Invoice
Receiving Report

4. List three items that would be deducted from "balance per books" in a bank reconciliation.

Bank Service charges
NSF funds chk
Misc. Charges

True-False

Circle T if the statement is true, F if it is false.

T (F) 1. A good system of internal control will guarantee that the accounting records are accurate.

T (F) 2. When a petty cash fund is established, Cash is debited, and Petty Cash is credited.

(T) F 3. Collusion refers to a secret agreement between two or more persons to defraud a company.

T (F) 4. Cash Over or Short is a contra account to Cash in the balance sheet.

(T) F 5. A system of authorization and approval is an example of an internal accounting control.

(T) F 6. The mail should be opened in the accounting department so that transactions may be recorded immediately.

T (F) 7. A company orders goods by sending the supplier a purchase requisition.

(T) F 8. A check that is outstanding for two consecutive months should be included in both months' bank reconciliations.

(T) F 9. A credit memorandum on a bank statement indicates an addition to the bank balance.

T (F) 10. After a bank reconciliation has been completed, the company must make journal entries to adjust for all outstanding checks.

T (F) 11. Only the purchase of merchandise may be recorded in the voucher register.

(T) F 12. The check register has a Vouchers Payable debit column.

(T) (F) 13. After a voucher has been recorded, it is placed in an unpaid voucher file in alphabetical order.

(T) (F) 14. A bank reconciliation for the month of September will begin with balance per books and balance per bank statement at September 1.

T (F) 15. Rotating employees in job assignments is poor internal control because employees would continually be forced to learn a new job skill.

Multiple-Choice

Circle the letter of the best answer.

1. In a system that uses special-purpose journals, the voucher register takes the place of the
   a. cash register
   b. cash payments journal.
   c. accounts receivable subsidiary ledger.
   d. purchases journal.

2. Which of the following is an example of an internal accounting control?
   a. Doing a time and motion study
   b. Separating record keeping from the handling of assets
   c. Hiring a quality control expert
   d. Preparing performance reports

3. The balance in the schedule of unpaid vouchers should equal
   a. the Vouchers Payable debit total from the voucher register minus the Vouchers Payable credit total from the check register.
   b. the Vouchers Payable credit total from the check register minus the Vouchers Payable debit total from the voucher register.
   c. the Vouchers Payable credit total from the voucher register minus the Vouchers Payable debit total from the check register.
   d. the Vouchers Payable debit total from the check register minus the Vouchers Payable credit total from the voucher register.

4. When a petty cash fund is replenished,
   a. Petty Cash is credited.
   b. Petty Cash is debited.

c. Cash is credited.
d. Cash is debited.

5. Cash on hand (as in a petty cash fund) should be included in a bank reconciliation as
   a. an addition to the bank statement balance.
   b. a deduction from the bank statement balance.
   c. an addition to the company's book balance.
   d. a deduction from the company's book balance.

6. Which of the following documents is prepared (by a buyer of goods) before all of the others?
   a. Purchase order
   b. Receiving report
   c. Check authorization (or voucher)
   d. Purchase requisition

7. Which of the following is an example of poor internal control?
   a. The receiving department comparing goods received with the related purchase order
   b. Forcing employees to take earned vacations
   c. Requiring someone other than the petty cash custodian to enter petty cash transactions into the accounting records
   d. Bonding employees

Applying Your Knowledge

Exercises

1. The facts that follow are needed to prepare a bank reconciliation for the Nelson Company as of March 31, 19xx. For each, provide the proper symbol (a, b, c, or d) to indicate where it should appear.
   a = Addition to the bank statement balance

b = Deduction from the bank statement balance
c = Addition to the company's book balance
d = Deduction from the company's book balance

<u>d</u> 1. The service charge by the bank was $8
<u>c</u> 2. A $1,700 note receivable was collected for the company by the bank. No collection fee was charged.
<u>b</u> 3. There were two outstanding checks, totaling $3,200.
<u>d</u> 4. A $355 NSF check drawn by a customer was deducted from the company's bank account and returned to the company.
<u>a</u> 5. A deposit of $725 was made after banking hours on March 31.
<u>d</u> 6. Check no. 185 was drawn for $342 but was erroneously recorded in the company's books as $324.

2. A petty cash fund of $100 was set up. Petty cash vouchers for the month totaled $86, and cash in the petty cash box totaled $12.50. The fund should be reimbursed in the amount of $ <u>87.50</u> .

3. Rand & Company uses a voucher system. Record each transaction in the journal provided, and indicate after each entry the journal of original entry in which the transaction would be recorded.
   a. Voucher no. 200 is prepared to establish a petty cash fund of $75.
   b. Voucher no. 201 is prepared to purchase merchandise from Axelson Company, $350.
   c. Check no. 601 is issued in payment of voucher no. 200.
   d. Check no. 602 is issued in payment of voucher no. 201.
   e. Voucher no. 202 is prepared to replenish the petty cash fund, which contains $20 in cash and the following receipts: cab fare, $12; postage, $34; and miscellaneous expense, $7.
   f. Check no. 603 is issued in payment of voucher no. 202.

General Journal				
Date	Description		Debit	Credit
	a Petty Cash		75		voucher
	A/P			75	
	To establish petty cash fund				
	b Purchases		350		voucher
	A/P			350	
	Merch. from Axelson Co.				
	c A/P		75		check
	Cash			75	
	To pay petty cash				
	d A/P		350		check
	Cash			350	
	To pay Axelson Co.				
	e Cab Fare		12		voucher
	Postage		34		
	Misc. Exp.		7		
	Cash Short		2		
	A/P			55	
	To replenish Petty Cash				
	f A/P		55		check
	Cash			55	
	To pay petty cash				

Crossword Puzzle
For Chapters 7 and 8

ACROSS

4. Bank document (2 words)
5. System of organization (2 words)
6. Send money
8. With 13-Down, sequence of written approval
10. Central processor part (2 words)
11. Cash _____ or short
12. _____/benefit principle
15. Ledger to support controlling account
16. Recorded by hand

DOWN

1. Tied directly to the computer (hyphenated)
2. Invoice
3. Bank document (2 words)
4. System to deal with information (2 words)
6. Fund for small expenditures (2 words)
7. Send money
9. Insuring against employee theft
13. See 8-Across
14. Column in check register

Internal Control Weaknesses in Small Business

CPAs are keenly aware of the high failure rates for small businesses and that often the reason for failure is the absence of effective internal controls. If the CPA can discern the weaknesses in the internal control system of a small business, he or she can offer the expertise to overcome them. In the following article, Robert A. Leitch, *CPA, Ph.D, professor,* Gadis J. Dillon, *CPA, Ph.D, assistant professor, and* Sue H. McKinley, *a doctoral student, all of the School of Accounting at the University of Georgia, Athens, Georgia 30602, present the findings of a study of internal control systems in small business and some weaknesses in them.*

The results of our study of more than 120 small businesses indicated several areas in which these businesses were hampered by major internal control problems. An understanding of these areas can help the practitioner in reviewing the accounting system and statements of a small business client. It can also highlight specific areas about which the practitioners can give advice to the client, such as how to improve an accounting system so the client has confidence in it and ultimately is able to use it to improve management effectiveness.

Small businesses usually are far less complex than large businesses and tend to be dominated by the talents of the owners and managers. As a result, the control system can be much simpler while making effective use of the physical presence of the owner in the shop, manufacturing facility or office. For example, effective control can be established if the owner approves all credit sales above a predetermined dollar amount. It is a real challenge to a CPA to design an effective and efficient internal control system for a small business client in spite of the relatively simple accounting system needed. Some factors that can complicate the task include the following:

1. An owner or manager who is not primarily concerned with internal control.
2. A lack of awareness on the part of the owner or manager of the need for such controls.

Source: Article by Robert A. Leitch et al. Reprinted from the December 1981 issue of *The Journal of Accountancy.* Copyright © 1981 by the American Institute of Certified Public Accountants, Inc.

3. Not enough employees to effectively separate control functions.
4. Too easy access to the company assets and accounting records.
5. Limits on the financial resources that can be used for the accounting system.
6. A decision-making process not based on information from the accounting system.

Obviously, the CPA serving small business clients is interested in concentrating on control areas most likely to cause problems for those clients. We hope the survey results presented here will be useful in this effort. To this end, we have highlighted them for different degrees of owner involvement, different types of accounting systems and, in a limited sense, different types of clients. Given these general areas of concern, the practitioner may find it helpful to use a weighted questionnaire, such as the one used here, to identify a client's specific problem areas.

Students in the graduate accounting systems course at the university conducted a system audit of a small business. One hundred twenty-two such surveys were used for the study, and they represent a wide cross section of small businesses throughout the Southeast.

Exhibit 1 summarizes the responses to the questionnaire. The first column of numbers lists weights suggested by Richard C. Rea in an article appearing in [*Journal of Accountancy*] three years ago [July 1978, pp. 53-54], and the last column indicates situations where the question was either not relevant or insufficient information was available.

The questions marked with asterisks are the ones which drew more negative than positive responses, thus indicating areas frequently deficient. Four of the questions—1(c), 1(d), 1(e) and 6(d)—relate to budgeting, planning and interim reporting, implying that management may not use financial information in the decision-making process. Others—such as 1(a), 2(b), 2(c), 3(i), 4(d), and 8(a)—indicate the informality of most small business systems and some of these may not be especially telling. But cash control problem areas such as 2(b), 2(c), 3(c) and 3(i) would seem to warrant special attention.

To assess the overall quality of internal control, the aforementioned weights were applied to obtain an internal control score for each company. That is, the total weighted *yes* answers were divided by the sum

Exhibit 1
Internal Control Questionnaire Summary of Results

	Weight	Yes	No	N/A or N/R
1. General				
a. Are accounting records kept up to date and balanced monthly?	5	89	33	0
*b. Is a chart of accounts used?	3	57	65	0
*c. Does the owner use a budget system for watching income and expenses?	1	28	94	0
*d. Are cash projections made?	1	23	99	0
*e. Are monthly or quarterly financial reports available to the owner?	3	59	60	3
f. Does the owner take a direct and active interest in the financial affairs and reports which are available?	5	114	8	0
g. Are the personal funds of the owner and his personal income and expenses completely segregated from the business?	4	114	8	0
h. Is the owner satisfied that all employees are honest?	2	117	4	1
*i. Is the bookkeeper required to take annual vacations?	2	13	16	93
2. Cash receipts				
a. Does the owner open the mail?	5	73	43	6
*b. Does the owner list mail receipts before turning them over to the bookkeeper?	5	26	73	23
*c. Is the listing subsequently traced to the cash receipts journal?	5	23	76	23
d. Are over-the-counter receipts controlled by cash register tapes, counter receipts, etc.?	5	91	23	8
e. Are receipts deposited intact daily?	5	88	32	2
*f. Are employees who handle funds bonded?	5	9	108	5
g. Do two different people reconcile the bank records and make out the deposit slip?	10	71	36	15
3. Cash disbursements				
a. Are all disbursements made by check?	5	95	27	0
b. Are prenumbered checks used?	5	120	2	0
*c. Is a controlled, mechanical check protector used?	5	23	99	0
d. Is the owner's signature required on checks?	5	102	19	1
e. Does the owner sign checks only after they are properly completed?	5	102	19	1
f. Does the owner approve and cancel the documentation in support of all disbursements?	5	78	44	0
g. Are all voided checks retained and accounted for?	5	115	7	0
h. Does the owner review the bank reconciliation?	5	67	22	33
*i. Is an imprest petty cash fund used?	5	35	70	17
j. Does the owner *never* sign blank checks?	5	65	24	33
k. Do different people reconcile the bank records and write the checks?	10	66	40	16
4. Accounts receivable and sales				
a. Are work order and/or sales invoices prenumbered and controlled?	5	65	36	21
b. Are customers' ledgers balanced regularly?	5	74	14	34
c. Are monthly statements sent to all customers?	5	61	27	34
*d. Does the owner review statements before mailing them himself?	5	29	57	36
e. Are account write-offs and discounts approved only by the owner?	5	83	7	32
f. Is credit granted only by the owner?	3	62	28	32

(continued)

Exhibit 1 (cont.)

	Weight	Yes	No	N/A or N/R
5. Notes receivable and investments				
a. Does the owner have sole access to notes and investment certificates?	5	26	5	91
6. Inventories				
a. Is the person responsible for inventory someone other than the bookkeeper?	3	108	7	7
b. Are periodic physical inventories taken?	5	83	34	5
c. Is there physical control over inventory stock?	5	68	48	6
*d. Are perpetual inventory records maintained?	2	33	83	6
7. Property assets				
a. Are there detailed records available of property assets and allowances for depreciation?	5	57	8	57
b. Is the owner acquainted with property assets owned by the company?	4	69	1	52
c. Are retirements approved by the owner?	4	65	2	55
8. Accounts payable and purchases				
*a. Are purchase orders used?	5	49	72	1
b. Does someone other than the bookkeeper always do the purchasing?	5	99	18	5
c. Are suppliers' monthly statements compared with recorded liabilities regularly?	4	85	23	14
d. Are suppliers' monthly statements checked by the owner periodically if disbursements are made from invoice only?	2	82	30	10
9. Payroll				
a. Are the employees hired by the owner?	3	107	13	2
b. Would the owner by aware of the absence of any employee?	3	103	16	3
c. Does the owner approve, sign and distribute payroll checks?	5	94	23	5

*Indicates predominantly negative responses.

Exhibit 2
Weighted Internal Control Scores

		Owner Involvement		Type of System			
Score	Total Sample	Owner Managed	Employee Managed	Double Entry	Single Entry	Small Computer	Service Bureau
90.0–99.9	4	2	2	4	0	0	0
80.0–89.9	16	15	1	12	4	0	0
70.0–79.9	35	28	7	21	9	5	0
60.0–69.9	35	33	2	22	11	1	1
50.0–59.9	18	13	5	10	6	1	1
40.0–49.9	9	4	5	4	4	0	1
30.0–39.9	5	3	2	1	4	0	0
	122	98	24	74	38	7	3

of the total weighted *yes* and *no* answers. As might have been anticipated, the scores varied widely.

The overall average for all businesses in the sample was a low 68 percent. The high score was 96 percent, indicating that some small businesses have excellent internal control, but the low score was 33 percent. Exhibit 2 shows the frequency distribution of the scores, both in total and by various classifications.

Accumulating scores by type of system resulted in considerable differences in averages, with double-entry manual systems generally showing the best internal control. Average scores for each type of control were

Double-entry manual—70.36 percent.
Single-entry manual—62.83 percent.
Small computer—67.34 percent.
Service bureau—55.10 percent.

The added control shown by the double-entry system probably reflects a greater interest in the system and perhaps indicates that the companies are larger and have more resources. A surprising result is the decline in control when a computer or an outside party is used to maintain accounting records. In situations such as the last two, the CPA could be of great help in advising the client on systems and in particular in matching the client's needs to the capabilities of a service.

The study found that each type of internal control system usually indicated certain other factors. For instance, single-entry systems are usually kept by the owner or a relative rather than by an employee and do not use charts of accounts. Many of the controls, such as listing mail receipts, sending monthly statements, taking physical inventories, maintaining perpetual inventories and implementing review procedures are less likely to be present in a single-entry system. Overall, internal control was found to be most strong in companies using double-entry manual systems.

Comparison of internal control scores based on owner involvement indicated that, on average, active participation by the owner as an owner-manager resulted in more effective control. The average score for owner-managed small businesses was 68.64 percent compared to 62.91 percent for employee-managed small businesses. This evidence seems to support the theory that participation by the owner enhances the effectiveness of the internal control system. Other owner-related findings were that the owner tends to use budgets, projections and financial reports more often when an employee manages the business. But when the owner is also manager, he tends to take an active part in control activities such as opening the mail, reviewing bank reconciliations and making employment decisions.

In terms of the type of business and its impact on the effectiveness of controls, two findings seem significant. First, in the wholesale durable goods business, there was a tendency toward a lack of control over counter receipts (question 2(d)). And, second, miscellaneous retail stores (liquor, drug, flowers, sporting goods) tended to have no records of property and to use single-entry manual systems (question 7(a)).

The study pointed out some general areas that present problems for small businessess, such as budgeting and planning and cash control procedures. Needless to say, these are the very areas where a CPA's expertise is required. Both in theory and in practice the accounting profession seems to have much left to do in helping the small business entrepreneur improve internal control. But no one would doubt that improved internal control procedures might lower the rate of failures among this important segment of the business community.

Chapter Nine

General-Purpose External Financial Statements

Reviewing the Chapter

1. Financial reporting should fulfill three objectives. It should (a) provide information that is useful in investment and credit decisions; (b) provide information useful in assessing cash flow prospects; and (c) provide information about business resources, claims to those resources, and changes in them. **General-purpose external financial statements** are the main way of presenting financial information to interested parties. They consist of the balance sheet, income statement, statement of owner's equity, and statement of changes in financial position.

2. Accounting attempts to provide decision makers with information that meets the following **qualitative characteristics**, or standards: understandability, usefulness, relevance, and reliability.
   a. **Understandability** refers to the ease of interpretation by the decision maker.
   b. The **usefulness** of accounting information to the decision maker depends on the qualitative characteristics of relevance and reliability.
   c. **Relevance** includes the standards of **predictive value, feedback value,** and **timeliness.** It means that the information is capable of influencing the decision maker.

   d. **Reliability** includes the standards of **representative faithfulness, verifiability,** and **neutrality.** It means that accounting information accurately reflects what it is meant to represent.

3. To aid in the interpretation of financial information, accountants depend on the following conventions: comparability, consistency, materiality, conservatism, full disclosure, and cost/benefit.
   a. **Comparability** means that the information allows the decision maker to compare the same company over two or more accounting periods, or different companies for the same accounting period.
   b. **Consistency** means that a particular accounting procedure, once adopted, should not normally be changed from period to period. However, if a company does change a procedure, it must justify the change and disclose the dollar effect on the statements.
   c. The **materiality** convention states that an item should be disclosed separately or treated specially if knowledge of it would probably influence the user's decision.

d. The **conservatism** convention states that an accountant who has a choice of acceptable accounting procedures should choose the one that would be least likely to overstate assets and income. Applying the lower-of-cost-or-market rule to inventory valuation is an example of conservatism.

e. The **full disclosure** convention states that financial statements and their accompanying footnotes should contain all relevant information.

f. The **cost/benefit** convention states that the cost of providing additional accounting information should not exceed the benefits to be gained from it.

4. **Classified financial statements** divide assets, liabilities, owner's equity, revenues, and expenses into subcategories to offer more useful information to the reader.

5. On a classified balance sheet, assets are usually divided into four categories: (a) current assets; (b) investments; (c) property, plant, and equipment; and (d) intangible assets. (Sometimes another category called other assets is added for miscellaneous items.)

6. These categories are usually listed in their order of liquidity—the ease with which an asset can be turned into cash.

7. **Current assets** are cash and assets that are expected to be turned into cash or used up within the normal operating cycle of the company or one year, whichever is longer. (From here on we will call this time period the current period).

a. The normal operating cycle of a company is the average time between the purchase of inventory and the collection of cash from the sale of that inventory.

b. Cash, short-term investments, accounts receivable, notes receivable, prepaid expenses, supplies, and inventory are current assets.

8. Examples of **investments** are stocks and bonds held for long-term investment, land held for future use, plant and equipment not used in the business, special funds, and a controlling interest in another company.

9. **Property, plant, and equipment** include things like land, buildings, delivery equipment, machinery, and office equipment. All except land are subject to depreciation.

10. **Intangible assets** have no physical substance. They represent certain long-lived rights or privileges. Examples are patents, copyrights, goodwill, franchises, and trademarks.

11. The liabilities of a classified balance sheet are usually divided into current and long-term liabilities.

a. **Current liabilities** are obligations for which payment (or performance) is due in the current period. They are paid from current assets or by incurring new short-term liabilities. Examples are notes payable, accounts payable, taxes payable, and unearned revenues.

b. **Long-term liabilities** are debts that are due after the current period or that will be paid from noncurrent assets. Examples are mortgages payable, long-term notes payable, bonds payable, employee pension obligations, and long-term leases.

12. The owner's equity section of a classified balance sheet is usually called owner's equity, partners' equity, or stockholders' equity. The exact name depends on whether the business is a sole proprietorship, a partnership, or a corporation.

13. In a sole proprietorship or partnership, the owner's equity section shows the name of the owner or owners. Each is followed by the word *capital* and the dollar amount of investment as of the balance sheet date.

14. In a corporation, the stockholders' equity section consists of contributed capital (also called paid-in capital) and retained earnings.

a. **Contributed capital** represents the amount invested by the stockholders, and is further divided into the par value of the issued stock and paid-in or contributed capital in excess of par value.

b. **Retained earnings** reflect the earnings record of the company since its beginning. Dividends (assets distributed to stockholders) reduce the Retained Earnings account balance, as do net losses.

15. The income statement measures **comprehensive income**, or the change in the owner's equity of a business other than the owner's investments and withdrawals. A **condensed income statement**, which contains the statement's major categories with little or no detail, may be presented in either multistep or single-step form.
    a. The **multistep form** is the more detailed of the two, containing several subtractions and subtotals. It has separate sections for cost of goods sold, operating expenses, and **other** (nonoperating) **revenues and expenses**. One important subtotal is **income from operations**, which equals gross margin from sales minus operating expenses.
    b. In the **single-step form**, the revenues section lists all revenues including other revenues, and the operating costs section lists all expenses including other expenses. The difference is labeled net income or net loss.

16. Ledger accounts are arranged in the order in which they appear in the financial statements, with balance sheet accounts coming before income statement accounts. The **chart of accounts** is a systematic numbering scheme for identifying the accounts.

17. Classified financial statements help the reader evaluate liquidity and profitability.

18. **Liquidity** refers to a company's ability to pay its bills when they are due and to meet unexpected needs for cash. Two measures of liquidity are working capital and the current ratio.
    a. **Working capital** equals current assets minus current liabilities. It is the amount of current assets that would remain if all the current debts were paid.
    b. The **current ratio** equals current assets divided by current liabilities. A current ratio of 1:1, for example, shows that current assets are barely enough to pay current liabilities. A 3:1 current ratio would be considered more satisfactory.

19. **Profitability** means more than just a company's net income. And to draw conclusions, one must compare profitability measures with industry averages and past performance. Four common measures of profitability are profit margin, return on assets, debt to equity ratio, and return on equality.
    a. The **profit margin** equals net income divided by sales. A 12.5 percent profit margin, for example, means that 12½¢ has been earned on each dollar of sales.
    b. **Return on assets** equals net income divided by average total assets. This measure shows how efficiently the company is using its assets.
    c. The **debt to equity ratio** measures the proportion of a business financed by creditors relative to the proportion financed by the owner. It equals total liabilities divided by owner's equity. A debt to equity ratio of 1.0, for instance, indicates equal financing by creditors and owners.
    d. **Return on equity** shows what percentage was earned on the owner's investment. It equals net income divided by average owner's equity.

20. Financial statements of corporations are usually complicated and have a number of features not found in a sole proprietorship's or partnership's statements. Published statements appear in the company's **annual report**, a publication distributed to stockholders each year. The annual report also gives nonfinancial information.

21. **Consolidated** financial statements are the combined statements of a company and its controlled subsidiaries. (Chapter 20 explains them in more detail.) A company's financial statements may show data from consecutive periods side by side for comparison. Such statements are called **comparative financial statements**.

22. A corporation's income statement should disclose **provision for income taxes** or **income tax expense** separately from the other expenses. Sole proprietorships and partnerships are not taxable units.

23. **Earnings per common share**, also called **net income per share**, equals net income divided by the number of shares of common stock. It usually appears below net income in the income statement and is a measure of the company's profitability.

24. A section called **notes to the financial statements** is usually needed to help the reader interpret some of the complex financial statement items.

25. A **summary of significant accounting policies** discloses the generally accepted accounting principles used in preparing the statements. It usually follows the last financial statement.

26. Corporations are often required to issue **interim financial statements**. These statements give financial information covering less than a year (for example, quarterly data).

27. The **accountant's report** is issued by an independent auditor. It conveys to third parties that the financial statements were examined in accordance with generally accepted auditing standards (**scope section**), and expresses the auditor's opinion on how fairly the financial statements reflect the company's financial condition (**opinion section**).

Testing Your Knowledge

Matching

Match each term with its definition by writing the appropriate letter in the blank.

_e_ 1. Classified financial statements

_m_ 2. Liquidity

_h_ 3. Current assets

_b_ 4. Property, plant, and equipment

_j_ 5. Intangible assets

_o_ 6. Normal operating cycle

_d_ 7. Current liabilities

_l_ 8. Long-term liabilities

_i_ 9. Contributed capital

_g_ 10. Retained earnings

_n_ 11. Comprehensive income

_p_ 12. Chart of accounts

_c_ 13. General-purpose external financial statements

_r_ 14. Comparative financial statements

_f_ 15. Earnings per common share

_q_ 16. Summary of significant accounting policies

_k_ 17. Notes to the financial statements

_a_ 18. Accountant's report

a. The auditor's opinion concerning the financial statements
b. Long-lived tangible assets
c. The balance sheet, income statement, statement of owner's equity, and statement of changes in financial position
d. Short-term obligations
e. Financial reports broken down into subcategories
f. Net income divided by outstanding shares of common stock
g. Total earnings since a corporation's beginning that have been kept in the business
h. The subcategory of assets that are expected to be turned into cash or used up within one year or the operating cycle, whichever is longer
i. The amount invested by stockholders
j. Assets that lack physical substance and that grant rights or privileges to their owner
k. A section that interprets or supplements financial statement information
l. Obligations due after the current period
m. The ability to pay bills when due and to meet unexpected needs for cash
n. The change in the owner's equity of a business, exclusive of investments and withdrawals
o. The average time span between the purchase of inventory and collection of cash from its sale
p. A systematic numbering scheme for the ledger
q. A listing of the accounting principles used in preparing the financial statements
r. Financial statements with data from consecutive periods placed side by side for analysis

Completion

Use the lines provided to complete each item.

1. List the three forms of business organization, with each one's name for the owner's equity section in the balance sheet.

Business Organization

a. _Sole proprietorship_

b. _partnership_

c. _corporation_

Name for Owner's Equity Section

a. _owner's equity_

b. _partner's equity_

c. _stockholder's equity_

2. What does each of the following ratios have to do with a company's profitability?

Profit margin _compares N.I. to sales (shows x¢ earned per x$ sales)_

Return on assets _— ~~shows~~ compares average total assets to N.I. (shows how efficiently company is using assets)_

Return on equity _compares N.I. to avg ~~total~~ o.e. (shows what % was earned on owners investment)_

Debt to equity ratio _measures portion financed by debtors to creditors_

3. What does each of the following ratios have to do with a company's liquidity?

Working capital _shows how much assets are left if all liabilities paid_

Current ratio _shows what % of assets to liabilities_

4. Explain the basic point of each of the following conventions:

Consistency and comparability _using same acctg procedures from one period to next_

Materiality _relative importance of an item or event_

Cost/benefit _cost should not exceed benefit (of providing addl. info_

Conservatism _least likely to overstate assets & income_

Full disclosure _showing all relevant info in statements_

True-False

Circle T if the statement is true, F if it is false.

T (F) 1. Receivables are not current assets if collection requires more than one year.

T (F) 2. Retained Earnings is a cash account set aside for the payment of dividends.

(T) F 3. Gross margin from sales minus operating expenses equals income from operations.

T (F) 4. Operating expenses are made up of selling expenses and cost of goods sold.

(T) F 5. The chart of accounts classifies and helps one locate the ledger accounts.

(T) F 6. The net income figure is needed to figure the profit margin, the return on assets, and the return on equity.

(T) F 7. A statement of retained earnings would include dividends declared during the period.

(T) F 8. One meaning of the term *liquidity* is the ease with which an asset can be converted into cash.

T F 9. The normal operating cycle of a company cannot be less than one year.

T F 10. Net worth refers to the current value of a company's net assets.

T F 11. Other revenues and expenses is a separate classification in a multistep income statement.

T F 12. The net income figures for a multi-step and a single-step income statement will differ, given the same accounting period for the same company.

T F 13. A partnership would not prepare a statement of retained earnings.

T F 14. Working capital equals current assets divided by current liabilities.

T F 15. The proportion of a company financed by the owners is shown by the debt to equity ratio.

T F 16. The qualitative characteristic of relevance means that accounting information can be confirmed or duplicated by independent parties.

Multiple-Choice

Circle the letter of the best answer.

1. The basis for classifying assets as current or noncurrent is the period of time normally required by the business to turn cash invested in
   a. noncurrent assets back into current assets.
   b. receivables back into cash, or 12 months, whichever is shorter.
   c. inventories back into cash, or 12 months, whichever is longer.
   d. inventories back into cash, or 12 months, whichever is shorter.

2. Which of the following will not be found anywhere in a single-step income statement?
   a. Cost of goods sold
   b. Other expenses
   c. Gross margin from sales
   d. Operating expenses

3. The current ratio would probably be of *most* interest to
   a. stockholders.
   b. creditors.
   c. management.
   d. customers.

4. Which item below will *not* appear in the stockholders' equity section of a corporation's balance sheet?
   a. Retained earnings
   b. Common stock
   c. Paid-in capital in excess of par value
   d. James Esmay, Withdrawals

5. The accountant's report
   a. expresses an opinion as to the fairness of the financial statements audited.
   b. states whether or not a company is a sound investment.
   c. is prepared by a company's own internal auditors.
   d. should include forecasts to help the reader assess future profitability.

6. Net income divided by sales equals
   a. the profit margin.
   b. return on assets.
   c. working capital.
   d. income from operations.

7. Operating expenses consist of
   a. other expenses and cost of goods sold.
   b. selling expenses and cost of goods sold.
   c. selling and general and administrative expenses.
   d. none of the above.

8. Applying the lower-of-cost-or-market rule to inventory valuation and short-term investments follows the convention of
   a. consistency.
   b. materiality.
   c. conservatism.
   d. full disclosure.

9. A corporation began the accounting period with retained earnings of $5,000, ended with retained earnings of $12,000, and earned a $20,000 net income during the period. Apparently, how much did they declare in dividends during the period?
   a. $3,000
   b. $12,000
   c. $13,000
   d. $27,000

10. Which of the following is *not* an objective of financial reporting, according to FASB *Statement of Financial Accounting Concepts No. 1?*
   a. To provide information about the timing of cash flows
   b. To provide information to investors, creditors, and others
   c. To provide information about business resources
   d. To provide information not found in the accountant's report

Applying Your Knowledge

Exercises

1. Assume that Springfield Company uses the following group headings on its classified balance sheet:
   a. Current assets
   b. Investments
   c. Property, plant, and equipment
   d. Intangible assets
   e. Current liabilities
   f. Long-term liabilities
   g. Owner's equity

   Indicate by letter where each of the following should be placed. Write an "X" next to items that do not belong on the balance sheet.

   d 1. Franchises
   e 2. Short-term advances from customers
   c 3. Accumulated depreciation
   g 4. Mark Mathews, Capital
   a 5. Prepaid rent
   c 6. Delivery truck
   a 7. Office supplies
   b 8. Fund for the purchase of land
   f 9. Notes payable due in ten years
   e 10. Bonds payable currently due (payable out of current assets)
   d 11. Goodwill
   a 12. Short-term investments
   X 13. Provision for income taxes
   a 14. Inventory
   e 15. Accounts payable

2. The following information relates to Spiffy Appliances, Inc., for 19xx.

Current assets	$ 60,000
Average total assets	200,000
Current liabilities	20,000
Long-term liabilities	30,000
Average owner's equity	150,000
Sales	250,000
Net income	25,000

   In the spaces provided, indicate each measure of liquidity and profitability.
   a. Working capital = $ 40,000
   b. Current ratio = 3 to 1
   c. Profit margin = 10 %
   d. Return on assets = 12.5 %
   e. Return on equity = 16.7 %

3. The following data relate to the Confrey
   Company for 19xx.

Cost of goods sold	$150,000
Interest revenues	2,000
Income tax expense	5,000
Net sales	200,000
Common stock outstanding	3,500 shares
Operating expenses	30,000

   a. In the space provided, complete the
      condensed multistep income statement
      in good form. Include earnings per share
      information in the proper place.

Confrey Company
Income Statement (Multistep)
For the Year Ended December 31, 19xx

Sales	200,000
~~Interest Revenue~~ C/o/s	150,000
Gross Margin	50,000
Operating expenses	30,000
Income from Operations	20,000
Add Interest Rev.	2,000
Income before Taxes	22,000
Less Income Tax Expense	5000
N/I	17,000
Earnings Per Share @ 3500 shares	$4.86

---

   b. In the space provided, complete the
      condensed single-step income statement
      in good form. Include earnings per share
      information in the proper place.

Confrey Company
Income Statement (Single-Step)
For the Year Ended December 31, 19xx

Revenues	52,000
Expenses	35,000
N.I.	17,000
Earnings Per share @ 3500 shares	$4.86

Wrong because

Conditions Necessary for Developing a Conceptual Framework

Reed K. Storey, CPA, assistant director of research and technical activities at the Financial Accounting Standards Board, believes that three conditions are necessary for the FASB to develop a useful conceptual framework for financial accounting and reporting: the concepts must be rooted in the real world, attitudes and modes of thought must be changed and the FASB and its staff must take the concepts seriously. He describes these conditions in the following adaptation of an article that appeared in the March 3, 1981, issue of the FASB's Viewpoints, *which was based on a talk Storey presented at the 1980 annual meeting of the American Accounting Association in Boston, Massachusetts, last August.*

One of my favorite scenes in the musical comedy (and movie) *1776* is one that should have happened even if it actually did not. Jefferson has written the declaration stating why the United States ought to be independent, and it has just been read to the Congress. It is a masterpiece, but Congress, as committees are wont to do, immediately begins to nitpick and rewrite it, changing or deleting words, sentences or even whole paragraphs. After several of those changes, someone suggests that, since the colonists' quarrel is with King George rather than with the British people or Parliament, they should avoid giving offense by deleting a reference to Parliament. John Adams has finally had enough: "This is a revolution, dammit; we've got to offend somebody."

The Financial Accounting Standards Board's conceptual framework is no revolution, but it will offend both those who think it is revolutionary and those who think it should be. It will require change. Concepts that merely (to borrow board member Ralph Walters' description) "embalm the status quo" are useless in forming a basis for standards unless we are willing to assert or concede that what we are now doing is, like the House of Peers in Gilbert and Sullivan's *Iolanthe*," not susceptible to any improvement whatsoever." (I use *we*, and *us* and *our*, broadly, to include all who are concerned with financial reporting.)

I wish to describe, at least partially, three conditions

Source: Article by Reed K. Storey. Adapted from the March 3, 1981, issue of *FASB Viewpoints.*

that I think are necessary for the FASB to develop a useful conceptual framework for financial accounting and reporting. The first condition relates to the concepts themselves. The others relate to the environment in which the conceptual framework is being developed.

Concepts Rooted in the Real World

Concepts, to be useful, must involve limits, and the first condition for a useful conceptual framework is probably the most fundamental limit needed by concepts that are to underlie financial statements: The concepts themselves must be rooted in the real world. That condition flows from the utilitarian and representational nature of financial accounting and financial statements. Just as lines of various shapes and sizes in a road map represent different kinds of highways and roads, rivers and political boundaries, so also various descriptions and amounts in financial statements represent cash in bank, buildings, wages due, sales, use of labor, earthquake damage to property and a host of other things owned or owed by particular business enterprises as well as events and circumstances that affect them or their values. The items in financial statements are quantitative representations of economic things and events in the real world relating to and affecting actual business enterprises.

The usefulness of quantitative representations lies in the accuracy of their representation—in their essential agreement with the things or events represented. Representations in financial statements are intended to be utilitarian. They are supposed to be useful in the same way that the lines in a road map help a traveler reach a destination. Utilitarian representations contrast with aesthetic representations, which do not necessarily require accuracy. An artist may change the number or location of eyes, ears, arms, legs and the like and may use colors in any way desired—for example, green nose or purple hair—and still describe a painting as representing a person. A composer can describe certain music as representing the babbling of a brook or happiness felt on arriving in the country even though listeners do not hear that. However, a cartographer cannot add roads and bridges where none exist, or remove some that do exist, to enhance the aesthetic impact of a map without spoiling the usefulness of the representation. It may then be nice artwork, but it is no longer a road map. Similarly, accountants cannot add imaginery things and events to financial statements, or remove things and events that do exist, without spoiling the usefulness of the representation.

Assets and Things

For about five years, I have spent a good part of my waking hours on a project called elements of financial statements. It has to do with definitions of assets, liabilities, revenues, expenses, etc. Now, why should it take five years to define a few simple concepts that we use every day? After all, most of us think we know an asset or liability when we see one. And indeed we do. The problem is in accounting, not in our basic perceptions.

The crux of the problem is (1) that we have some definitions that have grown out of practice that do not meet the condition of being related to real world things and events and (2) that many of us are extremely reluctant to let go of those definitions. For example, here is a definition from Accounting Principles Board Statement no. 4, *Basic Concepts and Accounting Principles Underlying Financial Statements of Business Enterprises*, that describes assets in existing practice:

"*Assets*—economic resources of an enterprise that are recognized and measured in conformity with generally accepted accounting principles. Assets also include certain deferred charges that are not resources but that are recognized and measured in conformity with generally accepted accounting principles."[1]

That definition begins with a reference to something in the real world, but it falls off after only five words. It is not a concept at all but a set of instructions on where to find out what an asset is, namely, look at generally accepted accounting principles. An asset is whatever GAAP recognizes as one.

That kind of definition is not much help to the FASB (or anyone else) in deciding what should be an asset. Since the FASB is the arbiter of GAAP, the definition says, in effect, that an asset is whatever the FASB says it is. As any number of people have pointed out, the definition is circular. A little background on how we got it will illustrate why it is so hard to change.

At least as far back as 1907, we had definitions of assets that met the condition of representing things

in the real world. Charles Ezra Sprague described assets as "consisting of property and claims upon property" in *The Philosophy of Accounts*[2] in that year. And here is part of William A. Paton's discussion of "resources, assets, or *properties*" in *Accounting Theory* (1922).

"What is meant by the term 'properties'? In brief, a property is any consideration, material or otherwise, owned by a specific business enterprise and of value to that enterprise. . . .

". . . Two main types of assets are involved: (1) structures, equipment, commodities, and all other tangible things possessed by business enterprises and having value, and (2) all recognized securities, privleges, and claims which give the holder definite right to money, valuable services, or commodities, and all valuable considerations arising from monopolistic conditions."[3]

John B. Canning's definition in *The Economics of Accountancy* (1929), which is perhaps the most quoted of all, is in more abstract terms but agrees in substance with those of Sprague and Paton.

"In general, then, the professional accountant's implied definition may be said to be: *An asset is any future service in money or any future service convertible into money (except those services arising from contracts the two sides of which are proportionately unperformed) the beneficial interest in which is legally or equitably secured to some person or set of persons. Such a service is an asset only to that person or set of persons to whom it runs.*'" [Emphasis in the original.][4]

Assets and Costs

The American Accounting Association made a significant contribution to changing the definition of assets from one based on things in the real world to that in APB Statement no. 4. In 1936 the executive committee of the association issued "A Tentative Statement of Accounting Principles Underlying Corporate Financial Statements." The statement contained no definitions of assets, but each of its propositions embodied a corollary of a "fundamental axiom," namely: "Accounting is . . . not essentially a process of valuation, but the allocation of historical costs

1. Accounting Principles Board Statement no. 4, *Basic Concepts and Accounting Principles Underlying Financial Statements of Business Enterprises* (New York: AICPA, 1970), par. 132.

2. Charles Ezra Sprague, *The Philosophy of Accounts* (New York: Charles Ezra Sprague, 1907), p. 20.
3. William A. Paton, *Accounting Theory with Special Reference to the Corporate Enterprise* (Chicago, Ill.: A.S.P. Accounting Studies Press, Ltd., 1962), pp. 30 and 32.
4. John B. Canning, *The Economics of Accountancy* (New York: Ronald Press Co., 1929), p. 22.

and revenues to the current and succeeding fiscal periods."[5]

Two members of the 1936 executive committee undertook to elaborate and expand the basic concepts of the tentative statement to a "sound fundamental structure of corporate accounting." The result was, of course, *An Introduction to Corporate Accounting Standards*, by W. A. Paton and A. C. Littleton,[6] published in 1940, which laid out in detail what the "fundamental axiom" of the 1936 tentative statement meant in practice.

The monograph was a startling exception to the general proposition that academic writing has had little effect on accounting practice. Although the monograph took exception to certain existing practices—such as Lifo and cost or market, whichever is lower—it was generally a rationalization of existing practice and provided that practice with a theoretical basis that had previously been lacking. Generations of accountants learned to use it as scripture.

The monograph contained no explicit definition of assets, but it set out a definite concept of assets. Most assets were "deferred charges to revenue," costs waiting to be "matched" against future revenues.

"It should not be overlooked . . . that these 'assets' are in fact 'revenue charges in suspense' awaiting some future matching with revenues as costs or expenses. . . .

"It is admitted that not all assets are 'costs' in the sense of technical factors related to the generation of revenue. 'Money resources'—cash, marketable securities, and receivables—are in some respects distinct from the pool of technical cost factors. Such resources represent the current funds of the enterprise, including recognized revenue elements in process of collection. . . .

"The balance sheet thus serves as a means of carrying forward unamortized acquisition prices, the not-yet-deducted costs. . . ."[7]

During the 40 years since the Paton and Littleton monograph, accounting practice has developed substantially along the lines specified in the monograph,

and rationalization and theory consistent with the monograph have been widely used and have been common in authoritative pronouncements.

A legacy of that practice and theory has been the common use of the expression "assets are costs." That sounds innocent enough, but apparently accountants sometimes have not been able, or have not tried, to distinguish the assets from the attribute measured. The result has been proliferation of "what-you-may-call-its"—debits (and credits) in balance sheets that are recorded without much consideration of whether they refer to anything in the real world. They are the sources of the "deferred charges that are not resources but that are recognized and measured in conformity with generally accepted accounting principles" that APB Statement no. 4 includes in its definition of assets.

The mischief maker here is not so much the what-you-may-call-its themselves, which on closer examination often turn out to represent assets in the sense meant by Sprague, Paton and Canning, but the mode of thought that led to them. It was a mode of thought that made "matching" into a religion, a doctrine sufficient to justify some highly questionable procedures. It made accounting results much more a matter of opinion and judgment than they need to be. What-you-may-call-its were recorded not because they represented anything in the real world but because they were said to be necessary "to match costs and revenues properly" or "to avoid distorting periodic net income." That reasoning presumes that we know what net income for a period should be. Apparently, what net income "should be," as well as what constitutes "proper matching of costs and revenues" and what "distorts periodic income," can be known by experience, gut feeling, intuition, management desire or similar source.

I think it is no coincidence that virtually all what-you-may-call-its smooth *reported* income—make it more stable than it would be without them.

In my opinion, financial accounting's excursion into fantasy-land over the last 40 years—our ignoring of correspondence of items in financial statements with the things and events they are supposed to represent while we were using opinion and judgment to "match costs and revenues properly" and "avoid distorting periodic net income"—has been the source of a significant number of our major problems and remains one of the greatest dangers we face. I quote my comments in Accounting Research Study no. 12,

5. Executive Committee of the American Accounting Association. "A Tentative Statement of Accounting Principles Underlying Corporate Financial Statements," *Accounting Review*, June 1936, pp. 187–191.

6. W. A. Paton and A. C. Littleton, *An Introduction to Corporate Accounting Standards* (Evanston, Ill.: AAA, 1940).

7. Ibid., pp. 25, 26 and 67.

Reporting Foreign Operations of U.S. Companies in U.S. Dollars, in 1972:

"As accounting numbers increasingly incorporate devices that are merely inventions of accounting rather than representations of things and events in the real world, the numbers will increasingly be irrelevant and useless to those who rely on financial statements."[8]

During the years that financial accounting was making costs into assets and matching into a religion, the authoritative literature did not say much about what the resulting information was supposed to be good for, or even whether it was supposed to be good for anything. Emphasis on usefulness, particularly decision usefulness, came much later and was not explicitly stated in American Institute of CPAs pronouncements until APB Statement no. 4 in 1970. Financial accounting had more or less turned inward. It was not much concerned with the relation of the items in financial statements to things and events in the real world.

Robert Sterling gives a good example of what can happen when we turn inward so much that we mistake the numbers in the accounts for the real world outside.[9] "The auditors' problems in the McKesson-Robbins case sprang from their reliance on the accounts without going into the real world to find out whether the client actually had receivables and inventories. However, they were following what we would now call generally accepted auditing standards. Auditors could give clean opinions in those days without confirming receivables or observing physical inventories. That case brought auditors into the real world for quantities of inventories and receivables. Now, 40 years later, it is high time for us to stop talking (and thinking) about assets as costs in accounts, to start thinking about them as resources that benefit an enterprise and to ask whether the descriptions and numbers that we put in financial statements represent something that is really there rather than merely entries in accounts.

Changing Attitudes: Time and Patience

The habits and modes of thought that I have described have developed over many years, and I have no illu-

sions that they will be changed easily or quickly. That brings me to the next condition for a successful conceptual framework: We need to change some attitudes and modes of thought, and that will take a long time and require a lot of patience.

Professor Maurice Moonitz has probably devoted more thought than anyone to the question of why it is so hard to establish accounting standards. To appreciate his analysis, I refer you to his research study for the AAA in 1974, *Obtaining Agreement on Standards in the Accounting Profession*,[10] but I think it is fair to say that he found a powerful inhibitor to be the affected parties' resistance to change.

All of us resist change. It takes time to get used to new ideas or procedures. Moreoever, our society has created institutional factors that put tremendous pressure on people to show certain kinds of results, including certain kinds of accounting results. Thus, I do not find it surprising that folks—including management, accountants and even financial analysts—are prone to defend the status quo, which they find known and comfortable, and resist change, which they find uncertain and unsettling.

The preceding paragraph is meant as a preface to some observations about the inevitability of change, the inevitability of resistance to change and the contribution of a conceptual framework. First, I think the handwriting is already on the wall for the present model (which is often mislabeled "historical cost accounting") because, among other things, it can't cope with everyday complications, such as changing prices and fluctuating foreign exchange rates. Those kinds of problems magnify the faults of the existing model's particular mixture of historical costs, current costs, current exit values, net realizable values and present values in a way that all can see them, although our propensity to defend the status quo leads us to seek explanations for those faults other than in the existing model and to seek solutions that patch it up.

For example, almost everybody know that revenues result from the whole process of buying, converting and selling assets or services and collecting the selling price rather than merely from the act of sale, and that we use the sale basis of recognition primarily because of questions about the reliability of most revenue

8. Leonard Lorensen, Accounting Research Study no. 12, *Reporting Foreign Operations of U.S. Companies in U.S. Dollars* (New York: AICPA, 1972), p. 106.
9. Robert R. Sterling, *Toward A Science of Accounting* (Houston, Tex.: Scholars Book Co., 1979), ch. 12.

10. Maurice Moonitz, Studies in Accounting Research no. 8, *Obtaining Agreement on Standards in the Accounting Profession* (Sarasota, Fla.: AAA, 1974).

measures before sale. However, few seem to understand that to delay revenue recognition until the time of sale does not significantly diminish the problem of reliability of measures but merely transfers it from revenue recognition to expense recognition. Costs of goods sold that have resulted from several allocations within a cost accounting system as well as a cost-flow assumption, such as Lifo or Fifo, or depreciation expenses that have resulted from a straight-line or sum-of-the-years'-digits allocation procedure are not verifiable, and we have no way of knowing the extent to which they faithfully represent or fail to represent the *cost* of the goods sold or the *depreciation* during the period. As Financial Accounting Concepts Statement no. 2, *Qualitative Characteristics of Accounting Information*,[11] notes, only the methods for obtaining those results are verifiable, not the results themselves.

I am not arguing that, by itself, earlier revenue recognition would avoid all cost allocations or that it would not involve significant concerns about its reliability. My point is that cost deferrals created in the existing model by delaying revenue recognition make the result much less reliable than we usually admit, perhaps as unreliable or more unreliable than those of earlier recognition. I emphasize that point because it seems not well understood, probably because it is obscured by the widely accepted myth that "historical costs are more objective or more verifiable than current costs or current values."

Moreover, even if the weaknesses of deferring costs are magnified enough for all to see, as they are by changing prices or fluctuating foreign exchange rates, we are more inclined to attempt to patch up the existing model than to admit that it is the basic source of our problems. For example, we try to introduce "deferred gains," and perhaps even "deferred losses," that are, at best, valuation accounts that in effect nullify the revaluation of assets or liabilities and, at worst, are pure what-you-may-call-its that represent nothing at all in the real world.

I expect changes in the existing model to be evolutionary, perhaps over a long time. The conceptual framework won't cause those changes—they are already inevitable. But the concepts can make clear the reasons for the changes, guide the changes that need to be made and make the process of change orderly and consistent rather than ad hoc and potentially inconsistent.

Those changes, no matter how inevitable or needed, will be resisted. I think it is accurate to say that most managers and a good many practicing CPAs have, figuratively speaking, been dragged along kicking and screaming by virtually every significant change in financial reporting that has resulted from pronouncements of standard-setting bodies. That resistance is natural and, within limits, healthy. I do not hold that all change is progress, although I do think that those who have opposed the pronouncements have more often than not been mistaken in their opposition. That is, the majority of those pronouncements have improved financial reporting; moreover, the vast majority of those who resisted them have learned to live with them and in retrospect have even come to brag about them, at least indirectly. We have all heard the boast that "U.S. financial reporting is the best in the world." A good dose of skepticism about the need for change is, nevertheless, healthy. Resistance to pronouncements commonly results in better pronouncements, and the FASB's due process procedures are specifically intended to assure that the necessary skepticism is heard.

One of the factors that can help smooth the way for change is education. I hope to see the FASB's conceptual framework documents replace the Paton and Littleton monograph as the basic sourcebook in accounting education. Then, as students who have the newer background rise in CPA firms and industry, they will feel as comfortable with the concepts as those now in high positions feel with the Paton and Littleton model.

I see the full development of a conceptual framework—especially our learning to use it, feeling comfortable with it and fully accepting it—to be a long process. It will involve significantly a process of education with the FASB leading out. I am, of course, disappointed that we are starting so late; many of the steps we are now tentatively taking should have been taken years ago. But, I have also described in some detail why we went down what is essentially a blind alley—making "matching and attaching" a religion without much concern about what in the real world the numbers were supposed to represent. It will take time to back out of that blind alley completely, and we must be patient. The point is, however, that we have taken some tentative steps in what I assess to be the right direction, and I hope we can now press on toward the objectives we have set.

11. Financial Accounting Concepts Statement no. 2, *Qualitative Characteristics of Accounting Information* (Stamford, Conn.: Financial Accounting Standards Board, 1980), pars. 81–89.

The Board and the Concepts

The last condition for a conceptual framework that I wish to mention is that the board and its staff must take the concepts seriously if they expect others to do so. It goes without saying that the board and its staff must use the concepts and be seen to use them. The board's example of how to use the concepts will do more to enhance their stature and make them operational than any number of admonitions.

Even more significant, perhaps, is that the board's example not abuse the concepts. Nothing will undercut the concepts quicker and more fatally than for the board to change them merely because they result in unpopular answers. I do not mean that concepts should not be changed, but if they are to mean anything, they should be changed only for causes such as changing environmental conditions and discoveries of errors in reasoning, not merely because they produce answers we don't like.

If the concepts in the conceptual framework are at all effective, the FASB will inevitably be faced with a situation in which the pressure and temptation to change a concept rather than an existing procedure will be strong. Most of us have little experience with trying to use concepts to solve problems. We have, for reasons I have already noted, acquired the habit of doing it the other way around. Stephen Zeff has described it succinctly: "Too often, accounting theory is invoked more as a tactic to buttress one's preconceived notions rather than as a genuine arbiter of contending views."[12] Because of that habit, it will usually be much easier to change the concept rather than an existing procedure. But, should the board yield to that temptation, we will be right back to APB Statement no. 4. I think there is a better way.

All our measurement bases, including the mixture of bases we call the existing accounting model, have weaknesses. We may find ourselves facing the dilemma that we can't measure what we want, and what we can measure isn't very relevant in the circumstances. Thus, we must resort to practical but imperfect solutions to many problems. I think that, in trying to set a standard in that kind of situation, the FASB should recognize and admit that there is no sufficiently reliable measure that is consistent with the concepts

and that it is choosing a practical solution for what it considers to be good reasons. In contrast, to change concepts to fit an essentially expedient solution can only undercut concepts by weakening or destroying the limits they set, thereby weakening or destroying their major contribution.

Summary and Prognosis

I have briefly noted and discussed some conditions for a successful conceptual framework:

☐ The concepts themselves must be rooted in the real world.
☐ We need to change some attitudes and modes of thought, and that will take a long time and require a lot of patience.
☐ The board and its staff must take the concepts seriously if they expect others to do so.

What is the outlook? I suppose that depends on your perspective. The way one views the outlook for the conceptual framework probably depends significantly on what one expects or hopes for. Those who feel threatened by the conceptual framework or hope that it will maintain the status quo will be disappointed. Change is coming, even if the conceptual framework is never adopted, because of weaknesses in the existing accounting model. To use the concepts to "embalm the status quo" would not prevent the changes; it would merely make the concepts useless and promote continued ad hoc tinkering with the existing model.

Disappointment is also in store for those who expect the conceptual framework to lead unequivocally to a unique solution for each problem—the only solution that logically follows from the concepts. That is not even a goal of the FASB's conceptual framework; it is concerned not with a search for ultimate truth but with rigorous, internally consistent and useful concepts that are based in the real world.

Since my frustrations in this business have taught me patience and my expectations are modest, I see reasons to be optimistic. After Financial Accounting Concepts Statement no. 1, *Objectives of Financial Reporting by Business Enterprises*,[13] was issued in late 1978, I heard the criticism that after five years and several millions of dollars, the FASB was still

---

12. Stephen Zeff, "Comments on Accounting Principles—How They Are Developed," in Robert R. Sterling, ed., *Institutional Issues in Public Accounting* (Lawrence, Kans.: Scholars Book Co., 1974), p. 177.

13. Financial Accounting Concepts Statement no. 1, *Objectives of Financial Reporting by Business Enterprises* (Stamford, Conn.: FASB, 1978).

where the AICPA Study Group on the Objectives of Financial Statements (the Trueblood group) was in 1973. The implication was clear—no progress.

I think that criticism completely misses the point, and not just in overstating the money spent on the conceptual framework. The FASB asked what people thought of the Trueblood group's objectives in 1974. Only 37 percent of the respondents said that the board should adopt the first objective: "The basic objective of financial statements is to provide information useful for making economic decisions." Even fewer, 35 percent, recommended adopting the third objective: "to provide information useful to investors and creditors for predicting, comparing, and evaluating potential cash flows to them in terms of amount, timing, and uncertainty."[14]

Now, however, you hear many people speak approvingly of decision usefulness and the significance of information useful in assessing amounts, timing and uncertainty of potential cash flows. The point is that between 1973 and 1978, the FASB submitted the objectives to its due process procedures twice, changed some parts as a result of comments received (the most significant change was probably from objectives of financial *statements* to objectives of financial *reporting*) and got the objectives accepted.

It may be unfortunate that it took five years and substantial cash for the FASB to get the objectives accepted, but that's the way the real world works. Changing people's minds takes time. When you consider that acceptance of the objectives involved reversing long-held attitudes, five years is not so long. Rather than a basis for criticism, those five years practically produced a miracle.

14. Report of the Study Group on the Objectives of Financial Statements, *Objectives of Financial Statements* (New York: AICPA, 1973), pp. 61–62.

Chapter Ten

Short-Term Liquid Assets

Reviewing the Chapter

1. **Short-term liquid assets** consist of cash, short-term investments, accounts receivable, and notes receivable.

2. Cash consists of coin and currency on hand, checks and money orders, and bank deposits. A company's cash account may include a **compensating balance**. This balance is a minimum amount that a bank requires a company to keep in its bank account.

3. Companies frequently have excess cash on hand for short periods of time. To put this idle cash to good use, most companies purchase **short-term investments** (also called **marketable securities**).
   a. When cash is first invested, Short-Term Investments is debited and Cash credited. When income from the investment is received, Cash is debited and Dividend Income or Interest Income is credited. The account used depends on whether the investment is in equity securities (such as stock) or debt securities (such as bonds).
   b. On the balance sheet, short-term investments in equity securities are presented at the lower of cost or market. This presentation is justified by the conservatism convention. It shows immediate recognition of a potential loss but puts off recognition of a potential gain until it is realized. Short-term investments in debt securities are presented on the balance sheet at cost, unless the value of the securities has been permanently impaired.
   c. When a short-term investment is sold, Cash is debited, Short-Term Investments is credited, and a loss is debited or a gain is credited for any difference between the original purchase price and the sale price.

4. **Accounts receivable** are classified as current assets and represent payment due from credit customers.

5. Wholesalers and retailers usually allow customers to pay for merchandise over a period of time (that is, they extend credit). They do so because the customer might decide against a purchase that required full payment immediately. This type of credit is often called **trade credit**. It makes expensive items affordable and increases sales for the merchant. Most companies that sell on credit have credit departments, whose responsibility is to approve or refuse credit to individuals or companies. **Uncollectible accounts** (also called bad debts), the accounting term for credit accounts that are not paid, are an expense of selling on credit.

6. The matching rule requires that an uncollectible accounts expense must appear on the same income statement as the corresponding sale, even if the customer defaults in a future period. At the time of a credit sale, however, the company does not know which customers will or will not pay. So an estimate of uncollectible accounts must be made at the end of the accounting period. An adjusting entry is then made debiting Uncollectible Accounts Expense and crediting Allowance for Uncollectible Accounts for the estimated amount. Uncollectible Accounts Expense is closed out much as other expenses are and appears on the income statement. **Allowance for Uncollectible Accounts** is a contra account to Accounts Receivable, reducing Accounts Receivable to the amount estimated to be collectible.

7. The two most common methods for estimating uncollectible accounts are the percentage of net sales method and the accounts receivable aging method.

8. Under the **percentage of net sales method**, the estimated percentage for uncollectible accounts is multiplied by net sales for the period. The resulting figure is then used in the adjusting entry for uncollectible accounts. Any previous balance in Allowance for Uncollectible Accounts represents estimates from previous years that have not yet been written off. It has no bearing on the adjusting entry under this method.

9. Under the **accounts receivable aging method**, customer accounts are placed into a "not yet due" category or into one of several "past due" categories. The amounts in each category are totaled. Each total is then multiplied by a different percentage for estimated bad debts. The sum of these products represents estimated bad debts on ending Accounts Receivable. Again, the debit is to Uncollectible Accounts Expense and the credit to Allowance for Uncollectible Accounts. However, the entry is for the amount that will bring Allowance for Uncollectible Accounts to the figure arrived at under the aging method.

10. When it becomes clear that a specific account will not be collected, it should be written off by a debit to Allowance for Uncollectible Accounts and a credit to Accounts Receivable. The debit is *not* made to Uncollectible Accounts Expense. After a specific account is written off, Accounts Receivable and Allowance for Uncollectible Accounts decrease by the same amount, but the net figure for expected receivables stays the same.

11. When a customer whose account has been written off pays in full or in part, two entries must be made. First, the customer's receivable is reinstated by a debit to Accounts Receivable and a credit to Allowance for Uncollectible Accounts for the amount now thought to be collectible. Second, Cash is debited and Accounts Receivable is credited for each collection.

12. The **direct charge-off method** charges uncollectible accounts to an expense in the period of default, which may or may not coincide with the period of the related sale. There is no estimate for bad debts at the end of the period. When an account is deemed uncollectible, a debit to Uncollectible Accounts Expense and a credit to Accounts Receivable are made. The direct charge-off method often violates the matching rule because accounts may be written off in periods after the sale.

13. When a customer overpays, his or her account will have a credit balance. When a balance sheet is prepared, Accounts Receivable should be shown for the sum of all accounts with debit balances. An account called Credit Balances in Customer Accounts should appear under current liabilities for the sum of all accounts with credit balances.

14. When a firm has made sales to and purchases from the same company, it should maintain two separate accounts and should not offset them against each other.

15. **Installment accounts receivable** are receivables that will be collected in a series of payments, and are usually classified on the balance sheet as current assets.

16. Companies that allow customers to use national credit cards (such as Master Card) must follow special accounting procedures. The credit card company reimburses the company for the sale, less a service charge. The credit card company levies a service charge because it is responsible for establishing credit and collecting the money from the customer.

17. When loans and sales are made to the company's officers, employees, or stockholders, they should be shown separately on the balance sheet with a title such as Receivables from Employees and Officers.

18. A **promissory note** is a written promise to pay a definite sum of money on demand or at a future date. The person who signs the note and thereby promises to pay is called the maker of the note. The person to whom money is owed is called the payee. The payee records long- or short-term Notes Receivable and the maker records long- or short-term Notes Payable.

19. Either the **maturity date** and **duration of note** must be stated on the promissory note or it must be possible to figure them out from the information on the note.

20. To the borrower, **interest** is the cost of borrowing money. To the lender, it is the reward for lending money. The principal is the amount of money borrowed or loaned. The interest rate is the annual charge for borrowing money, and is expressed as a percentage. A note may be either interest-bearing or noninterest-bearing.

21. Interest (not interest rate) is a dollar figure, which is figured as follows:

interest = principal
    × interest rate
    × time (length of loan)

For example, interest on $800 at 5 percent for 90 days is $10, calculated as ($800/1) × (5/100) × (90/360). A 360-day year is commonly used to simplify the computation. If the length of the note were expressed in months, then the third fraction would be the number of months divided by 12.

22. Interest of 12 percent for 30 days can quickly be found by moving the decimal point of the principal two places to the left. This 12 percent method can also be modified to deal with variations from 30 days and 12 percent.

23. The **maturity value** (of an interest-bearing note) is the face value of the note (principal) plus interest.

24. It is common for banks to deduct the interest in advance when lending money on promissory notes. This practice is called **discounting** a note. The **discount** is the amount of interest deducted, and it is computed as follows:

discount = maturity value
    × discount rate
    × discount period

The **proceeds from discounting** is the amount received by the borrower and equals the maturity value minus the discount.

25. A **dishonored note** is one that is not paid at the maturity date. The payee would debit Accounts Receivable for the principal plus interest plus any **protest fee**, credit Notes Receivable, and credit Interest Earned.

26. To raise immediate cash, companies often sell notes receivable to banks or financing companies before maturity. This practice is called discounting because the bank deducts the interest from the maturity value of the note to determine the proceeds. The company then debits Cash for the proceeds, credits Notes Receivable for the principal, and credits Interest Earned for the difference.

27. On the maturity date, the maker of a note that has been discounted must pay the bank or financing company directly. The original payee must make good on the note if the maker does not, and is therefore said to have a **contingent liability**.

28. End-of-period adjustments must be made for notes that apply to both the current and future periods. In this way interest may be properly divided among the periods.

Testing Your Knowledge

Matching

Match each term with its definition by writing the appropriate letter in the blank.

_j_ 1. Credit
_g_ 2. Notice of protest
_f_ 3. Uncollectible accounts expense
_m_ 4. Allowance for uncollectible accounts
_p_ 5. Installment accounts receivable
_e_ 6. Promissory note
_a_ 7. Maker
_l_ 8. Payee
_i_ 9. Maturity date
_k_ 10. Maturity value
_c_ 11. Interest rate
_o_ 12. Interest
_b_ 13. Principal
_h_ 14. Discount
_d_ 15. Dishonored note
_n_ 16. Discounting a note

a. The debtor named in a promissory note
b. The amount of money borrowed or loaned
c. The annual charge for borrowing money, expressed as a percentage
d. A note that is not paid at the maturity date
e. A written promise to pay
f. Estimated bad debts as represented on the income statement
g. A statement indicating that a discounted note has been dishonored
h. The amount of interest deducted in advance from the maturity value of a note
i. The time when payment is due on a note
j. Allowing customers to pay for merchandise over a period of time
k. A note's principal plus interest
l. The creditor named in a promissory note
m. Estimated bad debts as represented on the balance sheet
n. Selling a note prior to maturity
o. The annual charge for borrowing money, expressed in dollars
p. Receivables that will be collected in a series of payments

Completion

Use the lines provided to complete each item.

1. List three methods used in figuring uncollectible accounts.

   % of net sales
   aging accts receivable
   direct charge - off

2. Explain the concept of _contingent liability_ as it relates to discounted notes receivable.

   The responsibility of the payee to reimburse the bank for a dishonored note

3. Under what circumstance would there be a debit balance in Allowance for Uncollectible Accounts?

   Too many accts written off

True-False

Circle T if the statement is true, F if it is false.

T F 1. Under the direct charge-off method, Allowance for Uncollectible Accounts does not exist.

T F 2. The percentage of net sales method violates the matching principle.

T F 3. Under the accounts receivable aging method, the balance in Allowance for Uncollectible Accounts is ignored in making the adjusting entry.

T F 4. Allowance for Uncollectible Accounts is a contra account to Accounts Receivable.

T F 5. Loans to officers of the company should *not* be included in Accounts Receivable on the balance sheet.

T F 6. When a customer overpays, his or her account on the company's books will have a credit balance.

T F 7. Interest of 5 percent on $700 for 90 days would be computed as follows: .05 × 700 × 90.

T F 8. Interest of 12 percent for 30 days can be determined by moving the decimal point of the principal two places to the left.

T F 9. When a note is discounted at the bank, the maker must make good on the note if the payee defaults.

T F 10. A 60-day note dated December 14 is due on February 14.

T F 11. It is possible for the proceeds of a discounted note receivable to be less than its face value.

T F 12. Under the allowance method, the entry to write off a specific account as uncollectible will decrease total assets.

T F 13. The maturity value of a note equals interest plus principal.

T F 14. Under the allowance method, a specific account is written off with a debit to Uncollectible Accounts Expense and a credit to Accounts Receivable.

T F 15. When a note is dishonored, the payee should nevertheless record interest earned.

T F 16. Uncollectible accounts may be viewed as an expense of selling on credit.

Multiple-Choice

Circle the letter of the best answer.

1. A company has credit card sales of $1,000 for the day. If there is a 5 percent charge by credit card companies, then the company's entries to record sales and the eventual receipt of cash would include a
   a. credit to Sales for $950.
   b. debit to Accounts Receivable, Credit Card Companies for $1,050.
   c. credit to Credit Card Revenue for $50.
   d. debit to Cash for $950.

2. Which of the following does not equal the others?
   a. $600 for 60 days at 6 percent 6
   b. $1,200 for 120 days at 3 percent 12
   c. $300 for 120 days at 6 percent 6
   d. $600 for 30 days at 12 percent 6

3. A company estimates at the balance sheet date that $1,500 of net sales for the year will not be collected. A debit balance of $600 exists in Allowance for Uncollectible Accounts. Under the percentage of net sales method, Uncollectible Accounts Expense and Allowance for Uncollectible Accounts would be debited and credited for
   a. $600.
   b. $1,100.
   c. $1,500.
   d. $2,100.

4. A contingent liability exists when
   a. a note is discounted.
   b. a note is dishonored.
   c. interest accrues on a note.
   d. a note reaches maturity.

5. Under the direct charge-off method, a specific customer's account is written off by
   a. debiting Uncollectible Accounts Expense and crediting Allowance for Uncollectible Accounts.
   b. debiting Accounts Receivable and crediting Allowance for Uncollectible Accounts.
   c. debiting Allowance for Uncollectible Accounts and crediting Accounts Receivable.
   d. debiting Uncollectible Accounts Expense and crediting Accounts Receivable.

6. Under the aging of accounts receivable method, a specific customer's account is written off by
   a. debiting Uncollectible Accounts Expense and crediting Allowance for Uncollectible Accounts.
   b. debiting Accounts Receivable and crediting Allowance for Uncollectible Accounts.
   c. debiting Allowance for Uncollectible Accounts and crediting Accounts Receivable.
   d. debiting Uncollectible Accounts Expense and crediting Accounts Receivable.

7. Which of the following cannot be determined from the information on a note?
   a. Discount rate
   b. Interest rate
   c. Interest
   d. Maturity date

8. Which method for handling bad debts often violates the matching principle?
   a. Percentage of net sales method
   b. Direct charge-off method
   c. Accounts receivable aging method
   d. None of the above

9. Which of the following is *not* considered a short-term liquid asset?
   a. Notes receivable
   b. Short-term investments
   c. Inventory
   d. Cash

10. On the balance sheet, short-term investments in stock are presented at
    a. cost, in accordance with the historical cost principle.
    b. market, only if the assets are permanently impaired.
    c. lower of cost or market.
    d. market, regardless of original cost.

Applying Your Knowledge

Exercises

1. Calculate interest on the following amounts:

    a. $7,200 at 4% for 20 days = $ _16_

    b. $52,000 at 7% for 3 months = $ _910_

    c. $4,317 at 6% for 60 days = $ _43.17_

    d. $18,000 at 8% for 1 day = $ _4.00_

2. For the following set of facts, make the necessary entries for Green's Department Store in the journal provided on the next page.

Dec. 31 Interest of $75 has accrued on notes receivable.

   31 Net sales for the year were $600,000. It is estimated that 4 percent will not be collected. Make the entry for uncollectible accounts.

Jan. 3 Anna Kohn has purchased $10,000 worth of goods on credit in November. She now issues Green's her $10,000, 30-day, 6 percent note, thus extending her credit period.

8 Tom O'Brien goes bankrupt and notifies Green's that he cannot pay for the $1,000 worth of goods he had purchased last year on account.

14 The only credit card that Green's accepts is Master Card. The store now records its credit-card sales of $4,000 for the first two weeks in January. Master Card will send payment to Green's upon receipt of invoices, and charges 5 percent for this service.

18 Green's discounts Anna Kohn's note at the bank, receiving $10,020.

24 A check is received from Master Card for the first two week's credit sales, less the service charge.

25 Tom O'Brien notifies Green's that he will in fact be able to pay $600 of the $1,000 that he owes.

28 A check for $200 is received from Tom O'Brien.

Feb. 2 Anna Kohn dishonors her note, and Green's must pay the bank the maturity value of the note plus a $10 protest fee.

General Journal

Date	Description	Debit	Credit
Dec 31	Interest Receivable	75	
	Interest Income		25
31	Uncollectible Accts Expense	24,000	
	Allowance for Uncollectibles		24,000
Jan 3	N/R (30 day, 6%)	10,000	
	A/R - Anna Kohn		10,000
8	Allowance for Uncollectibles	1000	
	A/R - John O'Brien		1000
14	A/R - Mastercard	4000	
	Sales		4000
18	Cash	10,020	
	N/R - Anna Kohn		10,000
	Interest Income		20
24	Cash	3800	
	A/R - Mastercard		4000
	Credit Card Expense (Discount)	200	
25	A/R - Tom O'Brien	600	
	Allowance for Uncollectibles		600
28	Cash	200	
	A/R - Tom O'Brien		200
Feb 2	A/R - Anna Kohn	10,060	
	Cash		10,060
	(includes $10 protest fee)		

Crossword Puzzle
For Chapters 9 and 10

ACROSS

4. Interest deducted on a note
6. Section of accountant's report
8. Measure of profitability (3 words)
9. Promissory _____
10. Charge for default on note (2 words)
14. Length of note
16. Property
17. Income statement form (hyphenated)
18. A current asset

DOWN

1. Source of information about a company (2 words)
2. Normal operating _____
3. Measure of liquidity (2 words)
4. _____ to equity ratio
5. See 11-Down
7. Combined, as financial statements
11. With 15-Down and 5-Down, income statement measure
12. Financial statements of less than a year
13. Method for estimating bad debts
15. See 11-Down

Chapter Eleven

Inventories

Reviewing the Chapter

1. **Monetary assets** consist of cash and assets that represent the right to receive cash. **Nonmonetary assets** are unexpired costs that will become expenses in the future accounting periods that they benefit. They are all assets except cash, short-term investments, receivables, and long-term investments. **Short-term nonmonetary assets** are classified as current assets, and include inventory, supplies, and prepaid expenses. **Long-term nonmonetary assets** benefit more than the current period, and include property, plant, equipment, natural resources, and intangibles.

2. To measure income properly and observe the matching rule, the following two questions must be answered:
   a. How much of the nonmonetary asset has been used up (expired) during the current period and should be transferred to expense?
   b. How much of the nonmonetary asset is unused (unexpired) and should remain on the balance sheet as an asset?

3. **Merchandise inventory** consists of all goods owned and held for sale in the regular course of business. It appears in the current asset section of the balance sheet below receivables.

4. Beginning inventory plus purchases equals cost of goods available for sale. Cost of goods sold is indirectly determined by deducting ending inventory from cost of goods available for sale.

5. Because the cost of ending inventory is needed to compute cost of goods sold, it affects net income dollar for dollar. It is most important to match cost of goods sold with sales so that net income will be accurate.

6. This year's ending inventory automatically becomes next year's beginning inventory. Because beginning inventory also affects net income dollar for dollar, an error in this year's ending inventory will result in misstated net income for both this year and next year.
   a. When ending inventory is understated, net income for the period will be understated.
   b. When ending inventory is overstated, net income for the period will be overstated.
   c. When beginning inventory is understated, net income for the period will be overstated.
   d. When beginning inventory is overstated, net income for the period will be understated.

7. Ending inventory is figured by (a) counting the items on hand, (b) finding the cost of each item, and (c) multiplying unit cost by quantity. Inventory includes all items to which a company has title, even if they haven't been delivered yet.

8. Goods in transit should be included in inventory only if the company has title to the goods. When goods are sent FOB shipping point, title passes to the buyer when the goods reach the common carrier. When goods are shipped FOB destination, title passes when the goods reach the buyer. Goods that have been sold but are still on hand should not be included in the seller's inventory count.

9. **Inventory cost** is defined as the purchase price plus any charges incurred in bringing the inventory to its existing condition and location.

10. When identical items of merchandise are purchased at different prices during the year, it is usually impractical to monitor the actual **goods flow** and record their corresponding costs. Instead, the accountant will make an assumption of the **cost flow**, and will use one of the following methods: (a) specific identification, (b) average-cost, (c) first-in, first-out, or (d) last-in, first-out.

    a. Under the **specific identification method**, the units of ending inventory can be identified as having come from specific purchases. The flow of costs reflects the actual flow of goods in this case. However, the specific identification method is not practical in most cases.

    b. Under the **average-cost method**, the average cost per unit is first figured for the goods available for sale during the period. That is, the cost of goods available for sale is divided by the units available for sale. Then, the average cost per unit is multiplied by the number of units in ending inventory to get the cost of ending inventory.

    c. Under the **first-in, first-out (FIFO) method**, the cost of the first items purchased is assigned to the first items sold. Therefore, ending inventory cost is figured from the prices of the most recent purchases. During periods of rising prices, FIFO yields the highest net income of the four methods.

    d. Under the **last-in, first-out (LIFO) method**, the last items purchased are assumed to be the first items sold. Therefore, the ending inventory cost is figured from the earliest purchases. During periods of rising prices, LIFO yields the lowest net income of the four methods. But it best matches current merchandise costs with current sales prices.

11. During periods of rising prices, FIFO will produce a higher net income than LIFO. During periods of falling prices, the reverse is true. The average-cost and specific identification methods will produce net income figures that are somewhere between those of FIFO and LIFO. Even though LIFO best follows the matching rule, FIFO provides a more up-to-date ending inventory figure for balance-sheet purposes.

12. The market value of inventory may fall below its cost, owing to physical deterioration, obsolescence, or decline in price level. Accordingly, it should be valued at the **lower of cost or market**. The three basic methods of valuing inventory at lower of cost or market are the **item-by-item method**, the **major category method**, and the **total inventory method**. However, the total inventory method is not acceptable for federal income taxes.

13. The **retail method** of inventory estimation may be used when the difference between the cost and sales prices of goods is a constant percentage over a period of time. It may be used whether or not the business makes a physical count of goods. To apply the retail method, goods available for sale are first figured at cost and at retail. Then, a cost-to-retail ratio can be computed. Sales for the period are then subtracted from goods available for sale at retail to produce ending inventory at retail. Finally, ending inventory at retail is multiplied by the cost-to-retail ratio to produce an estimate of ending inventory at cost.

14. The **gross profit method** of inventory estimation assumes that the ratio of gross margin for a business remains relatively stable from year to year. It is used when inventory records are lost or destroyed, and when records of beginning inventory and purchases are not kept at retail. To apply the gross profit method, cost of goods available for sale is first determined by adding purchases to beginning inventory. Then cost of goods sold is estimated as follows:

$$\text{sales} \times (1 - \text{gross margin \%})$$

The resulting estimated cost of goods sold is subtracted from cost of goods available for sale to arrive at estimated ending inventory.

15. When the **periodic inventory method** is used, a physical inventory is taken at the end of the period, and cost of goods sold is derived by subtracting ending inventory from cost of goods available for sale.

16. The **perpetual inventory method** is used by companies that want more control over their inventories. A continuous record is kept of the balance of each inventory item. Thus a physical count is not needed (although one should be taken periodically to confirm the perpetual records).

17. The journal entries for the cost of merchandise purchased and sold are different for the periodic and perpetual systems. The periodic system records all purchases of goods in a Purchases account, closes out Purchases and beginning inventory at the end of the period, and records ending inventory. The perpetual system records all purchases of goods with a debit to Merchandise Inventory, and records Cost of Goods Sold and a reduction in Merchandise Inventory after each sale. No Purchases account is needed, and the only merchandise-related entry made at the end of the period is to close out Cost of Goods Sold.

Testing Your Knowledge

Matching

Match each term with its definition by writing the appropriate letter in the blank.

_b_ 1. Nonmonetary assets

_h_ 2. Merchandise inventory

_d_ 3. Specific identification

_g_ 4. FIFO

_j_ 5. LIFO

_a_ 6. Average-cost

_f_ 7. Lower of cost or market

_i_ 8. Retail method

_c_ 9. Gross profit method

_k_ 10. Periodic system

_e_ 11. Perpetual system

a. The inventory method that utilizes an average-cost-per-unit figure

b. All assets except cash, receivables, and investments

c. The inventory estimation method used when inventory is lost or destroyed.

d. The inventory method in which the assumed flow of costs matches the actual flow of goods

e. The inventory system that maintains continuous records

f. The rule that governs how inventory should be valued on the financial statements

g. The inventory method that yields the highest ending inventory during rising prices

h. Goods held for sale in the regular course of business

i. The inventory estimation method that uses a cost-to-retail ratio

j. The inventory method that best follows the matching principle

k. The inventory system that does not maintain continuous records

Completion

Use the lines provided to complete each item.

1. List the four basic cost-flow assumptions used to determine the cost of merchandise inventory.

   specific id.

   average-cost

   FIFO

   LIFO

2. List the three basic methods of valuing inventory at lower of cost or market.

   item by item

   major category

   total inventory

3. List two methods of estimating ending inventory.

   retail

   gross profit

4. Briefly distinguish between the periodic and perpetual inventory systems in terms of record keeping and inventory taking.

True-False

Circle T if the statement is true, F if it is false.

(T) F 1. The unexpired portion of a non-monetary asset will appear on the balance sheet.

(T) F 2. When beginning inventory is understated, cost of goods sold for the period will also be understated.

(T) F 3. When ending inventory is overstated, net income for the period will also be overstated.

(T) F 4. An error in 19x1's ending inventory will cause net income to be misstated in both 19x1 and 19x2.

(T) (F) 5. Goods in transit belong in the buyer's ending inventory only if the buyer has paid for them.

(T) F 6. If prices never changed, then all four methods of inventory valuation would result in identical net income figures.

(T) (F) 7. Under FIFO, the goods are sold in exactly the same order as they are purchased.

T **(F)** 8. Of the four inventory methods, LIFO will result in the lowest income during periods of falling prices.

(T) (F) 9. Under the retail method, each item sold must be recorded at both cost and (retail).

(T) F 10. Under the gross profit method, cost of goods sold is estimated by multiplying the gross profit percentage by sales.

(T) F 11. A perpetual inventory system does not close out beginning inventory at the end of the period.

T **(F)** 12. Under rising prices, the average cost method will result in a lower net income than LIFO will.

T **(F)** 13. When a periodic inventory system is used, a subsidiary file of inventory accounts must be kept.

Multiple Choice

Circle the letter of the best answer.

1. Which of the following is *least* likely to be included in the cost of inventory?
   a. Freight in
   b. Cost to store goods
   c. Purchase cost of goods
   d. Excise tax on goods purchased

2. Under rising prices, which inventory method will most likely result in the highest tax liability?
   a. FIFO
   b. LIFO
   c. Both LIFO and average cost
   d. Average cost

3. Forgetting to inventory the merchandise in a warehouse will result in
   a. overstated net income.
   b. overstated total assets.
   c. understated owners' equity.
   d. understated cost of goods sold.

4. Which inventory method is best suited for low-volume, high-priced goods?
   a. FIFO
   b. LIFO
   c. Specific identification
   d. Average-cost

5. Which of the following is not used or computed in applying the retail inventory method?
   a. Ending inventory at retail
   b. Freight in at retail
   c. Beginning inventory at cost
   d. Sales during the period

6. The cost of inventory becomes an expense in the period in which
   a. (the inventory is sold.
   b. the merchandiser obtains title to the inventory.
   c. the merchandiser pays for the inventory.
   d. the merchandiser is paid for inventory that he has sold.

7. Goods in transit should be included in the inventory of
   a. neither the buyer nor the seller.
   b. the buyer when the goods have been shipped FOB destination.
   c. the seller when the goods have been shipped FOB shipping point.
   d. (the company that has title to the goods.

Applying Your Knowledge

Exercises

1. Swanson Company had beginning inventory of 100 units at $20. The firm made successive purchases as follows:

   Feb. 20 Purchased 200 units at $22
   May 8 Purchased 150 units at $20
   Oct. 17 Purchased 250 units at $24

   Calculate the cost that would be assigned to the ending inventory of 310 units as well as cost of goods sold under the following methods:

   15400

	Cost of Ending Inventory	Cost of Goods Sold
a. LIFO	$ *6600*	$ ~~13800~~ *8800*
b. FIFO	$ *7200*	$ *8200*
c. Average-cost	$ *6820*	$ *8580*

   avg = $22

2. The records of Monahan Company show the following data for the month of May:

Sales	$156,000
Beginning inventory (at cost)	70,000
Beginning inventory (at retail)	125,000
Net purchases (at cost)	48,000
Net purchases (at retail)	75,000
Freight in	2,000

   Compute the estimated cost of ending inventory, using the retail inventory method.

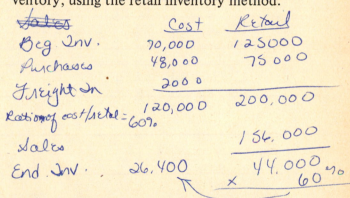

3. At the beginning of the accounting period, the cost of merchandise inventory was $150,000. Net sales during the period were $300,000, net purchases totaled $120,000, and the historical gross margin has been 20 percent. Compute the estimated cost of ending inventory, using the gross profit method.

Beg Inv.   150,000
Purchases   120,000
Cost avail.   270,000
c/o/s   240,000 = (1-20%) × 300,000
~~Sales~~   300,000
End Inv.   30,000

4. Rudena Enterprises uses the perpetual LIFO method for valuing its inventory. On May 1, its inventory consisted of 100 units that cost $10 each. Successive purchases and sales for May were as follows:

May 4 Purchased 60 units at $12.00 each
May 8 Sold 50 units
May 17 Purchased 70 units at $11.00 each
May 25 Sold 100 units

In the perpetual inventory record card provided below, enter all inventory data for the month of May.

5. Assume the same facts as in exercise 4 and that the goods retail for $20 each. In the journal at the bottom of this page, prepare the journal entries to record the May 17 purchase (assume a credit purchase) and the May 25 sale (assume a cash sale). You will need to refer to the completed perpetual inventory record card in exercise 4 to answer this question.

	Purchased			Sold			Balance		
Date	Units	Cost	Total	Units	Cost	Total	Units	Cost	Total
May 1							100	10	1000
4	60	12	720				100	10	
							60	12	1720
8				50	12	600	100	10	
							10	12	1120
17	70	11	770				100	10	
							10	12	
							70	11	1890
25				70	11				
				10	12				
				20	10	1090	80	10	800

	General Journal		
Date	Description	Debit	Credit
May 17	Merch. Inv.	770	
	A/P		770
25	Cash	2000	
	Sales		2000
25	C/O/S	1090	
	Merch. Inv.		1090

Paying FIFO Taxes: Your Favorite Charity?

In one of the most puzzling rituals of American business behavior, thousands of U.S. companies are once again preparing their annual reports using FIFO rather than LIFO inventory accounting. By so doing, they will pay as extra taxes funds which could be used for expansion, capital replacement or dividends.

Under FIFO, or the first-in, first-out assumption, inventory costs flow through the firm as if on a conveyor belt. Costs are assigned to units sold in the same order the costs entered inventory. As a result, during periods of rising prices, older and thus *lower* costs are subtracted from revenues when determining reported (and taxable) earnings.

In contrast, under LIFO, or the last-in, first-out assumption, inventory costs are accumulated as if on a coal pile, with the newest costs being removed from the top and assigned to units sold. Unless a cost layer is liquidated by depleting inventories, it can remain in the base of the pile indefinitely. Thus, during periods of rising prices older and lower costs can remain in the balance sheet inventory accounts while the newer and *higher* costs are used to calculate earnings. Compared to FIFO, reported earnings in most cases drop. But so do taxable earnings. The company can keep more cash for itself and for shareholders.

According to their latest annual reports, three long-time LIFO users—Amoco, General Electric and U.S. Steel—have together saved more than $3 billion in taxes compared to what they would have paid using FIFO.

LIFO was deemed acceptable for tax purposes in 1939, and it's been used widely in selected industries, notably steel and petroleum, since the late 1940s. A large number of firms switched to LIFO in 1974, a year of high inflation. And for 1980, American Hospital Supply, Eli Lilly, Clorox and Williams Cos., among others, have announced they're making the switch.

Yet the vast majority of companies continue to use FIFO. Some managers are perhaps reluctant to incur additional LIFO bookkeeping costs. Some have perhaps dismissed LIFO's tax advantages in light of variable year-end inventory levels or less than galloping

*FIFO Firms LIFO Competitors	1974–1978	
	Additional FIFO Taxes	LIFO Tax Savings
	(in millions of dollars)	
*Federal Paper Board	$ 8	
Mead Corp.		$ 46
*J.P. Stevens	29	
Burlington Inds.		44
Cone Mill		28
*Jewel Companies	36	
American Stores		18
*Matsco Corp.	15	
Wallace-Murray		13
*Minn. Mining & Mfg.	118	
Eastman Kodak		204
*Smith International	32	
Dresser Inds.		125
Hughes Tool Co.		22

prices. Others may believe that since LIFO would result in lower reported earnings, stockholders are content to pay the extra FIFO taxes.

How much extra are stockholders willing to pay? In a forthcoming study in the "Supplement to the Journal of Accounting Research, 1980," I compare the inventory levels and accounts of 105 New York Stock Exchange firms which used FIFO, with those of 105 competitors that adopted LIFO between 1973 and 1975. From 1974 to 1978, by my estimates, the 105 FIFO firms paid an average of nearly *$26 million* each in additional federal income taxes, thanks to their policy of sticking with FIFO. For 1974 alone, these additional taxes averaged nearly $12 million per firm—more than 1½% of their sales.

Indeed there are good reasons to suspect that the additional taxes paid by FIFO firms put them at a competitive disadvantage. The accompanying table compares estimates of the additional taxes paid by six FIFO firms, with the amounts saved by direct competitors that adopted LIFO or extended its use in 1974.

FIFO firms, of course, do not typically disclose the additional taxes they have paid. I have estimated these amounts, however, using industry-specific price indexes and assumptions about procurement, to come up with the differences betweeen FIFO- and LIFO-based earnings. The additional FIFO taxes shown in the table equal these differences multiplied by the corporate income tax rate (then 48%).

The estimates of additional FIFO taxes assume that LIFO is applicable to all of a FIFO firm's inventories. As a result, these amounts may be overstated for firms like Smith International which hold significant portions of their inventories in other countries where LIFO is not permitted. However, the amounts that have been saved by LIFO competitors may understate the potential savings in cases like American Stores where LIFO has been adopted for only a portion of domestic inventories.

The amounts presented suggest that a number of firms have paid millions of dollars each in additional taxes by using FIFO rather than LIFO for domestic inventories. It is unlikely that bookkeeping costs could account for such sums. And fears of negative stockholder reaction appear unfounded in light of the efficient markets research documenting investor preferences for cash flows. While there are some unusual circumstances (like falling prices or inventory levels) in which LIFO could yield smaller cash flows, it is puzzling why so many firms in so many industries have continued to use FIFO.

Perhaps companies sticking to FIFO are showing their support for some worthy federal program. But wouldn't it make more sense to contribute some LIFO tax savings to a favorite *tax-deductible* charity? Or perhaps I have ignored an important LIFO cost or FIFO benefit. If so, please let me know.

Pros and Cons of Switching to LIFO

I want to commend you on the Jan. 19 editorial page article by Gary C. Biddle on FIFO.

It is important that more investors become aware of the fact that many companies have huge LIFO reserves (the differential between the estimated current market of the inventory and original cost) which are not reflected in the present market value of the securities. There are a number of companies where the LIFO reserve is greater than the present market value of the stock.

J.P. Stevens, for example, has finally realized the advantage of LIFO and in the annual report to be issued shortly will show a reduction of current income tax payments of $16.7 million as a result of having adopted LIFO in 1980.

J. Edward Roney
Detroit

Prof. Biddle writes as if the LIFO inventory method causes a tax forgiveness. LIFO causes only a tax deferment—thus, an interest-free loan of tax due, plus the wealth transfer of inflation on the money due. Not a small matter in many cases.

But the deferred tax must be paid sometime—usually when the firm is cash short—unless the firm is immortal and never has a LIFO layer liquidation or a fall in prices. The deferred tax liability is not shown on the balance sheet. It can be in billions of dollars, as we shall learn if we have deflation and a depression.

LIFO is base on the zany idea that the value of an inventory is determined by the order it is withdrawn from stock. Only in the U.S. is this thought to make sense.

H. Morris Hansen
Fairfax, Calif.

Source: Letters to the editor, *Wall Street Journal*, January 27, 1981. Used by permission.

Further Thoughts on FIFO Accounting

In his Jan. 19 editorial page article, Prof. Biddle questions why so many industries have continued to use FIFO inventory accounting.

One reason may be that the managements of industries using FIFO are reluctant to reduce reported earnings. Although their reasons may appear myopic, they are nevertheless real. A recent survey by the Conference Board showed that more than 80% of medium-sized and large manufacturers had annual bonus plans for executives. The survey indicated that all plans linked bonuses to corporate performance. It appears likely that corporate performance is often measured by the amount of and by the increase in reported earnings. To reduce reported earnings even in the short-term would mean reduced compensation for these executives. This alone may account for some of the FIFO inventory companies. Until corporate managers lengthen their time horizons for determining improved corporated performance there will be reluctance to change anything that has an immediate negative impact on reported earnings.

When contemplating a change to the LIFO inventory costing method, management should also be told that LIFO could cause erratic if not poor production habits in the future. This occurs when management continues to produce, to make certain that old lower costs remain in inventory and are not assigned to the cost of goods sold, while sales fall short of expectations. The result, at the very least, is a temporary involuntary buildup of inventory. This in turn often leads to the furloughing of production employees while sales catch up with past production. Once the catchup takes place the furloughed employees need to be recalled. The problem is that sometimes they have found other jobs and are not available. This is expecially painful in industries where the learning curve is important.

LIFO inventory accounting does provide a company with a number of benefits, including tax benefits and improved cash flow. However, the benefits may not offset some of the problems it creates and that perhaps explains why so many New York Stock Exchange companies continue to use FIFO.

John Cerepak
Professor, Department of Accounting
Fairleigh Dickinson University
Teaneck, N.J.

Source: Letters to the editor, *Wall Street Journal*, January 28, 1981. Used by permission.

I, too, have long been puzzled why so many firms continue to use FIFO. While FIFO does permit the firm to report higher "earnings" per share, it is unlikely that the stock market is fooled. Given the impressive scientific evidence supporting market efficiency, it seems more likely that share prices are geared primarily to real magnitudes, especially the ability to pay dividends, rather than to reported earnings. Surely the general decline in real stock prices witnessed during the past twelve years can be explained, in part, by widespread use of FIFO working in conjunction with ongoing inflation.

FIFO accounting harms the public in two important ways. First, the public is led to believe that profits are greater than they really are. This not only arouses public antagonism, it also fosters intervention. For example, some of the commotion during the "obscene oil profits" episode of 1973–74 owed its origin to FIFO accounting. By overstating their profits, the oil companies seemingly almost invited the price controls and other waste-creating regulations which ensued. Second, since FIFO enriches the Treasury at the expense of stockholders, it induces a shift in scarce economic resources from the private to the public sector. This overpayment of taxes, which is unlegislated and represents a magnitude in the billions of dollars, fosters a transfer system which, because of bracket creep, already overtaxes the private sector during inflation.

Geoffrey E. Nunn
Professor of Economics
San Jose State University
San Jose, Calif.

Chapter Twelve

Current Liabilities and Payroll Accounting

Reviewing the Chapter

1. **Liabilities** are present obligations for either the future payment of assets or the future performance of services. A liability generally should be recorded when an obligation arises. But it is also necessary to make end-of-period adjustments for accrued and estimated liabilities. On the other hand, contracts representing future obligations are not recorded as liabilities until they become current obligations.

2. Liabilities are valued at the actual or estimated amount due, or at the fair market value of goods or services that must be delivered.

3. **Current liabilities** are present obligations that are expected to be satisfied within one year or the normal operating cycle, whichever is longer. Payment is expected to be out of current assets or by taking on another current liability. **Long-term liabilities** are obligations that are not expected to be satisfied in the current period.

4. Current liabilities consist of definitely determinable liabilities and estimated liabilities.

5. **Definitely determinable liabilities** are obligations that can be measured exactly. They include trade accounts payable, short-term notes payable, dividends pay-able, sales and excise taxes payable, current portions of long-term debt, accrued liabilities, payroll liabilities, and unearned or deferred revenues.

   a. Trade accounts payable are current obligations due to suppliers of goods and services.

   b. Short-term notes payable are current obligations evidenced by promissory notes. Interest may be either stated on the face of the note or deducted in advance (discounted).

   c. Dividends payable is an obligation to distribute the earnings of a corporation to its stockholders. It arises only when the board of directors declares a dividend.

   d. Most states and many cities levy a sales tax on retail transactions. The federal government also charges an excise tax on some products. The merchant must collect the taxes at the time of the sale and would record both the receipt of cash and the proper tax liabilities.

   e. An accrued liability is an actual or estimated liability that exists at the balance sheet date but is unrecorded. An end-of-period adjustment is needed to record both the expenses and the accrued liabilities.

f. Unearned or **deferred revenues** represent obligations to deliver goods or services in return for advance payment. When delivery takes place, Deferred Revenues is debited and a revenue account is credited.

6. **Estimated liabilities** are definite obligations. However, the amount of the obligation must be estimated at the balance sheet date because the exact figure will not be known until a future date. Examples of estimated liabilities are income taxes, property taxes, product warranties, and vacation pay.

   a. A corporation's income tax depends on its net income, a figure that often is not determined until well after the balance sheet date.

   b. Property taxes are taxes levied on real and personal property. Very often a company's accounting period ends before property taxes have been assessed. Therefore, the company must make an estimate. The debit is to Property Taxes Expense, and the credit is to Estimated Property Taxes Payable.

   c. When a company sells its products, many of the warranties will still be in effect during the next accounting period. However, the warranty expense and liability must be recorded in the period of the sale no matter when the company makes good on the warranty. Therefore, at the end of each accounting period, the company should make an estimate of future warranty expense that will apply to the present period's sales.

   d. In most companies, employees earn vacation pay for working a certain length of time. Therefore, the company must estimate the vacation pay that applies to each payroll period. The debit is to Vacation Pay Expense, and the credit is to Estimated Liability for Vacation Pay.

7. A **contingent liability** is a potential liability that may or may not become an actual liability. The uncertainty about its outcome is settled when a future event does or does not occur. Contingent liabilities arise from things like pending lawsuits, tax disputes, discounted notes receivable, the guarantee of another company's debt, and failure to follow pollution regulations.

8. The three general types of liabilities associated with payroll accounting are (a) liabilities for employee compensation, (b) liabilities for employee payroll withholding, and (c) liabilities for employer payroll taxes. An employee is under the direct supervision and control of the company. An independent contractor (such as a lawyer or a CPA) is not, and is therefore not accounted for, under the payroll system.

9. **Wages** are hourly or piecework pay. **Salaries** are the monthly or yearly rate paid generally to administrative or managerial employees.

10. The employer is required by law to withhold certain taxes from the employee's wages and to remit those taxes to government agencies. The employer also makes other withholdings for the employee's benefit.

    a. FICA taxes provide for retirement and disability benefits, survivor's benefits, and medical benefits.

    b. Federal income taxes depend on (1) the amount that the employee earns, and (2) the number of exemptions claimed on the employee's W-4 form (Employee's Withholding Exemption Certificate). The amount that the employer withholds and remits to the government should be close to the employee's actual federal income tax liability. State income taxes require similar withholding procedures.

    c. Withholdings may also be made for pension plans, insurance premiums, union dues, and savings plans.

11. An employee's take-home pay equals his or her gross earnings less total withholdings. To help make payroll procedures easier, the company must keep a separate **employee earnings record** for each employee, listing all payroll data (earnings, deductions, and payment). Each year, the firm must inform the employee of his or her yearly earnings and withholdings on a W-2 form (Wage and Tax Statement). The

employee uses this form to complete the individual tax return.

12. The **payroll register** is a detailed listing of the company's total payroll each payday. Each employee's name, regular and overtime hours, gross earnings, deductions, net pay, and payroll classification are listed for that payroll period. The journal entry for recording the payroll is based on the column totals of the payroll register.

13. Independent of employee's taxes, the employer must pay (a) FICA taxes, (b) federal unemployment insurance taxes (FUTA), and (c) state unemployment compensation taxes. These taxes are considered operating expenses, and require a debit to Payroll Taxes Expense and a credit to each of the three tax liabilities.

14. To pay salaries, many companies use a special payroll bank account against which payroll checks are drawn. In addition, monthly or quarterly payments must be made to the proper agencies for withholdings.

15. It is important to keep firm internal control over the payroll system to lessen the possibility of payroll fraud. For this reason, the business should separate the duties of (a) the personnel function, (b) the timekeeping function, (c) the accounting function, and (d) the distribution function.

Testing Your Knowledge

Matching

Match each term with its definition by writing the appropriate letter in the blank.

_B_ 1. Current liabilities

_L_ 2. Long-term liabilities

_G_ 3. Definitely determinable liabilities

_E_ 4. Estimated liabilities

_O_ 5. Deferred revenues

_J_ 6. Vacation pay

_H_ 7. Withholdings

_C_ 8. FICA taxes

_K_ 9. W-2 form

_I_ 10. W-4 form

_F_ 11. Take-home pay

_N_ 12. Employee earnings record

_a_ 13. Payroll register

_M_ 14. Payroll taxes expense

_Q_ 15. Contingent liabilities

_D_ 16. Wages

_P_ 17. Salaries

a. A listing of payroll data for all employees for one payday

b. Obligations that are expected to be satisfied within one year or the normal operating cycle, whichever is longer

c. A tax paid by both the employer and the employee

d. Hourly or piecework pay to an employee

e. Obligations that exist but cannot be exactly measured at the balance sheet date

f. Gross earnings less total withholdings

g. Obligations that can be measured exactly

h. A portion of earnings retained by the employer and remitted to appropriate agencies

i. A statement listing exemptions claimed

j. Pay received during one's earned time off

k. A yearly statement of earnings and withholdings

l. Obligations that are not expected to be satisfied in the current period

m. FICA and unemployment taxes levied on the employer

n. A record containing all payroll data for one employee

o. Obligations to deliver goods or services in return for advance payment

p. Monthly or yearly pay to (usually) a manager or administrator

q. Potential liabilities that may or may not become actual liabilities.

Completion

Use the lines provided to complete each item.

1. Current liabilities fall into two principal categories. What are they?

Definitely determinable

Estimated

2. Give three examples of contingent liabilities.

Pending lawsuits

Discounted N/R

Tax disputes

3. Give three examples of estimated liabilities.

Income Tax

Property Tax

Vacation Pay   _Warranty Expense_

4. Give three examples of definitely determinable liabilities.

_A/P_

_N/P_

Sales tax   Excise tax

5. List three withholdings from an employee's salary that are always or almost always required.

FICA

FWT

State Tax

6. List the three components of payroll taxes expense.

FICA

FUTA

MUCF

True-False

Circle T if the statement is true, F if it is false.

T (F) 1. Deferred revenues can be found on the income statement.

(T) F 2. A contract to purchase goods in the future does not require the recording of a current liability.

(T) F 3. Failure to record an accrued liability will result in an overstatement of net income.

(T) F 4. The current portion of a long-term debt is a current liability (assume that it is to be satisfied with cash).

T (F) 5. Sales tax is an example of an estimated liability.

T (F) 6. Warranties fall under the category of definitely determinable liabilities.

(T) F 7. Federal income taxes withheld depend on the number of exemptions claimed on the W-4 form.

(T) F 8. The journal entry for recording the payroll is based on the column totals of the payroll register.

T (F) 9. FUTA is a tax paid by both the employer and the employee.

(T) F 10. Every contingent liability must eventually become an actual liability or no liability at all.

T (F) 11. The account Discount on Notes Payable is associated with notes whose interest is stated separately on the face of the note.

(T) F 12. Paychecks should not be distributed by the payroll department.

(T) F 13. A CPA is an example of an independent contractor.

T (F) 14. If a refrigerator is sold in year 1, and repairs are made in year 2, Product Warranty Expense should be recorded in year 2.

(T) F 15. When the payroll is recorded, Salaries Payable is credited for total take-home pay.

Multiple-Choice

Circle the letter of the best answer.

1. Which of the following is not a definitely determinable liability?
   a. Dividends payable
   b. Deferred revenues
   (c.) Property taxes payable
   d. Excise taxes payable

2. Estimated liabilities would not apply to
   a. warranties.
   b. vacation pay.
   c. a corporation's income tax.
   (d.) pending lawsuits.

3. Which of the following is not an employee withholding?
   a. FUTA tax
   b. Union dues
   c. FICA tax
   d. Charitable contributions

4. The amount of federal income tax withheld is recorded as a
   a. payroll expense.
   b. contra account.
   c. current asset.
   d. current liability.

5. Payment to an employee for more hours than he or she has actually worked suggests a flaw in the
   a. personnel function.
   b. timekeeping function.
   c. accounting function.
   d. distribution function.

6. When an employee receives vacation pay, the company should
   a. debit Vacation Pay Expense and credit Cash.
   b. debit Vacation Pay Receivable and credit Cash.
   c. debit Estimated Liability for Vacation Pay and credit Cash.
   d. debit Vacation Pay Expense and credit Estimated Liability for Vacation Pay.

7. A company, which uses a calendar year, receives a property tax bill each March (for that particular calendar year) to be paid by April 10. If entries are made at the end of each month to record property tax expense, the April 10 entry to record payment would include a
   a. debit to Cash.
   b. credit to Estimated Property Taxes Payable.
   c. debit to Property Taxes Expense.
   d. debit to Prepaid Property Taxes.

8. Marina Pools, Inc., purchased some equipment by executing a $10,000 noninterest-bearing note due in three years. The equipment should be recorded by Marina at
   a. $10,000 minus the discounted interest on the note.
   b. $10,000 plus the discounted interest on the note.
   c. the amount of the discounted interest on the note.
   d. $10,000.

Applying Your Knowledge

Exercises

1. During 19x1, White's Appliance Store sold 300 washing machines, each with a one-year guarantee. It was estimated that 5 percent will eventually require some type of repair, with an average cost of $35. Prepare the adjusting entry that White's would make concerning the warranty. Also, prepare the entry that the store would make on April 9, 19x2, for one such repair that cost $48.

\multicolumn{6}{c}{General Journal}					
\multicolumn{2}{c}{Date}	Description		Debit	Credit
19x1 10	31	Warranty Expense		525	
		Estimated Warranty Liability			525
		300 × 5% × 35 = $525			
19x2 4	9	Estimated Warranty Liability		48	
		Service or Parts			48
		Repair washer			

2. Frank Nelson, an office worker who is paid $6.50 per hour, worked 40 hours during the week of May 7. FICA taxes are 7.0 percent, union dues are $5, state taxes withheld are $8, and federal income taxes withheld are $52. In addition, Nelson's employer must pay (on the basis of gross earnings) FICA taxes of 7.0 percent, federal unemployment taxes of .7 percent, and state unemployment taxes of 2.7 percent. Prepare journal entries that summarize Nelson's earnings for the week and that record the employer's payroll taxes. Round off amounts to the nearest cent.

\multicolumn{6}{c}{General Journal}					
\multicolumn{2}{c}{Date}	Description		Debit	Credit
5	7	Wages Expense		260	
		FICA pay			18.20
		Union Dues pay			5
		SWT pay			8
		FWT pay			52
		Wages pay			177.80
		Frank Nelson earnings			
		Payroll Taxes Expense		27.04	
		FICA pay			18.20
		FUTA pay			1.82
		MUCT pay			7.02

Crossword Puzzle
For Chapters 11 and 12

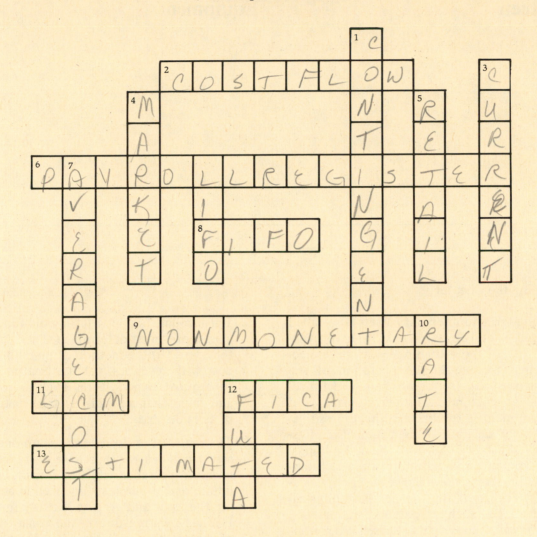

ACROSS

2. Inventory-movement assumption (2 words)
6. Listing of employees on payday (2 words)
8. Inventory method
9. Asset not involving cash
11. Inventory pricing method (abbreviation)
12. Employer and employee withholding
13. Type of liability

DOWN

1. Potential liability
3. Short-term
4. Replacement cost of inventory
5. Inventory estimation method
7. Method for pricing inventory (2 words)
10. Tax percentage
12. Tax assessed against employers

Chapter Thirteen

Property, Plant, and Equipment

Reviewing the Chapter

1. **Long-term nonmonetary assets** (also called **fixed assets**) are assets that (a) have a useful life of more than one year, (b) are acquired for use in the operation of the business, and (c) are not intended for resale to customers. Property, plant, and equipment is the balance sheet classification for **tangible assets**, which have physical substance, such as land, buildings, equipment, and natural resources. **Intangible assets** is the balance sheet classification for assets that do not have physical substance, such as patents, trademarks, goodwill, copyrights, leaseholds, franchises, and organization costs.

2. In dealing with long-term nonmonetary assets, the major accounting problems are to figure out how much of the asset has benefited the current period, and how much should be carried forward as an asset to benefit future periods. This allocation of costs to different accounting periods is called **depreciation** in the case of plant and equipment (plant assets), **depletion** in the case of natural resources, and **amortization** in the case of intangible assets. Because land has an unlimited useful life, its cost is never converted into an expense.

3. To account for long-term nonmonetary assets, one must determine (a) the cost of the asset, (b) the method of matching the cost with revenues, (c) the treatment of subsequent expenditures such as repairs and maintenance, and (d) the treatment of asset disposal.

4. The cost of a long-term nonmonetary asset includes the purchase cost, freight charges, insurance while in transit, installation, and other costs involved in acquiring the asset and getting it ready for use. Interest incurred during the construction of a plant asset is included in the cost of the asset. However, interest incurred for the purchase of a plant asset is expensed when incurred.

5. When land is purchased, the Land account should be debited for the price paid for the land; real estate commissions; lawyers' fees; and such expenses as back taxes assumed, draining, clearing, and grading costs, assessments for local improvements, and the cost (less salvage value) of tearing down a building on the property.

6. Land improvements, such as driveways, parking lots, and fences, are subject to depreciation and require a separate Land Improvements account.

7. When long-term nonmonetary assets are purchased for a lump sum, the cost should be divided among the assets acquired in proportion to their appraisal values.

8. *Depreciation*, as used in accounting, refers to the allocation of the cost (less the residual value) of a plant asset to the periods benefited by the asset. It does not refer to the physical deterioration or the decrease in market value of the asset. That is, it is a process of allocation, not valuation.

9. A plant asset should be depreciated over its estimated useful life in a systematic and rational manner. Plant assets have limited useful lives because of physical deterioration and **obsolescence** (the process of becoming out-of-date).

10. Depreciation is recorded by debiting Depreciation Expense and crediting Accumulated Depreciation. Accumulated Depreciation is a contra asset account, and its balance is deducted from the corresponding plant asset in the balance sheet. The difference is called the book value or **carrying value**, and represents the unexpired cost of the asset. Generally, separate Depreciation Expense and Accumulated Depreciation accounts are maintained for each type of plant asset.

11. Depreciation may be figured after determining the asset's cost, residual value, depreciable cost, and estimated useful life. **Residual value** is the estimated value at the disposal date and is often referred to as **salvage value** or **disposal value**. **Depreciable cost** equals the asset's cost less its residual value. **Estimated useful life** may be measured in time or in units, and requires careful consideration by the accountant.

12. The most common depreciation methods are (a) straight-line, (b) production, (c) sum-of-the-years'-digits, and (d) declining-balance. The last two are examples of **accelerated methods** because depreciation is greatest in the first year and declines each year thereafter.

13. Under the **straight-line method**, the depreciable cost is spread evenly over the life of the asset. Under this method, depreciation for each year is computed as follows:

$$\frac{\text{cost} - \text{residual value}}{\text{estimated useful life in years}}$$

14. Under the **production method**, depreciation is based not on time but on use of the asset in units. Under this method, depreciation for each year is computed as follows:

$$\frac{\text{cost} - \text{residual value}}{\text{estimated useful life in units}}$$

$$\times \text{ actual units of output}$$

15. Under the **sum-of-the-years'-digits method**, depreciation is computed by multiplying depreciable cost by a fraction that changes every year. Under this method, depreciation for the first year (where n = estimated useful life) is computed as follows:

$$(\text{cost} - \text{residual value}) \times \frac{N}{1 + 2 + \cdots + n}$$

In each succeeding year, the numerator decreases by one, but the denominator remains the same.

16. Under the **declining-balance method**, depreciation is figured by multiplying the existing carrying value of the asset by a fixed percentage. The **double-declining-balance method** is a form of the declining-balance method, and uses a fixed percentage that is twice the straight-line percentage. Under the double-declining-balance method, depreciation for each year is computed as follows:

$$2 \times \frac{100\%}{\text{useful life in years}} \times \frac{\text{existing}}{\text{carrying value}}$$

Under the declining-balance or double-declining-balance method, the asset may not be depreciated below its residual value.

17. When an asset is purchased after the beginning of the year or discarded before the end of the year, depreciation should be recorded for only part of the year. The accountant figures the year's depreciation and multiplies this figure by the fraction of the year that the asset was in use.

18. Often, the estimated useful life or residual value is found to be over- or understated after some depreciation has been taken. The accountant must produce a revised figure for the remaining useful life or remaining depreciable cost. Future depreciation is then calculated by spreading the remaining depreciable cost over the remaining useful life, leaving previous depreciation unchanged.

19. Assets of low unit cost, such as small tools, generally are not depreciated on an individual basis. Instead, they are either charged as expenses or recorded in an inventory account when purchased. In the latter case, an inventory of small tools must be taken at the end of each period to determine the amount consumed in that period.

20. When a company has several plant assets that are similar, it will probably use **group depreciation** rather than individual depreciation. Under group depreciation, the original costs of all similar assets are lumped together in one summary account. Then depreciation is figured for the assets as a whole, using the straight-line or declining-balance method.

21. Under the **accelerated cost recovery system (ACRS)**, each depreciable asset is placed in one of four categories for tax purposes (three, five, ten, and fifteen years), and depreciated according to percentages established by Congress. Automobiles, trucks, and small tools typically fall in the three-year category. Depreciable real estate typically falls in the fifteen-year category.

22. When an asset is still in use after it has been fully depreciated, no more depreciation should be taken, and the asset should not be written off until its disposal. Disposal occurs when the asset is discarded, sold, or traded in.

23. When a business disposes of an asset, depreciation should be recorded for the period preceding disposal. This will bring the asset's Accumulated Depreciation account up to the date of disposal.

24. When a machine, for example, is discarded (thrown out), Accumulated Depreciation, Machinery is debited and Machinery is credited for their present balances. If the machine has not been fully depreciated, then Loss on Disposal of Machinery must be debited for the carrying value to balance the entry.

25. When a machine is sold for cash, Accumulated Depreciation, Machinery is debited, Cash is debited, and Machinery is credited. If the cash received is less than the carrying value of the machine, then Loss on Sale of Machinery would also be debited. On the other hand, if cash received is greater than the carrying value, then Gain on Sale of Machinery would be credited to balance the entry.

26. When an asset is traded in (exchanged) for a similar one, the gain or loss should first be computed, as follows:

    Trade-in allowance
    – Carrying value of asset traded in
    = Gain (loss) on trade-in

    a. For financial reporting purposes, losses should be recognized (recorded) on the exchange of similar assets, but gains should not be. When there is a loss, the asset acquired should be debited for its list price (cash paid plus trade-in allowance). When there is a gain, however, the asset acquired should be debited for the carrying value of the asset traded in plus cash paid (this will result in nonrecognition of the gain).

    b. For income tax purposes, no gain or loss should be recognized on the exchange of similar assets. All assets acquired should be recorded at the carrying value of the asset traded in plus cash paid.

27. Most companies maintain a subsidiary ledger for each type of asset, detailing the purchase, depreciation, and disposal of each particular asset within that asset group. This practice enables the company to exercise adequate control over the assets and to provide tax, insurance, and depreciation information to the accounting department.

28. **Natural resources** are tangible nonmonetary assets in the form of valuable substances that may be extracted and sold. They are sometimes referred to as **wasting assets**, and include standing timber, oil and gas fields, and mineral deposits.

29. **Depletion** refers to the allocation of a natural resource's cost to accounting periods based on the amount extracted in each period. Depletion for each year is figured as follows:

$$\frac{\text{cost} - \text{residual value}}{\text{estimated units to be extracted}}$$

$\times$ actual units extracted during period

Units removed but not sold in that year are recorded as inventory, to be charged as expense in the year sold.

30. Assets that are acquired in conjunction with the natural resource, and that cannot be used after the natural resource is depleted, should be depreciated on the same basis as depletion is figured.

31. In accounting for the exploration and development of oil and gas resources, two methods have been used. Under **successful efforts accounting**, the method now required, the cost of a dry well is written off immediately as a loss. The **full-costing method**, which is no longer acceptable, capitalizes and depletes costs of both successful and dry wells.

32. The SEC has rejected both of the above methods and has proposed **reserve recognition accounting**. This method emphasizes the current value of reserves discovered. It may be a long while, however, before the issue of oil and gas accounting is settled.

Testing Your Knowledge

Matching

Match each term with its definition by writing the appropriate letter in the blank.

_E_ 1. Long-term nonmonetary assets (fixed assets)

_F_ 2. Depreciation

_N_ 3. Obsolescence

_G_ 4. Carrying value (book value)

_L_ 5. Residual value (salvage or disposal value)

_I_ 6. Accelerated method

_A_ 7. Straight-line method

_H_ 8. Production method

_D_ 9. Sum-of-the-years'-digits method

_J_ 10. Double-declining-balance method

_B_ 11. Group depreciation

_O_ 12. Natural resources (wasting assets)

_M_ 13. Depletion

_C_ 14. Amortization

_K_ 15. Successful efforts accounting

a. The depreciation method that charges equal depreciation each year

b. Using one depreciation rate for several similar items

c. The allocation of an intangible asset's cost to the periods benefited by the asset

d. The accelerated depreciation method that involves a changing fraction

e. Assets to be used in the business for more than one year

f. The allocation of the cost of a plant asset to the periods benefited by the asset

g. The unexpired cost of an asset

h. The depreciation method whose cost allocation is based on units, not time

i. The practice of charging the highest depreciation in the first year, and decreasing depreciation each year thereafter.

j. The accelerated depreciation method based on twice the straight-line rate

k. The method required in accounting for oil and gas reserves

l. The estimated value of an asset at the disposal date

m. The allocation of a natural resource's cost to the periods in which it is removed

n. One reason for an asset's limited useful life

o. Assets in the form of valuable substances that may be extracted and sold

Completion

Use the lines provided to complete each item.

1. Briefly distinguish between depreciation expense and accumulated depreciation.

Instate   Depr. Exp. is cost expensed
_____   during a particular period
contra to   Accum depr. is the amt.
asset on   of an asset that has been
bal sh.   depreciated.

2. For each asset category, provide the accounting term for the allocation of its cost to the periods benefited.

Category	Term for Cost Allocation
Intangible assets	amortization
Plant and equipment	depreciation
Natural resources	depletion

3. When a plant asset is sold for cash, under what unique circumstance would no gain or loss be recorded?

if it is sold for exactly the salvage value carrying

4. Plant assets have *limited* useful lives for two reasons. What are they?

become obsolete or deteriorate

5. List four pieces of information necessary to compute the depletion expense of an oil well for a given year.

# of units produced year cost per unit est # units left cost of well & to compute salvage value & cost/unit

True-False

Circle T if the statement is true, F if it is false.

T F 1. Land is not subject to depreciation.

T F 2. As accumulated depreciation increases, carrying value will decrease.

T F 3. Land held for speculative reasons is not classified as property, plant, and equipment.

T **F** 4. Depreciation is a process of valuation, not allocation.

T F 5. Depreciation may be calculated for a machine by having an appraiser determine to what extent the machine has worn out.

T F 6. When land is purchased for use as a plant site, its cost should include the cost of tearing down a building and clearing and draining the land.

T F 7. Each type of depreciable asset should have its own accumulated depreciation account.

T F 8. Estimated useful life in years is irrelevant when applying the production method of depreciation.

T **F** 9. Under the straight-line method, if depreciation expense is $1,000 in the first year, it will be $2,000 in the second year.

T **F** 10. When the estimated useful life of an asset is revised after some depreciation has been taken, the accountant should not go back to previous years to make corrections.

T F 11. The full-costing method capitalizes the cost of both successful and dry wells.

T **F** 12. Under the income tax method, a gain or loss should be recorded when an asset is exchanged for another asset.

T F 13. When a machine is sold for less than its carrying value, one of the debits is to Loss on Sale of Machinery and one of the credits is to Accumulated Depreciation, Machinery.

T F 14. The carrying value of an asset represents its unexpired cost.

T **F** 15. Accelerated depreciation will result in less net income than will straight-line depreciation in the asset's last year of depreciation.

T F **16.** Of the four basic depreciation methods, the straight-line method most resembles the method used to compute depletion.

T **F** 17. Under the double-declining-balance method, the carrying value of an asset will equal zero at the end of its estimated useful life if no residual value has been assumed.

T **F** 18. When a company has several plant assets that fall into one functional group, such as delivery equipment, information detailing the purchase, depreciation, and disposal of each particular asset should be included in the ledger's controlling account.

T F 19. ACRS, the new method for depreciating assets for tax purposes, ignores estimated useful life and residual value.

Multiple-Choice

Circle the letter of the best answer.

1. If a building and land are purchased for a lump-sum payment of $66,000, how much would be allocated to land if the land is appraised at $20,000 and the building at $60,000?
   a. $22,000
   b. $20,000
   c. $16,500
   d. $13,750

2. The expired cost of a plant asset is referred to as its
   a. accumulated depreciation.
   b. carrying value.
   c. depreciable cost.
   d. residual value.

3. A machine that cost $9,000 with a carrying value of $2,000 is sold for $1,700, and an entry is made. Which of the following is true about the entry?
   a. Accumulated Depreciation is debited for $2,000.
   b. Machinery is credited for $2,000.
   c. Loss on Sale of Machinery is credited for $300.
   d. Accumulated Depreciation is debited for $7,000.

4. Which depreciation method, when applied to an asset in its first year of use, will result in the greatest depreciation charge?
   a. Straight-line
   b. Production
   c. Sum-of-the-years'-digits
   d. Impossible to determine without more information

5. When a certain machine was purchased, its estimated useful life was 20 years. However, after it had been depreciated for 5 years, the company decided that it had originally overestimated the machine's useful life by 3 years. What should be done?
   a. Go back and adjust depreciation for the first 5 years.
   b. Depreciate the remainder of the depreciable cost over the next 15 years.
   c. Depreciate the remainder of the depreciable cost over the next 12 years.
   d. Both a and b

6. Which of the following is not a long-term nonmonetary asset?
   a. A copper mine
   b. Inventory
   c. Goodwill
   d. Office equipment

7. Land improvements
   a. should be included in the cost of land.
   b. are subject to depreciation.
   c. should be deducted from the cost of land.
   d. should be charged as expense in the year purchased.

8. Overestimating the number of barrels that can be pumped from an oil well over its lifetime will result in
   a. understating net income each year.
   b. understating depletion cost per unit each year.
   c. overstating depletion expense each year.
   d. understating total assets each year.

Applying Your Knowledge

Exercises

1. A machine that cost $26,000 had an estimated useful life of five years and a residual value of $2,000 when purchased on January 1, 19x0. Fill in the amount of depreciation expense for 19x1, as well as the accumulated depreciation and carrying value of the machine as of December 31, 19x1, under each of the listed methods.

		Depreciation Expense for 19x1	Accumulated Depreciation as of 12/31/x1	Carrying Value as of 12/31/x1
a.	Straight-line	$ _4800_	$ _9600_	$ _16,400_
b.	Sum-of-the-years'-digits	$ _6400_	$ _14,400_	$ _11,600_
c.	Double-declining balance	$ _6240_ _10 400_	$ _16,640_	_9360_

2. A machine that was to produce a certain type of toy was purchased for $35,000 on April 30, 19xx. The machine was expected to produce 100,000 toys during the ten years that the company expected to keep the machine. The company estimated that it could then sell the machine for $5,000. Calculate depreciation expense in 19xx when it produced 7,500 toys.

35000 cost
- 5000 sv
30,000/100,000 = .30
by prod

.30 × 7500 = $ 2250

3. On October 12, 19xx, a machine that cost $25,000 and has a carrying value of $8,000 is traded in, along with $15,500 in cash, for a new machine with a retail price of $23,000. On the next page, prepare the journal entry that would conform to APB *Opinion No. 29*, as well as the entry that would conform to income tax rulings.

23000
-15500
TIA 7500
- 8000
Loss 500

General Journal

Date		Description	Debit	Credit
19xx				
Oct	12	Machinery (new)	23,000	
		Accum Depr. (old)	17,000	
		Loss on trade in	500	
		Machinery (old)		25,000
		Cash		15,500
		APB #29 rules		
Oct	12	Machinery (new)	23,500	
		Accum Depr (old)	17,000	
		Machinery (old)		25,000
		Cash		15,500
		Income Tax rules		

4. In 19xx the Porter Coal Company purchased a coal mine for $800,000. It is estimated that 2 million tons of coal can be extracted from the mine. In the space provided, prepare Porter's adjusting entry for December 31, 19xx, to reflect the extraction of 100,000 tons during the year and the sale of three-fourths of the coal mined.

General Journal

Date		Description	Debit	Credit
19xx 12	31	Depletion Expense	30,000	
		Coal Inv.	10,000	10,000
		Accum Depletion		40,000
	31	C/o Deplet'n of Coalmine 19xx		

$800,000/2,000,000 = .40 × 100,000 =$

What's Clogging the CPA's 'Supreme Court'

In a four-story building in a Connecticut industrial park, some 50 accounting experts often put in 70-hour weeks—largely trying to plug an infinite variety of loopholes in corporate financial reports. By the end of 1983, these thinkers for the Financial Accounting Standards Board in Stamford will have expanded by 10% its existing body of rules that binds the nation's public and private companies.

But as the FASB ends a roller-coaster decade of existence at the end of this month, the federally blessed "supreme court" of accounting has come under mounting criticism—from accounting professionals as well as corporate executives—for letting itself become mired in narrow, single-industry problems. "Even if you had a thousand standards, brilliant minds could find ways to circumvent them," says Stanley J. Scott, a retired Arthur Young & Co. partner who recently studied the "standards overload" issue for the American Institute of Certified Public Accountants (AICPA).

Instead of this costly but largely ineffective attack on accounting abuses, critics contend, the board should first complete its long-delayed "conceptual framework" project, which promises to rework accounting theory to cope with today's economic conditions. For example, the board has yet to decide whether real estate purchased in 1970 should be carried on the balance sheet for what it cost then or whether it should be inflated to today's value. Also on the docket is the controversial question of how to record pension liabilities.

Bogged Down?

Financial executives fret that new theory will render the current standard-setting activity obsolete. "The FASB is issuing all these standards and interpretations," worries John F. Chironna, director of accounting practices for International Business Machines Corp., "but the board has said they'll all have to be reexamined after completion of the conceptual framework."

Critics say the FASB's latest proposed standard is a good example of how the board is getting bogged down with "cookbook" regulations. Entitled "Reporting a Change in Accounting for Railroad Track Structures—an Amendment of APB Opinion No. 20," the proposal tells railroads how to switch to a new depreciation method mandated by the Interstate Commerce Commission. Instead of railroads absorbing the cumulative effect on profits in the current year, the FASB would have them restate their accounts for prior years. Unfortunately, that instruction collides with an opinion of the FASB's predecessor—the Accounting Principles Board—that says restating old accounts to reflect any kind of accounting change is to be avoided unless the situation fits one of four exceptions. The proposal would create a fifth exception for APB 20, which was written more than a decade ago. Although critics would have FASB give up such patchwork actions in favor of a sweeping rewrite of the basic rules, ignoring the nitty-gritty could create a vacuum.

"It's tough for executives and the accounting

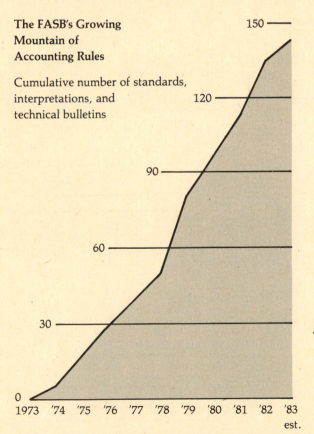

The FASB's Growing Mountain of Accounting Rules

Cumulative number of standards, interpretations, and technical bulletins

150
120
90
60
30
0

1973 '74 '75 '76 '77 '78 '79 '80 '81 '82 '83 est.

Data: Financial Accounting Standards Board

profession to keep up with all these new standards, no question about it," concedes Edmund Coulson, deputy chief accountant at the Securities & Exchange Commission. But he warns, "To stop addressing issues in so-called narrow areas would just force us to step in." The commission has the power to set accounting rules but has always allowed the accounting profession to do the job. For some 40 years, the responsibility rested with the AICPA, but by the end of the go-go 1960s companies were increasingly exaggerating their profits, and critics charged that the institute was too dominated by the accounting establishment to address the problem effectively.

Years of Tumult

So in 1973, the FASB—representing CPAs and industry—began its perilous decade of congressional challenges, uproars over the way floating exchange rates affected profits, and today's growing discontent with the volume and narrowness of new rules.

The board recently incurred scathing criticism from a formidable source after issuing FAS 72, "Accounting for Certain Acquisitions of Banking or Thrift Institutions," which removes paper profits from the acquirer's books by speeding up the write-off of goodwill (BW—Apr. 18). "Numerous other industries are suffering from the same economic conditions as thrifts," wrote Price Waterhouse & Co. in a message to clients. "Was it worth creating yet another exception in a system already riddled with them? We think this is the wrong way to set standards."

But according to Donald J. Kirk, chairman of the FASB, this was an example of a previously issued "broad" principle that did not work. "There already was in existence a standard that said goodwill shall not be amortized over a period longer than 40 years," says Kirk. "There was plenty of room for judgment here. Yet the financial institutions used exactly 40 years as the write-off period, maximizing income. How can you possibly justify 40 years when you have one troubled S&L buying another?"

Despite the critics, it appears that the FASB will stick with the current approach. "Where there is wide latitude," Kirk says, "the most liberal accounting prevails."

Chapter Fourteen

Revenue and Expense Issues and Inflation Accounting

Reviewing the Chapter

1. Applying the matching rule involves (a) recognizing the revenues earned in the period, and (b) allocating the expired costs to the period.

2. The two bases commonly used to determine when revenues should be recognized are (a) point-of-sale basis and (b) cash basis.
   a. Under the **point of sale basis**, revenues are recognized when title to the goods sold passes to the buyer, or when services are rendered completely.
   b. Under the **cash basis**, revenues are recognized when cash is received, regardless of when the sale is made.

3. **Capital expenditures** are **expenditures** (payments or incurrence of liabilities) for plant and equipment, **additions** (such as a building wing), **betterments** (such as the installation of an air-conditioning system), and intangible assets. A capital expenditure is recorded as an asset because it will benefit several accounting periods. **Revenue expenditures** are expenditures for repairs, maintenance, fuel, and anything else necessary to maintain and operate the plant and equipment. A revenue expenditure is charged as expense in the period incurred, under the theory that it benefits only the current accounting period. To make accounting simpler, however, many companies set a dollar amount and treat any expenditure greater than that amount as a capital expenditure and any below that amount as a revenue expenditure.

4. **Ordinary repairs** are expenditures necessary to maintain an asset in good operating condition, and are charged as expense in the period incurred. **Extraordinary repairs** are expenditures (as for a major overhaul) that either increase the asset's residual value or lengthen its useful life. They are recorded by debiting Accumulated Depreciation and crediting Cash.

5. Intangible assets are long-term nonmonetary assets that have no physical substance. They represent certain rights and advantages to their owner. Examples of intangible assets are patents, copyrights, trademarks, goodwill, leaseholds, leasehold improvements, franchises, licenses, brand names, formulas, and processes. An intangible asset should be written off over its useful life (not to exceed 40 years) through amortization.

6. Research and development involves developing new products, testing existing ones, and doing pure research. The costs associated with these activities should normally be charged to expense in the period incurred.

7. **Goodwill**, as the term is used in accounting, refers to the ability of a company to earn more than is normal for its particular industry. Goodwill should be recorded only when a company is purchased; it equals the excess of the purchase cost over the fair market value of the net assets. There are several methods available to place a cost value on goodwill when a business is purchased. It often is (a) arbitrarily set by the buyer and seller, (b) arbitrarily valued at some multiple of the expected above-average earnings, or (c) determined by capitalizing above-average earnings at the industry's average rate of return. Once it is recorded, goodwill should be amortized over its estimated useful life, not to exceed 40 years.

8. Net income is affected greatly by the accounting estimates and procedures chosen when applying the matching principle. These choices must be made when dealing with uncollectible accounts, inventory, depreciation, depletion, and amortization.

9. One of the most difficult challenges in accounting is dealing effectively with changes in the **purchasing power** of the dollar. Changes in **specific price levels** relate to a specific item or service. Changes in **general price levels** relate to a group of goods and services. **Inflation** refers to an increase in the general price level, while **deflation** refers to a decrease in the general price level.

10. A **price index** shows changes (between periods) in the relative price of the same group of goods and services. The percentage change in the index from one year to the next is as follows:

$$\frac{\text{change in index}}{\text{previous year's index}}$$

The Consumer Price Index for All Urban Consumers (CPI-U) is the index used in adjusting financial statements for changes in the general price level.

11. The two methods of accounting for changing prices are constant dollar accounting and current value accounting.

12. **Constant dollar accounting** involves restating historical cost statements for changes in the general price level. That is, all amounts are stated in dollars that have the same general purchasing power.
   a. Changes in the general price level affect monetary and nonmonetary items differently. Monetary items (cash, receivables, and liabilities) are stated in terms of current dollars at all times. Since these items are fixed in dollar amount regardless of inflation or deflation, **purchasing power gains and losses** will occur. On the other hand, nonmonetary items (inventory, investments, plant assets, intangibles, owners' equity, revenues, and expenses) are sensitive to changes in the general price level and therefore do not create purchasing power gains and losses.
   b. To restate an amount in terms of current dollars, use this formula:

$$\text{recorded amount} \times \frac{\text{current price level}}{\begin{array}{c}\text{price level when}\\\text{item originated}\end{array}}$$

Nonmonetary items on the balance sheet are adjusted for changes in the price level since the item's origin, except for retained earnings, which is computed as a balancing figure.

13. **Current value accounting** moves away from historical cost accounting and involves disclosure of current value information. Current value may be measured in terms of **net realizable value** (the amount a company could sell its assets for) or **replacement cost** (the cost of buying equivalent, new assets).

14. The FASB requires that certain large publicly held companies disclose supplemental information (for the current year and the most recent five years) on both a constant dollar and current value basis. The current value used is the lower of net realizable value or replacement cost at the balance sheet date.

Testing Your Knowledge

Matching

Match each term with its definition by writing the appropriate letter in the blank.

F 1. Capital expenditure

I 2. Revenue expenditure

L 3. Goodwill

B 4. Patent

N 5. Copyright

D 6. Leasehold

E 7. Leasehold improvements

J 8. Trademark

H 9. Constant dollar accounting

A 10. Current value accounting

G 11. Purchasing power gains and losses

K 12. Price index

C 13. Net realizable value

M 14. Replacement cost

a. According to the FASB, disclosure of the lower of net realizable value or replacement cost

b. The exclusive right to sell a particular product or use a specific process for 17 years

c. The amount a company could sell its assets for

d. Payment for the right to rent property

e. Additions to property being rented

f. An item recorded as an asset because it will benefit future periods

g. The result of holding monetary items during periods of changing prices

h. Restatement of historical cost statements for changes in the general price level

i. An item charged as an expense in the period incurred

j. An identifying symbol or name for a product or service that may only be used by its owner

k. A published measurement of the change in the purchasing power of the dollar from one time period to another

l. The excess of the price paid for the net assets of a company over their fair market value

m. The cost of buying equivalent, new assets

n. The exclusive right to publish literary, musical, or artistic materials, or computer programs for the author's life plus 50 years

Completion

Use the lines provided to complete each item.

1. Distinguish between capital and revenue expenditures.

C - for plant & equip + improvements that will benefit future periods, amortized
R - minor improvements + repairs that will not affect future value charged to expense

2. List three examples of monetary items.

Cash
N/P (all payables)
A/R (all receivables)

True-False

Circle T if the statement is true, F if it is false.

T (F) 1. A copyright is a name or symbol that may be used only by its owner.

(T) F 2. Goodwill should not be recorded unless it has been purchased.

T (F) 3. Accounts payable is an example of a nonmonetary item.

(T) F 4. During a period of rising prices, holding more in monetary liabilities than in monetary assets will result in a purchasing power gain.

T (F) 5. Research and development costs should be capitalized when they can be associated with a specific new product.

(T) F 6. The cash basis of revenue recognition normally violates the matching rule.

(T) F 7. If ordinary maintenance were erroneously capitalized instead of being charged as expense, then net income for the period would be overstated.

T (F) 8. A betterment is an example of a revenue expenditure.

T (F) 9. Recording an extraordinary repair will leave the carrying value of the asset unchanged.

(T) F 10. The two principal types of price changes are current value accounting and constant dollar accounting.

(T) F 11. Constant dollar accounting adjusts historical costs for changes in the general price level.

(T) F 12. Current value accounting represents a departure from historical cost accounting.

T F 13. Companies that must disclose supplemental information on changing prices must choose between constant dollar disclosure and current value disclosure.

Multiple-Choice

Circle the letter of the best answer.

1. If land was purchased for $24,000 when the general price index was 120, what amount should be used in restating the cost of the land (under constant dollar accounting) when the index is 150?
   a. $24,000
   b. $28,000
   c. $30,000
   d. $36,000

2. Which of the following is not a revenue expenditure?
   a. Ordinary maintenance of a machine
   b. Replacing the old roof with a new one
   c. The installation of new light bulbs
   d. A tire repair on the company truck

3. Which of the following should be charged as expense in the period of expenditure?
   a. Goodwill
   b. Leaseholds
   c. Leasehold improvements
   d. Research and development costs

4. Charging a depreciable item as expense when it should have been capitalized will result in
   a. overstated total assets.
   b. understated net income for the succeeding period.
   c. overstated depreciation expense for the succeeding period.
   d. understated net income for the period.

5. A long-term note for $33,000 was issued by Harris Corporation when the price index was 110. What amount should be used in restating the note payable (under constant dollar accounting) when the index is 120?
   a. $33,000
   b. $36,000
   c. $36,300
   d. $39,600

6. During inflationary periods, a purchasing power loss arises when
   a. monetary assets exceed monetary liabilities.
   b. monetary liabilities exceed monetary assets.
   c. nonmonetary assets exceed nonmonetary liabilities.
   d. nonmonetary liabilities exceed nonmonetary assets.

Applying Your Knowledge

Exercises

1. Net income figures for Superior Company are as follows: 19x1: $20,000; 19x2: $30,000; 19x3: $25,000. Net assets are $200,000, and the normal rate of return is 8 percent. Calculate goodwill if average superior earnings for 19x1–19x3 are to be capitalized at 8 percent.

   19x1 – 4000
   19x2   18,000
   19x3   9,000
   ─────────────
   27,000 ÷ 3 = 9000 ÷ 8% =

   112,500

2. Classify each of the following expenditures as a capital or revenue expenditure by placing a C or an R next to each item.

   _C_ a. Replacement of the roof on a building
   _R_ b. Replacement of the battery in a company vehicle
   _R_ c. The cost of painting the executive offices
   _C_ d. Installation of aluminum siding on a building
   _C_ e. Replacement of the motor in a machine
   _R_ f. The cost to repair an air-conditioning unit
   _C_ g. The cost to install a piece of machinery
   _C_ h. Addition of a building wing
   _R_ i. Tune-up of a company vehicle

3. The net monetary assets of Balboa Company were $240,000 on January 1, 19xx, and $429,000 on December 31, 19xx. For the year, cash receipts totaled $504,000 and cash payments totaled $315,000. Its collections and payments occurred evenly throughout the year. General price index information is as follows:

January 1, 19xx	120
December 31, 19xx	130
Average during the year	126

   a. Was there a purchasing power gain or loss? _loss_
   b. The gain or loss was in the amount of $ _26,000_.

   ```
    240,000      130/120      260,000
   + 504,000      130/126     + 520,000
   - 315,000      130/126     - 325,000
   ─────────                  ─────────
    429,000                    455,000

    429,000                    429,000
                             ─────────────
                              ( 26,600 )
   ```

Crossword Puzzle
For Chapters 13 and 14

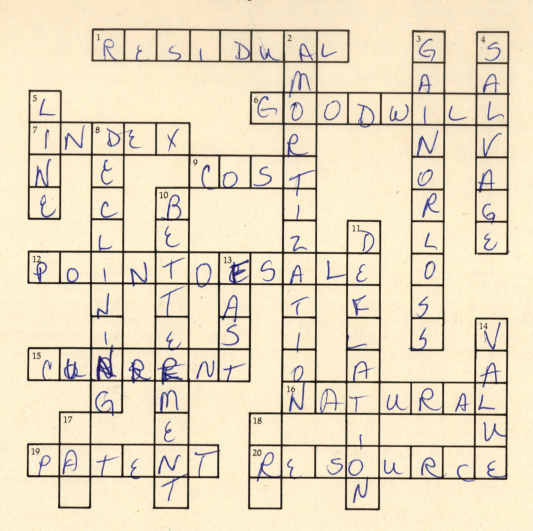

ACROSS

1. Estimated proceeds upon disposal
6. Intangible arising from purchase of business
7. The CPI-U is one
9. Depreciable _____
12. Basis of revenue recognition (3 words)
15. With 3-Down, measure of a dollar's purchasing power
16. With 20-Across, a wasting asset
19. Intangible with a 17-year legal life
20. See 16-Across

DOWN

2. Allocation of an intangible's cost
3. See 15-Across (2 words)
4. Estimated proceeds upon disposal
5. Straight- _____ method
8. _____ -balance method
10. A capital expenditure
11. Increase in a dollar's purchasing power
13. _____ -costing method of depletion
14. Carrying _____
17. Branch of accounting that requires ACRS
18. Oil and gas accounting method (abbreviation)

Inflation Scoreboard: How 400 Companies Really Performed in 1981

If the glowing corporate press releases and glossy annual reports are taken at face value, most of the nation's largest industrial companies fared very well during 1981 despite the drag of recession and high interest rates. Average sales were up 10%, and the typical company managed to turn a slightly larger profit than it had the year before.

But a closer look at other financial figures, often buried in minuscule type amid a myriad of confusing footnotes, reveals a far less rosy picture: When the numbers are adjusted for inflation, overall sales were flat for the year, while reported earnings were only half as large as they first appeared to be. Even if the unrealized paper gains from having more debt than monetary assets are added in—under the theory that because of inflation those debts will be repaid with cheaper dollars—the profits that appear in corporate financial reports still are overstated by one-third. And inflation's impact on sales and profits was proportionately as severe as it was the year before, even though the consumer price index's climb slowed from an average 12.4% in 1980 to 8.9% in 1981.

Those are the major conclusions of *Business Week's* second annual Inflation Scoreboard, which tracks both the reported and inflation-adjusted sales and earnings for 400 of the largest industrial corporations in 35 key industries. The data were gleaned from the latest corporate annual reports for fiscal 1981—some still hot off the press—and quickly entered in *Business Week's* computer for analysis. The Inflation Scoreboard gives executives, investors, and analysts the first comprehensive look at "real" corporate profits for the year just ended—data that are not yet available from any single source.

Apples and Oranges

In this year's survey, companies in five industries that are part of *Business Week's* regular quarterly scoreboards are not included. Those industries—banking, savings and loan, utilities, and nonbank financial, which covers insurance and brokerage companies—have their own unique problems in accounting for the effect of inflation. That is because they deal in money

Source: Reprinted from the May 3, 1982 issue of *Business Week* by special permission, © 1982 by McGraw-Hill, Inc., New York, NY 10020. All rights reserved.

itself rather than in goods and nonfinancial services or because, in the case of utilities, revenues and costs are affected by the regulatory process. Adjusted profit numbers for such industries cannot easily be compared with those of industrial industries.

This is the second year that all major companies have had to include inflation-related figures in their annual reports to shareholders. Under mandate from the Financial Accounting Standards Board (FASB), corporations now must show sales, dividends, and market price per share for the past five years, expressed in 1981 dollars, by applying the consumer price index.

Sales are easily adjusted for inflation. For most companies, revenue from the sale of products and services comes in fairly evenly throughout the year. Thus, reported sales for 1981 are already expressed in something akin to average 1981 dollars of purchasing power, even in the traditional historical-cost financial statements. And sales for prior years can be translated into 1981 dollars simply by applying an appropriate index. Similar conversions for inflation can be made for dividends and market price per share to enable shareholders to gauge how well their investment has kept pace with inflation. In the current Inflation Scoreboard, historical-cost sales for the average large company have grown at an annual rate of 15% for the past five years, while growth adjusted for inflation comes to only 4%. Dividend growth shows an almost identical pattern.

The Real Controversy

At present, the FASB requires companies to use the consumer price index because it is issued on a monthly basis and because it is very rarely revised. Many executives feel that another index, such as the gross national product deflator, might be more appropriate for translating business revenues, but that index appears only quarterly and frequently is restated.

Profits, however, are not so easily adjusted for the effect of changing prices; therein lies the real controversy over inflation accounting. It also explains why it has been so long in coming. One rather simplistic way is to apply the CPI to reported earnings, just as is done for sales and dividends. Under such a computation, the companies in the Inflation Scoreboard showed an average annual growth rate of only 1%

during the past five years, compared with a growth in reported profits of 12% yearly. But that calculation does not even come close to measuring inflation's real and often hidden impact on corporate earnings.

The problem comes when accountants try to measure costs. One key goal in good financial reporting is to match the revenues that a company takes in during the year with the costs of making its products and services. Such costs include labor, materials, and depreciation—the arbitrary proportional annual charge for "using up" plant and equipment. But unlike sales, most of these costs are not in 1981 dollars. The raw materials that are to be matched with the current year's sales may have been bought in prior years when prices were considerably lower. And the annual depre-

ciation charge may be based on the cost of plant and equipment dating back 20 years or more.

Two distinct systems—known as the constant-dollar and current-cost methods—have been used to perform the matching task and to come up with a definitive inflation-adjusted profit figure. Both tend to provide the same result when applied broadly across multi-industry lines, but depending on which scheme is chosen, the results can vary widely from industry to industry. Predictably, since most executives are anxious to interpret profits in the most favorable light, each method has its share of vigorous supporters and vociferous critics. And more than a few corporate managers oppose any adjustment for inflation. Since it still considers its inflation-accounting directive

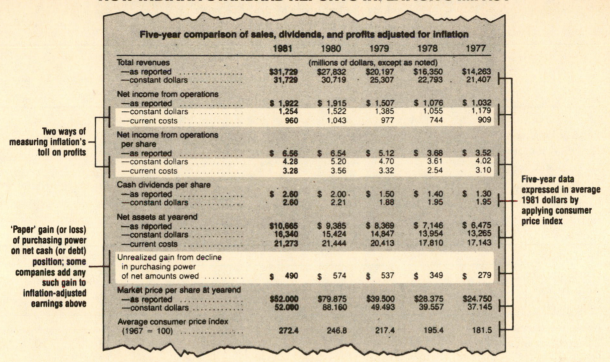

Five-year comparison of sales, dividends, and profits adjusted for inflation

	1981	1980	1979	1978	1977
	(millions of dollars, except as noted)				
Total revenues					
—as reported	$31,729	$27,832	$20,197	$16,350	$14,263
—constant dollars	31,729	30,719	25,307	22,793	21,407
Net income from operations					
—as reported	$ 1,922	$ 1,915	$ 1,507	$ 1,076	$ 1,032
—constant dollars	1,254	1,522	1,385	1,055	1,179
—current costs	960	1,043	977	744	909
Net income from operations per share					
—as reported	$ 6.56	$ 6.54	$ 5.12	$ 3.68	$ 3.52
—constant dollars	4.28	5.20	4.70	3.61	4.02
—current costs	3.28	3.56	3.32	2.54	3.10
Cash dividends per share					
—as reported	$ 2.60	$ 2.00	$ 1.50	$ 1.40	$ 1.30
—constant dollars	2.60	2.21	1.88	1.95	1.95
Net assets at yearend					
—as reported	$10,665	$ 9,385	$ 8,369	$ 7,146	$ 6,475
—constant dollars	16,340	15,424	14,847	13,954	13,265
—current costs	21,273	21,444	20,413	17,810	17,143
Unrealized gain from decline in purchasing power of net amounts owed	$ 490	$ 574	$ 537	$ 349	$ 279
Market price per share at yearend					
—as reported	$52.000	$79.875	$39.500	$28.375	$24.750
—constant dollars	52.000	88.160	49.493	39.557	37.145
Average consumer price index (1967 = 100)	272.4	246.8	217.4	195.4	181.5

Two ways of measuring inflation's toll on profits

'Paper' gain (or loss) of purchasing power on net cash (or debt) position; some companies add any such gain to inflation-adjusted earnings above

Five-year data expressed in average 1981 dollars by applying consumer price index

experimental and because the issue still is so controversial, the FASB requires companies to show two adjusted profit numbers, one calculation for each method used.

Using the constant-dollar plan, a company's cost of goods sold is translated into average dollars for the current period, in this case 1981 dollars, using the CPI. Similarly, the cost of its plant and equipment also is expressed in 1981 dollars and a new annual depreciation figure computed. Once these costs are adjusted, they are subtracted, with such unadjusted costs as labor, overhead, and taxes, from sales. The result: constant-dollar profits—profits adjusted for general inflation.

But changes in costs for individual companies may show a pattern completely different from that of the CPI. For industries with heavy investments in natural resources, the cost of comparable new assets has risen far faster over the years than general inflation. Conversely, for many high-technology companies, new processes and economies of scale often make the present cost of production far lower than in the developmental stages.

So some companies prefer the other inflation-accounting scheme: the current-cost method. Depreciation and raw material costs first are adjusted for what it would cost to replace their own plant and inventory at today's prices. When other costs are subtracted from sales, the resulting profit figure shows earnings adjusted for changes in each com-

pany's specific costs. Some theorists see the current-cost profit figures as a measure of "distributable income"—what a company could afford to pay out in dividends while maintaining the same level of productive capacity.

The Debt Side

For 1981, average profits under the constant-dollar method come to just 46% of historical-cost profits, compared with 48% in 1980. Current-cost profits for the year just ended are 44% of reported profits, a slight improvement from the 43% recorded in the Inflation Scoreboard a year ago.

Some executives who are disgruntled with both inflation-adjustment methods complain that each concentrates only on assets and fails to take account of the equally significant impact of inflation on the debt side. They argue that if a company has more debt than it has monetary assets, such as cash and marketable securities, it gains purchasing power during inflation because it will be able to pay off its liabilities in cheaper dollars.

The FASB does require a separate calculation of such annual purchasing power gains or losses, and a few companies—all of which reported gains—have chosen to add those "paper" profits to both constant-dollar and current-cost profit figures in their annual reports. The risk, of course, is that any such gain will be realized only in the future, if at all, and the com-

Ranking the Industries by Profit Growth
Average Compound Growth Rate 1977–1981

| | Percent | | | | | |
| Industry | Growth in Profits | | Growth in Sales | | Growth in Dividends | |
	Reported	Indexed*	Reported	Indexed*	Reported	Indexed*
Steel	54%	35%	9%	− 2%	2%	− 6%
Food & lodging	30	16	20	8	31	17
Natural resources (fuel)	28	15	24	11	25	11
Oil service & supply	28	14	25	12	13	13
Metals & mining	26	15	13	2	24	11
Service industries	24	12	25	12	20	7
Instruments	22	10	24	11	26	13
Railroads	21	9	18	6	12	1
Tobacco	20	7	17	5	20	8
Conglomerates	19	7	15	3	16	4
Aerospace	16	5	19	7	17	6
General machinery	14	3	15	4	16	4
Food processing	13	2	12	1	11	0
Leisure time industries	13	2	15	3	23	10
Beverages	12	1	16	4	12	1
Chemicals	12	1	16	4	10	− 1
Drugs	12	1	14	3	12	1
Misc. manufacturing	12	1	14	2	10	− 1
Publishing, TV	12	1	15	4	16	5
All-industry average	*12%*	*1%*	*15%*	*4%*	*14%*	*4%*
Electrical	11	0	14	3	14	3
Personal care products	10	− 1	13	2	11	0
Real estate	10	2	28	16	34	20
Office equipment	9	− 2	15	3	9	− 2
Retailing (food)	8	− 2	11	0	16	4
Textiles & apparel	7	− 3	12	1	12	1
Containers	5	− 5	10	− 1	8	− 3
Trucking	5	− 6	9	− 1	17	5
Paper	3	− 6	9	− 1	12	1
Special machinery	3	− 7	12	1	12	1
Appliances	1	−10	8	− 3	− 3	−13
Tire & rubber	1	−12	4	− 6	− 2	− 9
Retailing (nonfood)	− 1	−11	8	− 2	24	10
Building materials	− 2	−11	10	0	13	1
Airlines	Loss	Loss	16	5	−14	−20
Automotive	Loss	Loss	1	− 9	NM	NM

NM = not meaningful
*Consumer price index

pany still has to generate cash from its ongoing operations to pay off its debt. Including monetary gains as part of earnings also can make a dangerously leveraged company appear to be performing handsomely.

Since profit figures for years past are somewhat difficult to recalculate on an inflation-adjusted basis, the FASB did not make companies restate reported profits for years prior to adoption of the rule. As a result, the majority of companies in the survey have only two or three years of inflation-adjusted profit data, and it will be several years before meaningful trends can be calculated.

Chapter Fifteen

Accounting for Partnerships

Reviewing the Chapter

1. According to the Uniform Partnership Act, a **partnership** is "an association of two or more persons to carry on, as co-owners, a business for profit." It's chief characteristics are as follows:
   a. Voluntary association: Partners choose each other when they form their business.
   b. **Partnership agreement**: Partners may have either an oral or a written agreement.
   c. **Limited Life**: Certain events may dissolve the partnership.
   d. **Mutual agency**: Each partner may bind the partnership to outside contracts.
   e. **Unlimited liability**: Each partner is personally liable for all debts of the partnership.
   f. Co-ownership of partnership property: Business property is jointly owned by all partners.
   g. Participation in partnership income: Each partner shares income and losses of the business.

2. A partnership has several advantages. It is easy to form and dissolve. It is able to pool capital resources and individual talents. It avoids the corporation's tax burden. It gives freedom and flexibility to its partners' actions.

3. The disadvantages of a partnership are limited life, mutual agency, unlimited liability, capital limitation, and difficulty of transferring ownership interest.

4. The owners' equity section of a partnership's balance sheet is called **Partners' Equity**, and a separate capital and withdrawals account must be maintained for each partner. When a partner makes an investment, the assets contributed are debited at their fair market value, and the partner's capital account is credited.

5. The method of distributing partnership income and losses should be specified in the partnership agreement. The most common methods base distribution on (a) a stated ratio only, (b) a capital investment ratio only, and (c) a combination of fixed salaries, interest on each partner's capital, and the stated ratio. Net income is distributed to partners' equity by debiting Income Summary and crediting each partner's capital account; the reverse is done for a net loss.

6. When income and losses are based on a stated ratio only, partnership income or loss for the period is multiplied by each partner's ratio (stated as a fraction or percentage) to arrive at each partner's share.

7. When income and losses are based on a capital investment ratio only, partnership income or loss for the period is multiplied by each partner's proportion of (a) total capital invested at the beginning of the period or (b) average capital during the period.

8. When income and losses are based on salaries, interest, and a stated ratio, a certain procedure must be followed. First, salaries and interest must be allocated to the partners regardless of the net income figure for the period. Then, any net income left over after the salary and interest must also be allocated to the partners, in the stated ratio. On the other hand, if the salary and interest is greater than net income, then this excess must be deducted from each partner's allocation, in the stated ratio.

9. When a partnership is legally dissolved, it loses the authority to continue business as a going concern. **Dissolution** of a partnership occurs upon the (a) withdrawal of a partner, (b) bankruptcy of a partner, (c) incapacity of a partner, (d) death of a partner, (e) admission of a new partner, (f) retirement of a partner, or (g) expiration of the partnership agreement.

10. A new partner may be admitted into a partnership by either (a) purchasing an interest in the partnership from one or more of the original partners or (b) investing assets into the partnership.
    a. When a new partner purchases an interest from another partner, the selling partner's capital account is debited and the buying partner's account credited for the interest in the business sold. The purchase price is ignored in making this entry.
    b. When a new partner invests his or her own assets in the partnership, the contributed assets are debited and the new partner's capital account is credited. The amount of the debit and credit may or may not equal the value of the assets. It depends on the value of the business and the method applied.

When the partners feel that the business is worth more than its net assets indicate, they will probably ask the entering partner to pay them a **bonus**. Under the opposite set of circumstances, a partnership may give the new partner a greater interest in the business than the value of the assets contributed.

11. A partner may withdraw from a partnership in one of two ways. (a) The partner may take assets from the partnership that are greater than, less than, or equal to his or her capital investment. (b) The partner may sell his or her interest to new or existing partners.

12. **Liquidation** of a partnership is the process of (a) selling partnership assets, (b) paying off partnership liabilities, and (c) distributing the remaining assets to the partners. The liquidation transactions are summarized in a statement of liquidation.
    a. The sale of partnership assets is recorded by debiting Cash, crediting the assets, and debiting or crediting Gain or Loss from Realization for the difference. The gain or loss must then be distributed to the partners in their stated ratio. If a partner's account shows a deficit after the distribution of a loss, then he or she must pay personal assets to the business to cover the deficit. If the partner cannot pay, the remaining partners must absorb the deficit, in their stated ratio.
    b. The payment of liabilities is recorded by debiting the liabilities and crediting Cash.
    c. The distribution of cash to the partners is recorded by crediting Cash and debiting the partners' capital accounts for their remaining balances (not in their stated ratio).

Matching

Match each word with its definition by writing the appropriate letter in the blank.

_E_ 1. Partnership

_K_ 2. Voluntary association

_J_ 3. Partnership agreement

_B_ 4. Limited life

_C_ 5. Mutual agency

_H_ 6. Unlimited liability

_F_ 7. Stated ratio

_I_ 8. Dissolution

_a_ 9. Liquidation

_L_ 10. Bonus method

_D_ 11. Partners' equity

_G_ 12. Statement of liquidation

a. The sale of partnership assets, and payment to creditors and owners

b. The fact that any change in partners will cause the business to dissolve

c. The power of each partner to enter into contracts that are within the normal scope of the business

d. The balance sheet section that lists the partners' capital accounts

e. An association of two or more persons to carry on, as co-owners, a business for profit

f. A formula that may be used to compute the allocation of net income or loss to the partners

g. A summary of liquidation transactions

h. The claim to the partners' personal assets by creditors if the partnership cannot pay its debts

i. The end of a partnership as a going concern

j. The specifics of how the partnership is to operate

k. The partners' consent to join one another in forming a partnership

l. The crediting of the new partner's capital account for more or less than the value of the assets contributed.

Completion

Use the lines provided to complete each item.

1. List seven events that dissolve a partnership.

Partner Withdraws

New Partner added

Death of partner

Bankruptcy of partner

Incapacity of partner

Retirement of partner

Expiration of agreement

2. List the three steps involved in partnership liquidation.

Sell assets

Pay off creditors

Divide profits or Losses

3. List four advantages of the partnership form of business.

Easy to form + dissolve
Pool capital + indiv. ressources
Avoids corp. tax burden
Freedom + flexibility to
_ partners' actions_

4. List five disadvantages of the partnership form of business.

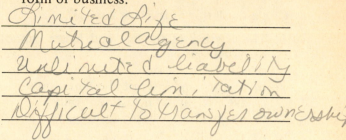

Limited Life
Mutual agency
Unlimited liability
Capital limitation
Difficult to transfer ownership

True-False

Circle T if the statement is true, F if it is false.

T **F** 1. A partnership agreement is not legal unless it is in writing.

T F 2. One way in which a partnership may be dissolved is by the admission of a new partner.

T F 3. If a partner in the restaurant business signs a contract to purchase a tractor for the partnership, without the partners' knowledge, the contract would probably not be binding on the partnership.

T **F** 4. When partners A and B share income in a 3:2 ratio but no stipulation has been made for sharing losses, losses should be shared equally.

T **F** 5. When the salary and interest allocations for the partners exceed net income for the period, it is actually a net loss that has occurred.

T F 6. When a partner invests property in the partnership, the property ceases to belong to the partner.

T F 7. It is possible for a partnership to incur a net loss for the period and actually increase one or more of the owners' accounts at the time that the loss is allocated.

T **F** 8. If partner C sells his $20,000 interest in the partnership to D for $25,000, then D's capital account is credited for $25,000.

T **F** 9. When an entering partner must pay a bonus for a certain interest in a partnership, the original partners' capital accounts are unchanged.

T F 10. When the original partners allow the entering partner a bonus for a certain interest in the partnership, the original partners' capital accounts are unchanged.

T F 11. If a partner withdraws from a partnership for less than his or her capital investment, the remaining partners receive the remainder in their stated ratio.

T **F** 12. The last step in a liquidation is to pay the partners in the stated ratio.

T F 13. When the partners are paid at the conclusion of a liquidation, their capital accounts are debited.

T **F** 14. Upon liquidation, when a partner cannot eliminate a deficit in his or her account by contributing personal assets, then the remaining partners must contribute their personal assets.

Circle the letter of the best answer.

1. The sharing of income and losses cannot be based upon
   a. a stated ratio only.
   b. a salary and interest allowance only.
   c. average capital investment only.
   d. a salary and a stated ratio only.

2. Partners A and B receive a salary allowance of $8,000 and $2,000, respectively, and share the remainder equally. If the company earned $5,000 during the period, what is the effect on A's capital account?
   a. A $4,000 increase
   b. A $5,000 increase
   c. A $5,500 increase
   d. A $2,500 decrease

3. A partnership has $60,000 in equity. If L contributes $45,000 for a one-third interest, for how much should L's account be credited under the bonus method?
   a. $15,000
   b. $20,000
   c. $35,000
   d. $45,000

4. Partners M and N have capital balances of $20,000 and $30,000, respectively, and share income and losses in a 3:2 ratio. If P contributes $10,000 for a one-fourth interest under the bonus method, what will be the new balance in M's account?
   a. $17,000
   b. $17,500
   c. $18,000
   d. $20,000

5. Partners R, S, and T share income and losses equally and have capital balances of $10,000, $20,000 and $30,000, respectively. Because S wishes to withdraw from the partnership, the assets are revalued and are found to be undervalued by $6,000. How much should S be allowed to take upon withdrawal from the partnership?
   a. $18,000
   b. $20,000
   c. $22,000
   d. $26,000

6. Partners W, X, and Y have beginning capital balances of $5,000, $8,000, and $7,000, respectively. If income and losses are allocated on the basis of beginning investments, how much of 19xx's net income of $60,000 should be allocated to Y?
   a. $7,000
   b. $20,000
   c. $21,000
   d. $27,000

7. Gains and losses from assets sold upon liquidation of a partnership are
   a. ignored in the statement of liquidation.
   b. divided equally among the partners.
   c. divided among the partners in proportion to their existing capital balances.
   d. divided among the partners in their stated ratio.

Applying Your Knowledge

Exercises

1. Partners A, B, and C each receive a $10,000 salary, as well as 5 percent interest on their respective investments of $60,000, $40,000, and $50,000. If they share income and losses in a 3:2:1 ratio, how much net income or loss would be allocated to each under the following circumstances?

   a. A net income of $40,500

   A = $ 10,000 + 3000 + 1500 = 14,500

   B = $ 10,000 + 2000 + 1000 = 13,000

   C = $ 10,000 + 2500 + 500 = 13,000

   b. A net income of $25,500

   A = $ 10000 + 3000 - 6000 = 7000

   B = $ 10,000 + 2000 - 4000 = 8000

   C = $ 10,000 + 2500 - 2000 = 10,500

   c. A net loss of $4,500

   A = $ 10,000 + 3000 - 21,000 = (8,000)

   B = $ 10,000 + 2000 - 14,000 = (2,000)

   C = $ 10,000 + 2500 - 7000 = 5500

2. Partners D, E, and F have account balances of $7,000, $15,000, and $20,000, respectively, prior to liquidation. Assets total $65,000 and liabilities total $23,000. If the assets are sold for $45,000, and the partners' stated ratio is 5:3:2, how much will each partner receive as a result of liquidation (if deficits are absorbed by the other partners)?

   D = $ 0

   E = $ 9/25 x 20,000 = 7200

   F = $ 10/25 x 20,000 = 12,800

3. Partners G, H, and I have capital balances of $10,000 each, and share income and losses in a 2:2:1 ratio. They agree to allow J to purchase a one-third interest in the business. If they use the bonus method to record the transaction, provide the proper journal entry under each of the following assumptions:

   a. J contributes $12,000 in cash.
   b. J contributes $15,000 in cash.
   c. J contributes $21,000 in cash.

Date	Description	Debit	Credit
General Journal			
a	Cash	12,000	
	G	800	
	H	800	
	I	400	
	J		14,000
	Purchase of 1/3 interest by J		
b	Cash	15,000	
	J		15,000
	Purchase of 1/3 interest by J		
c	Cash	21,000	
	G		1600
	H		1600
	I		800
	J		17,000
	Purchase of 1/3 interest by J		

Chapter Sixteen

Corporations: Organization and Contributed Capital

Reviewing the Chapter

1. A **corporation** is a business organization authorized by the state to conduct business and is a separate legal entity from its owners. It is the dominant form of American business because it makes it possible to gather together large amounts of capital.

2. Before a corporation may do business, it must apply for and receive a charter from the state. The state must approve the **articles of incorporation**, which describe the basic purpose and structure of the proposed corporation.

3. Management of a corporation consists of the board of directors, who decide corporate policy, and the officers, who carry on the daily operations. The board is elected by the stockholders, and the officers are appointed by the board.

4. The stockholders usually meet once a year to elect directors and to carry on other important business. Each share of voting stock entitles its owner to one vote. A stockholder who cannot attend the meeting can legally authorize another to vote his or her shares by **proxy**.

5. Some specific duties of the board of directors are to declare dividends, authorize contracts, decide on executive salaries, and arrange major loans with banks. It is also common for the board to appoint an **audit committee** to serve as a channel of communication between the corporation and its independent auditor. The audit committee is made up of outside directors and helps ensure the board's objectivity in judging management's performance. Management's main means of reporting the corporation's financial position and results of operations is its annual report.

6. The corporate form of business has several advantages over the sole proprietorship and partnership. It is a separate legal entity and offers limited liability to the owners. It also offers ease of capital generation and ease of transfer of ownership. Other advantages are the lack of mutual agency in a corporation and its continuous existence. In addition, a corporate form of business allows centralized authority and responsibility and professional management.

7. The corporate form of business also has several disadvantages compared to the sole proprietorship and partnership. It is subject to greater government regulation and **double taxation**. Limited liability of the owners may limit how much a small corporation can borrow. In addition, separation of ownership and control may allow management to make harmful decisions.

8. The costs of forming a corporation (such as attorneys' fees and incorporation fees) are debited to an intangible asset account called **Organization Costs**. These costs are amortized over the early period of the corporation's life, usually five years.

9. A corporation's balance sheet contains assets, liabilities, and a stockholders' equity section. **Stockholders' equity** is made up of **contributed capital**, representing the stockholders' investment, and retained earnings, representing earnings that have remained in the business.

10. Ownership in a corporation is evidenced by a document called a **stock certificate**. A stockholder sells stock by endorsing the stock certificate and sending it to the corporation's secretary or its transfer agent. The secretary or transfer agent is responsible for transferring the corporation's stock, maintaining stockholders' records, and preparing a list of stockholders for stockholders' meetings and for the payment of dividends. In addition, corporations often engage an underwriter to assist in the initial issue of stock.

11. The articles of incorporation will indicate the number of **shares of stock** that a corporation is authorized to issue. Stock that has been **issued** to stockholders and has not been bought back by the corporation is called **outstanding stock**. **Par value** is the legal value of a share of stock.

12. When only one type of stock is issued, it is called **common stock**. A second type of stock, called **preferred stock**, may also be issued. Preferred stockholders receive prior claim over common stockholders to dividends when declared and to assets when distributed at liquidation.

13. When a dividend is declared by the board of directors, Dividends Declared is debited, and Dividends Payable is credited.

14. Each share of preferred stock entitles its owner to a dollar amount or percentage of par value each year before common stockholders receive anything. Once the preferred stockholders have received the annual dividends to which they are entitled, however, the common stockholders generally receive the remainder.

15. In addition, preferred stock (a) is cumulative or noncumulative, (b) is participating or nonparticipating, (c) is convertible or nonconvertible, and (d) may be callable. It usually has no voting rights. Because common stockholders' claim to assets upon liquidation ranks behind that of creditors and preferred stockholders, common stock is considered the **residual equity** of a company.
   a. When the preferred stockholders do not receive the full amount of their annual dividend, the unpaid amount is carried over to the next year when the preferred stock is **cumulative**. Unpaid back dividends are called **dividends in arrears** and should be disclosed either in the balance sheet or as a footnote. When the preferred stock is **noncumulative**, unpaid dividends are not carried over to the next period.
   b. When preferred stock is **participating**, its holders are entitled to more than the annual fixed amount, once the common stockholders have also received an equal percentage on their total par value. Preferred stock is fully participating when no limit is placed on additional dividends, and is partially participating when a limit does exist for additional dividends. Holders of **nonparticipating preferred stock**, on the other hand, are limited to their annual fixed amount.
   c. An owner of **convertible preferred stock** has the option to exchange each share of preferred stock for a set number of common stock shares.
   d. Some preferred stock is **callable**, meaning that the corporation has the right to buy it back at a specified call or redemption price. Convertible preferred stock can instead be converted to common stock if its holder so desires.

16. Capital stock (common or preferred) may or may not have a par value, depending on the specifications in the charter. When par-value stock is issued, the Capital Stock account is credited for the **legal capital** (par value), and any excess is recorded as Paid-in Capital in Excess of Par Value. In the stockholders' equity section of the balance sheet, the entire amount is labeled Total Contributed Capital. On rare occasions, stock is issued at a discount (less than par value), thereby creating a contingent liability (for the amount of the discount) for those stockholders upon liquidation.

17. **No-par stock** is stock for which par value has not been established, and it may be issued with or without a **stated value**. Stated value (when established by the board of directors) is the legal capital for a share of no-par stock. The total stated value is recorded in the Capital Stock account. Any amount received in excess of stated value is recorded as Paid-in Capital in Excess of Stated Value. If no stated value is set, however, the entire amount received is legal capital and is credited to Capital Stock.

18. Sometimes stock is issued in exchange for assets or for services rendered. Such a transaction should be recorded at the fair market value of the stock. If the stock's fair market value cannot be determined, the fair market value of the assets or services should be used.

19. An investor who signs a **stock subscription** agrees to pay a set price for a certain amount of stock at some later date or in installments. When subscriptions are received, Subscriptions Receivable is debited, and Capital Stock Subscribed (a contributed capital account) and Paid-in Capital in Excess of Par Value are credited. Upon collection, Cash is debited and Subscriptions Receivable is credited. When the stock is issued upon full payment, Capital Stock Subscribed is debited and Capital Stock is credited.

20. When stock is retired, all of the contributed capital associated with the retired shares must be removed from the accounts. When less is paid than was originally contributed, the difference is credited to Paid-in Capital, Retirement of Stock. When more is paid, the difference is debited to Retained Earnings.

21. When stock is donated to a corporation by its stockholders, only a memorandum entry should be made because assets, liabilities, and stockholders' equity are unaffected. In addition, the balance sheet should disclose the number of shares now in the treasury.

22. When assets are donated to a corporation, they are debited at their fair market value, and a contributed capital account is credited.

23. The **book value** of a share of stock equals the net assets represented by one share of a company's stock. If the company has common stock only, the book value per share is arrived at by dividing stockholders' equity by the number of outstanding and subscribed shares. When the company also has preferred stock, the liquidating value of the preferred stock plus any dividends in arrears are deducted from stockholders' equity in computing book value per share of common stock.

24. **Market value** is the highest price that investors are willing to pay for a share of stock on the open market.

Testing Your Knowledge

Matching

Match each term with its definition by writing the appropriate letter in the blank.

F 1. Corporation

O 2. Articles of incorporation

I 3. Board of directors

K 4. Organization costs

J 5. Proxy

L 6. Authorized stock

E 7. Outstanding stock

M 8. Common stock

G 9. Preferred stock

A 10. Dividends in arrears

P 11. Par value

N 12. No-par stock

D 13. Stated value

H 14. Stock subscription

B 15. Book value per share

C 16. Market value

a. Unpaid back dividends

- b. The net assets represented by one share of a company's stock

c. The price that investors will pay for a share of stock

- d. The amount of legal capital of a share of no-par stock

e. Stock that is presently held by stockholders

f. The dominant form of business in the United States

g. The type of stock whose holders have prior claim over common stockholders to dividends

h. An agreement by an investor to pay for stock at some later date or in installments

i. The corporate body that sets major business policies

j. A substitute authorized to vote for another

k. Expenditures necessary to form a corporation

l. The maximum amount of stock that a corporation may issue

m. The name of the stock when only one type of stock has been issued

n. Stock that may or may not have a stated value

o. A description of the basic purpose and structure of a corporation that is filed when applying for a charter

p. The legal value for stock that is stated in the charter

Completion

Use the lines provided to complete each item.

1. List eight advantages of the corporate form of business.

Separate legal entity — Limited Liability

Ease of capital Generation

Continuous Existence — Ease of Transfer of ownership

No mutual agency

Centralized authority

Professional mgmt.

2. List four disadvantages of the corporate form of business.

Govt. regulation

Double taxation

Limited liability — limit borrowing

Separate control — make harmful mgmt decisions

3. Name the two major portions of the Stockholders' Equity section of a balance sheet.

Capital (contrib.)

Retained Earnings

4. State the meaning of the following terms when used to describe preferred stock.

a. *Cumulative* — dividends are accumulated

b. *Noncumulative* — dividends not accumulated

c. *Participating* — participates in "extra dividends above the negotiated

d. *Convertible* — may be converted into common

e. *Callable* — can be recalled by co @ a specified $

True-False

Circle T if the statement is true, F if it is false.

T F 1. Corporate income is taxed at the corporate level and at the individual level when distributed as dividends.

T F 2. The concept of legal capital was established to protect the corporation's creditors.

T F 3. Unless stock is issued at a discount, creditors cannot attach the personal assets of the corporation's stockholders.

T **F** 4. Organization costs must be charged to expense in the year of the corporation's formation.

T F 5. Contributed capital consists of capital stock plus paid-in-capital in excess of par (stated) value.

T F 6. A transfer agent keeps records of stock transactions.

T **F** 7. Preferred stock may not be both convertible and participating.

T F 8. Dividends in arrears do not exist when all preferred stock is noncumulative.

T **F** 9. The worth of a share of stock can be measured by its par value.

T **F** 10. As cash is received on stock subscriptions, the stockholders' equity section of the balance sheet will increase in amount.

T F 11. The book value of a share of common stock will decrease when dividends are declared.

T **F** 12. Preferred stockholders are guaranteed annual dividends, whereas common stockholders are not.

T **F** 13. Preferred stock is considered the residual equity of a corporation.

T F 14. When stock is retired at more than its issue price, Retained Earnings is debited for the difference.

T F **15.** When stock is donated to a corporation by its stockholders, total stockholders' equity is unaffected.

T F **16.** When assets are donated to a corporation, Retained Earnings is credited for the fair market value of the assets received.

Multiple-Choice

Circle the letter of the best answer.

1. Which of the following should not appear in the stockholders' equity section of a balance sheet?
   a. Paid-in Capital in Excess of Par Value
   b. Capital Stock Subscribed
   c. Discount on Capital Stock
   d. Subscriptions Receivable

2. With a stock subscription, what account is credited when the stock is actually issued?
   a. Capital Stock
   b. Capital Stock Subscribed
   c. Subscriptions Receivable
   d. Paid-in Capital in Excess of Par (Stated) Value

3. Which of the following statements is true?
   a. Outstanding shares plus issued shares equals authorized shares.
   b. Unissued shares plus outstanding shares equals authorized shares.
   c. Authorized shares minus unissued shares equals issued shares.
   d. Unissued shares minus issued shares equals outstanding shares.

4. Howard Corporation has always paid dividends to both its preferred and common stockholders. In a corporation such as this, which type of stock probably has the least useful feature?
   a. Cumulative preferred
   b. Fully participating preferred
   c. Convertible preferred
   d. Partially participating preferred

5. When a corporation has issued only one type of stock and wishes to compute book value per share, it needs all the information below except for
   a. retained earnings.
   b. current year's dividends.
   c. total contributed capital.
   d. total shares outstanding and subscribed.

6. McFarland Corporation has outstanding 1,000 shares of $100 par value, 7 percent cumulative and nonparticipating preferred stock, and 20,000 shares of $10 par value common stock. Last year, the company paid no dividends, but this year it distributed $40,000 in dividends. What portion of this $40,000 will common stockholders receive?
   a. $0
   b. $2,800
   c. $26,000
   d. $33,000

7. The journal entry to record the issue of stock for less than par value should include a
   a. debit to Retained Earnings.
   b. debit to Discount on Capital Stock.
   c. credit to Paid-in Capital in Excess of Par Value.
   d. credit to Cash.

8. Which of the following is not a characteristic of corporations in general?
   a. Separation of ownership and management
   b. Ease of transfer of ownership
   c. Double taxation
   d. Unlimited liability of stockholders

9. When common stock is retired at a cost that is less than the issue price, which account will not be included in the journal entry?
   a. Paid-in Capital in Excess of Par (Stated) Value
   b. Retained Earnings
   c. Cash
   d. Common Stock

Applying Your Knowledge

Exercises

1. Hamilton Corporation paid no dividends in its first two years of operations. In its third year, it paid $51,000 in dividends. For all three years there have been 1,000 shares of 6 percent, $100 par value cumulative and nonparticipating preferred stock, and 5,000 shares of $10 par value common stock outstanding. How much of the $51,000 in dividends goes to preferred stockholders? to common stockholders?

Preferred stockholders receive $ _18,000_ .

Common stockholders receive $ _33,000_ .

2. Refer to the facts in exercise 1. If instead there were no dividends in arrears and the preferred stock were fully participating, how much of the $51,000 dividend would have gone to each class of stockholder?

Preferred stockholders receive $ _27,000_ .

Common stockholders receive $ _24,000_ .

3. On May 1, Burr Corporation accepted subscriptions to 1,000 shares of $50 par value common stock at $70 per share. A 20 percent down payment was also received on that date. On June 3, an additional 40 percent was received. On June 18, the remaining 40 percent was received, and the stock was issued. Prepare all necessary entries in the journal provided.

General Journal

Date		Description	Debit	Credit
May	1	Subscriptions Receivable	70,000	
		Common Stock Subscribed (1000 shares of $50 par)		50,000
		Paid in Capital Excess of Par Common ($70/share)		20,000
	1	Cash	14,000	
		Subscriptions Receivable		14,000
		20% down on stock subscriptions		
June	3	Cash	28,000	
		Subscriptions Receivable		28,000
		additional 40% received on stock subscriptions		
	18	Cash	28,000	
		Subscriptions Receivable		28,000
		Remaining 40% received		
	18	Common Stock Subscribed	50,000	
		Common Stock		50,000

4. Carter Corporation's balance sheet as of December 31, 19xx, includes the following information regarding stockholders' equity:

Contributed Capital		
Preferred Stock, $50 par value, 7% cumulative and nonparticipating, 4,000 shares authorized, issued, and outstanding	$200,000	P
Common Stock, no-par, 30,000 shares authorized, issued, and outstanding	360,000	C
Paid-in Capital in Excess of Par Value, Preferred	40,000	P
Total Contributed Capital	$600,000	
Retained Earnings	80,000	
Total Stockholders' Equity	$680,000	

Dividends in arrears total $28,000.

In the space that follows, compute book value per share of both preferred stock and common stock.

Preferred

Stock - 200,000
Excess Capital 40,000
240,000 ÷ 4000 = $60/share
Div. arrears 28,000
w/excess 268,000 ÷ 4000 = $67/share
w/o excess 228,000 ÷ 4000 = $57/share

Common
680,000 - 268,000 = 412,000 Equity attributable to common

412,000 ÷ 30,000 = $13.73/share

680,000 - 228,000 = 452,000 ÷ 30,000 = $15.07/share

Crossword Puzzle
For Chapters 15 and 16

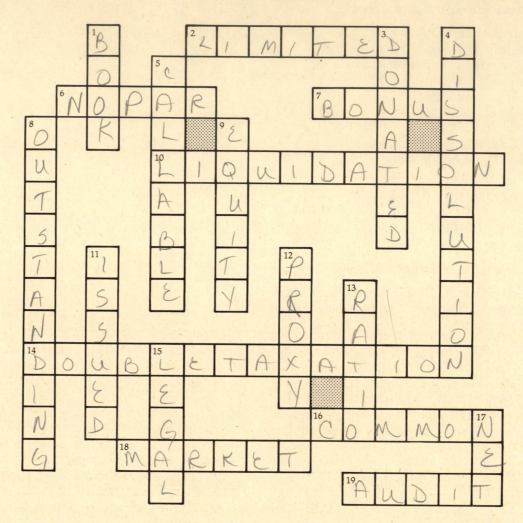

ACROSS

2. Like a stockholder's liability
6. Stock that may or may not have a stated value (hyphenated)
7. Excess paid for admission of new partner
10. Sale of the partnership assets
14. Disadvantage unique to a corporation (2 words)
16. Type of stock
18. True value of a share of stock
19. Corporate committee

DOWN

1. Value designating equity per share
3. Stock given to a corporation as a gift
4. The result of a change in ownership of a partnership
5. Stock that may be bought back by a corporation
8. Currently in the hands of stockholders
9. Common stock is a corporation's residual _____
11. Sold to stockholders at one time
12. Authority to vote for another
13. Basis for dividing partnership earnings
15. Capital equal to par or stated value
17. After deducting depreciation

Chapter Seventeen

Retained Earnings and Corporate Income Statements

Reviewing the Chapter

1. The stockholders' equity section of a corporation's balance sheet is composed of contributed capital and retained earnings. Contributed capital represents the owners' capital investment. **Retained earnings** are the profits that a corporation has earned since its beginning, minus any losses, dividends declared, or other transfers out of retained earnings.

2. Ordinarily, Retained Earnings will have a credit balance. However, when a debit balance exists, the corporation is said to have a **deficit**.

3. The Retained Earnings account may be increased through (a) net income from operations and (b) certain prior period adjustments. It may be decreased through (a) net loss from operations, (b) cash dividend declarations, (c) stock dividend declarations, (d) certain prior period adjustments, and (e) certain treasury stock transactions. A corporation's net income is closed at the end of the period by debiting Income Summary and crediting Retained Earnings. The reverse is done for a net loss.

4. As already explained, a **dividend** is a distribution of assets by a corporation to its stockholders, normally in cash. Dividends are usually stated as a specified dollar amount per share of stock and are declared by the board of directors. Dividends are declared on the date of declaration, specifying that the owners of the stock on the date of record will receive the dividends on the date of payment. A **liquidating dividend** is the return of contributed capital to the stockholders, and is normally paid when a company is going out of business.

5. When cash dividends are declared, the Dividends Declared account is debited and Cash Dividends Payable is credited; when they are paid, Cash Dividends Payable is debited and Cash is credited. The Dividends Declared account is closed to Retained Earnings at the end of the year. No journal entry is made on the date of record.

6. A **stock dividend** is a proportional distribution of shares of stock to a corporation's stockholders. Stock dividends are declared to (a) give evidence of the company's success without paying a cash dividend, (b) reduce the stock's market price, and (c) allow a nontaxable distribution. The result of a stock dividend is the transfer of a part of retained earnings to contributed capital. For a small stock dividend (less than 20–25 percent), the market value of the shares distributed is transferred from retained earnings. For a large stock dividend (greater than 20–25 percent), the par or stated value is transferred. A stock dividend does not change total stockholder's proportionate equity in the company.

7. A **stock split** is an increase in the number of shares of stock outstanding, with a corresponding decrease in the par or stated value of the stock. For example, a 3 for 1 split on 40,000 shares of $30 par value stock would result in the distribution of 80,000 additional shares. (That is, a former owner of one share now owns two more shares.) The par value would be reduced to $10. The balances in stockholders' equity would not be affected.

8. The purpose of a stock split is to improve the stock's marketability by causing the stock's market price to go down. In the above example, if the stock were selling for $180 per share, a 3 for 1 split would probably cause the market price to fall to about $60 per share. A memorandum entry should be made for a stock split, disclosing the decrease in par or stated value as well as the increase in shares of stock outstanding.

9. **Treasury stock** is common or preferred stock that has been issued and reacquired by the issuing company. That is, it is issued but no longer outstanding stock. Treasury stock is purchased (a) to distribute to employees through stock option plans, (b) to maintain a favorable market for the company's stock, (c) to increase earnings per share, and (d) to use in purchasing other companies.

10. Treasury stock may be held indefinitely, reissued, or canceled, and has no rights until reissued. Treasury stock, the last item in the stockholders' equity section of the balance sheet, appears as a deduction.

11. When treasury stock is purchased, its account is debited for the purchase cost. It may be reissued at cost, above cost, or below cost. When cash received from reissue exceeds the cost, the difference is credited to Paid-in Capital, Treasury Stock Transactions. When cash received is less than cost, the difference is debited to Paid-in Capital, Treasury Stock Transactions (and Retained Earnings if needed). In no case should a gain or loss be recorded.

12. **Prior period adjustments** are entries made in the current period for certain transactions that relate to, but were not determinable in, prior accounting periods. A prior period adjustment can be made only for one of two reasons. First, it may be done to correct an error in the financial statements of a prior period. Second, it may be done to record a tax gain from carrying forward a preacquisition operating loss of a purchased subsidiary. Prior period adjustments appear on the current period's retained earnings statement as an adjustment to the beginning balance, but not on its income statement. All other items of income and loss during the period that do not qualify as a prior period adjustment must appear on the income statement.

13. The **statement of retained earnings** is a labeled summary of the changes in retained earnings during the accounting period.

14. Retained earnings may be divided into appropriated and unappropriated retained earnings. Unappropriated retained earnings show the asset amount that may be distributed to stockholders as dividends. **Appropriated retained earnings** show the asset amount that is to be retained in the business for other purposes. Retained earnings are appropriated for contractual, legal, or voluntary reasons, and by the board of directors only. Retained Earnings is not a cash account, but is merely a guide to asset distribution.

15. Appropriations of retained earnings should be disclosed in the retained earnings portion of the balance sheet or as notes to the financial statements.

16. Corporate taxable income is determined by subtracting allowable business deductions from includable gross income. Some special features of corporate tax provisions are a special dividends received deduction, carry-forwards and carry-backwards for net operating loss deductions and capital losses, a limit on the deduction for charitable contributions, and tax credits for certain expenditures.

17. **Capital assets** are stocks and bonds owned by individuals, as well as certain business property. Capital assets are classified as long-term or short-term depending on whether they have been held for more or less than one year. The combined total for all gains and losses on short-term capital assets during a tax year is called the **net short-term capital gain (or loss).** The combined total for all gains and losses on long-term capital assets is called the **net long-term capital gain (or loss).** The combined total of these two amounts is the **net capital gain (or loss).** A corporation's net long-term capital gain is taxed at 28 percent. However, a net capital loss may be used only to offset net capital gains in the three preceding and five successive years.

18. Corporations are subject to a tax rate that ranges from 15 percent to 46 percent.

19. **Tax credits** are dollar-for-dollar deductions from the computed tax liability. An **investment tax credit** of 6 or 10 percent is allowed on certain expenditures for plant assets.

20. An income statement should contain all revenues and expenses of the period, as well as discontinued operations, extraordinary items, accounting changes, and earnings per share.

21. The results of operations for the period and any gains or losses from the **discontinued operations** of a segment of a business should be disclosed (net of taxes) after Income from Continuing Operations. A segment is defined as a separate major line of business or class of customer.

22. An **extraordinary item** is an event that is unusual and occurs infrequently. Extraordinary items should be disclosed separately in the income statement (net of taxes) after Discontinued Operations.

23. A company may change from one accounting principle to another (as from FIFO to LIFO) only if it can justify the new method as better accounting practice. Once an accounting change is made, the company must disclose the nature and justification for the change, as well as its effect on income before extraordinary items, net income, and earnings per share. In addition, the cumulative effect of the change on prior years (net of taxes) should appear on the income statement after extraordinary items.

24. Investors use the **earnings per share** figure to judge the performance of a company, to estimate its future earnings, and to compare it with other companies. Earnings per share figures should be disclosed for (1) income from continuing operations, (2) income before extraordinary items, (3) cumulative effect of accounting changes, and (4) net income. These figures should appear on the face of the income statement.

25. A company that has issued no securities that are convertible into common stock has a **simple capital structure**. In this case, earnings per share is figured by dividing net income applicable to common stock by the weighted-average shares outstanding.

26. A company that has issued securities that may be converted into common stock has a **complex capital structure**. In this case, a dual presentation of primary and fully diluted earnings per share is required. **Primary earnings per share** is figured as follows:

$$\frac{\text{net income applicable to common stock}}{\text{weighted-average common shares}\atop\text{plus common stock equivalents}}$$

Fully diluted earnings per share is figured as follows:

$$\frac{\text{net income applicable to common stock}}{\text{weighted-average common shares}\atop{\text{plus common stock equivalents}\atop\text{plus other potentially dilutive securities}}}$$

Common stock equivalents are convertible securities that are roughly equal to the common stock they could be converted into.

Testing Your Knowledge

Matching

Match each term with its definition by writing the appropriate letter in the blank.

J 1. Retained earnings

C 2. Deficit

R 3. Prior period adjustment

E 4. Dividend

M 5. Simple capital structure

B 6. Complex capital structure

N 7. Discontinued operations

F 8. Liquidating dividend

I 9. Stock dividend

L 10. Stock split

P 11. Appropriated retained earnings

D 12. Treasury stock

O 13. Statement of retained earnings

A 14. Extraordinary item

K 15. Earnings per share

H 16. Accounting change

G 17. Capital assets

Q 18. Investment tax credit

a. An unusual and infrequent gain or loss
b. The make-up of a corporation when convertible securities have been issued
c. A negative figure for retained earnings
d. Issued stock that has been reacquired by the corporation
e. A distribution of assets to a corporation's stockholders
f. The return of contributed capital to a corporation's stockholders
g. Stocks and bonds owned by individuals, and certain business property
h. Use of a different but more appropriate accounting method
i. A proportional distribution of stock to a corporation's stockholders
j. The profits that a corporation has earned since its inception, minus any losses, dividends declared, or transfers to contributed capital
k. A measure of net income earned for each share of stock
l. A corporate stock maneuver in which par or stated value is changed
m. The make-up of a corporation when no convertible securities have been issued
n. The income statement section immediately before extraordinary items
o. A summary of the changes in retained earnings during the period
p. The quantity of assets that are unavailable for dividends
q. A deduction from the computed tax liability resulting from the purchase of certain plant assets
r. An entry made in the current period that relates to an earlier period

Completion

Use the lines provided to complete each item.

1. List five ways in which the retained earnings account may be reduced.

   net loss from operations
   cash dividend & declarations
   stock dividend
   prior period adjustments
   treasury stock transactions

2. What are the two major distinctions between a stock dividend and a stock split?

   Stock split lowers par value & increases stock shares outstanding)
   Stock dividend doesn't
   Stock dividend transfers retained earnings to contrib. capital, & split does not

3. What two conditions must be met for an item to qualify as extraordinary?

   Infrequent
   unusual

4. What is the difference between treasury stock and unissued stock?

   Treasury stock has been issued but bought back (not outstanding) unissued has never been issued

True-False

Circle T if the statement is true, F if it is false.

T F 1. A prior period adjustment should never appear in the current period's income statement.

T **F** 2. Appropriated Retained Earnings represents cash set aside for a special purpose.

T F 3. On the date of payment of a dividend, total assets and total stockholders' equity decrease.

T **F** 4. After a stock dividend is distributed, each stockholder owns a greater percentage of the corporation.

T F 5. When a 30 percent stock dividend is declared, the market value of the stock on that date is irrelevant in making the journal entry.

T **F** 6. The main purpose of a stock split is to reduce the stock's par value.

T F 7. The purchase of treasury stock will reduce total assets and total stockholders' equity.

T **F** 8. When treasury stock is issued at more than its cost, Gain on Sale of Treasury Stock should be recorded by the corporation.

T **F** 9. Treasury stock is listed in the balance sheet as an asset.

T **F** 10. A gain on the sale of a plant asset qualifies as an extraordinary item.

T **F** 11. Extraordinary items should appear on the statement of retained earnings.

T F 12. The effect of the change from straight-line depreciation to sum-of-the-years'-digits should be reported in the income statement immediately after extraordinary items.

T **F** 13. Stock Dividends Distributable is a current liability in the balance sheet.

T F 14. Both primary and fully diluted earnings per share data should be provided for a corporation with a complex capital structure.

T **F** 15. If an extraordinary gain of $20,000 has occurred, it should be reported net of taxes at more than $20,000.

T **F** 16. Capital assets that have been held for more than six months are classified as long-term capital assets.

Multiple-Choice

Circle the letter of the best answer.

1. Which of the following has no effect on retained earnings?
   a. A stock split
   b. A stock dividend
   c. A cash dividend
   d. A prior period adjustment

2. A company with 10,000 shares of common stock outstanding distributed a 10 percent stock dividend and then split its stock 4 for 1. How many shares are now outstanding?
   a. 2,750
   b. 41,000
   c. 44,000
   d. 55,000

3. When retained earnings are appropriated, which of the following is true?
   a. Retained Earnings is credited.
   b. The company is no longer limited in the amount of dividends it can pay.
   c. The appropriation is debited.
   d. Total stockholders' equity remains the same.

4. On the date that a stock dividend is distributed,
   a. Common Stock Distributable is credited.
   b. Cash is credited.
   c. Retained Earnings remains the same.
   d. no entry is made.

5. When treasury stock is reissued below cost, which of the following will never be true?
   a. Retained Earnings is debited.
   b. Treasury Stock is credited.
   c. Contributed Capital, Treasury Stock Transactions is debited.
   d. Loss on Reissue of Treasury Stock is debited.

6. The purchase of treasury stock will not affect
   a. the amount of stock outstanding.
   b. the amount of stock issued.
   c. total assets.
   d. total stockholders' equity.

7. An extraordinary item should appear
   a. on the income statement.
   b. on the balance sheet.
   c. on the statement of retained earnings.
   d. as a footnote.

8. The BNJ Corporation had 60,000 shares of common stock outstanding from January 1 to October 1, and 40,000 shares outstanding from October 1 to December 31. What is the weighted-average number of shares used for earnings per share calculations?
   a. 45,000 shares
   b. 50,000 shares
   c. 55,000 shares
   d. 100,000 shares

9. If retained earnings were $70,000 on January 1, 19xx, and $100,000 on December 31, 19xx, and if cash dividends of $15,000 were declared and paid during the year, net income for the year must have been
   a. $30,000.
   b. $45,000.
   c. $55,000.
   d. $85,000.

Applying Your Knowledge

Exercises

1. For each of the following sets of facts, prepare the proper entry in the journal provided.

Sept. 1 Patterson Corporation began operations by issuing 10,000 shares of $100 par value stock at $120 per share.

Dec. 31 The net income for the first four months of operations was $800,000.

Jan. 10 The board of directors declared a cash dividend of $2.50 per share.

31 This is the date of record for the cash dividend.

Feb. 20 The cash dividend is paid.

Mar. 7 A 5 percent stock dividend is declared. The market price of the stock is $130 per share on March 7.

30 This is the date of record for the stock dividend.

Apr. 13 The stock dividend is distributed.

Date		Description	Debit	Credit

General Journal

2. Quigley Corporation began operation on August, 10, 19x1, by issuing 50,000 shares of $10 par value stock at $105 per share. As of January 1, 19x3, its capital structure was the same. For each of the following sets of facts for January of 19x3, prepare the proper entry in the journal provided. In all cases, assume sufficient cash and unappropriated retained earnings.

Jan. 2 All stock is split 2 for 1.

12 The corporation purchases 5,000 shares of stock from the stockholders at $60 per share.

18 Retained earnings of $70,000 are appropriated for the purchase of a building.

19 A $1 per share cash dividend is declared on outstanding stock.

30 The corporation reissues 2,000 shares of treasury stock at $65 per share.

31 The cash dividend is paid.

General Journal				
Date		Description	Debit	Credit

3. The RHJ Corporation earned $360,000 during 19xx. There were 100,000 shares of $10 par-value common stock outstanding during the entire year. In addition, there were 30,000 shares of $5 par-value, cumulative, convertible preferred stock outstanding during the entire year. These shares are not considered common stock equivalents. The dividend rate is $2 per share, and each share is convertible into two shares of common stock. Compute both primary and fully diluted earnings per share.

	Primary	Fully Diluted
30,000 shares — $5 par preferred	60,000	

4. A company has $100,000 in net operating income before taxes. It also had an extraordinary loss of $30,000 when lightning struck one of its warehouses. The company must pay a 40 percent tax on all items. Complete the partial income statement in good form.

Net operating income before taxes	$100,000

Emerging Trends in Financial Reporting

An analysis of the changes taking place in the reporting environment

For the past decade, the financial reporting environment has been in a state of rapid evolution, and the current activities of the Financial Accounting Standards Board, the Securitites and Exchange Commission and governmental accountants suggest that this process is continuing. Under such circumstances, it seems important to step back to try to gain a perspective on the direction of the changes taking place. Understanding the consequences of official pronouncements means not only being aware of their issuance but also recognizing the motivating factors behind them. Furthermore, if the profession is to avoid facing the future with misguided expectations and obsolete skills, the shifts in the financial reporting environment should be closely monitored.

Changing Role of Financial Statements

One of the most significant changes in financial reporting is the steady erosion of the relative importance of financial statements. At one time, financial statements were the whole of financial reporting. Over the past decade, however, more financial reporting innovation has taken place outside the financial statements. This tendency is partly the result of efforts by the accounting profession and the corporate reporting community to reduce their legal exposure and partly in recognition of the deficiencies of the financial statement format for purposes of communicating uncertain, interpretive and subjective data. In addition, the hesitation of both the FASB and the SEC to try to substantially reduce the major elements of inconsistency now existing among financial statements as a result of alternative accounting treatments of some major items has contributed to the relative decline in the statements' importance in achieving the FASB's articulated objectives of financial reporting.

This fundamental change is evidenced by a number of pronouncements and actions taken in recent years. It is significant, for example, that FASB Financial Accounting Concepts Statement no. 1,

Objectives of Financial Reporting by Business Enterprises,[1] was directed at the objectives of financial reporting rather than at financial statement objectives, which was the charge of the committee chaired by Robert M. Trueblood a few years earlier whose work served as the basis for most FASB conclusions.[2] In its 1977 report,[3] the SEC Advisory Committee on Corporate Disclosure further emphasized the need for interpretation and analysis of results by management in its discussion of operations, and the commission's significant enlargement of requirements for management's discussion and analysis of operations[4] adopted in fall 1980 continued the process of implementing the advisory committee's recommendations.

The FASB also has issued a number of its important standards dealing with information not required to be included in the basic financial statements. FASB Statement no. 33, *Financial Reporting and Changing Prices*[5] (and three statements which expand it to certain specific industries[6]) requires disclosures only outside the financial statements. Business segment reporting also is not required in the basic statements or notes, although the board does view the separate disclosures required by Statement no. 14, *Financial Reporting for Segments of a Business Enterprise,*[7] as "an integral part of the financial statements." Both the FASB and the SEC now seem willing to permit

---

1. Financial Accounting Standards Board Financial Accounting Concepts Statement no. 1, *Objectives of Financial Reporting by Business Enterprises* (Stamford, Conn.: FASB, 1978).
2. Study Group on the Objectives of Financial Statements, *Objectives of Financial Statements* (New York: AICPA, 1973).
3. "SFC Corporate Disclosure Group Issues Final Report," JofA, Dec. 77, pp. 22, 24.
4. See "New SEC Rulings on Disclosures Change Annual Reports and Other Forms," p. 84.
5. FASB Statement no. 33, *Financial Reporting and Changing Prices* (Stamford, Conn.: FASB, 1979).
6. FASB Statement no. 39, *Financial Reporting and Changing Prices: Specialized Assets—Mining and Oil and Gas* (Stamford, Conn.: FASB, 1980); FASB Statement no. 40, *Financial Reporting and Changing Prices: Specialized Assets—Timberlands and Growing Timber* (Stamford, Conn.: FASB, 1980); and FASB Statement no. 41, *Financial Reporting and Changing Prices: Specialized Assets—Income-Producing Real Estate* (Stamford, Conn.: FASB, 1980).
7. FASB Statement no. 14, *Financial Reporting for Segments of a Business Enterprise* (Stamford, Conn.: FASB, 1976).

disclosure of oil and gas reserve data outside the financial statements, and both are exercising great restraint in responding to the congressional mandate for a single method of accounting for the historical costs related to oil and gas production.

The result of this trend ultimately seems likely to make the financial statements increasingly a well-defined ritual where objective data are arrayed without great regard for their relevance. The most important and relevant information for investment decision making will be presented supplementally, and management will be assigned a reporting role of greater significance in interpreting results, performing some of the functions previously assigned to the user of financial statements.

The impact of this trend on the role of the FASB and the auditing role of the public accounting profession is still in the process of evolution. The FASB has clearly attempted to expand its turf to consider the broader field of financial reporting although it still spends a large part of its time on issues directly related to the financial statements. The conceptual framework effort deals with issues such as relevance and the use of financial reporting to predict future cash flows, but also with specific issues such as the formatting of the income statement.

I hope the conceptual framework, when finally completed, will help the board sort out the issues and provide a matrix of sorts in which its decision-making process can be set. To date, the board's determination to seek consensus and to avoid threatening its various constituencies has led it to defer some of the hard decisions about the conceptual framework. In the next two years, some of these decisions must be made if the framework is to have any meaning. While no one with reasonable expectations believes that the framework will resolve all specific issues, it has the potential for providing decision guidelines to the board that should enhance (but certainly not ensure) the consistency and neutrality of its standard-setting efforts. From this, the role of financial statements and other financial reporting should emerge with greater clarity.

The impact of changing reporting trends on the auditor is more difficult to predict. Auditors are torn between their desire to be an important part of the reporting action and their concern about the potential liabilities they may incur by so doing. To date, the auditing standards board of the American Institute of CPAs has addressed this issue several times with ambivalent results, and it seems likely that, in the absence of a major reconstruction of the auditor's role, this conflict will continue.

Future-Oriented Reporting

Related to the growth in supplemental information is the increasing emphasis on the future-oriented objectives of financial reporting. Over the past decade, there has been substantial movement toward articulating the importance of financial data in the predictive process and decreasing the emphasis on the stewardship role of statements. The FASB, following the lead of the Trueblood committee, described the principal objective of financial reporting as providing information which would assist investors in predicting the amount, timing and uncertainty of future cash flows to the company. While the board emphasized that this objective did not imply explicit forecasts, it clearly suggested an obligation of preparers and auditors to be aware of investors' uses of the statements in their forecasting processes.

During the decade, the SEC has evidenced consistent and continuing interest in the forecasting process and the role of financial statements in it. In 1971, then Chairman William Casey indicated that the commission's historical policy of rejecting forecasts of all kinds in disclosure documents was "not cast in stone," and he initiated hearings on projections in 1972 that led to a statement of policy in 1973 which officially lifted the ban on forecasts and adopted a neutral attitude toward them. In 1974, the commission adopted a requirement for the presentation of a management discussion and analysis of the summary of operations that would, among other things, require management to discuss any "material facts, whether favorable or unfavorable, . . . which in the opinion of management may make historical operations or earnings as reported . . . not indicative of current or future operations or earnings."[8] In 1977, the Advisory Committee on Corporate Disclosure recommended that the commission move from a policy of neutrality on forecasts to one of encouragement, and, in 1979, the commission adopted this recommendation.[9] It then adopted a "safe harbor rule," which offered legal protection to those who did prepare and disclose forecasts in good faith even if they were not subsequently achieved.

8. Securities and Exchange Commission Accounting Series Release no. 159, *Notice of Adoption of Amendments to Guide 22 of the Guides for Preparation and Filing of Registration Statements Under the Securities Act of 1933 and Adoption of Guide 1 of the Guides for Preparation and Filing of Reports and Registration Statements Under the Securities Exchange Act of 1934 (Textual Analysis of Summary of Earnings or Operations),* August 14, 1979.
9. SEC Release no. 33–5992, *Guides for Disclosure of Projections of Future Economic Performance,* November 7, 1978.

Finally, in the fall of 1980, the SEC adopted a substantial expansion of the requirement for management's discussion and analysis which further emphasized the requirement for a discussion of future-oriented variables. The new requirement, included as item 11 in regulation S-K, calls for a description of "any known trends or uncertainties which have lead or which the registrant reasonably expects will have a material favorable or unfavorable impact on net sales or revenues or income from continuing operations."[10] The instructions which accompany this requirement include the following:

"The discussion and analysis should specifically focus on material events and uncertainties known to management which would cause reported financial information not to be necessarily indicative of future operating results or of future financial condition. This would include description and amounts of (a) matters which would have an impact on future operations and have not had an impact in the past, and (b) matters which have had an impact on reported operations and are not expected to have an impact upon future operations."[11]

Perhaps of equal importance to the adoption of rules is the indication of the commission's staff that monitoring compliance with the intent of this requirement will be a major priority of the Division of Corporation Finance in 1981 and 1982. The director of the division has indicated in seminars that his staff will be issuing helpful and constructive comments on disclosures made and on occasion seeking additional information regarding the disclosures. He has suggested that if internal company forecasts show any substantial deviation from the trend line fitted to past year's sales and income from continuing operations, a disclosure obligation exists, and he has indicated that the division staff will be paying special attention to cases where significant changes in sales and earnings are observed if there is no indication of such changes in the previous year's management discussion and analysis of operations.

These various developments suggest that the trend toward future-oriented disclosure is not likely to abate. It seems likely that the FASB will be testing accounting principles adopted in the future by the degree to which they assist in the predictive process, and the more controversial issue of required explicit forecasting will receive continued attention both from the board and the SEC.

Liquidity Disclosure

The emphasis on future cash flows has also led to increasing attention to liquidity and the problems of reporting funds flows in a business. These areas are currently receiving consideration at both the FASB and the SEC, and this examination is likely to lead to substantial changes in historical reporting patterns.

The SEC has had an interest in funds flows for a number of years. In 1973, the commission noted its concern that some companies were using "cash flow" as a proxy for income measurement and prohibited the presentation of cash flow per share data; at the same time the SEC noted the importance of funds flow analysis in reflecting managerial decisions about the use of funds generated and the sources of this capital.[12] Former Chairman Harold M. Williams frequently expressed his view that the analysis of cash inflows and outflows might be of greater use to investors than conventional income measurement.

In its rules adopted September 1980,[13] the commission specifically mandated new disclosures about liquidity, capital resources and financial position. In its expanded management's discussion requirements, the SEC directed management to discuss the registrant's financial condition and changes in financial condition as well as results of operations. The discussion is to include an analysis of the company's liquidity and capital resources as well as any other information necessary to understand its financial condition. This disclosure should identify any known trends or known demands, commitments, events or uncertainties likely to result in any material increase or decrease in liquidity. If a material deficiency is identified, the registrant is to indicate the course of action management has taken or proposes to take to remedy the deficiency. Also, the SEC has charged management to identify sources of liquidity and briefly describe and discuss any material unused sources of liquid assets. These directives impose comprehensive, tight disclosure requirements on many companies.

The rule also required disclosure of the company's capital resources. The registrant is to describe any material commitments for capital expenditures as of the end of the latest fiscal period. The disclosure is to indicate the general purpose of such commitments and the anticipated source of funds needed to fulfill them. This is to be followed by a description of

---

10. SEC Regulation S-K, *Part 229—Standard Instructions for Filing Forms Under Securities Act of 1933 and Securities Exchange Act of 1934*, December 23, 1977; item 11, par. 3ii, of reg. 229.20, September 2, 1980.
11. Ibid., par. 3iv, "Instructions," par. 3.

12. SEC ASR no. 142, *Reporting Cash Flow and Other Related Data*, March 15, 1973.
13. SEC ASR no. 279, *Amendments to Annual Report Form, Related Forms, Rules, Regulations and Guides; Integration of Securities Acts Disclosure Systems*, September 2, 1980.

any new material trends, both favorable and unfavorable, in the company's capital resources. Also to be disclosed are any indications of expected material changes in the mix and the relative costs of resources. The management discussion is to include changes in equity, debt and any off-balance-sheet financial arrangements.

It is important to be aware that the SEC, in adopting these rules on liquidity disclosure, is not designing regulations to force registrants to compute a lot of ratios. It is looking at liquidity in dynamic terms: as funds flows, financial flexibility and the ability of the company to meet commitments and its plans for meeting commitments.

It would have been useful if the SEC had laid out the conceptual underpinnings of its liquidity and captial resource requirements. Item 11 in regulation S-K defines liquidity as "the ability of an enterprise to generate adequate amounts of cash to meet the enterprise's needs for cash" and says that liquidity should be discussed on both a long-term and a short-term basis.[14] Presumably, therefore, the objective is to help investors recognize potential constraints on a company's activities. In a sense, the traditional pattern of warning about potential difficulties rather than emphasizing opportunities is still evident. However, it seems likely that the commission is equally interested in the implications of liquidity for future success. If such was the objective, one would have hoped that greater emphasis might have been placed on the characteristics of expected future investments, with some indication whether that level would simply sustain current operating levels or provide for real economic growth. The commission's recent further encouragement of capital expenditure projections,[15] in which the commission expressed its belief that projections of capital expenditures are "extremely meaningful," suggests the direction in which the commission intends liquidity disclosure to move.

In December 1980, the FASB, also working in the area of funds flow and liquidity, produced a discussion memorandum entitled *Reporting Funds Flows, Liquidity, and Financial Flexibility*.[16] In it the FASB lays out some fundamental issues in regard to what a funds statement should show and just what it should be. It raises such basic problems as whether to retain the old definition of funds as working capital or to redefine funds as liquid assets. It questions whether the funds statement should be segmented in more ways than is the current practice. It asks whether more information should be required about capital expenditures. It suggests that perhaps capital expenditures should be broken into those for maintaining current capacity, those for increasing capacity and those for complying with environmental and other regulations. It is likely that one of the results of this discussion will be the adoption of a radically different funds statement, perhaps as early as next year. At a minimum, information will be presented in a different format, and additional information regarding the areas noted above will be included.

As a result of this activity in both Washington, D.C., and Stamford, Connecticut, users of financial reporting are likely to see much more data about cash inflows and outflows. This does not mean, however, that income will be ignored. The FASB has frequently noted that income or some segment of it may be the best measure of future cash flows, and, accordingly, the board is currently working on the reformatting of the income statement. It seems likely that what will emerge from this process is some segmentation of income into separate recurring and nonrecurring segments, perhaps with the exclusion of certain items from any income definition. The board's Financial Accounting Concepts Statement no. 3, *Elements of Financial Statements of Business Enterprises*,[17] identifies an all inclusive concept of comprehensive income, defined as the change in equity resulting from all non-owner sources. Other definitions leave unanswered the question of what items will be identified as the components of comprehensive income, such as earnings, operating results, etc. Many arguments remain to be resolved in this area, despite the fact that most of the research on efficient markets suggests that a lot of effort in reformatting financial reporting is not of enormous benefit, since the market seems able to see through format and accounting differences in financial reporting.

Inflation Accounting

Issues of funds flow, income measurement and future orientation of reporting all are influenced by the significant changes in the environment caused by rapidly changing prices. Inflation in many respects has dominated accounting issues in recent years, and

14. SEC reg. S-K, item 11, par. 3iv, "Instructions," par. 5.
15. SEC Release no. 33–6293, *Revision of Property, Plant and Equipment Disclosure Requirements*, February 25, 1981.
16. FASB Discussion Memorandum, *Reporting Funds Flows, Liquidity, and Financial Flexibility* (Stamford, Conn.: FASB, December 15, 1980).

17. FASB Financial Accounting Concepts Statement no. 3, *Elements of Financial Statements of Business Enterprises* (Stamford, Conn.: FASB, 1980).

unfortunately it seems likely to do so in the years to come. With price stability, predictability of results is enhanced, funds flows and income flows tend to come together in the long run and the implicit assumption of accounting that a dollar of cost produces a dollar of value has relative stability over time. Under inflationary conditions, however, the weaknesses of accounting are magnified and the traditional accounting model cannot be applied without distortions appearing in virtually every application where significant time lags occur in recording related events.

Since double digit inflation first appeared in the U.S. in 1974-75, both the FASB and the SEC have been active in trying to ensure that investors obtain information which will enable them to determine the effect of changing prices on business enterprises. The SEC adopted ASR no. 190[18] in 1976 requiring supplemental disclosure of replacement cost data relating to inventories, fixed assets, cost of sales and depreciation. In 1979, the FASB adopted Statement no. 33, which supplanted disclosure, either in footnotes or a separate section, of general price level adjusted data (the constant dollar approach) and current cost data (which reflect the current costs of the particular products being manufactured or sold and the current cost of facilities).

The 1980 annual reports of large companies for the first time include all the data mandated by Statement no. 33. These reports provide required supplemental data in a variety of formats, and researchers are now beginning the process of analyzing the information. The FASB has proposed a research plan that will include the creation of a data bank to assist researchers in appraising the data and testing hypotheses regarding its usefulness.

Users are now developing techniques for the interpretation of the data. Some are most concerned with the asset valuation implications. Statement no. 33 data more accurately reflect the value of assets, which has been gravely distorted in financial statements by the use of historical cost and nominal dollars. Current cost disclosure provides data for at least an approximation of the current cost of inventories and property, plant and equipment. Current cost is not the equivalent of the assets' current market price and is therefore not their liquidation value, but it does offer an approximation of what the assets might be worth in an operating entity. Other analysts are looking for more stable relationships between income statement variables when current costs are used and

for better approximations of future cash flows. As experience is gained and research completed, a more systematic picture of the value of these data will emerge, and conclusions can then be drawn about the feasibility of revising the basic accounting model.

Up to the present, it is rather strange that more time and effort have been devoted by the accounting profession to developing measurement techniques to reflect inflation's effect on financial statements than seems to have been spent by management in creating techniques for managing in an inflationary environment. Only recently have some managements begun to consider the use of the measurement techniques to provide data for planning and operating decisions. In the next few years, it is likely that greater development will come in this area than in external financial reporting.

Any management can deal with inflation intuitively as long as the rate is both known and predictable, even if the rate is high. The major managerial problems arise when the rate is uncertain and variable. Under such conditions, techniques must be developed to deal with a dynamic environment and minimize the impact of change, and here sophisticated measurement and analytical techniques must be developed. Managers must pay more attention to asset and liability balance relationships as well as budgeting operating fund flows. Controls must factor in diverse inflationary assumptions, and the sensitivity of results to changing prices must be known, particularly when long-run investment decisions are being made.

While the managerial impact is based primarily on the unexpected variability of the inflation rate, the direction taken in inflation accounting for external reporting purposes is probably dependent on the average level of the rate of inflation. If the rate should drop to 5 percent, a lot of today's important issues will recede. If the rate goes up to 30 percent, there will probably be mounting pressure for including inflation-adjusted numbers in basic financial statements. By way of illustration, the United Kingdom, with a higher basic inflation rate, now gives companies the option of presenting current cost data either in the basic financial statements or as supplemental data. Both historical and current cost are required, but the company is allowed to choose the presentation method.

Pension Cost

Since inflation causes the greatest accounting problems when a long time span exists between the point where measurement is required and that where cash is transferred, it is not surprising that the FASB is

18. ASR no. 190, *Notice of Adoption of Amendments to Regulation S-X Requiring Disclosure of Certain Replacement Cost Data*, March 23, 1976.

faced with difficulties in the pension accounting area. To date the board has faced only the problem of how pension plans themselves should account. In the near future, however, it must face the far more significant problem of how pension costs should be accounted for by employers, and it is here where the most controversy will arise. Decisions made by the board in this area will likely have the largest effect on reported results of any faced in the decade of the 1980s, since the proportion of compensation represented by deferrals is growing steadily.

Unfortunately, the board's record in dealing with the lesser problem of pension plan liabilities does not provide much confidence that analysts' interest in the approach leading to the most valid prediction of long-run future cash flows will be well served. In 1980, when the FASB issued Statement no. 35, *Accounting and Reporting by Defined Benefit Pension Plans*,[19] it had to make a number of significant decisions. First, it decided that in pension fund accounts assets must be carried at market value. When considering how to measure the liability for pensions in the pension fund's accounts (not the corporation's statements), the board then had three choices to make. All three of its decisions served to minimize the liability reported by these funds.

First, the FASB mandated use of an accrued benefit method. This in effect means that instead of charging an equal amount each year to build up the amount that will be paid at retirement, the fund will record an amount the first year which will ultimately accrue, by compounding, into an amount sufficient to pay a proportionate share of the value of the payment needed at retirement under the plan's terms. The board thus says that in earlier years a smaller amount is recorded as an increase to the fund's liability and in later years more must be added than under other methods. The result is that the use of the so-called accrued benefit method tends to make the reported liability small in relation to the liability measured in economic terms based on the most likely payments.

Second, the FASB opted for using current salary levels in making the estimate of future disbursements for pensions. That means that even though a pension plan may say that a pension is based on salaries in the last three years prior to retirement, the estimates do not include any provisions for increased salaries resulting from inflation.

Third, the FASB decided that current rates of return are to be used in computing the discount

factor. Since current rates of return take inflation into account, they are certainly higher than a pure monetary rate of return, but the salaries used to figure the benefits—the outflows in this actuarial calculation—don't take inflation into account. Thus, each of the FASB's three choices tended to lower the fund's liability.

As the board proceeds with its re-examination of pension issues from the perspective of the employer, it will face a number of these issues again as it evaluates the problem of pension cost. It has indicated that employer cost and the related question of pension liabilities are not simply mirror images of pension plan accounting by issuing a discussion memorandum which addresses issues without the presumption that employer accounting will follow from the decisions made in Statement no. 35. As this project progresses to its scheduled completion in 1983, the board will be faced with significant decisions. If it adopts a similar liability approach to that in Statement no. 35, it will necessarily adopt a measure of pension costs which is loaded toward the closing years of an employee's service, thus allocating this important element of compensation disproportionately over this period. If, as seems likely, companies conform their accounting and their cash contributions to the plan, this will mean that a significant cash outflow will occur in later periods, perhaps affecting the firm's long-run liquidity and financial flexibility. Even if a company elected to pay out cash in a different pattern, the accounting method based on Statement no. 35 would overstate earning power by failing to reflect a realistic pension cost. I hope that the board will listen to the concerns expressed by analysts and others and develop an approach to cost measurement which reflects pension cost at a level at least equal to an equal percentage of pay over working life. The issues are not simple—they are highly technical and warrant serious attention because of the magnitude of these costs in the future.

Foreign Currency Translation

The obvious troubles caused by inflation in measuring financial position and results of operations domestically are compounded when an enterprise is subject to various rates of price change throughout the world fluctuating relatively with each other and then is faced with the necessity of translating these results into a single currency unit for presentation to stockholders and other investors. It is not surprising, therefore, that foreign currency translation has caused no end of difficulty for the FASB and other standard-setting bodies around the world.

19. FASB Statement no. 35, *Accounting and Reporting by Defined Benefit Pension Plans* (Stamford, Conn.: FASB, 1980).

There is little question that of all the statements published by the FASB, the one that is most faithful to the historical cost accounting model, and the one that is most rigorously logical, is Statement no. 8, *Accounting for the Translation of Foreign Currency Transactions and Foreign Currency Financial Statements.*[20] Its requirements provide fundamental, theoretical consistency with today's accounting model. There is a general perception, however, that its application does not produce economic information which makes sense. In large part the complaints relate to deficiencies in the accounting model but in this case they reached a crescendo which required board attention. To do something about the statement, the FASB had a range of choices which basically fell into two categories.

One option was to tinker with Statement no. 8 and try to make some changes that would ameliorate some of the perceived problems. The other was to make a very fundamental change in the basic principles of consolidations and foreign currency translation. In its first exposure draft, the FASB opted for the second approach. It made fundamental changes. It moved from the so-called temporal method, where items were reflected on the basis of historical cost and exchange rates when assets were acquired, to a current exchange rate basis. In effect, therefore, current value accounting was introduced, at least as far as foreign currencies were concerned. This was inconsistent with the accounting model, but many found the approach to be more understandable.

This change did not solve the problem of removing large and unstable translation gains and losses from income but simply reflected gains and losses on equity investment rather than on net liquid assets investment. To deal with fluctuations, the FASB made another surprising decision. It offered up the long discredited direct charge to surplus and said in the exposure draft that gains and losses on foreign currency translations (those that arise from the accounting process) may be charged into a separate surplus account and need not appear in the income statement. These were two very fundamental changes. They prejudged a number of issues that the conceptual framework was to address, and various people were very critical. After hearings last December, which failed to produce a clear majority of views among commentators or board members, FASB Chairman Donald J. Kirk said that the board may have to withdraw the draft for reconsideration. The board will issue a new exposure draft, and it is unlikely that any statement will be effective until calender year 1983.[21]

Municipal Accounting

A final area of financial reporting which is generating controversy and activity at present and which seems likely to be a place where considerable accounting innovation and change will occur in the 1980s is state and local governmental accounting. There seems to be general agreement that state and local governmental financial reporting is deficient, and that it does not provide a sound basis for economic accountability. What is not clear is how this problem should be dealt with. There are broad disagreements both about accounting and reporting issues and about what entity should take responsibility for standard setting in the area.

The "turf" issue is most active at the present time. The FASB views its franchise as broad and believes that it is an appropriate extension of its authority to set standards for governmental units. The representatives of government view this as dangerous, unsatisfactory and unconstitutional. Accordingly, people in the government have said they will resist standards set by the FASB. Basically they argue that those in government know most about its problems and therefore should be the ones to make determinations regarding standards of accountability. This logic was rejected long ago in the private sector. There was a time when it was argued that it should be companies and financial officers who set accounting standards; since then the consensus has held that the authority is best vested in an independent body.

A recent suggestion by a committee made up of members of the AICPA and governmental organizations that a governmental accounting standards board be created seems to be a grave error. Someone with an independent perspective should make standards decisions and the creation of two standards boards will lead to continuing conflicts and possibly the weakening of the FASB. Although testimony at recent hearings held by the committee on its proposal resulted in diverse views, no one stepped forward to provide financing for the proposed GASB, nor were "turf" issues resolved.

Underlying the controversy is a fundamental substantive issue regarding the differences which exist between governmental and nongovernmental ac-

20. FASB Statement no. 8, *Accounting for the Translation of Foreign Currency Transactions and Foreign Currency Financial Statements* (Stamford, Conn.: FASB, 1975).

21. "FASB Statement no. 8 Replacement May Not Take Effect Till 1983, FASB Official Discloses," JofA, June 81, p. 7.

counting. Views range from extreme positions that see no similarities on the one hand and no differences on the other. Actually, a middle ground seems likely to emerge. It is clear that governmental accounting does not have a qualitative bottom line such as net income and that performance in the public sector requires a balancing of intransitive service efforts and service outputs. At the same time, cost measurement in economic terms is a legitimate objective of both private and public sectors, and the largest number of "accounting" problems seem to arise in this process.

I hope that over time the FASB will be able to move into this area with adequate recognition of the differences which exist between government and the private sector and with adequate staff resources and industry assistance to do the standard-setting job.

Summary

These various trends in financial reporting promise a decade of continuing evolution in the financial reporting scene. As each of these trends is examined, the impact of an inflationary environment on both business and government is a consistent thread, as is the presence of the FASB. If we see a continuation of changing and unpredictable inflationary move-ments, it is unlikely that any solutions will provide stability in financial reporting, and the most probable projection is for continuing rapid and evolutionary changes in the reporting environment. Under such conditions, the need for an authoritative standard-setting body with a coherent framework for viewing problems is very great. Such a body must provide intellectual leadership in accounting measurement, with due recognition of the problems of the world. While the comments above indicate some disagreements with specific actions taken by the FASB, that board still seems to have a solid institutional structure and to offer the greatest hope for sound, consistent and rigorous standard setting.

The combination of a private sector standard-setting body with oversight and occasional creative stimulation by the SEC has provided us with a generally sound accounting structure in the past. Under conditions of economic strain which test the underpinnings of the accounting model, any system will be challenged to sustain its viability. The emerging trends noted in this article suggest a dynamism in the development of financial reporting that bodes well for its creative and responsive evolution in the decade ahead.

Chapter Eighteen

Corporations: Long-Term Liabilities

Reviewing the Chapter

1. Corporations frequently issue long-term **bonds** or notes to raise funds. The holders of these bonds or notes are creditors of the corporation. They are entitled to periodic interest, plus the principal of the debt on some specified date. As is true for all creditors, their claims for interest and principal take priority over stockholders' claims.

2. Bonds are normally due ten to fifty years after issue, and interest is usually paid semiannually. When bonds are issued, the corporation executes a contract with the bondholders called a **bond indenture**. In addition, the company issues **bond certificates** as evidence of its debt to the bondholders. A **bond issue** is made up of the total number of bonds available at the same time. Bonds are usually issued with a face value that is some multiple of $1,000, and carry a variety of features.
   a. **Secured bonds** give the bondholders a claim to certain assets of the company upon default. **Unsecured bonds** (called **debenture bonds**) do not.
   b. When all the bonds of an issue mature on the same date, they are called **term bonds**. When the bonds mature over several maturity dates, they are called **serial bonds**.
   c. When **registered bonds** are issued, the corporation maintains a record of all bondholders and pays interest by check to the bondholders of record. **Coupon bonds**, on the other hand, entitle the bearer to interest when the detachable coupons are deposited with the bank.

3. Bonds payable due in the current period can be classified as a current liability only if they will be paid with current assets. In addition, the characteristics of all bonds should be disclosed in the notes to the financial statements.

4. Bond prices are expressed as a percentage of face value. For example, when bonds with a face value of $100,000 are issued at 97, the company will receive $97,000.

5. When the bond interest rate equals the market rate for similar bonds on the issue date, the company will probably receive face value for the bonds.

6. Regardless of the issue price, bondholders are entitled to interest, which is based on the face amount. Interest for a period of time is computed by the formula

   interest = principal × rate × time

   A 360-day year is used.

7. When bonds are issued between interest dates, the interest that has accrued since the last interest date is collected from the investor upon issue. It is then returned to the investor (along with the interest earned) on the next interest date.

8. When the bond interest rate is less than the market rate for similar bonds on the issue date, the bonds will probably sell at a **discount** (less than face value).

9. Unamortized Bond Discount is a contra account to Bonds Payable on the balance sheet. The difference between the two amounts is called the carrying value. The carrying value increases as the discount is amortized and equals the face value of the bonds at maturity.

10. A discount on bonds payable is considered an interest charge that must be amortized (spread out) over the life of the bond. Amortization is generally recorded on the interest payment dates, using either the straight-line or effective interest method.

11. Under the straight-line method of amortization, the amount to be amortized each interest period equals the bond discount divided by the number of interest payments during the life of the bond.

12. The effective interest method of amortization is more difficult to apply than the straight-line method but should be used instead when the amounts differ significantly.

13. To apply the **effective interest method** when a discount is involved, the market rate of interest must first be determined for similar securities when the bonds were issued (called the effective rate of interest). This interest rate (halved for semiannual interest) is multiplied by the existing carrying value of the bonds for each interest period to obtain Bond Interest Expense to be recorded. The actual interest paid is then subtracted from the bond interest expense recorded to obtain the discount amortization for the period. Because the unamortized discount is now less, the carrying value is now greater. This new carrying value is applied to the next period, and the same amortization procedure is applied.

14. When the bond interest rate is greater than the market rate for similar bonds on the issue date, the bonds will probably sell at a **premium** (greater than face value).

15. Premium on Bonds Payable is added to Bonds Payable in the balance sheet to produce the carrying value. Amortization of the premium acts as an offset against interest paid in determining Interest Expense to be recorded. Under the straight-line method, the premium to be amortized in each period equals the bond premium divided by the number of interest payments during the life of the bond.

16. The effective interest method is applied to bond premiums in the same way that it is applied to bond discounts. The only difference is that the amortization for the period is figured by subtracting the Bond Interest Expense recorded from the actual interest paid (the reverse is done for amortizing a discount).

17. When the accounting period ends between interest dates, the accrued interest as well as the proportionate discount or premium amortization must be recorded.

18. **Callable bonds** are bonds that may be retired by the corporation before the maturity date. When the market rate for bond interest drops, a company may wish to call its bonds and substitute debt with a lower interest rate. When bonds are called (for whatever reason), an entry is needed to eliminate Bonds Payable and any unamortized premium or discount, and to record the payment of cash at the call price. In addition, a gain or loss on the retirement of the bonds would be recorded.

19. **Convertible bonds** are bonds that may be exchanged for other securities (usually common stock) at the option of the bondholder. When a bondholder converts his or her bonds into common stock, the common stock is recorded by the company at the carrying value of the bonds. Specifically, the entry will eliminate Bonds Payable as well as any unamortized discount or premium, and will record common stock and paid-in capital in excess of par value. No gain or loss is recorded.

20. **A bond sinking fund** is established by corporations to assure that bondholders will be paid at maturity. Over the life of the bonds, the corporation will make fixed deposits to the sinking fund trustee, who invests the funds. At the maturity date, the sum of the fixed deposits plus sinking fund earnings should approximately equal the maturity value of the bonds. Bond sinking funds are classified on the balance sheet as long-term investments. In addition to, or instead of, the sinking fund, an appropriation of retained earnings may be set up.

21. A deposit into a bond sinking fund is recorded with a debit to Bond Sinking Fund and a credit to Cash. Sinking fund earnings are recorded with a debit to Bond Sinking Fund and a credit to Income from Bond Sinking Fund. A loss from the sale of sinking fund investments would be recorded with a debit to Loss on Sale of Sinking Fund Investment and a credit to Bond Sinking Fund. When the bonds are retired with the use of the sinking fund, Bonds Payable would be debited, Bond Sinking Fund credited, and Cash debited or credited, depending on whether there was an excess or a deficiency.

22. **A mortgage** is a long-term debt payable in equal monthly installments, and secured by real property. Upon payment of the mortgage, both Mortgage Payable and Mortgage Interest Expense are debited, and Cash is credited. Each month, the interest portion of the payment decreases, while the principal portion of the payment increases.

23. A lease is a contract that allows a business or individual to use an asset for a specific length of time in return for periodic payments. A **capital lease** is so much like a sale (as determined by certain criteria) that it should be recorded by the lessee as an asset (to be depreciated) and a related liability. An **operating lease** is a lease that does not meet the criteria for capital leases, and should be recorded only as Rent Expense for each period leased.

24. **A pension plan** is a program whereby a company agrees to pay benefits to its employees after they retire. Benefits to retirees are usually paid out of a **pension fund**. The two costs associated with pension plans are normal pension costs and past service costs. **Normal pension costs** measure service credit earned for the current year as translated into payments to the employee upon retirement. **Past service costs**, on the other hand, measure service credit earned during years *prior* to the initiation of the pension plan.

25. Computing income taxes for financial reporting differs from computing income taxes due the government for the same accounting period. This difference is caused by the fact that financial reporting income is governed by generally accepted accounting principles, whereas taxable income is governed by the Internal Revenue Code. Accordingly, when income for financial reporting differs materially from taxable income, the income tax allocation technique should be used. Under this method, the difference between the current tax liability and income tax expense is debited or credited to an account called Deferred Income Taxes.

Testing Your Knowledge

Matching

Match each term with its definition by writing the appropriate letter in the blank.

_I_ 1. Bonds
_D_ 2. Bond indenture
_Q_ 3. Secured bonds
_A_ 4. Debenture bonds
_O_ 5. Term bonds
_T_ 6. Serial bonds
_J_ 7. Registered bonds
_F_ 8. Coupon bonds
_C_ 9. Callable bonds
_R_ 10. Convertible bonds
_E_ 11. Bond discount
_M_ 12. Bond premium
_L_ 13. Effective interest method
_B_ 14. Capital lease
_G_ 15. Operating lease
_S_ 16. Bond sinking fund
_N_ 17. Pension plan
_H_ 18. Normal pension cost
_K_ 19. Past service cost
_P_ 20. Income tax allocation

a. Unsecured bonds
b. A lease that amounts to a sale
c. Bonds that may be retired by the company before maturity
d. The contract between the bondholder and the corporation
e. The difference between par and a lower amount paid for bonds
f. Bonds with detachable forms that are redeemed for interest
g. A true lease, recorded with debits to Rent Expense
h. Service credit earned during the current year, as translated into payments at retirement
i. Long-term debt instruments
j. Bonds whose owners receive interest by check directly from the company
k. Service credit earned during prior years, as translated into payments at retirement
l. The amortization method based on carrying value
m. The difference between par and a greater amount paid for bonds
n. A program whereby a company agrees to pay benefits to its employees when they retire
o. Bonds that mature on one specific date
p. A technique that reconciles the difference between financial reporting taxes and the actual tax liability
q. Bonds that are backed by certain assets
r. Bonds that may be exchanged for stock
s. An investment used to pay off bonds at maturity
t. Bonds that mature in installments

Completion

Use the lines provided to complete each item.

1. Distinguish between the terms _debenture_ and _indenture_.

Indenture is the agreement between bondholders + corp issuing ; Debenture is a bond not secured by any specific assets

2. Under what circumstance would a premium probably be received on a bond issue?

If mrkt interest is higher than face interest.

3. What is the formula for computing interest for a period of time?

principal × rate × time = interest

True-False

Circle T if the statement is true, F if it is false.

T F **1.** Bondholders are creditors of a corporation.

T F **2.** A term bond matures on one particular date.

T **F** **3.** Bond interest expense can be paid only when declared by the board of directors.

T F **4.** Bonds with a lower interest rate than market (for similar bonds) will probably sell at a discount.

T **F** **5.** When a bond premium is amortized, the bond interest expense recorded will be greater than the cash recorded.

T F **6.** When the effective interest method is used to amortize a bond discount, the amount amortized will increase each year.

T **F** **7.** When bonds are issued between interest dates, Bond Interest Expense is debited for accrued interest since the last interest date.

credited

T F **8.** As a bond premium is amortized, the carrying value of bonds payable will decrease.

T **F** **9.** A bond sinking fund will probably increase in size more in year 2 than it will in year 5.

T F **10.** When bonds are converted into stock, no gain or loss should be recorded.

T F **11.** When bonds are retired, all of the premium or discount associated with the bonds must be canceled.

T **F** **12.** When the effective interest method is used to amortize a premium on bonds payable, the premium amortized will decrease in amount each year.

T **F** **13.** Bond sinking funds are classified as current assets in the balance sheet.

T F **14.** Under capital leases, assets should be recorded at the present value of future lease payments.

T F **15.** Pension Expense is usually difficult to measure because it is based on many estimates, such as employee life expectancy and employee turnover.

T F **16.** If taxable income were always equal to accounting income, there would be no need for income tax allocation.

Multiple-Choice

Circle the letter of the best answer.

1. Assume that $900,000 of 5 percent bonds are issued (at face value) two months before the next semiannual interest date. Which of the following statements correctly describes the journal entry?
a. Cash is debited for $800,000.
b. Cash is debited for $807,500.
c. Bond Interest Expense is credited for $7,500.
d. Bond Interest Expense is credited for $15,000.

2. A company has $600,000 in bonds payable with an unamortized premium of $12,000. If one-third of the bonds are converted to common stock, the carrying value of the bonds payable will decrease by
a. $196,000.
b. $200,000.
c. $204,000.
d. $208,000.

3. As a mortgage is paid off,
   a. the principal portion of the fixed payment increases.
   b. the interest portion of the fixed payment increases.
   c. the principal and interest portions do not change each interest period.
   d. the monthly payments increase.

4. Premium on Bonds Payable is presented on the balance sheet as
   a. a long-term asset.
   b. an addition to Bond Sinking Fund.
   c. a deduction from Bonds Payable.
   d. an addition to Bonds Payable.

5. When the interest dates on a bond issue are May 1 and November 1, the adjusting entry to record Bond Interest Expense on December 31 might include a
   a. debit to Bond Interest Payable.
   b. credit to Cash.
   c. credit to Unamortized Bond Discount.
   d. credit to Bond Interest Expense.

6. Under the effective interest method, as a discount is amortized,
   a. the amount amortized will decrease each period.
   b. the Interest Expense recorded will increase each period.
   c. interest paid to bondholders will increase each period.
   d. the bonds' carrying value will decrease each period.

7. Which of the following would probably be considered an operating lease?
   a. A 6-year lease on equipment with an option to renew for another 6 years
   b. A 5-year lease on machinery, cancelable at the end of the lease period by the lessor
   c. A 40-year lease on a building equal to its useful life
   d. A 7-year lease on a company vehicle with an option to buy the vehicle for $1 at the end of the lease period

8. A $200,000 bond issue with a carrying value of $195,000 is called at 102 and retired. Which of the following statements is true about the journal entry prepared?
   a. A gain of $5,000 is recorded.
   b. A loss of $4,000 is recorded.
   c. A loss of $9,000 is recorded.
   d. No gain or loss is recorded.

Applying Your Knowledge

Exercises

1. A corporation issues $600,000 of 7 percent, 10-year bonds at 98½ on one of its semiannual interest dates. Assuming straight-line amortization, answer each of the following questions.
   a. What is the amount of the bond discount? $ 9000

   b. How much interest is paid on the next interest date? $ 21,000

   c. How much bond interest expense is recorded on the next interest date?
      $ 21,450
      450 = 9000 ÷ 20

   d. After 3 years, what is the carrying value of the bonds? $ 593,700

2. A corporation issues $500,000 of 7 percent, 20-year bonds at 110. Interest is paid semiannually, and the effective interest method is used for amortization. Assume that the market rate for similar investments is 6 percent, and the bonds are issued on an interest date.

a. What amount was received for the bonds? $ _550,000_

b. How much interest is paid each interest period? $ _17,500_

c. How much bond interest expense is recorded on the first interest date? $ _16,500_

d. How much of the premium is amortized on the first interest date? $ _1000_

e. What is the carrying value of the bonds after the first interest date? $ _549,000_

3. Pennco issued $600,000 of 8 percent, 10-year bonds at 106. In the space provided, calculate the total interest cost.

600,000 × 8% = 48000 × 10 =

$480,000

−premium = 36,000 ÷ 10 = 3600/yr

480,000 − 36,000 = 444,000

4. Jamison Corporation had taxable income of $80,000, $20,000, and $60,000 in 19x1, 19x2, and 19x3, respectively. Its income for accounting purposes was $60,000, $30,000, and $70,000 for 19x1, 19x2, and 19x3, respectively. The difference between tax and accounting income was due to $30,000 in revenues that were recognized in full for tax purposes in 19x1, but were recognized one-third per year for accounting purposes. Make the correct journal entry to record income taxes in each of the three years. Assume a 40 percent tax rate.

General Journal

Date		Description	Debit	Credit
12/31	81	Income Taxes ~~Payable~~ Expense	24,000	
		Deferred Tax	8000	
		Current Tax Payable		32,000
	82	Income Tax Expense	12,000	
		Deferred Tax		4000
		Current Tax Payable		8000
	83	Income Tax Expense	28,000	
		Deferred Tax	~~4000~~	4000
		Current Tax Payable		28,000

Crossword Puzzle
For Chapters 17 and 18

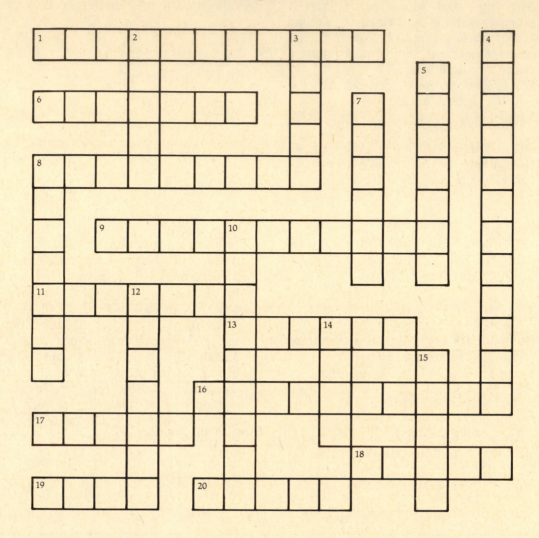

ACROSS

1. Arrangement for retirement income (2 words)
6. Bonds _____ (liability account)
8. Unsecured bond
9. Item given special tax treatment (2 words)
11. Type of capital structure
13. Bond whose interest is paid to the bearer
16. Bond whose owner is recorded by the company
17. See 20-Across
18. Sale (of bonds)
19. Bonds with one maturity date
20. With 17-Across, a corporate move to lower the market price of stock

DOWN

2. Primary earnings per _____
3. Use another's property for a fee
4. Retained earnings set aside
5. Fund to retire bonds
7. Bonds that mature in installments
8. Negative retained earnings
10. Deduction from IRS liability (2 words)
12. Opposite of bond discount
14. _____ service cost
15. 1974 law regulating 1-Across

Pension Accounting: The Liability Question

Do pension obligations belong on the balance sheet?

Financial reports are not telling the whole story about pensions. But how should that story be told? Should some part of the pension obligations not currently recognized as a liability be included on the balance sheet of the employer? Is there an unrecorded liability for pensions under existing generally accepted accounting principles?

We want to discuss this aspect of pension accounting for three reasons. First, the many questions in the pension accounting area are so complex that they all cannot be effectively discussed at once, and the answer to the liability question does not appear to depend on answers to other questions. Second, and more important, the question is one of the most significant in terms of the changes from current accounting that could result from the Financial Accounting Standards Board's pension accounting project. That significance can help us to achieve our primary objective—to stimulate thinking about and discussion of the issues involved in the board's project. Third, a majority of the speakers at the FASB's July 13–15 public hearings in New York on its discussion memorandum (DM), *Employers' Accounting for Pensions and Other Postemployment Benefits,*[1] took positions against including pension obligations on employers' balance sheets and provided a variety of supporting arguments. We believe an interesting case can be made *for* recognizing pension liabilities, and that case should be considered and debated by those who are interested in pension accounting questions.[2]

To understand better how the weight of pension liabilities can affect major decisions of management, consider the following report in the press: "Esmark announced recently that it was putting its meat-packing subsidiary, Swift Fresh Meats Division, on the market—and funding the subsidiary's 'sizable' unfunded pension liabilities.

"'They had to do that to make it saleable,' one Esmark analyst commented."

The same article also included a description of another situation: "One instance where pension liabilities were not adequately covered in the original deal—and later came back to haunt a firm—involved the spin-off in 1976 of Facet Enterprises from The Bendix Corp. The divestiture was ordered by the Federal Trade Commission, and Bendix formed Facet as a subsidiary, transferred certain business units to Facet and in 1976 distributed all of the stock of Facet to the common stockholders of Bendix. Included in the transfer to Facet were large unfunded pension liabilities.

"Facet eventually filed suit against Bendix, charging the company was aware of 'highly detrimental finan-

Source: Article by Timothy S. Lucas and Betsy Ann Hollowell. Reprinted from the October 1981 issue of *The Journal of Accountancy*. Copyright ©1981 by the American Institute of Certified Public Accountants, Inc.

1. Financial Accounting Standards Board Discussion Memorandum, *Employers' Accounting for Pensions and Other Postemployment Benefits* (Stamford, Conn.: FASB, 1981).

2. The liability question is one of eight issues addressed in the DM. This article does not attempt to cover other closely related questions, including how to measure the liability if it is to be recorded and the nature of the offsetting debit that arises if a liability is recorded. Measuring or determining the amount of the liability is complex and involves two problems. First, any measure of the pension obligation involves estimating future events, such as how long retirees will live and how many employees will leave before vesting or die before retiring. Second, even after all the estimates are made, there are different attributes of the obligation that may be measured, including vested benefits, accumulated benefits and prior service cost determined under one or more actuarial cost methods. Determining the amount that might be recorded as a liability is beyond the scope of this article, but it involves understanding events related to the growth of the pension obligation as an employee's career progresses from hiring to retirement. The possible choices with regard to the nature of the offsetting debit that arises if a liability is recorded discussed in the DM include recording the debit as an intangible asset or as some kind of charge on the income statement.

cial consequences' the transfer of the obligation would have on Facet."[3]

Facet Enterprises subsequently notified the Pension Benefit Guaranty Corp. that it was terminating the pension plan, which covered some twenty-two hundred employees and retirees. Facet said that terminating the pension plan was necessary to rescue its financially troubled automotive parts divisions and that the plan's unfunded liabilities of about $31 million exceeded the net worth of the three units it covered.

At about the same time, *Fortune* reported:

"When Kaiser Steel was considering liquidation last September . . . some people saw an opportunity for a quick profit in the stock. They believed the sell-off of Kaiser's various properties would fetch considerably more than the $44 per share its stock was going for. This reasoning, however, overlooked the company's unfunded vested pension liability of about $9 per share *and* the even larger amount Kaiser says it would have had to fork over to provide health insurance and other benefits to retirees. When Kaiser's directors eventually voted not to liquidate, they gave as one reason the size of these burdens. The board concluded the liquidation value could actually be *below* the $44 market price."[4]

In these situations, which unfortunately are not unique, a pension obligation had an unexpected and newsworthy effect on the economic potential and well-being of the company. The pension obligation was not suddenly created in any of these situations. It existed all along, but it was not reported as a liability. Although each company had prepared financial statements in accordance with GAAP, the pension situation was not fully understood, even by knowledgeable readers of those statements.

Current Pension GAAP

Employer accounting for pensions is based, at present, on Accounting Principles Board Opinion no. 8, *Accounting for the Cost of Pension Plans,*[5] as amended by FASB Statement no. 36, *Disclosure of Pension Information.*[6] Opinion no. 8 allows pension cost to be determined under any of a number of acceptable actuarial cost methods. Typically, the method used to determine funding of a pension plan (the annual contribution to the pension fund or trust) is also used for accounting.

Under current GAAP, most balance sheets do not include a line item labeled "pension liability." Nevertheless, under Opinion no. 8 part of the pension obligation is recorded as a liability. The amount of liability recorded (debit expense, credit liability) typically is equal to the amount of liability discharged by the contribution (debit liability, credit cash). This is because contributions to the pension plan are recorded as discharges of the pension liability and because most companies fund pension cost accrued. The resulting net liability—the amount appearing on the balance sheet—is zero. But the amount expensed and contributed to the plan cannot be called an unrecorded liability in the usual sense. It does not appear on the balance sheet only because the transfer of assets to the pension fund is regarded as payment of the liability. If, instead, we view the transfer as a segregation or setting aside of assets, it would be logical to add the accumulated amounts expensed (the liability) and the assets held by the plan to the balance sheet.

But for most employers and most plans another part of the pension obligation has not yet been expensed, recorded as a liability or "discharged" by contributions to the plan. The pension obligation that is not recorded as a liability under current GAAP results, primarily, from plan amendments. Parts of that obligation also may result from establishment of new plans and from cumulative experience gains and losses, but for simplicity we will focus on plan amendments. When a pension plan is amended to increase benefits, the increased benefits usually are granted based on service, including service rendered before the date of the change. In some cases benefits also are increased for former employees who are already retired. After such an amendment, the employer's pension obligation is larger than it was before. It is this incremental obligation that some believe should be recorded as a liability. This view is based on the idea that the employer has an obligation for benefits already earned by employees. The amount of benefits earned (however measured) will not necessarily coincide with the accumulation of prior years' normal costs and amortization of prior service costs recorded under Opinion no. 8.

For convenience, let's assume that we are dealing with a typical company that sponsors a single-employer, defined-benefit pension plan. The plan provides a retirement income benefit of, say, $50 per month for each year of an employee's service. In the current year, the company amends the plan to increase the benefits to $60 per month per year of ser-

3. Maria Crawford Scott, "Pension Liabilities May Hurt Merger," *Pensions and Investments*, October 13, 1980, p. 4.
4. Mary Greenebaum, "The Market Has Spotted Those Pension Problems," *Fortune*, December 1, 1980, p. 146.
5. Accounting Principles Board Opinion no. 8, *Accounting for the Cost of Pension Plans* (New York: AICPA, 1966).
6. FASB Statement no. 36, *Disclosure of Pension Information* (Stamford, Conn.: FASB, 1980).

vice for all active employees and for retirees who are receiving pensions. The amendment provides for increased benefits based on all of an employee's years of service, past as well as future. Actuaries will review the change and compute the new, increased amount of contribution the company will pay over a period of years to fund the increased benefits. The accounting question is, When the plan is amended, does a recordable liability arise for that part of the increased benefits attributed to past years of service?

Opinion no. 8 accounting reflects such an amendment prospectively, usually based on the way the cost of the amendment will be funded. No increase in liability is recorded immediately as a result of the event that occurred when the plan was amended. Instead, it is provided for and recorded as expense and a liability a little bit at a time.

Whether a recordable liability arises when the plan is amended depends on what kinds of things belong on balance sheets. Accountants and users of financial statements generally understand the nature of items on balance sheets, including liabilities. That knowledge makes the balance sheet useful. Liabilities such as accounts payable, notes payable and bonds payable all have something in common. And, most important, all accounts, notes and bonds payable are included. If each company had the flexibility to omit some of these items in the footnotes, the usefulness of the balance sheet would be reduced. Analysts would doubtless add the "footnote liabilities" to those on the statement and construct their own adjusted balance sheets (as some do today with pension disclosures), but the convenience of having a complete balance sheet would be lost and some users might be misled because they expect all liabilities to be included.

The FASB has begun the process of describing the kinds of things that belong on the right-hand side of a balance sheet by providing a definition of liabilities. Financial Accounting Concepts Statement no. 3, *Elements of Financial Statements of Business Enterprises,* defines liabilities as "probable future sacrifices of economic benefits arising from present obligations of a particular entity to transfer assets or provide services to other entities in the future as a result of past transactions or events."[7]

The concepts statement also identifies three essential characteristics of a liability inherent in the definition: ". . . (a) it embodies a present duty or responsibility to one or more other entities that entails settlement by probable future transfer or use of assets at a speci-

fied or determinable date, on occurrence of a specified event, or on demand, (b) the duty or responsibility obligates a particular enterprise, leaving it little or no discretion to avoid the future sacrifice, and (c) the transaction or other event obligating the enterprise has already happened."[8]

In addition, it discusses other features often found in liabilities: "Liabilities commonly have other features that help identify them—for example, most liabilities require the obligated enterprise to pay cash to one or more identified other entities and are legally enforceable. However, those features are not essential characteristics of liabilities. Their absence, by itself, is not sufficient to preclude an item's qualifying as a liability. That is, liabilities may not require an enterprise to pay cash but to convey other assets, to provide or stand ready to provide services, or to use assets. And as long as payment or other transfer of assets to settle an existing obligation is probable, the identity of the recipient need not be known to the obligated enterprise before the time of settlement. Similarly, although most liabilities rest generally on a foundation of legal rights and duties, existence of a legally enforceable claim is not a prerequisite for an obligation to qualify as a liability if the future payment of cash or other transfer of assets to settle the obligation is otherwise probable."[9]

A careful reading of the above excerpts reveals that the definition of liabilities is primarily a description of current practice; it is not a radical change but a formal description of the kinds of things that we already think of as liabilities. Accountants are likely to agree, for example, that accrued salaries payable is a liability because the company has a responsibility or obligation to employees who have performed services for which they have not yet been paid. The obligation probably will be satisfied by paying the accrued amounts (transferring assets) at a future date, and the event that obligated the company (the performance of the services) has already occurred.

On the other hand, a budgeted expenditure to replace a machine is not a liability, even though the transfer of assets may be virtually certain and the need to replace the machine acute. The budgeted expenditure does not entail the essential obligation—the duty or responsibility to another entity. That obligation will be created by a future event.

The same understanding of a liability (as formalized by Concepts Statement no. 3) can be used in considering the pension liability question. In the example described earlier, when the plan is amended is there an

---

7. Financial Accounting Concepts Statement no. 3, *Elements of Financial Statements of Business Enterprises* (Stamford, Conn.: FASB, 1980), par. 28.

8. Ibid., par. 29.
9. Ibid., par. 29

obligation to make a probable future payment? Has the event that obligated the company already happened? It seems clear to us that a case can be made for an affirmative answer to those questions. If so, the pension obligation is similar to other obligations that are recorded as liabilities, and the balance sheet would be incomplete—its usefulness diminished—if the pension liability was excluded, just as it would be incomplete without bank loans or accounts payable.

The news excerpts quoted earlier suggest that economic decisions sometimes are affected by the failure of decision makers to fully understand or consider pension obligations. As noted, the pension obligations that are not recorded and may therefore be overlooked result primarily from plan amendments. The incremental pension obligations that result from a plan amendment are now recorded as liabilities only over future periods. If those obligations were included on the balance sheet as liabilities when incurred, it seems to us, they would be less likely to be overlooked, and the balance sheet would provide a more complete picture of the financial position of the company. We also noted that some analysts adjust present balance sheets to consider some measure of pension obligations. If, as we have suggested, the unrecorded pension obligation looks like other obligations afforded balance sheet status, why do some people still want to exclude pension obligations from balance sheets?

Arguments for and Against Deferred Recognition of Pension Liabilities

The remainder of this article explores some of the reasons advanced for continuing the present practice of deferred recognition of pension liabilities resulting from plan amendments. Our opinions as to why those reasons have not been convincing also are discussed. The arguments for and against recognition generally apply equally to the obligation resulting from plan amendments and to that resulting from other factors such as experience gains and losses.

The company's obligation is only to make contributions. Some people suggest that the company does not have an obligation directly to the employees but only an obligation to make scheduled contributions to the plan. They conclude that there is no liability if contributions called for (by the actuary) have been made.

We believe this confuses the existence of a liability with its maturity date. If there is an obligation to the plan—an obligation to make future contributions—resulting from past events such as plan amendments and past service, that obligation may qualify as a lia-

bility. The fact that the contributions are scheduled for payment in future years does not mean that the obligation should remain unrecorded; most liabilities have scheduled future payment dates. The obligation to the plan and the obligation to the employees are two different ways to describe the same thing. The crucial question is whether there is a present obligation as a result of past transactions or events, not the identification of the obligee.

In addition, the idea that the existence of the pension plan or trust as a separate legal entity somehow avoids what would otherwise be the company's liability leads to other questions. Suppose a company set up a similar trust to be funded over a period of years to pay off a major lawsuit settlement. Should the full amount of the agreed on settlement be recorded as a liability or is it only an obligation of the trust?

It Is Not a Legal Liability. Some argue that the pension liability should be excluded from the balance sheet because it is not a "legal" liability. As the excerpt we quoted from Concepts Statement no. 3 notes, legal status is not required for an obligation to be recorded as a liability. In addition, the meaning of the term *legal liability* in this context is unclear. Pension obligations have been held to be legally enforceable in various circumstances.

It Will Never Have to Be Paid. If a pension plan is assumed to continue in effect, the liability will never be fully paid since there will always be active employees whose pensions are not yet payable. Some people suggest that the pension obligation need not be recorded on this basis.

The same thing may be said, however, of many other liabilities. For example, if a company continues in business, it is unlikely ever to reduce the balance of accounts payable to zero, but it is still considered useful to record and report the total amount of the obligation at the end of each period. This argument seems to be more relevant to funding decisions than to accounting questions.

The Amount of the Obligation Can't Be Measured. Some argue that the pension obligation should be excluded from the balance sheet because it is too uncertain or too hard to measure. They note that several future events must be estimated to calculate the amount of the obligation and that it is expected that these estimates will have to be adjusted as experience unfolds. The need to estimate and project future events is not unique to pensions. Accounting unavoidably involves many estimates and must be able to deal with changes in those estimates. The best current estimate of the amount of the pension obligation, based on the experience and knowledge of the professional actuary, is useful information. Pension accounting is already based on the same estimates; the only difference is that the amounts are spread over a number of future periods.

Spreading the effect of a plan amendment over a number of future periods tends to obscure, rather than report, the effect of the change. The obligation for future pension payments or contributions clearly is greater after a plan amendment than it was before the amendment. Financial Accounting Concepts Statement no. 1, *Objectives of Financial Reporting to Business Enterprises*, states:

"Financial reporting should provide information about the economic resources of an enterprise, the claims to those resources (obligations of the enterprise to transfer resources to other entities and owners' equity), and the effects of transactions, events, and circumstances that change its resources and claims to those resources."[10]

Since the plan amendment is an event that changes the employer's obligation—an event that increases employees' claims to the company's resources—financial statements should reflect that event.

The Increased Benefits Are Granted in Exchange for Future Service.
Some suggest that increases in pension benefits are granted in anticipation of future employee services, even though the amount of increase may be computed based on the number of years of prior service. In this view, the employer would be unlikely to increase benefits unless he expected to receive something of value in return. Since the value of past services cannot be enhanced retroactively, the employer must expect to receive benefits in the form of future services. The suggested conclusion is that the liability arises only as the future service is rendered.

The use of this line of reasoning for benefit increases granted to those already retired is based on the idea that current employees will provide services in exchange for benefits paid to other individuals already retired because they expect to receive similar increases after they retire.

The problem with that argument is it does not address whether the employer has a liability—a present obligation to transfer assets as a result of past transactions or events. After a plan amendment becomes effective, that obligation exists. What the employer receives in return for incurring the liability is another issue. An asset can exist as a result of the amendment, for example, if employees are motivated to work harder. Concepts Statement no. 3 has defined assets as "probable future economic benefits obtained or controlled by a particular entity as a result of past transactions or events."[11] Whether an intangible asset exists after a plan amendment is beyond the scope of this article.

Liability Recognition Would Have Economic Consequences.
Some suggest that recognizing the unrecorded pension liability would cause some employers to go bankrupt, to be denied access to credit markets or to be unwilling to improve pension plans. These and other predicted economic consequences are perceived as undesirable. They are said to be costs that exceed any possible benefit that might result from changes in pension accounting.

The FASB addressed the relationship between economic consequences and accounting standards in Financial Accounting Concepts Statement no. 2, *Qualitative Characteristics of Accounting Information:*

"While rejecting the view that financial accounting standards should be slanted for political reasons or to favor one economic interest or another, the Board recognizes that a standard-setting authority must be alert to the economic impact of the standards that it promulgates. The consequences of those standards will usually not be easy to isolate from the effects of other economic happenings, and they will be even harder to predict with confidence when a new standard is under consideration but before it has gone into effect. Nevertheless, the Board will consider the probable economic impact of its standards as best it can and will monitor that impact as best it can after a standard goes into effect. For one thing, a markedly unexpected effect on business behavior may point to an unforeseen deficiency in a standard in the sense that it does not result in the faithful representation of economic phenomena that was intended. It would then be necessary for the standard to be revised.

"Neutrality in accounting is an important criterion by which to judge accounting policies, for information that is not neutral loses credibility. If information can be verified and can be relied on faithfully to represent what it purports to represent—*and if there is no bias in the selection of what is reported*—it cannot be slanted to favor one set of interests over another. It may in fact favor certain interests, but only because the information points that way, much as a good examination grade favors a good student who has honestly earned it.

---

10. Financial Accounting Concepts Statement no. 1, *Objectives of Financial Reporting by Business Enterprises* (Stamford, Conn.: FASB, 1978), par. 40.

11. Concepts Statement no. 3, par. 19.

"The italicized words deserve comment. It was noted earlier in this Statement that reliability implies completeness of information, at least within the bounds of what is material and feasible, considering the cost. An omission can rob information of its claim to neutrality if the omission is material and is intended to induce or inhibit some particular mode of behavior."[12]

The board also has recognized its responsibility to limit changes in existing practice to situations in which the perceived benefits exceed the perceived costs of the change.

Economic consequences, however, can work both ways. There also may be economic consequences of failing to change accounting rules that do not reflect economic reality or that are not neutral and unbiased. The costs of not improving accounting are probably as hard to measure as the costs of changes, but they may be significant.

The economic consequences argument against recognizing the pension liability presumes that markets and decision makers will not become aware of the liability if it is not recorded. It also assumes that situation to be desirable. That assumption conflicts with the basic objective of reporting neutral and unbiased information that is relevant to decision makers.

Consider, for example, the suggestion that recording the pension liability will deny some companies access to credit. Decisions to grant or deny credit to a particular company are not made by the FASB; they are made by people, such as bankers, who are concerned with the ability of the company to repay. Credit decisions are based, in part, on accounting information, and those who must decide to grant or deny credit rely on having unbiased information, including information about a company's liabilities. It is inappropriate for the FASB to refuse to recognize a liability that exists just because knowledge of that liability might cause the banker to deny credit to a particular company. Indeed, that may be a persuasive reason to require recognition of the liability.

12. Financial Accounting Concepts Statement no. 2, *Qualitative Characteristics of Accounting Information* (Stamford, Conn.: FASB, 1980), pars. 106, 107, 108.

Conclusion

Based on our work to date, we are not convinced by the arguments against recording a liability when a pension plan is established or amended. We believe that an accounting liability does exist and that including it with other liabilities in the balance sheet will significantly improve the usefulness of financial statements.

CPAs may or may not agree with our conclusion. However, even if they, and the members of the FASB, ultimately do agree, a number of important related questions must be resolved before any change in pension accounting can be implemented, including

☐ What is the appropriate measure of the liability? Is it vested benefits, accumulated benefits, prior service cost or something else?
☐ If a liability is recorded, what is the nature of the offsetting debit? Is it expense, an extraordinary charge, an intangible asset or something else?
☐ How should the assets held by the plan be reflected on the employer's balance sheet? Depending on the measure of the liability, plan assets might exceed the liability for many companies.

These and other related issues are now being considered as part of the FASB's project on employers' accounting for pensions and other postemployment benefits. The answers to the issues may have a significant effect on how financial statements reflect pension activities. We encourage accountants to help in finding answers that improve financial reporting by participating in the board's process.

Chapter Nineteen

Statement of Changes in Financial Position and Cash Flow Statement

Reviewing the Chapter

1. The **statement of changes in financial position** is a major financial statement that is presented with the balance sheet, income statement, and statement of retained earnings. Its main purpose is to summarize the important financing and investing activities of a company during a given period.

2. In accounting, **funds** are usually defined as working capital (current assets minus current liabilities), and not as cash. Accountants take this view because working capital is more closely related than cash to a company's operating cycle. So the statement of changes in financial position generally uses the working capital concept of funds rather than the cash concept.

3. The change in working capital is calculated by subtracting one year's ending working capital from the subsequent year's. It may be expressed as an increase or a decrease.

4. An increase in a current asset or a decrease in a current liability will result in an increase in working capital. A decrease in a current asset or an increase in a current liability will result in a decrease in working capital.

5. If a transaction is to affect working capital, at least one current and one noncurrent account must be involved. For example, the purchase of inventory for cash would not affect working capital because both accounts are current in nature.

6. Business transactions that increase working capital are called **sources of working capital**. These transactions are described as financing activities, and include (a) net income from operations, (b) the sale of noncurrent assets, (c) long-term borrowing, and (d) the sale of capital stock.

   a. Net income from operations increases working capital. It means that cash receipts and receivables that arise from the sale of goods and services exceed cash payments and payables that arise when expenses are incurred. However, to find working capital from operations, certain items must be added to, or subtracted from, net income. For example, although depreciation was a deduction in arriving at net income, it must be added back because depreciation does not cause a change in working capital. On the other hand, the year's amortization of bond premium would be deducted.

b. The sale of a noncurrent asset increases cash and decreases the noncurrent asset, resulting in an increase in working capital. Working capital increases by the amount of the sale, whether or not there is a gain or loss.

c. Long-term borrowing increases both cash and long-term liabilities, resulting in an increase in working capital.

d. The issuance of the company's stock increases both cash and stockholders' equity, resulting in an increase in working capital.

7. Business transactions that decrease working capital are called **uses of working capital**. These transactions are described as investing activities, and include (a) an operating loss, (b) the purchase of noncurrent assets, (c) the declaration of a cash dividend, (d) the purchase or retirement of stock, and (e) the retirement or reclassification of a long-term debt. In preparing the uses of the working capital section of the statement of changes in financial position, one should remember that nonworking capital expenses such as depreciation must still be added back to a net loss to arrive at working capital applied to operations. In addition, the declaration of a cash dividend reduces working capital, but the eventual payment of the dividend does not affect working capital (since no noncurrent account is involved). Finally, when a long-term debt is reclassified as a current liability because it is currently due, it results in a decrease in working capital.

8. An **exchange transaction** is a transaction that involves only noncurrent accounts, and therefore has no effect on working capital. Such a transaction is viewed, however, as both a source and a use of working capital, according to the **all financial resources** concept of funds. Examples of exchange transactions are the purchase of land in exchange for a long-term note, and the conversion of bonds payable into common stock.

9. On the formal statement of changes in financial position, total uses of working capital is subtracted from total sources of working capital to arrive at an increase (or decrease) in working capital. An accompanying schedule of changes in working capital is required. It must show how each working capital account has changed and should back up the working capital change previously obtained.

10. The following steps should be taken in preparing a statement of changes in financial position.

a. Find the change in working capital from last year to this year.

b. Prepare a work sheet for the statement of changes in financial position.

c. Classify changes in noncurrent accounts as sources or uses of working capital.

d. Prepare the statement of changes in financial position, as well as the supporting schedule of changes in working capital.

11. The work sheet for the statement of changes in financial position is designed to aid in the preparation of the statement by (a) providing a mechanism for analyzing each transaction that affects working capital, and (b) classifying the effect of those transactions as sources or uses of working capital.

12. The **cash flow statement** provides information about a company's debt-paying ability. It presents the company's sources and uses of cash during the period, as well as the increase or decrease in cash.

a. In preparing the cash flow statement, cash flow from operations is first found by converting the income statement from an accrual basis to a cash basis or by the short-cut method.

b. Cash flow from operations is now listed with all other sources of cash and totaled. All uses of cash are listed below that and totaled. The difference between the total sources and total uses of cash will be the increase or decrease in cash for the period.

Testing Your Knowledge

Matching

Match each term with its definition by writing the appropriate letter in the blank.

<u>D</u> 1. Statement of changes in financial position

<u>B</u> 2. Working capital

<u>G</u> 3. Funds

<u>E</u> 4. Sources of working capital

<u>A</u> 5. Uses of working capital

<u>F</u> 6. Exchange transaction

<u>H</u> 7. All financial resources (concept of funds)

<u>C</u> 8. Cash flow statement

a. Business transactions that decrease working capital

b. Current assets minus current liabilities

c. The statement that reports sources and uses of cash during the period

d. The statement that reports the important financing and investing activities of a business during the period

e. Business transactions that increase working capital

f. A transaction that affects only noncurrent accounts

g. In accounting, another term for working capital

h. The viewpoint that an exchange transaction is really both a source and a use of working capital

Completion

Use the lines provided to complete each item.

1. List four sources of working capital.

Sale of Bonds (L.T. Borrowing)
Sale of Assets
Sale of Stock
Net income from operations

2. List five uses of working capital.

Operating loss
purchase of assets
declaration of cash dividend
purchase of stock
retirement of L.T. debt

3. Provide two examples of transactions that do not affect working capital but must be included in the statement of changes in financial position (that is, exchange transactions).

Convert bonds pay to common stock
exchange land for L.T. note

4. List two items in the statement of changes in financial position that must be added to net income to produce working capital provided from operations.

depreciation
amortization of bond discount

True-False

Circle T if the statement is true, F if it is false.

T F 1. The cash collection of an account receivable increases working capital.

T F 2. The term *funds*, as it applies to the statement of changes in financial position, refers to working capital in most cases.

T F 3. Financing activities are described under Sources of Working Capital in the statement of changes in financial position.

T F 4. The statement of changes in financial position provides information covering a period of time rather than as of a certain date.

T F 5. The purchase of inventory on credit does not affect working capital.

T F 6. Accumulated depreciation must be added back to net income to produce working capital provided from operations.

T F 7. The declaration of a cash dividend is not a use of working capital until it is paid.

T F 8. Reclassifying a long-term debt as a short-term debt does not affect working capital.

T F 9. The statement of changes in financial position work sheet utilizes a comparative income statement.

T F 10. An increase in the Land account by $10,000 from the end of one year to the end of the next always signifies that the company purchased additional land for $10,000 during the year.

T F 11. The issuance of preferred stock for services rendered to the company is both a source and a use of working capital.

T F 12. The declaration of a cash dividend requires a credit in the analysis columns of the work sheet opposite Dividends Payable.

T F 13. The change in each working capital item need not be presented with the statement of changes in financial position.

T F 14. An operating loss for the year will always result in a decrease in working capital.

T F 15. Net purchases equal cost of goods sold minus a decrease in inventory.

Multiple-Choice

Circle the letter of the best answer.

1. When an asset with a book value of $8,000 is sold for $6,000, the transaction should be recorded in the statement of changes in financial position as
   a. a $2,000 extraordinary loss.
   b. a $2,000 use of working capital.
   c. a $6,000 source of working capital.
   d. an $8,000 use of working capital.

2. When net income is recorded (debited) in the analysis columns of the statement of changes in financial position work sheet, which item is credited?
   a. Net Income
   b. Income Summary
   c. Cash
   d. Retained Earnings

3. In the statement of changes in financial position, depreciation expense is
   a. a use of working capital.
   b. added to net income.
   c. subtracted from net income.
   d. omitted.

4. The Calumet Corporation had cash sales of $30,000 and credit sales of $70,000 during the year, and the Accounts Receivable account increased by $14,000. Cash receipts from sales totaled
   a. $70,000.
   b. $86,000.
   c. $100,000.
   d. $114,000.

5. Which of the following will affect cash flow from operations but not changes in working capital?
   a. Depreciation expense
   b. The issuance of common stock
   c. The payment of a current liability
   d. The purchase of inventory on credit

6. In the statement of changes in financial position, bad debts expense is
   a. added to net income.
   b. subtracted from net income.
   c. neither added to nor subtracted from net income.
   d. added to net income sometimes, and subtracted from net income at other times.

7. Cash payments for purchases equal net purchases plus
   a. an increase in inventory.
   b. a decrease in inventory.
   c. an increase in accounts payable.
   d. a decrease in accounts payable.

8. Which of the following would be added to operating expenses when computing cash payments for expenses?
   a. Increases in prepaid assets
   b. Increases in accrued liabilities
   c. Noncash expense
   d. None of the above

9. Which of the following would *not* appear on a cash flow statement, but *would* appear on a statement of changes in financial position?
   a. Cash dividend paid
   b. Purchase of inventory on credit
   c. Issuance of bonds
   d. Purchase of equipment on credit

10. A company that uses the allowance method for recording uncollectible accounts records Bad Debt Expense of $5,000 at the end of a given year, and records $2,000 in specific write-offs during that year. As a result of the above facts, working capital
    a. decreased by $7,000.
    b. decreased by $5,000.
    c. decreased by $3,000.
    d. increased by $3,000.

70.000
- 14.000
56.000

Applying Your Knowledge

Exercises

1. The comparative balance sheets of Dexter Corporation are shown below. In the column provided, compute the change in each working capital item as well as the total change in working capital.

Dexter Corporation
Comparative Balance Sheets
As of December 31, 19x1, and December 31, 19x2

	19x2	19x1	Increase (Decrease) in Working Capital
Assets			
Cash	$ 2,000	$16,000	(14,000)
Short-term Investments	0	10,000	(10,000)
Accounts Receivable	8,000	2,000	6000
Inventory	32,000	8,000	24,000
Buildings	60,100	24,000	
Accumulated Depreciation, Buildings	(13,200)	(9,000)	
Total Assets	$88,900	$51,000	
Liabilities and Stockholders' Equity			
Notes Payable	$10,000	$ 1,600	(8400)
Accounts Payable	6,400	9,400	3000
Bonds Payable	24,000	0	
Common Stock	40,000	30,000	
Retained Earnings	8,500	10,000	
Total Liabilities and Stockholders' Equity	$88,900	$51,000	
Increase (Decrease) in Working Capital			600

2. In the space provided, use the following information to prepare (in good form) a statement of changes in financial position for Lewis Corporation. Omit an analysis of working capital changes. Although a work sheet would ordinarily be prepared first, leave this step out in your answer.
   a. Net income (after taxes) for the current year was $200,000.
   b. Depreciation expense amounted to $10,000.
   c. Land was purchased for $80,000.
   d. Dividends declared totaled $100,000. However, dividends paid totaled $91,000.
   e. Machinery with a book value of $13,500 was sold for $13,500.
   f. Common stock was issued in exchange for $7,000 worth of office equipment.
   g. $10,000 of bonds payable were reclassified as a current liability.
   h. Income tax expense amounted to $70,000.

Lewis Corporation
Statement of Changes in Financial Position
For the Year Ended December 31, 19x1

Sources of Working Capital

Operations

Net Income — ~~200,000~~ — 200,000

Add Expenses Not Requiring Outlay of Working Capital in the Current Period:

Depreciation — 10,000 — 10,000

Working Capital Provided from Operations — 210,000

Other Sources of Working Capital

Machinery Sale — 13,500

Common Stock — 7000

Total Sources of Working Capital — 20,500 / 230,500

Uses of Working Capital

Purchase of Land — 80,000

Dividends Declared — 100,000

Office Equip. — 7000

BP-current (reclass) — 10,000 — 197,000

Total Uses of Working Capital

Increase (Decrease) in Working Capital — (33,500)

Solvency: The Forgotten Half of Financial Reporting

Increased attention must be given to providing information useful in solvency evaluation.

The management of a business enterprise is concerned with two broad objectives: to operate the business profitably and to maintain its solvency. Profitability refers to a company's ability to increase its wealth. Solvency refers to its ability to pay its debts when due.

During the first three decades of this century, issues of solvency evaluation clearly dominated financial reporting. Income statements were not in common use, the balance sheet was referred to as *the* financial statement and short-term creditors, particularly bankers, were assumed to be the primary users of that statement. In 1927, Paul-Joseph Esquerré observed:

"It is undeniable that today almost every business balance sheet proceeds on the assumption that it is going to be used to obtain bank loans; and as the banker is presumed to loan only on the security of liquid assets, all the efforts of the statement of financial status are directed towards the proof of that liquidity."[1] Beginning around 1930, accountants began to shift their attention from issues of solvency evaluation to those of profitability. By 1952 the pendulum had swung completely:

". . . the determination of periodical profit or loss from enterprise operations constitutes the crux of the accounting problem, the central issue around which all other considerations revolve and to which they are unavoidably related."[2]

Since 1952, the focus of financial reporting has remained on profitability. Accounting theorists, accounting educators, groups responsible for promulgating accounting standards, practicing accountants and auditors have been concerned with profitability reporting almost exclusively. With few exceptions, reporting information useful in evaluating the solvency of a company has either been ignored or given a role that is clearly secondary to that of reporting profitability. Financial reporting for solvency evaluation is the forgotten half of financial reporting.[3]

The Relationship Between Solvency and Profitability

Solvency and profitability are clearly related. Long-run solvency depends on long-run profitability. No method of obtaining money to pay debts will be available in the long run to an enterprise that is not profitable. In the short run, however, solvency and profitability do not necessarily go together. An unprofitable enterprise may remain solvent for years because its cash collections continue to exceed its required cash payments. On the other hand, a profitable enterprise in need of cash to finance increasing receivables, inventory and plant may tie itself to an unrealistic debt repayment schedule that could eventually result in its insolvency:

Though my bottom line is black, I am flat upon my back,
My cash flows out and customers pay slow.
The growth of my receivables is almost unbelievable;
The result is certain—unremitting woe!
And I hear the banker utter an ominous low mutter,
"Watch cash flow."[4]

The Importance of Solvency

Investors and creditors, the primary users of general purpose financial statements, need to evaluate the solvency as well as the profitability of companies in which they have interest. Creditors are obviously concerned with solvency. In fact, evaluation of solvency is often referred to as credit analysis, although

Source: Article by Loyd C. Heath and Paul Rosenfield. Reprinted from the January 1979 issue of *The Journal of Accountancy.* Copyright © 1979 by the American Institute of Certified Public Accountants, Inc.

1. Paul-Joseph Esquerré, *Accounting* (New York: Ronald Press Company, 1927), p. 41. See also Hector R. Anton, *Accounting for the Flow of Funds* (New York: Houghton Mifflin Co., 1962), p. 5; A.C. Littleton and V.K. Zimmerman, *Accounting Theory: Continuity and Change* (Englewood Cliffs, N.J.: Prentice-Hall, Inc., 1962), pp. 113-17; and Eldon S. Hendriksen, *Accounting Theory,* 3d ed. (Homewood, Ill.: Richard D. Irwin, 1977), pp. 56-59.
2. Maurice Moonitz and Charles C. Staehling, *Accounting: An Analysis of Its Problems,* vol. 1 (Brooklyn, N.Y.: Foundation Press, Inc., 1952), p. 107.

3. Some of the material for this article was developed in connection with the preparation of Accounting Research Monograph no. 3, *Financial Reporting and the Evaluation of Solvency,* by Loyd C. Heath (New York: AICPA, 1978).
4. Herbert S. Bailey, Jr., "Quoth the Banker, 'Watch Cash Flow,'" *Publishers Weekly,* January 13, 1975, p. 34.

that term should not be taken to mean that creditors are the only parties interested in a company's solvency or even that creditors are more interested in solvency than other financial statement users. If a company becomes insolvent, equity investors are likely to lose even more than creditors because creditors' rights are senior to those of stockholders in bankruptcy and reorganization proceedings.

Even if a company never reaches the point of insolvency, the mere threat or suspicion of insolvency is likely to result in losses to stockholders. The more obvious consequences are that the market value of their shares is likely to decline and that increased credit costs will tend to reduce profits. But less obvious consequences may be just as serious. Even if there is no imminent threat of insolvency, a company that is short of cash will have to pass up profitable investment opportunities and restrict cash payments in ways that are likely to affect long-run profitability.

Other financial statement users are also concerned with a company's solvency. Employees, suppliers and customers are concerned because loss of solvency usually means loss of jobs, loss of customers and disruption of sources of supply. The U.S. government's guarantees of loans to Lockheed Aircraft Corp. several years ago illustrate society's concern over the solvency of at least one major corporation.

Evaluating Solvency

Solvency is a money or cash phenomenon. A solvent company is one with adequate cash to pay its debts; an insolvent company is one with inadequate cash.[5] Evaluating solvency is basically a problem of evaluating the risk that a company will not be able to raise enough cash before its debts must be paid.

Solvency analysis is not simply a matter of evaluating a company's so-called current assets and liabilities to determine the adequacy of its working capital "cushion." During the last 25 years the emphasis in solvency analysis by sophisticated users of financial statements has shifted from static analysis of working capital position (or "proof of . . . liquidity" as Esquerré called it) to dynamic analysis of cash receipts and payments in much the same way that the emphasis in security analysis shifted from static analysis of balance sheet values to dynamic analysis of net income during the 1930s and 1940s. Today, it is recognized that most of the cash a company

will receive within the next year is not represented by assets classified as current (or any other assets now on the balance sheet, for that matter); and most of the obligations it will have to pay during that time are not represented by liabilities classified as current.

Any information that provides insight into the amounts, timing and certainty of a company's future cash receipts and payments is useful in evaluating solvency. Statements of past cash receipts and payments are useful for the same basic reason that income statements are useful in evaluating profitability: both provide a basis for predicting future performance.[6] Information about the due dates of receivables and payables is also useful in predicting future cash receipts and payments and, therefore, in evaluating solvency.

Since cash receipts and payments can never be predicted with certainty, solvency evaluation also involves evaluating a company's capacity to control or adjust cash receipts and payments to survive a period of financial adversity, a concept that has been called financial flexibility.[7] Some of the things included under the concept of financial flexibility are a company's unused borrowing capacity and its ability to liquidate assets without adversely affecting the profitability of its remaining assets.

Information about a company's cash receipts and payments is also relevant in evaluating a company's profitability but in a different way. The timing of a company's receipts and payments is irrelevant in the measurement of income except insofar as timing affects the amounts at which assets and liabilities are recorded. The sale of an item for $10,000 cash and the sale of that item for a $10,000 note receivable due in five years with interest at 10 percent are regarded as equivalent transactions in evaluating profitability. They are not equivalent, however, in evaluating solvency because the timing of the cash receipts differs greatly in the two cases. The timing of future cash receipts and payments is the sine qua non of solvency evaluation and the heart of the distinction between issues of solvency reporting and profitability reporting.

Evidence of Neglect

We have neglected solvency. Evidence of that neglect and bias toward the income measurement or profitability point of view can be found in both accounting practice and discussions of accounting problems.

5. Liquidity is closely related to solvency but it is a narrower concept. The term "liquidity" is usually used to refer to a company's asset characteristics or to its asset and liability structure. As discussed later in this article, a company's ability to remain solvent depends on more than its present financial position as reflected in its balance sheet.

6. For a specific proposal that enterprises publish statements of past cash receipts and payments, see Loyd C. Heath, "Let's Scrap the 'Funds' Statement," JofA, Oct. 78, pp. 94–103, and the monograph referred to in footnote 3.
7. The concept of financial flexibility is discussed more fully in chapter 2 of the monograph referred to in footnote 3.

Misleading balance sheet classification. One of the principal methods now used to report information for use in solvency evaluation is to classify assets and liabilities as current or noncurrent. That practice began shortly after the turn of the century in response to the needs, or at least the perceived needs, of commercial bankers. The bulletin that governs current-noncurrent classification today, chapter 3A of Accounting Research Bulletin no. 43, *Restatement and Revision of Accounting Research Bulletins,* first appeared in 1947 as ARB no. 30 and has remained virtually unchanged since that time. That bulletin is defective in many ways. It is based on an outmoded, simplistic, static model of solvency evaluation; it contains incomprehensible definitions of current assets and current liabilities together with lists of assets and liabilities that appear to contradict those definitions; it ignores basic principles of classification; and it not only fails to provide information useful in evaluating solvency but it also provides misleading information.[8] The fact that a bulletin that provides guidance on the major device in financial statements intended for solvency evaluation is so defective and has been allowed to remain in effect for over thirty years with no serious effort to change it is a prime example of how little attention has been given to solvency issues by accounting policymakers.

Misdirect "funds" statements. "Where got—where gone" statements, the forerunners of statements of changes in financial position (fund statements), were viewed as tools for use in solvency analysis. William Morse Cole, credited with being the father of funds statements, observed in 1915:

"It is obvious that an important result of constructing such a table . . . is the possibility of seeing from it at a glance the changes in solvency."[9]

During the 1920s when H.A. Finney popularized funds statements that explained changes in working capital, providing information for use in solvency evaluation was still the principal objective of those statements. Working capital was considered to be *the* measure of a company's debt-paying ability, and the funds statement was viewed as a way of explaining changes in that measure.

In spite of the fact that financial statement users have shifted their emphasis from working capital analysis to analysis of a company's cash receipts and payments, nearly all funds statements found in

practice today are still based on the outmoded and useless concept of working capital.

To make matters even worse, beginning with APB Opinion no. 3, *The Statement of Source and Application of Funds,* in 1964, companies were required to report "significant" financing and investing activities that did not affect working capital as if they did, so that even changes in working capital are not now reported in an understandable way. Duff and Phelps, Inc., an investment research firm, describes the current form of funds statement as "not much more than a miscellaneous collection of plus and minus changes in balance sheet items" and observes that "the predominant emphasis on working capital serves little purpose since working capital is not an important analytical figure."[10] Earl A. Spiller and Robert L. Virgil note that, under APB Opinion no. 19, *Reporting Changes in Financial Position,* "as long as certain types of transactions are disclosed in the required way, apparently any, all, or no underlying concept of funds is appropriate."[11]

The important point is that the original objective of funds statements—that of providing information for solvency analysis by explaining changes in some measure of debt-paying ability—has been lost. Funds statements are now viewed as the residual or "third" financial statement whose function is to report any "significant" information not reported elsewhere.[12]

Rejection of users' demands. Some of the strongest evidence of pro-income measurement, anti-solvency bias appears in the accounting profession's response to suggestions by financial statement users that statements of cash receipts and payments would be useful in solvency evaluation because income statements based on accrual accounting conceal the timing of cash movements. Those suggestions have often been interpreted as challenges to the supremacy of the income statement and contemptuously (perhaps fearfully) dismissed. For example, in 1961 J.S. Seidman, a prominent practitioner who was both president of the AICPA and a member of the Accounting Principles Board, stated:

". . . instead of studying various ways and terminology for presenting cash flow statements, I think the profession is called upon to report to companies, to

8. For a discussion of these points, see chapter 4 of the monograph referred to in footnote 3.
9. William Morse Cole, *Accounts: Their Construction and Interpretation,* rev. and enl. ed. (Boston, Mass.: Houghton Mifflin Co., 1915), p. 102.
10. Duff and Phelps, Inc., *A Management Guide to Better Financial Reporting* (New York: Arthur Andersen & Co., 1976), pp. 81-82.
11. Earl A. Spiller and Robert L. Virgil, "Effectiveness of APB Opinion no. 19 in Improving Funds Reporting," *Journal of Accounting Research,* Spring 1974, p. 115.
12. For suggestions on how to improve disclosure of some of the information now reported in funds statements, see the Heath article referred to in footnote 6.

analysts, to stockholders, and the exchanges that cash flow figures are dangerous and misleading and the profession will have no part of them."[13]

More recently, statements of cash receipts and payments were rejected by the Financial Accounting Standards Board in its exposure draft *Objectives of Financial Reporting and Elements of Financial Statements of Business Enterprises.* The board explained in paragraphs 33 and 34:

"Financial statements that show only cash receipts and payments during a short period, such as a year, [cannot] adequately indicate whether or not an enterprise's performance is successful.

"Information about enterprise earnings (often called net income or net profit) and its components measured by accrual accounting generally provides a better measure of enterprise performance than information about current cash receipts and payments. That is, financial information provided by accounting that recognizes the financial effects of transactions and other events when they occur rather than only when cash is received or paid is usually considered a better basis than cash receipts and payments for estimating an enterprise's present and continuing ability to bring in the cash it needs."[14]

Ruling out statements of cash receipts and payments on the grounds that they cannot "adequately indicate whether or not an enterprise's performance is successful" indicates the board considered only one aspect of a company's performance to be relevant in measuring success, that is, its earnings performance. Apparently the board did not consider a company's success in generating cash and paying off its liabilities to be part of its "performance." Obtaining cash needed to survive and obtaining increased wealth are both necessary parts of an enterprise's performance. Assuring survival and prospering require different kinds of achievement, not simply different amounts of achievement.[15]

The board's argument that enterprise earnings are a "better" indicator of cash-generating ability casts income statements and statements of cash receipts and payments as competing methods of disclosure although they are not. Income statements report the effects of a company's operations on its long-run cash-generating ability; the question of when cash has been or will be received or paid is ignored except as it affects amounts at which receivables and payables are recorded. Statements of cash receipts and payments, on the other hand, report the effects of operations on cash movements during the year; when those movements have affected or will affect income is ignored. Thus, income statements and statements of cash receipts and payments are complementary, not competing forms of disclosure. They report different things for different purposes. The board's rejection of statements of receipts and payments at the objectives level based on the argument that income statements are "better" indicators of cash-generating ability than cash flow statements indicates an insensitivity to the timing of cash movements and, therefore, an insensitivity to solvency issues.

Confusion between income effects and cash effects of operations. Undoubtedly one of the reasons that user's demands for statements of cash receipts and payments have not received more serious consideration is that income measurement so dominates the thinking of many accountants that they do not even distinguish between a company's income and the cash it has generated through operations; they speak of income as if it were synonymous with cash. Thus, they often refer to the retirement of debt and the purchase of plant and equipment "out of profits" when they really mean out of cash generated by operations, and they refer to the income statement as *the* statement of operations even though it shows only one effect of operations. Other effects of operations such as those on cash, on plant and equipment or on capital structure are not, of course, reported in that statement. In fact, before APB Opinion no. 19 became effective in 1971, CPAs routinely stated in their standard reports that a company's financial statements "present fairly . . . the results of its operations" even though only the income effects of operations were reported; no statement was required that even purported to report the effects of operations other than the income effects.

Further evidence of the confusion between the income effects and other effects of operating activities can be found in the common yet confusing and misleading practice of showing income as a "source" of working capital or "funds" on statements of changes in financial position even though this "attempt to tie in these statements with profit and loss misses the major point that these statements are neither segments nor elaborations of income-measuring data, but instead are reports on changes that have occurred in other directions."[16] If accountants are going to provide information useful in solvency evaluation, they must first recognize that net income is not the

13. J.S. Seidman, JofA, June 61, p. 31.
14. FASB, *Objectives of Financial Reporting and Elements of Financial Statements of Business Enterprises* (Stamford, Conn.: FASB, 1977).
15. For a discussion of this point, see Paul Rosenfield, "Current Replacement Value Accounting—A Dead End," JofA, Sept. 75, p. 72.

only effect of operations and that other effects, particularly the cash effect, may be as important as net income.

Effects of inflation on solvency.

A period of rising prices creates a cash problem and therefore a solvency problem for many companies, because increased amounts of cash are needed to replace higher priced assets. To meet that need, either cash receipts and payments from operations have to be adjusted or additional outside financing must be obtained. Information useful in evaluating the magnitude of a company's need for additional cash to replace higher priced assets is relevant for evaluating solvency under those conditions. Statements of cash receipts and payments, particularly if they are available for several years in which there have been different rates of inflation, and disclosure of the replacement costs of assets held are two types of information that would be useful in estimating a company's need for additional cash to replace assets.

The problem of financial reporting during a period of rising prices has usually been considered only from the perspective of income measurement rather than from the perspective of solvency. The use of replacement prices has been supported on the grounds that it provides a superior measure of income, not that it provides information for estimating a company's future cash requirements. Even when the solvency dimension of the problem has been recognized, the solution often suggested has been to exclude the excess of the replacement value of an asset over its cost from income to obtain a measure known as "distributable" income—a solution that combines and confuses the income measurement and the solvency dimensions of the problem.[17]

Economic v. legal entities.

The distinctions between separate legal entities are ignored when consolidated financial statements are prepared; companies within the consolidated group are treated as one economic entity. Legal distinctions between entities, however, are often necessary to evaluate solvency because creditors' rights attach to the separate entities, not to the consolidated entity. From the solvency perspective, a consolidated balance sheet may be misleading because "the pressing liabilities may be in the parent company, but the liquid assets which give promise of meeting these liabilities may be in a subsidiary . . . [where they are] unavailable to the parent. . . ."[18]

Similarly, one subsidiary may have adequate cash available, but the "pressing liabilities" may be those of another subsidiary and legal restrictions may prevent transfer of assets from one subsidiary to another.

Recently the Advisory Committee on Corporate Disclosure to the Securities and Exchange Commission noted this point and made the following suggestion:

"Where there are material blockages to free movements of cash within a consolidated entity (e.g., caused by loan indentures, foreign currency restrictions, or other legal constraints which limit a parent's or a subsidiary's movement of cash to another entity within the consolidated group), separate funds statements might be required for the entity in which the blockage had occurred in order to disclose adequately the significance of this blockage to the ability of the consolidated entity as a whole to meet its dividend, debt service, and other commitments from internally-generated cash."[19]

While separate statements of cash receipts and payments for some or all the companies comprising a consolidated entity probably would be useful in the situation described, they are not a complete solution to the problem described because balance sheets, too, can be misleading under those conditions. The point in raising this issue, however, is not to recommend a solution but to point out that consolidated financial statements raise an important issue in the evaluation of solvency that has received little or no attention from accountants.

Consolidated financial statements are usually justified with the argument that they are intended to portray the economic substance of parent-subsidiary relationships rather than their legal form. That argument is specious because a financial statement user concerned with solvency considerations often finds that the legal form of a relationship *determines* its economic substance, and legal form therefore cannot be ignored. The use of consolidated financial statements, like the problem of financial reporting during periods of changing prices, needs to be looked at from the

16. Maurice Moonitz and Louis H. Jordan, *Accounting: An Analysis of Its Problems,* rev. ed., vol 1 (New York: Holt, Rinehart and Winston, Inc., 1963), p. 103.

17. For discussion of this point, see FASB discussion memorandum, *An Analysis of Issues Related to Conceptual Framework for Financial Accounting and Reporting: Elements of Financial Statements and Their Measurement* (Stamford, Conn.: FASB, 1976), ch. 6. See also Rosenfield, pp. 72-73.

18. Ted J. Fiflis and Homer Kripke, *Accounting for Business Lawyers; Teaching Materials,* 2d ed. (St. Paul, Minn.: West Publishing Co., 1977) p. 604. For discussion of a recent example in which this issue is raised, see Abraham J. Briloff, "Whose 'Deep Pocket?' " *Barron's,* July 19, 1976, p. 5.

19. *Report of the Advisory Committee on Corporate Disclosure to the Securities and Exchange Commission,* printed for the use of the House Committee on Interstate and Foreign Commerce, 95th Congress, 1st sess., Committee Print 95-29, November 3, 1977, p. 505n.

solvency point of view as well as from the income measurement point of view.

Information on funding pension obligations. A company's obligation to make periodic payments to fund its pension plan often represents a significant cash drain and may be an important consideration in evaluating its solvency. The amount of that obligation cannot be determined by the amount of pension expense reported on its income statement because funding requirements may differ from pension expense reporting requirements.

Current generally accepted accounting principles do not require a company to provide any information about its obligation to provide funding for its pension plan over the next several years. They do not even require it to disclose the amount of its contribution to its pension fund for past periods. APB Opinion no. 8, *Accounting for the Cost of Pension Plans,* is, as its title suggests, concerned almost exlusively with the *cost*, that is, the income effect, of pension plans. It ignores their impact on a company's solvency.

Let's Not Forget Solvency

The solvency perspective that dominated U.S. financial reporting for the first three decades of this century was lost when accountants turned their attention to problems of income measurement during the 1930s. For the past 40 or 50 years nearly all financial reporting issues have been considered almost exclusively from the standpoint of income measurement. Reporting practices that have as their objective providing information useful in evaluating solvency, such as classification of assets and liabilities as current and noncurrent and providing a funds statement, are based on an old model of solvency evaluation that has since been rejected by financial statement users as naive or simplistic.

The solution to the problems discussed here does not lie simply in searching for a new basis of balance sheet classification, in replacing funds statements with statements of cash receipts and payments, in disclosing due dates of receivables and payables, in disclosing replacement costs of assets held, in presenting separate statements of companies comprising a consolidated entity or in disclosing more information about pension obligations—although all those steps would probably help. Those solutions deal only with the current symptoms.

The basic problem is that accountants have forgotten the solvency point of view—not just accounting policymakers but all accountants including management accountants, auditors and accounting educators. The only solution to that basic problem is for them to understand how today's users of financial statements look at solvency issues and to adopt that viewpoint when considering all matters of financial reporting. This does not, of course, mean neglecting the profitability point of view. But unless increased attention is given to providing information useful in solvency evaluation, the accounting profession is likely to find itself subject to increased criticism for failing to provide early warning signals of business failures, of which the Penn Central and W.T. Grant debacles are only two famous examples among thousands that occur every year.

Chapter Twenty

Intercompany Investments and International Accounting

Reviewing the Chapter

1. Two ways a company may expand are by increasing its operations and by investing in other companies. Companies that have expanded operations throughout the world are called **multinational** or **transnational corporations**.

2. A **closely held corporation** is one whose stock is owned by a few individuals and not traded publicly. On the other hand, a **publicly held corporation** is one whose securities are registered with the SEC and are traded by the public at large.

3. All long-term investments in the stock of other companies are recorded at cost. After purchase, the accounting treatment depends on the extent of influence exercised by the investing company. If the investing company can affect the operating and financing policies of the investee, even though it owns less than 50 percent of the investee's voting stock, it has **significant influence**. If the investing company can decide the operating and financing policies of the investee because it owns more than 50 percent of the investee's voting stock, it has **control**.

4. The extent of influence exercised over another company is often difficult to measure accurately. However, unless there is evidence to the contrary, long-term investments in stock are classified as (a) noninfluential and noncontrolling (generally less than 20 percent ownership), (b) influential but noncontrolling (generally 20 to 50 percent ownership), and (c) controlling (over 50 percent ownership).

5. The cost method should be used in accounting for noninfluential and noncontrolling investments. The equity method should be used in accounting for all other (that is, influential or controlling) investments. In addition, consolidated financial statements should usually be prepared when a controlling relationship exists.

   a. Under the **cost method**, the investor records investment income as dividends are received. In addition, the securities are recorded on the balance sheet at the lower of cost or market. Unrealized Loss on Long-Term Investments is debited and Allowance to Reduce Long-Term Investments to Market is credited for the excess of total cost over total market.

   b. Under the **equity method**, the investor records investment income as a debit to the Investment account and a credit to an Investment Income account. The amount recorded is the investee's periodic net income times the investor's ownership percentage. When the investor receives a cash dividend, the Cash account is debited and the Investment account is credited.

c. When a company has a controlling interest in another company, the investor is called the **parent company** and the investee is called the **subsidiary**. Companies in such a relationship must prepare **consolidated financial statements** (combined statements of the parent and its subsidiaries). The purchase method (described below) or the pooling-of-interests method (the subject of a more advanced accounting course) may be used.

6. The **purchase method** of consolidation must be used when two conditions apply. The parent company should own more than 50 percent of the subsidiary's voting stock. And the acquisition should not have been through an exchange of stock. Under this method, the parent records the investment at the purchase cost.

a. When the book value of the net assets purchased equals their cost, the assets and liabilities acquired should appear at cost on the consolidated balance sheet. No goodwill should be recorded.

b. The stockholders' equity section of the subsidiary at acquisition is not included in the consolidated balance sheet.

c. When less than 100 percent of the subsidiary has been purchased, the **minority interest** (outside ownership) must be disclosed on the consolidated balance sheet.

d. If the cost exceeds the book value of the net assets purchased, the extra amount should be allocated to the assets and liabilities acquired when consolidated financial statements are being prepared. The allocation should be based on fair market values at the date of acquisition. Any unassigned excess should be recorded as goodwill in the consolidated financial statements.

e. When the book value of the net assets purchased exceeds their cost, the carrying value of the assets should be reduced proportionately until the extra amount is eliminated.

f. Earnings of the subsidiary are combined with those of the parent only from acquisition date.

7. When consolidated financial statements are prepared, **eliminations** must be made on the consolidating work sheet for intercompany items. Among those items that must be eliminated are intercompany receivables, payables, sales, purchases, interest income, and interest expense, as well as the investment in the subsidiary company. As noted above, under the purchase method, the entire stockholders' equity section is eliminated.

8. When bonds are purchased as long-term investments, the investment account is debited at cost (which includes broker's commission). Accrued Interest Receivable is debited for accrued interest since the last interest date, and Cash is credited for cash paid. When interest is received on the investment, several accounts are involved. Cash is debited for cash received. Bond Interest Earned is credited for cash received plus the amortization of a bond discount or minus the amortization of a bond premium. And the investment account is debited (when there is a discount) or credited (when there is a premium) to balance the entry. Prior entries to accrue interest may slightly alter the above entry. Under this method of amortization, a bond discount or bond premium account is not used. At the maturity date, the bond investment account should equal the maturity value. However, if the bonds are sold before maturity, a gain or loss should be recorded for the difference between cash received and the bonds' carrying value.

9. When businesses expand internationally, two accounting problems arise. (a) The financial statements of foreign subsidiaries involve different currencies. Thus they must be translated into domestic currency by means of an **exchange rate**. (b) The foreign financial statements are not necessarily prepared in accordance with domestic generally accepted accounting principles.

10. Purchases and sales with foreign countries pose no accounting problem for the domestic company when domestic currency is being used. However, when the transaction involves foreign currency, the domestic company should record an exchange gain or loss. The exchange gain or loss reflects the change in the exchange rate from the transaction date to the date of payment.

11. When financial statements are prepared between the transaction date and the date of payment, an unrealized gain or loss should be recorded if the exchange rate has changed.

12. A foreign subsidiary that a parent company controls should be included in the parent company's consolidated financial statements. The subsidiary's financial statements must first be restated into the parent's **reporting currency**. The method of restatement depends on the foreign subsidiary's **functional currency**—that is, the currency with which it transacts most of its business.
    a. Type I subsidiaries are self-contained within a foreign country. Their financial statements must be translated from the functional currency (local currency in this case) to the reporting currency. Type II subsidiaries are simply an extension of the parent's operations. Their financial statements must be remeasured from the local currency to the functional currency (which in this case is the same as the reporting currency).

b. Depending on the type of subsidiary involved, the alternative exchange rates used are the current rate, the historical rate, and the average rate. A parent's investment in its subsidiary will probably change from year to year, and part of that change may be caused by exchange rate fluctuations called **translation adjustments**. For Type I subsidiaries, these translation adjustments should be included in the stockholders' equity section of the balance sheet, and not as part of net income. For Type II subsidiaries, however, **translation gains and losses** should be included in net income.

13. At present, there are no recognized world-wide standards of accounting. However, much progress has been made by the International Accounting Standards Committee (IASC) and the International Federation of Accountants (IFAC) in setting up international accounting standards. Despite the efforts of these bodies, there are still serious inconsistencies in financial statements among countries, and comparison remains a difficult task.

Matching

Match each term with its definition by writing the appropriate letter in the blank.

_E_ 1. Multinational corporation

_K_ 2. Closely held corporation

_B_ 3. Publicly held corporation

_H_ 4. Cost method

_N_ 5. Equity method

_L_ 6. Parent company

_I_ 7. Subsidiary

_F_ 8. Consolidated financial statements

_D_ 9. Purchase method

_J_ 10. Significant influence

_A_ 11. Minority interest

_P_ 12. Exchange rate

_O_ 13. Reporting currency

_C_ 14. Functional currency

_G_ 15. Translation adjustments

_M_ 16. Translation gains and losses

a. Outside ownership of a subsidiary

b. A corporation whose securities are registered and traded on the stock market

c. The type of money in which a company transacts most of its business

d. The consolidation method used when the parent owns more than 50 percent of the subsidiary's voting stock and did not acquire it through an exchange of stock

e. A corporation that has expanded operations throughout the world

f. Combined statements of the parent and its subsidiaries

g. Exchange rate fluctuations recognized on the balance sheet of a Type I subsidiary

h. The method used to account for noninfluential and noncontrolling investments

i. A company that is controlled by another company

j. The ability to affect the operating and financial policies of a company (usually when 20 percent or more of the voting stock is held)

k. A corporation whose stock is owned by a few individuals and is not traded publicly

l. A company that has a controlling interest in another company

m. Exchange rate fluctuations recognized on the income statement of a Type II subsidiary

n. The method to account for influential or controlling investments

o. The type of money in which a given set of consolidated financial statements are presented

p. The value of one currency in terms of another

Completion

Use the lines provided to complete each item.

1. List the three classifications for long-term investments in stocks, as well as the method that should be used after purchase to account for each investment.

Classification

Non-influential; non-controlling - < 20% ownership - cost method

Significant Influence - non-

Method

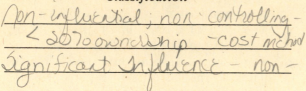

controlling - equity method - 20 - 50% ownership

Controlling - > 50% ownership purchase equity method & consolidate

2. Under what circumstance would a company record an exchange gain or loss?

Type II ~~consol~~ subsidiary

3. Briefly explain the accounting treatment for dividends received under the cost method and under the equity method.

Cost - dividends are treated as Cash, cr investment income

Equity - Dr Cash, cr. investment

4. Under what circumstance should goodwill be recorded in a consolidated balance sheet?

If stock is purchased for > value of equity

5. Why must certain items be eliminated when consolidated financial statements are prepared?

To eliminate inter-company transactions which distort the statements

True-False

Circle T if the statement is true, F if it is false.

T F 1. When one company has an influential but noncontrolling interest in another company, it must use the equity method to account for the investment.

T **F** 2. Under the cost method, the investor records investment income for a percentage (based on percentage ownership) of the investee's periodic net income.

T **F** 3. When one company owns at least 20 percent of another company, consolidated financial statements should be prepared.

T F 4. When consolidated financial statements are prepared, the parent's investment in the subsidiary must be eliminated.

T (F) 5. Under the purchase method of consolidation, the subsidiary's earnings for the entire year of acquisition are included in the consolidated financial statements.

(T) F 6. Under the equity method, the investor records a cash dividend by debiting Cash and crediting the investment account.

T (F) 7. A minority interest should be reported as an asset in the consolidated balance sheet.

(T) F 8. Goodwill from consolidation does not appear on the unconsolidated balance sheet of the parent or subsidiary, but may appear on the consolidated balance sheet.

(T) F 9. When long-term bonds are purchased at a premium, the carrying value of the investment prior to maturity will be greater than the maturity value.

(T) (F) 10. When long-term bonds are purchased at a discount, the amount of Bond Interest Earned that is recorded each interest period is greater than the amount of cash received.

T (F) 11. When preparing consolidated financial statements, purchases of goods and services from outsiders should be eliminated.

(T) F 12. When company A transacts business with foreign company B in the currency of company A, company A would not record an exchange gain or loss even if the exchange rate has changed between the transaction date and the date of payment.

(T) F 13. Given the data in statement number 12, company B should record an exchange gain or loss.

(T) F 14. When a given exchange rate remains constant over a period of time, no transaction involving the two currencies will result in an exchange gain or loss over that period.

T (F) 15. The IASC and the IFAC have developed standards of accounting that are recognized worldwide.

(T) F 16. When the book value of the net assets purchased equals their cost, the assets and liabilities purchased should appear at cost on the consolidated balance sheet.

T (F) 17. All assets and liabilities of a Type I subsidiary are restated at the current rate.

(T) F 18. Translation gains and losses are recognized in the income statement of a Type I subsidiary and in the balance sheet of a Type II subsidiary.

Multiple Choice

Circle the letter of the best answer.

1. The revenues and expenses (other than depreciation) of a British subsidiary would be translated into U.S. dollars for consolidated financial statement purposes by using the
   a. average exchange rate.
   b. historical exchange rate.
   c. current exchange rate.
   d. previous year's ending exchange rate.

2. The journal entry to record the receipt of a dividend under the cost method would include a
   a. debit to the investment account.
   b. credit to Dividend Income.
   c. debit to Goodwill.
   d. credit to the investment account.

3. When the book value of the net assets purchased exceeds their purchase cost,
   a. goodwill exists.
   b. the entire excess should appear as negative goodwill in the consolidated balance sheet.
   c. the subsidiary's assets should be increased until the extra amount is eliminated.
   d. the subsidiary's assets should be reduced until the extra amount is eliminated.

4. The elimination of an intercompany investment cannot include a
   a. debit to the investment account.
   b. debit to Goodwill.
   c. debit to Retained Earnings.
   d. credit to minority interest.

5. When an American company purchases goods from France and the transaction involves francs, what would the American company record on the date of payment if the value of the franc declined relative to the dollar between the purchase date and the payment date?
   a. An unrealized exchange gain
   b. An exchange loss
   c. An exchange gain
   d. No exchange gain or loss

6. The unconsolidated financial statements of a parent company may not include
   a. purchases from its subsidiary.
   b. goodwill from consolidation.
   c. an account reflecting the investment in its subsidiary.
   d. purchases from outsiders.

7. Which of the following items would not be eliminated when consolidated financial statements are prepared, assuming that the subsidiary is 100 percent owned?
   a. The subsidiary's capital stock
   b. The parent's investment in the subsidiary
   c. Interest owed to the subsidiary from the parent
   d. Profit on goods sold by the subsidiary to outsiders

8. Morse Company uses the cost method to account for its three long-term investments. The total cost of the investments is $95,000, and the total market value of the investments at the end of 19xx is $60,000. The account Allowance to Reduce Long-Term Investments to Market has a credit balance of $10,000 before the 19xx adjusting entry is made. The year-end adjusting entry for 19xx would include a
   a. debit to Unrealized Loss on Long-Term Investments for $35,000.
   b. debit to Allowance to Reduce Long-Term Investments to Market for $10,000.
   c. credit to Allowance to Reduce Long-Term Investments to Market for $60,000.
   d. debit to Unrealized Loss on Long-Term Investments for $25,000.

Applying Your Knowledge

Exercises

1. Weber Corporation purchased 80 percent of the common stock of Carter Corporation for $165,000. Carter's stockholders' equity included common stock of $60,000 and retained earnings of $90,000. On the lines provided, show the debits, credits, and amounts for the eliminating entry that would be made on the work sheet for consolidating the balance sheets of Weber and Carter. Assume that up to $10,000 of any excess of cost over carrying value is allocated to the building purchased.

Account Debited	Amount	Account Credited	Amount
Common Stock	$ 60,000	Investment - Carter	$ 165,000
Retained Earning	$ 90,000	Minority Interest	$ 30,000
Goodwill	$ 35,000		
Building	$ 10,000		

2. Fairfax Corporation owns 15 percent of the voting stock of Airdrome Company and 30 percent of the voting stock of Wilkins Company. Both are long-term investments. During a given year, Airdrome paid total dividends of $80,000 and earned $110,000, and Wilkins paid total dividends of $50,000 and earned $65,000. In the journal, prepare Fairfax's entries to reflect the above facts. Leave the date column empty, as no dates have been specified.

	General Journal			
Date		**Description**	**Debit**	**Credit**
		Cash	12,000	
		Investment Income - Airdrome		12,000
		Cash	15,000	
		Investment		15,000
		Investment	19,500	
		Investment Income		19,500

3. Randy Corporation, an American company, sold merchandise on credit to a Mexican company for 100,000 pesos. On the sale date, the exchange rate was $.05 per peso. On the payment date, the value of the peso had declined to $.045. Prepare the entries in the journal to record Randy Corporation's sale and receipt of payment. Leave the date column empty as no dates have been specified.

	General Journal			
Date		**Description**	**Debit**	**Credit**
		A/R - 100,000 pesos @ .05	5,000	
		A/R		5000
		Cash - 100,000 @ .045	4500	
		Loss on exchange	500	
		A/R		5000

1 = .25 or 4 = 1.00 $40 = $10

1 = .20 or 5 = 1.00 $40 = $8

4. On March 1, 19x1, Alt Company purchased ten $1,000 Pamco bonds at 94 plus a broker's commission of $200 plus accrued interest. The bonds had a face interest of $8\frac{4}{10}$ percent and paid interest each January 1 and July 1. In the journal provided, prepare Alt Company's journal entries based on the following facts (advice: keep running T-account for Investment in Bonds):

March 1, 19x1 Purchased the bonds.
July 1, 19x1 Received the interest and amortized the discount or premium. Assume a 9 percent effective interest rate.
Dec. 31, 19x1 Recorded accrued interest and amortized the discount or premium.
Jan. 1, 19x2 Received the interest.
March 1, 19x2 Sold all ten bonds at 95 less a $200 commission.

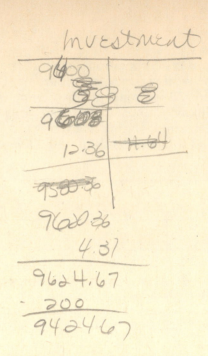

Handwritten T-account (Investment):
9600 / 8
9608
12.36 / 4.04
9580.36
9620.36
4.31
9624.67
- 200
9424.67

		General Journal		
Date		**Description**	**Debit**	**Credit**
19x1				
3	1	L.T. Investment	9600	
		Accrued Interest Receivable	140	
		Cash		9740
		Purchase of bonds @ 9400 + 200 commission		
		+ accrued interest		
7	1	Cash	420	
		Investment (288 - 280)	8	
		Bond Interest Income		288
		Accrued Interest Receivable		140
12	31	Accrued Interest Receivable	420	
		Investment (432.36 - 420)	12.36	
		Bond Interest Income		432.36
19x2				
1	1	Cash	420	
		Interest Receivable		420
3	1	Cash		
		L.T. Investment		
		Accrued Interest Receivable		
		Investment in Bonds	4.31	
3	1	Accrued Interest Receivable	140	4.31
		Bond Interest Income		140
		Loss on Sale	124.67	
	1	Cash	9440	
		Accrued Interest Receivable		140
		L.T. Investment		9624.67
		Sold @ 95 - 200 commission		

Handwritten calculations at bottom:
$9620.36 \times 9\% \times \frac{1}{6} = 144.31$
$10,000 \times 8.4\% \times \frac{1}{6} = 140$
4.31

Crossword Puzzle
For Chapters 19 and 20

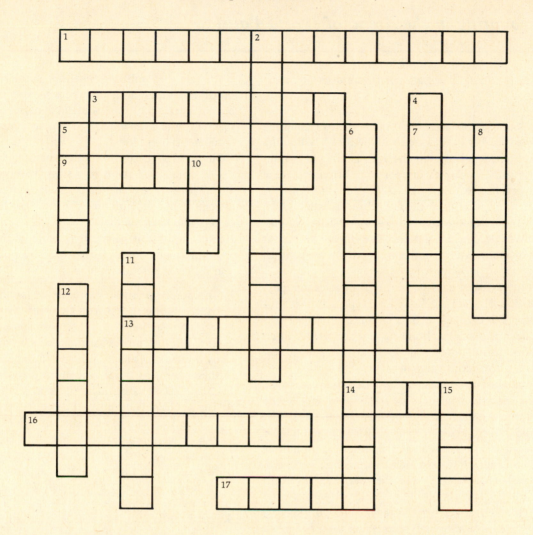

ACROSS

1. Broad definition of funds (2 words)
3. Outside interest in a subsidiary
7. Application of funds
9. _____ transaction (both source and application of funds)
13. A company controlled by another company
14. International accounting standards body
16. Significant _____ (ability to affect operations)
17. Working capital

DOWN

2. Selling stock to the general population (2 words)
4. Reporting or functional _____
5. Closely-_____ corporation
6. Consolidating work sheet adjustments
8. Method of accounting for long-term investments
10. _____ financial resources concept of funds
11. Statement similar to the statement of changes in financial position (2 words)
12. Company that controls another company
15. Method of accounting for long-term investments

Accounting in the Arena of World Politics

Crosscurrents of international standard-setting activities

It is no longer any secret that the affairs of accounting are inextricably intertwined with politics.[1] Within the profession, relatively mundane items like publication of a membership directory for firms belonging to the SEC practice section of the AICPA division for CPA firms, and the broader big GAAP versus small GAAP issue have become charged with political emotions. Their respective resolutions—like those of similar earlier issues—will be influenced heavily by political processes.

In the external environment of the profession, politicization of issues and resultant approaches to their solutions is even more of a factor. Professional governance, professional licensing and reciprocity in individual jurisdictions and disclosure of peer review results are standout examples.

Unparalled in intensity of politicization, however, is the matter of accounting standard setting.[2] Who should set standards and by what authority? Who should enforce standards and by what means? Should standard setting be broad and philosophical or narrow and procedural? Must standard setters "find" consensus in the community and then set their standards accordingly, or should they build consensus after they have already arrived at judgmental positions? Is one standard-setting body enough, or should there be several? One could easily fill an entire article with questions of this type.

Source: Article by Lane A. Daley and Gerhard G. Mueller. Reprinted from the February 1982 issue of *The Journal of Accountancy.* Copyright © 1982 by the American Institute of Certified Public Accountants, Inc.

1. S.J. Gray, J.C. Shaw and L.B. McSweeny, "Accounting Standards and Multinational Corporations," *Journal of International Business Studies,* Spring/Summer 1981, pp. 121–136; David Solomons, "The Politicization of Accounting," JofA, Nov. 78, pp. 65–72.
2. Canadian Institute of Chartered Accountants, "The Report of the Special Committee on Standard Setting (SCOSS), *CA Magazine,* June 1981, pp. 35–49; Donald J. Kirk, "Concepts, Consensus, Compromise and Consequences: Their Roles in Standard Setting," JofA, Apr. 81, pp. 83–86; Thomas A. Murphy, "Setting Accounting Standards—A Suggestion from a Businessman," *Financial Executive,* August 1979, pp. 52–57; Joshua Ronen and Michael Schiff, "The Setting of Financial Accounting Standards—Private or Public?" JofA, Mar. 78, pp. 66–73.

The fact that political dimensions attach to professional accounting affairs is no longer very interesting, but the question of how political dimensions manifest themselves and how they affect accounting-related outcomes is of interest.

Our article focuses on the international consequences of accounting standard setting. Worldwide, there are at least twenty national standard-setting organizations or boards with precious little synchronization of activities between them.

From a political perspective, national financial accounting standard setting the world over occurs from four different baselines:

1. The purely political approach, as found predominantly in France and West Germany. Here national legislation action decrees accounting standards.
2. The private, professional approach, exemplified by Australia, Canada and the United Kingdom. In these cases, financial accounting standards are set and enforced by private professional actions only.
3. The public/private mixed approach, for which the U.S. is the leading example and which countries like Japan appear to be emulating. Here standards are basically set by private sector bodies which behave as though they were public agencies and whose standards are enforced through governmental actions.
4. The broadly mixed system, like that in the Netherlands, where not only accounting professionals and governmental agencies but also labor unions, industry and trade associations take an active direct hand in setting and enforcing accounting standards.

No wonder, then, that the results of these various national standard-setting activities are heterogeneous and often contradictory. Moreover, this is a major reason why international political attention is being visited on accounting. In support of this assertion, consider the following:

Philips Industries of the Netherlands received highest marks for its annual report in the *Financial Times* (London) 1980 survey of annual reports of major companies worldwide. Yet currently Philips is considering a major change in its financial reporting based largely on replacement cost measurements. Its board of directors believes that the company's earnings are understated by world standards.

Just two years ago, the Royal Dutch Petroleum Company was unable to receive an unqualified report from its independent accountants, because British and U.S. standards for income tax allocation were contradictory. Whatever the company did in this respect caused a qualification by one of its joint auditors (Dutch/U.K./U.S.).

Swiss multinational companies are regularly publishing financial reports that materially exceed national requirements. Allegedly, this is done to secure better international financial credit, open the possibility of listing shares on stock exchanges outside of Switzerland and improve general market and product images.

□ In the competition for market shares, U.S./U.K.-based multinational accounting service firms claim to be better acquainted with world standards of financial accounting, to have more reliable transnational service networks and in general to be able to serve multinational companies more effectively.

□ Certain U.S. accounting standards, especially those relating to foreign exchange translations and the equity method of accounting for certain intercorporate investments, are said to have circumscribed the ability of U.S. enterprises to bid competitively in multinational merger negotiations.[3] The advent of the Foreign Corrupt Practices Act of 1977, together with comparatively conservative U.S. income tax laws as they affect multinational operations, have assertedly weakened the multinational competitive position of U.S.-based enterprises (e.g., in multinational corporate mergers and/or takeovers).

□ Third World countries clamor for accounting standards and rules that could be used to control the operations of multinational corporations within their borders. Broadly speaking, representatives of Third World countries often claim that today's financial accounting has a pervasive British-American bias and is tailored strongly to the needs of the highly industrialized countries.

□ U.S. corporate managements often claim that excessive "fine tuning" has given U.S. financial accounting an unwarranted emphasis on short-term profitability measurements. By contrast, Japanese financial accounting standards are thought to be more long-term oriented. Again, this is asserted to limit the multinational competitiveness of U.S.-based enterprises.

□ In many technical aspects (inflation accounting, financial statement consolidation, Lifo inventory pricing, lease accounting, pension accounting, research and development accounting, foreign exchange translation and other similar items), national accounting standards require different treatments of similar transactions and circumstances.[4] This is seen by many as a failure of underlying technical processes and full justification for political intervention.

Individually and in combination, reasons like those just enumerated have politicized accounting internationally. Next, we explore who the international accounting players are and what their game is.

Who Is Involved?

Accounting standard-setting efforts are taking place in three major international arenas. Both global and regional bodies are at work in each arena. Moreover, several groups best described as "lobbyists" are active throughout the entire international environment as they seek to represent the best interests of the constituencies.

The first international accounting arena is composed of international political bodies such as the United Nations (UN), the Organization for Economic Cooperation and Development (OECD), the European Economic Community (EEC) and the African Accounting Council (AAC). These agencies seek to formulate various financial and nonfinancial reporting requirements in a purely political manner. Representation on their accounting committees or working groups is by treaty, and the selection process to choose an individual to represent a country is not based on accounting expertise but, rather, on political considerations. For instance, the U.S. Department of State (with assistance from a national advisory committee) represents U.S. accounting interests at the UN and the OECD.

The second sphere of influence consists of the private standard-setting boards whose representation is from national professional accounting groups. Their predominant purpose is setting international financial reporting standards. The International Accounting Standards Committee (IASC) and the Association of Southeast Asian Nations Federation of Accountants (AFA) are in this group.

The third grouping consists of international pro-

3. Frederick D.S. Choi and Gerhard G. Mueller, *Introduction to Multinational Accounting* (Englewood Cliffs, N.J.: Prentice-Hall, Inc., 1978), p. 152–153. The Financial Accounting Standards Board issued FASB Statement no. 52, *Foreign Currency Translation* (see Official Releases, page 125), last December. See "FASB Replaces Standard on Foreign Currency Translation," JofA, Jan. 82, p. 9.

4. R.D. Nair and Werner G. Frank, "The Impact of Disclosure and Measurement Practices in International Accounting Classifications," *Accounting Review,* July 1980, pp. 426–450; R.D. Fitzgerald, A.D. Stickler and T.R. Watts, eds., *International Survey of Accounting Principles and Reporting Practices* (London: Price Waterhouse International, 1979).

fessional accounting organizations that deal with various professional issues such as auditing standards, educational requirements and ethical standards for the profession in the international setting. This arena includes the International Federation of Accountants (IFAC), the Union Européenne des Experts Comptables Economiques et Financiers (UEC) and the Asociación Interamericana de Contabilidad (AIC).

The "lobbyists" are widespread, representing many interested parties. National standard-setting bodies have obvious interests in the actions of the international bodies and thus may at times become lobbyists. One illustration of such "interface" is the June 1981 attendance of Donald J. Kirk, chariman of the Financial Accounting Standards Board, at a regular IASC meeting. Academic organizations sometimes act as lobbyists when topical research is undertaken and results are used as inputs to standard-setting processes. Other parties such as the International Chamber of Commerce, the National Foreign Trade Council, the International Confederation of Free Trade Unions, the Business and Industry Advisory Committee and the Trade Union Advisory Committee act as lobbyists to promote goals that are in their best interests.

In the preceding paragraphs only about one-half the groups and organizations active in the international accounting arena are identified by name. The large number of bodies directly involved provides one measure of the size and scope of what we are talking about. Hence, to keep the issue manageable and reasonably focused, we will concentrate on the international political and private standard-setting bodies. Interrelationships among these bodies are highlighted in exhibits 1, 2 and 3.

Exhibit 1 lists the countries most often represented in international bodies ranked by the incidence of international representation. Of the 37 countries listed (a country had to be represented on at least three bodies to be included) the "most represented" 7 are all Western, developed nations. Only 1 of the 37 is an African nation. None are from the Middle East.

Exhibit 2 examines the geographical distribution of the membership of the major international groups. Here we see an interesting pattern of fairly independent regional groups and highly interrelated global bodies. The developing world appears to be more highly represented in the global groups than exhibit 1 suggests. Although such additional representation is present, it is not made up of single countries represented in many bodies as is common for the Western nations. The Western countries may have comparatively greater access to international accounting standard-setting groups and agencies.

Exhibit 3 examines the cross representation among some major international accounting bodies. The results are very similar to those in exhibit 1, but the data in exhibit 3 point out much more clearly the high degree of correlation in the representation on the global bodies. The IASC is formed from a subset of the IFAC representation. Almost every OECD country is represented in both IASC and IFAC. Similarly the UEC is almost completely represented in the OECD, IASC and IFAC.

These are the participants in the international accounting standards efforts. Their activities are indicative of a large concern over issues of accounting and reporting practices worldwide. Both political and private professional groups are concerned enough to expend much time and money to influence the ongoing process of internationalization of accounting.

The following sections of this article take a brief look at the activities of international political and private accounting standard setters, discuss the goals of these international bodies and anticipate what evolutionary processes might be set into motion.

What is Happening?

In the political arena, three organizations are of primary interest—the UN, OECD and EEC. The UN has been at work since 1977 promulgating accounting standards at the committee level. Technical papers were developed to form the basis for the work of the Intergovernmental Working Group of Experts on International Standards of Accounting and Reporting. These technical papers contain many specific accounting standards regarding the substance of corporate annual reports as well as rules for such issues as consolidation.

The most notable portion of the papers is the extension of requirements to include data that heretofore were excluded from annual reports. These data are primarily oriented toward employment information and technology transfers. This focus appears to be a response to the desires of the developing nations to extract data from the multinational enterprises (MNEs) which they do not feel powerful enough to extract via national controls. Economic development and assisting and "protecting" employees of MNEs are other goals of the UN effort.

For the time being the UN accounting standards effort focuses on the MNEs. Eventually application to all companies the world over is envisioned. Should international accounting standards ever be adopted as a resolution by the UN, enforcement will require actions of either national standard-setting bodies or national governments to carry the force of law. Adop-

Exhibit 1*

**Selected Representation on International
Standard-Setting Bodies by Individual Country**

Country	AAC	AFA	CAPA	EEC	UEC	AIC	IASC	IFAC	OECD	UN**	
Canada	–	–	X	–	–	X	X	X	X	X	
France	–	–	–	X	X	–	X	X	X	X	
Germany	–	–	–	X	X	–	X	X	X	X	6 Group representation
Italy	–	–	–	X	X	–	X	X	X	X	
Netherlands	–	–	–	X	X	–	X	X	X	X	
Great Britain	–	–	–	X	X	–	X	X	X	X	
United States	–	–	X	–	–	X	X	X	X	X	
Belgium	–	–	–	X	X	–	X	X	X	–	
Denmark	–	–	–	X	X	–	X	X	X	–	
Ireland	–	–	–	X	X	–	X	X	X	–	
Japan	–	–	X	–	–	–	X	X	X	X	5 Group representation
Luxembourg	–	–	–	X	X	–	X	X	X	–	
Norway	–	–	–	–	X	–	X	X	X	X	
Philippines	–	X	X	–	–	–	X	X	–	X	
Australia	–	–	X	–	–	–	X	X	X	–	
Brazil	–	–	–	–	–	X	X	X	–	X	
Finland	–	–	–	–	X	–	X	X	X	–	
Greece	–	–	–	–	X	–	X	X	X	–	
India	–	X	X	–	–	–	–	X	–	X	
Malaysia	–	X	X	–	–	–	X	X	–	–	
Mexico	–	–	–	–	–	X	X	X	–	X	
New Zealand	–	–	X	–	–	–	X	X	X	–	4 Group representation
Nigeria	X	–	–	–	–	–	X	X	–	X	
Panama	–	–	–	–	–	X	X	X	–	X	
Pakistan	–	–	X	–	–	–	X	X	–	X	
Portugal	–	–	–	–	X	–	X	X	X	–	
Singapore	–	X	X	–	–	–	X	X	–	–	
Spain	–	–	–	–	X	–	X	X	X	–	
Sweden	–	–	–	–	X	–	X	X	X	–	
Argentina	–	–	–	–	–	X	–	X	–	X	
Bangladesh	–	–	X	–	–	–	X	X	–	–	
Cyprus	–	–	–	–	–	–	X	X	–	X	
Dominican Republic	–	–	–	–	–	X	–	X	–	X	3 Group representation
Fiji	–	–	X	–	–	–	X	X	–	–	
Iceland	–	–	–	–	X	–	–	X	X	–	
Sri Lanka	–	–	X	–	–	–	X	X	–	–	
Thailand	–	X	X	–	–	–	–	X	–	–	
Representatives	1	5	14	9	16	7	32	37	21	19	
Total number of representations in body	23	5	18	9	18	21	42	53	23	30	

*Adapted from United Nations Report E/C.10/AC.3/7 of September 9, 1980. Second session of the Ad Hoc Intergovernmental Working Group on International Standards of Accounting and Reporting–Commission on Transnational Corporations–UN Economic and Social Council.
**Member of the UN intergovernmental working group.

Exhibit 2*

Interrepresentation Among Major
International Standard-Setting Bodies

Body	Africa	Asia	Middle East	Europe	North America	Latin America	Australia/ New Zealand	Total
AAC	23	—	—	—	—	—	—	23
AFA	—	5	—	—	—	—	—	5
CAPA	—	13	1	—	2	—	2	18
EEC	—	—	—	9	—	—	—	9
UEC	—	—	—	18	—	—	—	18
AIC	—	—	—	—	2	19	—	21
IASC	5	9	1	16	2	7	2	42
IFAC	4	11	3	18	2	13	2	53
OECD	2	1	—	15	2	2	1	23
UN**	8	4	1	9	2	6	—	30

*Adapted from United Nations Report E/C.10/AC.3/7 of September 9, 1980. Second session of the Ad Hoc Intergovernmental Working Group on International Standards of Accounting and Reporting—Commission on Transnational Corporations—UN Economic and Social Council.

**Member of the UN intergovernmental working group.

Exhibit 3*

Interrepresentation Among Major
International Standard-Setting Bodies

Body	AAC	AFA	CAPA	EEC	UEC	AIC	IASC	IFAC	OECD	UN**
AAC	23	—	—	—	—	—	1	1	—	3
AFA	—	5	5	—	—	—	3	5	—	1
CAPA	—	5	18	—	—	2	13	16	5	5
EEC	—	—	—	9	9	—	9	9	9	5
UEC	—	—	—	9	18	—	16	16	17	5
AIC	—	—	2	—	—	21	5	11	2	7
IASC	1	3	13	9	16	5	42	39	20	17
IFAC	1	5	16	9	16	11	39	53	22	21
OECD	—	—	5	9	17	2	20	22	23	8
UN**	3	1	5	5	5	7	17	21	8	30

*Adapted from United Nations Report E/C.10/AC.3/7 of September 9, 1980. Second session of the Ad Hoc Intergovernmental Working Group on International Standards of Accounting and Reporting—Commission on Transnational Corporations—UN Economic and Social Council.

**Member of the UN intergovernmental working group.

tion by the UN certainly would change the political standing of the standards proposed (at a minimum, legitimize them), but it would not mean direct or immediate implementation.

The OECD began its international accounting standards efforts with its June 21, 1976, declaration by the governments of OECD member countries on international investment and multinational enterprises. Since the OECD is made up of developed countries, it represents a different view toward the MNE than does the developing world. This is evident in the reporting standards recommended by the OECD. These standards ignore the recommendations of the UN to expand the data set contained in corporate annual reports. They tend to be distillations of national standards already used in the countries represented. Unlike the UN, the OECD has not really broken any new ground with any of its recommendations. Like the UN, the OECD is powerless to enforce its recommendations aside from national adoption. The treaty creating the OECD does not extend police powers to the organization.

The EEC is unlike the UN and the OECD in a very important way. This body has been granted police powers via the Treaty of Rome. Thus it is setting accounting standards by fiat (not uncommon in Europe on the national level), and these standards must be adopted by the member countries in due course. Relevant activity so far is reflected in the Fourth Directive and the Seventh Directive (in draft form), which specify many measurement methods and reporting requirements to be used by companies in the EEC. Technical issues like consolidation rules are included. The noteworthy facet of this process is that the standards are actually being set by treaty—a mechanism we have not discussed. In fact, all accounting activity in the international political sector is premised on treaty agreements. The only difference is in the powers of enforcement that the underlying treaties specify.

At the private professional level, the IASC has been most active. At present, there are 16 definitive IASC standards. Forty-two countries are represented on the IASC and, as we have seen, Western countries dominate the organization. The IASC is setting standards in a manner very similar to that used by the American Institute of CPAs committee on accounting procedure in the 1950s. It has not broken any new ground; rather, the IASC attempts to review the procedures currently in use in countries around the world and distill or "harmonize" these by recommending a limited set of acceptable alternatives. The IASC has been beneficial to some countries as a source of information input to regional or national standard-setting processes. Frederick Choi notes that the AFA has used many of the IASC recommendations in preparing its own reporting standards.[5] As with the UN and the OECD, the IASC has no legitimate legal or political power. It acts as an adviser, and its recommendations must be adopted at the national level before any real implementation is possible. In addition, given its Western bias, many of the developing nations criticize the IASC for being insensitive to their situations and needs.

In summary, only one international organization presently promulgating accounting standards has the ability to enforce its recommendations. In addition, little is being done that might be described as new in character. The OECD and the IASC have not ventured into any new issues, and the EEC is still laying the groundwork for such an adventure. Only the UN has really extended itself. However, its work is still ongoing so that it is impossible to predict the nature of the final outcome.

What Goals Have Been Set?

With the plethora of parties involved in international accounting standard-setting activity, what can be said about the overall goal associated with this effort? Many accountants view the goal of this process as the "standardization" of worldwide financial reporting requirements for profit-oriented enterprises. In fact, the very term "accounting standard" underscores this fact. It is reinforced by the work of groups such as the UN that desire to develop requirements for the entire private sector the world over. Other groups like the OECD focus only on the MNEs but seem to desire ultimately the same uniformity (i.e., they don't want to "discriminate" unduly against MNEs).

Given that complete standardization has not been possible in many countries even at the national level, the likelihood for such development at the international level is small indeed. This has prompted groups like the EEC to adopt a position that does not seek uniformity but, rather, harmonization. The latter, as nearly as can be discerned, means that there will be acceptable alternatives but these alternatives must be such that they will not contradict each other (i.e., be fair and reasonable). This method of operations is typical of the British–American mode of standard-setting.

As yet no one has suggested that synchronization (or a method of providing means to resolve differen-

5. Frederick D.S. Choi, "ASEAN Federation of Accountants: A New International Accounting Force," *International Journal of Accounting Education and Research*, Fall 1979, pp. 53–66.

ces when the various national standards contradict one another as in the Royal Dutch Petroleum example cited earlier) might be the most appropriate mechanism—at least in short run. Synchronization would recognize that standards are only appropriate when enforceable by the legitimate powers of the state. Hence it is a problem of international politics as well as international economics when national accounting standards create barriers to economic activity. Contradictory national accounting standards may best be resolved at the political level with treaties binding the respective parties. This would not require the establishment of new standards; it would simply give recognition to the fact that situations occur in which it is in the best interests of national societies (as a whole) to allow some special "pardon" in selected matters of accounting and financial reporting.

The promise for the future of international standard setting in accounting lies in some form of a flexible interactive relationship, in which international standards are either interwoven directly into national standards or some mechanism for international resolution of specific conflicts evolves. At present the former is apparently farther along the road of development than the latter.

What Does the Future Hold?

It is inappropriate for anyone to project a single set of future outcomes. Therefore, we intend to provide three possible scenarios given the information currently available. The importance of these scenarios does not lie in their accuracy but, rather, in conjecturing the roles of involved international groups and their interaction(s) with national standard-setting bodies. It is this interaction that is of critical importance to the local practitioner as well as the national government.

Our first scenario focuses on the MNEs, since they are the companies most likely to be affected by international accounting standards developments. The second examines likely developments in the international political sector and the third assesses the ability of organizations like the IASC to develop into a leadership position in international standard-setting processes.

The MNEs are the parties bearing much of the cost of the lack of international agreement on accounting standards. Multiple sets of records and reports are needed for meeting each country's requirements. If published statements do not meet local requirements, the companies bear the cost of qualified audit opinions (as in the case of Royal Dutch Petroleum). To the extent that this imposes additional capital costs,

the lack of accounting agreement translates into real economic cost. Thus there is a possible incentive for the MNEs to impose accounting and financial reporting mechanisms in which they, either as a group or individually, choose a set of reporting standards and use their economic clout to encourage governmental units to adopt the mechanisms selected. Such a strategy could be particularly successful in countries where the national government is in a weak bargaining position relative to the MNE.

Since such behavior will not necessarily resolve the problem of the qualified audit opinion in all countries, managements of MNEs must either believe that in the long run their actions will result in resolution of the problem or that they will be able to convince capital contributors that the effects of opinion qualifications are trivial. Actions of this type must be weighed carefully, however, against possible political costs. MNEs are already under scrutiny for assorted disproportionate effects on the local political economy. MNEs' actions are bounded by the potential loss of profitable industry due to political decisions by national governments. It is for this reason that MNEs are unlikely to find it in their best interests to attempt to dictate public policy directly as it relates to accounting standards. If the MNEs were to become the primary force in accounting standard-setting processes, local professional accounting groups would lose power and influence regarding the process.

For purposes of the second scenario, international political processes provide the impetus for setting international accounting standards. This would require several major changes in the current environment but has the advantage of being a mechanism embraced at present by many societies for deciding public policy issues. It allows both general preference and intensity of preference to influence the decision process, and it would be done outside private professional organizations that might seek to work mainly in their own best interests. For such a scenario to develop, a much stronger set of international treaties must become available. Enforcement powers must be given to international political bodies or agreements consummated that stipulate binding national support for any standards set. This scenario also would require formal ties between national and international standard-setting processes. Either national bodies such as the FASB would become obsolete or they would be relegated to (1) dealing with issues left uncovered by the international bodies and (2) lobbying for interests of their local constituencies at the international level.

The second scenario seems plausible. First there is the actual activity of the EEC. Many regions of the world are attempting to use the EEC model to develop regional integration. Should they be successful (along EEC lines), several regionally oriented international groups could emerge that might be capable of setting regionally enforceable accounting standards. The question then would be whether these regional groups can find a mechanism to resolve interregional differences. At present, only the UN provides a theater for such activity, and there is no evidence that it can successfully deal with a situation as postulated.

The last scenario is a continuation or minor modification of the British–American model as used by the IASC. In this scenario the IASC would work with national standard-setting bodies to develop integrated accounting standards, which then would be adopted by the national groups as "accepted" alternatives. Several factors would have to be altered if the IASC were to accomplish this. First, the IASC would have to obtain a wider base of representation to become a truly global body. There are some indications that this is under way, but much more must be done.[6] Second, the IASC would have to begin to develop the types of formal working relationships with national bodies necessary for the conjectured development to take place. Third, the IASC would have to become a leader in dealing with accounting issues. This last step has huge costs, since the IASC would run the risk of exposing itself to disenchantment by members and may possibly lose support. Furthermore, IASC operations would have to be expanded significantly, including adequate research. Again, this would be very costly. If the IASC does not become the world leader in setting standards, it will never be a truly significant force except in providing information to areas of the world that are in the process of developing their own standards.

If the IASC becomes the dominant force in the international sphere, the national professions will serve a most important role in selecting representatives and in providing input to the entire process. It is in this scenario where the greatest amount of responsibility would rest with the national professions. Indeed, in almost any scenario one clear implication exists for the national professions. Decisions made on national accounting standards (which for a long time have been viewed as issues of national public policy) are in fact dynamically interrelated with issues of international

public policy.[7] It is not sufficient that CPAs in the U.S., as a national profession, attend only to issues that are relevant to their own interests. American CPAs must increasingly recognize the international effects of local decisions.

Summary

This article began with an examination of the activities in the international sector as they relate to the setting of accounting standards. We discovered a great deal of involvement in the international sphere of many different interest groups. There is a flavor of Western dominance in much of the representation on international accounting bodies and much interpollination in that representation. We suggested three views of what the goals of the international accounting standard-setting process might be and then examined three scenarios of possible future developments.

In all cases there is a long way to go. Formal ties between international groups and national governments are necessary if international standard setters are to develop police powers to enforce their own recommendations. Alternatively, private sector standard setting as constituted at present (i.e., no direct enforcement powers accruing to standard setters) must become more internationally oriented if it is to survive. Greater accounting "internationalization" is crucial to obtaining any kind of harmonization or synchronization of reporting requirements between nations.

Finally, we asserted that accounting professionals must cultivate an international orientation to understand the multidimensional effects of developing national standards. If nothing else, this will prepare them for a time when the promulgation of international standards may directly affect the CPA with a domestic practice because of the formal arrangements for national–international standard-setting interactions. The pressure for these interactions, we submit, is not coming from the political organizations (UN, OECD, EEC), the international professional bodies (IASC, IFAC, UEC) or the national standard setters (FASB, ASC in the U.K.). It is coming from the users of the products of accounting—MNEs, regulators, financial analysts, bankers, labor unions and all the other interested parties CPAs purport to serve.

---

6. The IASC Consultative Group, formed late in 1981, consists of participants nominated by the International Federation of Stock Exhanges, the International Association of Financial Executives Institutes, the International Chamber of Commerce, the International Confederation of Free Trade Unions, the International Coordinating Committee of Financial Analyst's Associations and the World Bank.

7. See *World Accounting Report* (London: Financial Times, July 1981), pp. iv–v, for public policy implications over standard setting within the EEC.

Reviewing the Chapter

1. Decision makers get specific information from general-purpose financial statements by means of **financial statement analysis**.

2. The users of financial statements are classified as either internal or external. The main internal user is management. The main external users are creditors and owners. Both creditors and owners will probably acquire a **portfolio**, or group of loans or investments, because the risk of loss is far less with several investments than with one investment.

3. Creditors and investors use financial statement analysis to (a) assess past performance and the current position, and (b) assess future potential and the risk connected with the potential. Information about the past and present is very helpful in making projections about the future. Moreover, the easier it is to predict future performance, the less risk is involved. The lower risk means the investor or creditor will require a lower expected return.

4. Decision makers assess performance by means of (a) rule-of-thumb measures, (b) analysis of past performance of the company, and (c) comparison with industry norms.
   a. Rule-of-thumb measures for key financial ratios are helpful but should not be the only basis for making a decision.

For example, a company may report high earnings per share, but may lack sufficient assets to pay current debts.
   b. Past performance of a company can help show trends. The skill lies in the analyst's ability to predict whether a trend will continue or will reverse itself.
   c. Comparing a company's performance with the performance of other companies in the same industry is helpful, but there are three limitations to using industry norms as standards. First, no two companies are exactly the same. Second, many companies, called **diversified companies** or **conglomerates**, operate in many unrelated industries, so that comparison is hard. (However, the recent requirement to report financial information by segments has been somewhat helpful.) Third, different companies often use different accounting procedures for recording similar items.

5. The chief sources of information about publicly held corporations are published reports, SEC reports, business periodicals, and credit and investment advisory services.
   a. A company's annual report provides useful financial information, and includes the following sections: (1) analysis of the past year's operations, (2) the financial statements, (3) footnotes,

(4) accounting procedures, (5) the auditor's report, and (6) a five- or ten-year summary of operations.

b. **Interim financial statements** may indicate significant changes in a company's earnings trend. They consist of limited financial information for less than a year (usually quarterly).

c. Publicly held corporations are required to file with the SEC an annual report (form 10-K), a quarterly report (form 10-Q), and a current report of significant events (form 8-K). These reports are available to the public and are sources of valuable financial information.

d. Financial analysts obtain information from such sources as the *Wall Street Journal, Forbes, Barron's, Fortune*, the *Commercial and Financial Chronicle*, Moody's, Standard and Poor's, and Dun and Bradstreet.

6. The most common tools and techniques of financial analysis are horizontal analysis, trend analysis, vertical analysis, and ratio analysis.

a. Comparative financial statements show the current and prior year's statements presented side by side to aid in financial statement analysis. **Horizontal analysis** shows absolute and percentage changes in specific items from one year to the next. The first of the two years being considered is called the **base year**, and the percentage change is computed by dividing the amount of the change by the base-year amount.

b. **Trend analysis** is the same as horizontal analysis, except percentage changes are calculated for several consecutive years. For percentage changes to be shown over several years, **index numbers** must be used.

c. **Vertical analysis** presents the percentage relationship of individual items on the statement to a total within the statement (for instance, cost of goods sold as a percentage of net sales). The result is a **common-size statement**. On a common-size balance sheet, total assets and total equities would each be labeled 100 percent. On a common-size income statement, sales would be labeled 100 percent. Common-size statements may be presented in comparative form to show information both within the period and between periods.

7. **Ratio analysis** determines certain relationships (ratios) between financial statement items, then compares the ratios with those of prior years or other companies. Ratios provide information about a company's liquidity, profitability, long-run solvency, and market strength. The most common ratios are as follows.

Ratio	Components	Use or Meaning
Liquidity Ratios		
Current ratio	$\dfrac{\text{current assets}}{\text{current liabilities}}$	Measure of short-term debt-paying ability
Quick ratio	$\dfrac{\text{cash + short-term investments + receivables}}{\text{current liabilities}}$	Measure of short-term liquidity
Receivable turnover	$\dfrac{\text{sales}}{\text{average accounts receivable}}$	Measure of relative size of accounts receivable balance and effectiveness of credit policies
Average days' sales uncollected	$\dfrac{\text{days in year}}{\text{receivable turnover}}$	Measure of time it takes to collect an average receivable
Inventory turnover	$\dfrac{\text{cost of goods sold}}{\text{average inventory}}$	Measure of relative size of inventory

Ratio	Components	Use or Meaning
Profitability Ratios		
Profit margin	$\dfrac{\text{net income}}{\text{sales}}$	Income produced by each dollar of sales
Asset turnover	$\dfrac{\text{sales}}{\text{average total assets}}$	Measure of how efficiently assets are used to produce sales
Return on assets	$\dfrac{\text{net income}}{\text{average total assets}}$	Overall measure of earning power or profitability of all assets used in the business
Return on equity	$\dfrac{\text{net income}}{\text{average owners' equity}}$	Profitability of owners' investment
Earnings per share	$\dfrac{\text{net income}}{\text{outstanding shares}}$	Means of placing earnings on a common basis for comparisons
Long-Term Solvency Ratios		
Debt to equity	$\dfrac{\text{total liabilities}}{\text{owners' equity}}$	Measure of relationship of debt financing to equity financing. A company with debt is said to be **leveraged**.
Interest coverage	$\dfrac{\text{net income before taxes}+\text{interest expense}}{\text{interest expense}}$	Measure of protection of creditors from a default on interest payments
Market Test Ratios		
Price/earnings(P/E)	$\dfrac{\text{market price per share}}{\text{earnings per share}}$	Measure of amount the market will pay for a dollar of earnings
Dividends yield	$\dfrac{\text{dividends per share}}{\text{market price per share}}$	Measure of current return to investor
Market risk	$\dfrac{\text{specific change in market price}}{\text{average change in market price}}$	Measure of volatility (called **beta**) of the market price of a stock in relation to that of other stocks

Testing Your Knowledge

Matching

Match each term with its definition by writing the appropriate letter in the blank.

G 1. Financial statement analysis
B 2. Portfolio
L 3. Diversified companies (conglomerates)
E 4. Interim financial statements
J 5. Horizontal analysis
F 6. Base year
H 7. Trend analysis
I 8. Index number
K 9. Vertical analysis
D 10. Common-size statement
M 11. Ratio analysis
A 12. Leverage
C 13. Beta

a. Debt financing
b. A group of investments or loans
c. A measure of market risk
d. A financial statement expressed in terms of percentages, the result of vertical analysis
e. Limited financial information for less than a year (usually quarterly)
f. The first year being considered when horizontal analysis is used
g. Getting specific information from general-purpose financial statements
h. A presentation of the percentage change in specific items over several years
i. A number used in trend analysis to show changes in related items over several years
j. A presentation of absolute and percentage changes in specific items from one year to the next
k. A presentation of the percentage relationships of individual items on a statement to a total within the statement
l. Companies that operate in many unrelated industries
m. The determination of certain relationships between financial statement items

Completion

Use the lines provided to complete each item.

1. Indicate five ratios that measure profitability.

Profit Margin
Asset Turnover
Return on Assets
Return on Equity
Earnings/Share

2. Briefly distinguish between horizontal and vertical analysis.

3. List the three methods by which decision makers assess performance.

Rule of Thumb

Analysis of Past Perform

Industry Norm Comparison

4. Why is it wiser to acquire a portfolio of small investments rather than one large investment?

_____

_____

_____

True-False

Circle T if the statement is true, F if it is false.

T F 1. Horizontal analysis is possible for both an income statement and a balance sheet.

T **F** 2. Common-size financial statements show dollar changes in specific items from one year to the next.

T **F** 3. A company with a 2.0 current ratio will experience a decline in the current ratio when a short-term liability is paid.

T F 4. The figure for inventory is not used in computing the quick ratio.

T **F** 5. Inventory turnover equals average inventory divided by cost of goods sold.

T **F** 6. The price/earnings ratio must be computed before earnings per share can be determined.

T F 7. When computing the return on equity, interest expense must be added back to net income.

T F 8. When a company has no debt, its return on assets equals its return on equity.

T **F** 9. The lower the debt to equity ratio, the riskier the situation.

T F 10. Receivable turnover measures the time it takes to collect an average receivable.

T F 11. A low interest coverage would be cause for concern for a company's bondholders.

T F 12. A stock with a beta of less than 1.0 indicates a risk factor that is less than that of the market as a whole.

T **F** 13. Dividends yield is a profitability ratio.

T **F** 14. On a common-size income statement, net income is given a label of 100 percent.

T F 15. Interim financial statements may serve as an early signal of significant changes in a company's earnings trend.

T F 16. Probably the best source of financial news is the _Wall Street Journal_.

T F 17. Return on assets equals the profit margin times asset turnover.

Multiple-Choice

Circle the letter of the best answer.

1. Which of the following is a measure of long-term solvency?
   a. Current ratio
   b. Interest coverage
   c. Asset turnover
   d. Profit margin

2. Short-term creditors would probably be _most_ interested in which ratio?
   a. Current ratio
   b. Earnings per share
   c. Debt to equity ratio
   d. Quick ratio

_200 / 100 = 2_

_150 / 50 = 3_

3. Net income is irrelevant in computing which ratio?
   a. Earnings per share
   b. Price/earnings ratio
   c. Asset turnover
   d. Return on equity

4. A high price/earnings ratio indicates
   a. investor confidence in high future earnings.
   b. that the stock is probably overvalued.
   c. that the stock is probably undervalued.
   d. little investor confidence in high future earnings.

5. Index numbers are used in
   a. trend analysis.
   b. ratio analysis.
   c. vertical analysis.
   d. common-size statements.

6. Which of the following would probably not be found in a company's annual report?
   a. The auditor's report
   b. A five- or ten-year summary of operations
   c. Interim financial statements
   d. Analysis of the past year's operations

7. The main internal user of financial statements is
   a. the SEC.
   b. management.
   c. investors.
   d. creditors.

8. Comparing performance with industry norms is complicated by
   a. the existence of diversified companies.
   b. the use of different accounting procedures by different companies.
   c. the fact that companies in the same industry will usually differ in some respect.
   d. all of the above.

9. A low receivable turnover indicates that
   a. few customers are defaulting on their debts.
   b. the company's inventory is moving very slowly.
   c. the company is making collections from its customers very slowly.
   d. a small proportion of the company's sales are credit sales.

10. In a common-size income statement, net income will be given a label of what percentage?
    a. 0 percent
    b. The percentage that net income is in relation to sales
    c. The percentage that net income is in relation to operating expenses
    d. 100 percent

Applying Your Knowledge

Exercises

1. Complete the horizontal analysis for the following comparative income statements. Round percentages to the nearest tenth of a percent.

	19x1	19x2	Increase or (Decrease) Amount	Percentage
Sales	$200,000	$250,000	50,000	25%
Cost of goods sold	120,000	144,000	24,000	20%
Gross margin	$ 80,000	$106,000	26,000	32.5%
Operating expenses	50,000	62,000	12,000	24%
Income before income taxes	$ 30,000	$ 44,000	14,000	46.7%
Income taxes	8,000	16,000	8,000	100%
Net income	$ 22,000	$ 28,000	6,000	27.2%

2. The following is financial information for Lassen Corporation for 19xx. Current assets consist of cash, accounts receivable, short-term investments, and inventory.

Average accounts receivable	$100,000
Average (and ending) inventory	180,000
Cost of goods sold	350,000
Current assets, Dec. 31	500,000
Current liabilities, Dec. 31	250,000
Market price, Dec. 31, on 21,200 shares	40/share
Net income	106,000
Sales	600,000
Average stockholders' equity	480,000
Average total assets	880,000

Compute the following ratios as of December 31. Round off to the nearest tenth of a whole number for a–i, to the nearest hundredth of a whole number in j–k.

a. The current ratio is ___2___ .

b. The quick ratio is ___1.28___ .

c. Earnings per share is ___5.00___ .

d. Inventory turnover is ___1.94x___ .

e. Return on assets is ___12%___ .

f. Return on equity is ___22.1%___ .

g. Receivable turnover is ___6x___ .

h. Average days' sales uncollected is ___60.8___ .

i. The profit margin is __17.67%__ .

j. Asset turnover is __6.68__ .

k. The price/earnings ratio is __8__ .

How Industry Perceives Financial Ratios

There is some agreement on which ratios are important but a lack of consensus on how they should be computed.

Financial statements serve as the primary financial reporting mechanism of an entity, both internally and externally. These statements are the method by which management communicates financial information to stockholders, creditors, and other interested parties. An analysis of this fianancial information should include the computation and interpretation of financial ratios.

However, at present, comprehensive financial ratio analysis is hampered by the lack of standard computations. Currently, no regulatory agency such as the Securities & Exchange Commission or the Financial Accounting Standards Board gives guidance in this area, except for the computation of earnings per share. As this study will indicate, there is some agreement on which ratios are important, but there is a lack of consensus on the computational methodology of these ratios.

In order to get the views of financial executives on important issues relating to financial ratios, a questionnaire was sent to the controllers of the companies listed in Fortune's 500 Largest Industrials for 1979. Companies that were 100%-owned subsidiaries of another company were excluded, leaving 493 companies to be surveyed. One hundred and three usable responses were received which represents a response rate of 20.9%. Considering both the length of the questionnaire and the amount of detailed questions, the response rate was good.

There were 57 industries represented in the responses; however, three industries had a significantly greater number of responses than the others. These industries were petroleum (10), motor vehicle parts & accessories (8), and chemicals and allied products (9). The other industries were represented by three or less responses. A separate review of the responses of the more highly represented industries indicated that, in general, their responses were not appreciably different than the summary of the overall responses. Any significant differences will be pointed out.

Source: Article by Charles H. Gibson. Reprinted from the April 1982 issue of *Management Accounting.* Copyright © 1982 by the National Association of Accountants.

The questionnaire was designed to accomplish the following objectives: (1) to determine the primary measure that a particular ratio provides, (2) to arrive at the significance of a specific ratio as perceived by financial management, (3) to gather information on the computational methodology used, (4) to find out what use is being made of inflation accounting data in ratio analysis, and (5) to determine which financial ratios are included as corporate objectives and to whom these ratios are reported.

Primary Measure and Significance of Individual Ratios

The first section of the questionnaire was designed to determine the perceived importance of specific financial ratios and what the ratio primarily measured. For this purpose 20 specific ratios were used. Two of these ratios (degree of operating leverage, and degree of financial leverage) proved to be confusing to respondents as indicated by both their lack of response and their written comments. It appears the respondent was not familiar with these ratios; therefore, these two ratios were deleted from the summary.

The 20 ratios were selected based upon a review of textbooks, and discussion with financial executives, and a review of ratios reported in annual reports. It was not considered practical to list all possible ratios nor would it be practical to expect companies to complete an unreasonably long survey. In addition to the 20 specific ratios, the respondents were asked to list other ratios that their company computes.

To determine the primary measure that a particular ratio provides, we asked this question: "Do you perceive this ratio as a primary measure of liquidity, long-term debt paying ability, profitability, or other?" The "other" could be anything perceived by the firm. In all probability it would be a measure of activity, or a stock indicator.

Many ratios indicate several measures of a firm. For example, inventory turnover could be an indication of liquidity, profitability, and activity. This question was designed to determine the primary measure indicated by the ratio.

To determine the perceived significance of a ratio, we asked: "How do you rate the significance of this ratio?"

0-2   low importance
3-6   average importance
7-9   high importance

A summary of the perceived primary measure and its significance rating for each of the 18 listed ratios (Table 1) indicates that there is a majority consensus on each ratio as to what the ratio primarily measures —an encouraging result that might help reduce some of the confusion about what a particular ratio is designed to measure. A number of the ratios that were rated primarily as an indication of liquidity were rated by approximately one-fourth of the companies as being a primary measure of something other than liquidity, for example, accounts receivable turnover. Ratios that received relatively high support in the "other" column often are listed in textbooks as activity ratios. Although they are an indication of activity, in my opinion activity is not a logical end objective. Activity is an indication of liquidity, debt, or profitability, depending on the particular ratio. The results of this survey indicate that the financial executives agree that ratios which indicate activity are a primary measure of liquidity, debt, or profitability.

Three ratios—price earnings, dividend payout, and book value per share—were indicated to have a primary measure other than liquidity, debt, or profitability. This result appears to be consistent with the widespread opinion that these ratios are primarily an indication of stock evaluation. A definite conclusion as to what these ratios measure cannot be made because the respondents were not asked to explain their interpretation of "other." This decision was a compromise in the design of the questionnaire in order to keep the response time reasonable.

Liquidity and Debt Ratios

Table 1 indicates the significance rating for each ratio. The significance rating given to the liquidity ratios is repeated below in order of their significance ratings.

Ratio	*Rating*
Working capital	6.62
Inventory turnover	6.52
Days' sales in receivables	6.46
Current ratio	6.39
Days' sales in inventory	5.31
Accounts receivable turnover	5.05

Note the range of significance does not appear to be material, which suggest that all of these ratios indicate some degree of liquidity. Probably all of these ratios need to be computed in order to get a reasonable view of liquidity based upon the interrelationship of these

ratios. For example, accounts receivable turnover and inventory turnover indicate a degree of quality of receivables and inventory, respectively. The perceived quality of receivables and inventory would reflect as to what would be a reasonable current ratio. If the quality of receivables and/or inventory is low, then a higher current ratio would be necessary in order to compensate for a low quality segment that influences the ratio.

The companies responding in the petroleum industry gave three of the liquidity ratios a much lower rating than the overall rating received by the ratio. These ratios were days' sales in accounts receivable, accounts receivable turnover, and inventory turnover. These liquidity ratios were each given a rating of 2.50 by the firms in the petroleum industry. Days' sales in inventory was given a much higher rating of 7.00 by the chemicals and allied products than the overall rating of 5.31.

Working capital was rated 8.70 by the motor vehicle parts and accessories industry which was much higher than the 6.2 overall average.

Although it might be expected that some industries would rate certain ratios much higher or lower than other industries, there were not enough responses by industry to draw any definite conclusion on this point. It is noteworthy that material differences in rating by industry were not indicated for the debt or profitability ratios.

There is a wide range of perceived significance for the debt ratio, as noted below:

Ratio	*Rating*
Debt to equity (or debt to capital	7.48
Times interest earned	6.14
Fixed charge coverage	5.44
Debt to assets	2.96

There are two views on a company's ability to carry debt. One relates to the balance sheet and the other relates to the income statement. The balance sheet view is concerned with how much debt the firm has in relation to funds provided by owners. The income statement view concentrates on the company's ability to service the outstanding debt. Both views are important and both need to be considered when drawing conclusions as to the company's ability to carry debt.

The balance sheet view is expressed with the ratio debt to equity (or debt to capital) and the debt to assets ratio. The debt to equity (or debt to capital) ratios were combined as one alternative because the pretesting of the questionnaire with financial executives and a review of annual reports indicated that there is agreement that a ratio which indicates the

Table 1

Primary Measure and Significance of Specific Ratios

Ratio	Primary measure					Significance	
	Liq.	Debt	Profit	Other	No. Responses	Avg. Rating	No. Responses
Days' sales in receivables	**68.0%**	1.0%	7.2%	23.8%	97	6.46	95
Accounts receivable turnover	**67.7%**	2.2%	6.5%	23.6%	93	5.05	88
Days' sales in inventory	**57.8%**	1.1%	12.2%	28.9%	90	5.31	93
Inventory turnover	**52.6%**	1.1%	17.9%	28.4%	95	6.52	91
Working capital	**91.0%**	2.0%	3.0%	4.0%	100	6.62	97
Current ratio	**94.0%**	3.0%	1.0%	2.0%	100	6.39	96
Times interest earned	7.4%	**71.3%**	12.8%	8.5%	94	6.14	96
Fixed charge coverage	7.9%	**69.7%**	15.7%	6.7%	89	5.44	89
Debt to assets	5.8%	**88.4%**	0.0%	5.8%	86	2.96	87
Debt to equity (or debt to capital)	6.2%	**85.6%**	2.1%	6.1%	97	7.48	95
Net profit margin	0.0%	0.0%	**100.0%**	0.0%	102	8.05	99
Total asset turnover	11.6%	2.3%	**51.2%**	34.9%	86	4.50	88
Return on investment (or capital)	0.0%	2.1%	**94.8%**	3.1%	96	8.52	94
Return on equity	1.1%	2.1%	**93.7%**	3.1%	95	8.07	94
Earnings per share	0.0%	0.0%	**98.0%**	2.0%	101	8.63	97
Price earnings ratio	0.0%	1.1%	28.7%	**70.2%**	94	6.12	90
Dividend payout	6.4%	2.1%	9.6%	**81.9%**	94	6.47	95
Book value per share	0.0%	0.0%	4.2%	**95.8%**	96	5.17	96

degree of debt carried on the balance sheet is needed. However, there is a great deal of disagreement as to the details of the computation. Usually a corporation will compute either the debt to equity or the debt to capital ratio, but not both. There are probably more than 15 different computations used to compute a ratio that indicates the degree of debt on the balance sheet.

The income statement view of debt is reflected by the firm's ability to meet fixed obligations in relation to income. Ratios that are designed to indicate a firm's ability to meet these fixed obligations are times interest earned, and fixed charge coverage. The difference between these ratios is that times interest earned only considers interest in relation to income while the fixed charge coverage considers interest plus other financing obligations a company considers fixed. An example of other fixed obligations would be the use of a portion of rent payments on operating leases.

The times interest earned coverage was rated to be moderately more significant than the fixed charge coverage. A firm probably should consider both of

these ratios to get an indication of its income ability to carry debt and related financing commitments.

Profitability and Other Ratios

Four of the profitability ratios received ratings over 8 out of a possible 9:

Ratio	Rating
Earnings per share	8.63
Return on investment (or capital). . . .	8.52
Return on equity.	8.07
Net profit margin	8.05
Total asset turnover	4.50

These ratios were rated the most significant of all of the ratios used in this study. This result seems to indicate that financial executives pay more attention to profitability than they do to liquidity or debt.

The one profitability ratio that was not given a high significance rating was the total asset turnover. Because the total asset turnover and the net profit

Table 2

Additional Financial Ratios (by Financial Executives)

Ratio	Primary Measure					Significance	
	Liq.	Debt	Profit	Other	No. Responses	Avg. Rating	No. Responses
Return on assets	0.0%	3.8%	**96.2%**	0.0%	26	8.33	26
Gross margin	0.0%	0.0%	**100.0%**	0.0%	11	7.30	12
Quick ratio (acid test)	**80.0%**	0.0%	20.0%	0.0%	10	6.25	9
Cash flow/debt	10.0%	**80.0%**	0.0%	10.0%	10	6.75	9
Sales per employee	0.0%	0.0%	**75.0%**	25.0%	4	6.00	4

margin are integral parts of the return on assets, they are both needed if a company wants to know why the return on assets is going up or down. Return on assets was not included in the list of ratios. It was excluded in an effort to minimize the list of ratios using the reasoning that if either or both net profit margin as total asset turnover were rated high, then the return on assets probably would be rated high.

It is probably necessary to compute all of the profitability ratios to get a reasonable view because each gives a different view of profitability.

As for the ratios rated primarily for other than an indication of liquidity, debt, or profitability, it was interesting that dividend payout (6.47) was rated to be more significant than the price/earnings ratio (6.12). This difference may have resulted because the survey's participants—financial managers—have placed more emphasis on their objective of dividend payout rather than the price/earnings ratio. A review of the financial ratios used in corporate objectives indicates this same point. Book value was rated 7.25 by the motor vehicle parts and accessories industry, which was materially higher than the overall rating for book value of 5.17.

The respondents were asked to list additional ratios that their company computes and to indicate the primary measure and significance of the ratio (Table 2). Many additional ratios were listed by less than four firms, but they are not included in Table 2 because they were not considered representative ratios.

The additional ratios indicate one more liquidity ratio, one more debt ratio, and three more profitability ratios. The liquidity ratio is the quick ratio (acid test), which is similar to the current ratio, except inventory has been removed from the current assets. The rating given to this ratio was approximately the same rating as was given the other liquidity ratios.

The additional debt ratio is the cash flow/debt ratio. The purpose of this ratio is to indicate the cash flow a

company is generating in relation to the debt that it is carrying. This ratio first appeared in the literature in 1966 in a bankruptcy study conducted by W.H. Beaver.[1] In his study the cash flow/debt ratio came out as the ratio with the greatest predictive ability in terms of bankruptcy. The executives who listed this ratio in the survey gave it a relatively high rating of 6.75.

The additional profitability ratios were return on assets, gross margin, and sales per employee. The return on assets ratio was given a relatively high rating and was listed far more times than the other ratios added. The gross margin was listed by several firms as a profitability measure and it was given a relatively high rating by these executives. It appears that this ratio possibly should be considered as an important profitability ratio. The third profitability ratio added was sales per employee. Only four firms added this ratio, but they were all in the retail industry. This ratio is possibly an important profitability measure in the retail industry.

Computational Methodology

The same ratio may be computed in different ways in practice. This is particularly true of the profitability ratios and the debt ratios. These differences essentially are caused by differences of opinion on how to handle special income statement and special balance sheet items. There is a difference of opinion on how to handle these items on the income statement:

1. Unusual or infrequent items,
2. Equity income,

1. W.H. Beaver, "Financial Ratios as Predictors of Failure," Empirical Research in Accounting: Selected Studies, 1966. Supplement to Vol. 4, *Journal of Accounting Research*, 71-127.

3. Minority share of earnings,
4. Discontinued operations,
5. Extraordinary items, and
6. Cumulative effect of change in accounting principle.

The special income statement items influence most of the profitability measures, and the times interest earned and fixed charge coverage in the debt ratios. To determine how financial management considers the special income statement items when computing these ratios, the question was asked for each special item in relation to a given ratio: "If your firm computes a given ratio, is the indicated special item included in net income in the numerator?" The firms were asked to assume that each item is material and is disclosed separately on the income statement.

Table 3 indicates that approximately 75% of the firms included unusual or infrequent items in the numerator. Whether to include unusual or infrequent items in the numerator is certainly a judgment decision.

A much higher percentage of firms included equity income in the numerator for the profitability ratios than they did for unusual or infrequent items. The percentage of firms that included equity income in the numerator when computing the times interest earned or fixed charge coverage dropped to approximately 70%. This drop in percentage probably was because equity income is a non-cash flow item to the extent that actual cash dividends were not received.

There is a logically correct response when considering equity income. The net profit margin is the relationship between income and net sales. None of the investee's sales are included in the investor's income statement; therefore, equity income should not be included in the numerator. Return on assets expresses the relationship between income and total assets. Since the investment account is included in the total assets, the equity income should be included in the numerator. Return on investment expresses the relationship between income and long term sources of funds. Therefore, equity income should be included in the numerator. Return on equity expresses the relationship between income and stockholders' equity. We would want to express the relationship between total income and stockholders' equity; therefore, the equity income should be included in the numerator. Times interest earned or fixed charge coverage ratio indicates the firm's ability to cover the interest or fixed charges; therefore, we would want to exclude the equity income from the numerator because it is a noncash flow item to the extent that actual cash dividends were not received.

Approximately 70% of the firms included minority share of earnings in the numerator when computing the given ratios. Is this a correct response? The net profit margin is the relationship between income and net sales. Since the sales of the subsidiary are consolidated with the parent company's sales, the minority share of earnings should be included with the parent company's income.

Return on assets expresses the relationship between income and total assets. Since subsidiary assets have been consolidated, the minority share of earnings should be included with the parent company's income. Return on investment expresses the relationship between income and long-term sources of

---

Table 3

Percentage of Firms Including the Special Item in the Numerator

	Special item					
Ratio	Unusual or Infrequent Items	Equity Income	Minority Share of Earnings	Discontinued Operations	Extraordinary Items	Cumulative Effect of Change in Accounting Principle
Net profit margin	69.3%	81.2%	70.7%	41.0%	29.5%	44.0%
Return on assets	70.3%	85.7%	66.1%	47.6%	26.6%	46.8%
Return on investment	77.6%	90.1%	73.5%	55.1%	32.9%	45.7%
Return on equity	79.8%	91.8%	68.8%	56.2%	38.6%	51.3%
Times interest earned or fixed charge coverage	73.1%	70.1%	70.3%	46.9%	34.3%	48.4%

funds; therefore, minority share of earnings should be included in the numerator. Return on equity expresses the relationship between income and stockholders' equity. Since the stockholders' equity does not include minority equity, the minority share of earnings should be excluded from the numerator. Times interest earned or fixed charge coverage indicates the firm's ability to cover the interest or fixed charge. The minority share of earnings is available for this coverage; therefore, we would want to include minority share of earnings in the numerator.

Discontinued operations were included in the numerator approximately 50% of the time; however, because discontinued operations are not recurring they should be excluded from the primary ratios. Approximately one-third of the time extraordinary items were included in the numerator. Again, extraordinary items are not recurring; therefore, should be excluded from the numerator. A little less than 50% of the time firms included the cumulative effect of the change in accounting principle in the numerator, but this item also should be excluded from the numerator because it is not recurring and it applies to prior periods.

Balance Sheet Items

The balance sheet items in the survey were deferred taxes, minority interest, and leases. To determine how deferred taxes are handled, the executives were directed to concentrate on deferred taxes that are presented as liabilities other than short-term. When computing financial ratios, such as the debt to equity ratio (total liabilities divided by shareholders' equity), they were asked: "Are deferred taxes considered to be a long-term liability?" Forty-three out of 101 firms stated that they include deferred taxes as a liability when computing debt ratios such as debt to equity. Twenty-four firms ignore the amount entirely and exclude it from the ratio. Three companies considered the deferred tax amount in equity as a free source of funds. Of the 31 respondents who indicated they did not include deferred tax in liabilities, none explained adequately how they did consider the deferred tax item.

How deferred taxes should be handled is a difficult judgment decision. The deferred tax amount is not likely to result in a cash outlay. But part or all of the deferred tax amount may result in a cash outlay. To be conservative, the deferred tax amount should be included in liabilities. In terms of the probable cash outlay the deferred tax amount should be excluded from liabilities.

When a subsidiary is consolidated in a parent company that owns less the 100% of the stock, an amount results on the balance sheet which is referred to as minority interest. This amount has alternative presentations including presentations with long-term liabilities and presentations between liabilities and stockholders' equity. The executives were asked to assume that they compute the debt to equity ratio. They were asked if the minority interest is included as part of debt, equity, or neither. Ninety-two responses were received on this question with 9.8% including it in debt, 17.4% in equity, and 72.8% not including it in the debt to equity computation.

FASB Statement No. 13 requires the capitalization of some leases on the balance sheet of the lessee. Operating leases are not capitalized but these commitments are disclosed in a footnote. The respondents were asked to consider capitalized leases which are presented as liabilities other than short-term. They were asked the question: "When computing financial ratios, such as the debt to equity ratio, are capitalized leases considered to be debt?" Ninety-two responses out of 97 considered capitalized leases to be part of debt while five did not.

The respondents were asked to consider operating (non-capitalized) leases. The question was: "Do you include the data on operating leases into ratio analysis?" Of the 101 responses, 18 companies indicated that they did include operating leases in ratio analysis. Most of the firms that included operating leases in ratio analysis do so by considering operating leases in the fixed charge coverage. How this is done varies by firm. Some examples of how operating leases are considered in a fixed charge computation are:

1. (a) Fixed charge coverage include 1/3
   (b) Total capital ratios include 7 x subsequent years' operating lease expenses
2. A portion of rent expense is included in the amount of fixed charges used in calculating fixed charge coverage.
3. An interest payment is imputed from the operating lease payment and this imputed interest is included as a fixed charge in determining the ratio of earnings to fixed charges.

One firm responded that operating leases are capitalized at the appropriate cost of debt after deducting implicit operating costs from the lease expense.

Inflation Accounting Data in Ratio Analysis

The respondents were asked if their firm uses any of the data called for in FAS No. 33, "Financial Reporting

Table 4

Key Financial Ratios Included as Corporate Objectives (100 Responses)

Ratio	No. Using This Ratio	Percentage Reported to:		
		Board	Key Employees	Stockholders
Return on equity	54	53%	51%	42%
Return on assets	53	49%	52%	13%
Net profit margin	43	41%	43%	24%
Earnings per share	38	38%	37%	32%
Return on capital	30	28%	30%	16%
Debt to capital	26	24%	23%	16%
Debt to equity	25	24%	24%	10%
Dividend payout	22	22%	19%	16%
Inventory turnover	18	15%	18%	2%
Days' sales in accounts receivable	13	10%	13%	2%
Current ratio	12	11%	12%	5%
Book value per share	10	10%	10%	9%
Earnings growth	9	9%	9%	6%
Working capital	9	8%	9%	8%
Fixed charge coverage	8	8%	7%	3%
Total asset turnover	7	6%	7%	0%
Accounts receivable turnover	6	4%	6%	0%
Days' sales in inventory	6	4%	5%	1%
Times interest earned	4	4%	4%	2%
Price-earnings ratio	4	3%	4%	2%
Operating margin	4	4%	4%	2%

and Changing Prices," in ratio analysis. One hundred responses were received on this question and 11 answered "yes." Examples of how this data is being used include:

1. Return on equity and return on capital employed are calculated using FAS No. 33 data and historical cost.
2. Income per share calculation only.
3. Ratios are computed on historical cost and inflation adjusted amounts for comparison.
4. Inflation-adjusted assets are used in calculating the ratios:
   (a) Market value of stock over inflation adjusted assets
   (b) Cash flow return on investment
5. Net income adjusted for general inflation (constant dollar) and changes in specific prices (current cost) is compared to net income on a historical cost basis.
6. When we measure such ratios as return on replacement cost of assets (for internal use only).

In light of the fact that only companies which report inflation accounting data were included in this survey, there does not appear to be much use made of the inflation accounting data in ratio analysis.

Key Financial Ratios as Corporate Objectives

Many firms have selected key financial ratios to be included as part of corporate objectives. Out of 100 respondents 93 indicated that their firms used financial ratios as part of their corporate objectives. Table 4 indicates the ratios that they use and to whom they are reported. Ratios reported by three or fewer firms are not listed.

In Table 4, the profitability ratios, which survey participants rated with the highest significance, were the same ratios used most frequently as corporate objectives. A couple of debt ratios were next in frequency of use. The most popular liquidity ratios were used less frequently than the most popular profitability or debt ratios.

The survey also indicates that a selected ratio is apt to be reported to both the board and to key employees, but a selected ratio is much less likely to be reported to stockholders.

In summary, financial ratios are an important tool in analyzing the financial results of a company and in managing a company. This survey of financial executives indicates the most significant ratios were rated to be profitability ratios. Overall, the debt and liquidity ratios were rated approximately the same.

The computational methodology used by the firms indicates that there is a need for guidance to enable them to compute more uniform ratios. This guidance probably should be provided by the Financial Accounting Standards Board.

Based on this survey, there does not appear to be much use made of inflation data in ratio analysis; however, the use of such data may improve as companies become more familiar with it.

Profitability ratios are those most likely to be used as corporate objectives. Ratios used as corporate objectives are as likely to be reported to the board as to key employees. It is much less likely that a key financial ratio will be reported to stockholders.

Measuring Financial Performance in an Inflationary Environment

There are numerous ways that an accounting concept such as current cost information can be used in conjunction with historical cost information to measure financial performance. How they may be calculated and their importance in helping companies contend with inflation are described in the following pages.

Financial Accounting Standards Board Statement 33, issued in late 1979, requires large, publicly held corporations to provide experimental current cost and constant dollar financial information to help measure the impact of inflation on business enterprises. Now that this information is available, the issue is what to do with it. How does one use it to manage a business more effectively or to make more intelligent investment decisions? Statement 33 does not address this point. It simply describes the information that is required and how it is to be calculated. Users are left to their own devices as to what to do with it, and many are puzzled how to proceed. This article forges into this uncharted territory by describing how current cost information can be used with historical cost information to measure financial performance in ways that can help businesses adopt strategies to more effectively cope with inflation.

My conclusions are based on research that was recently completed for the National Association of Accountants on the Impact of Inflation on Internal Planning and Control,[1] an analysis of the inflation-adjusted information contained in many annual reports, and the analyses of current cost information compiled by several public accounting firms. While methodologies associated with inflation accounting are still too experimental to codify financial measurement practices, certain measurements seem to merit consideration. Many of these measurements are familiar ratios that are often used with historical accounting information, but are not widely applied with current cost information. However, some measurements such as "holding gains," comparisons of historical costs and current cost information, and "gains and losses on net monetary assets or liabilities" are uniquely associated with inflation and the new accounting methodologies prescribed by FAS 33.

Two different accounting concepts, "current cost" and "constant dollar," are relevant. Current cost attempts to measure the effect of inflation in nominal dollars while the constant dollar concept seeks to eliminate its effect by using dollars with a uniform purchasing power. I will focus on current cost measure-

Source: Article by Allen H. Seed, III. Reprinted from the January 1982 issue of *Financial Executive*. Copyright ©1982 by Financial Executives Institute.

1. Allen H. Seed, *The Impact of Inflation on Internal Planning and Control,* National Association of Accountants, New York, N.Y., 1981.

ments because these measurements seem to be more useful than constant dollars for gauging the effect of inflation on financial performance at the corporate or business-unit level. However, before discussing current cost measurements, I should point out that many companies have found constant dollars to be quite useful for strategic analyses and capital expenditure evaluations. For purposes of strategic analysis, several years of historical information may be restated in constant dollars by a business unit to evaluate "real" growth in revenues, net income, and cash flows. Projected revenue, net income, and cash flows used for strategic planning and capital expenditure evaluations expressed in nominal dollars may similarly be deflated to constant dollars to appraise real growth and returns. As a participant in our recent research project put it, "The use of constant dollars helps management unclutter its thinking... The effect of inflation at even 7 to 8 per year boggles the mind."

Some companies, such as General Electric, consider current costs measured in constant dollars to be the best measure of "real" performance. This approach combines the two concepts that are called for under FAS 33. Unrealized gains or losses from holding net monetary assets and liabilities are required to be reported by FAS 33. Such gains or losses are part of the constant dollar concept and therefore are properly not included in a discussion of current cost measurements. Moreover, many preparers and users of financial information consider this information to be of questionable value because the benefits from inflation's effects on money that is borrowed should be viewed as an offset to interest expense that does not provide funds to the company.[2] Information is not reported to measure the present value of debt acquired at pre-inflation interest rates, so debt is not taken into consideration in current cost accounting.

There are at least a dozen useful ways that current cost information can be used in conjunction with historical cost information to measure financial performance. These measurements are listed below. How they may be calculated, why they behave the way they do, and their significance is described in the profiles that follow. Information contained in Borg-Warner Corporation's 1980 annual report was extracted and is restated to illustrate the calculations involved. Borg-Warner was selected as an example because the company is a typical, large industrial enterprise that has furnished its stockholders with the raw material needed to make the calculations. Furthermore, Borg-Warner's top management is keenly aware of the ef-

fect of inflation, and its president expounded at length on the problem in the annual report.

Suggested key ratios include:

1) Current Cost to Historical Cost Income
2) Income Growth
3) Margin on Sales
4) Effective Income Tax Rate
5) Dividend Payout Ratio
6) Operating Return on Investment
7) Holding Gain Return on Physical Assets
8) Physical Asset Ratio
9) Total Assets to Equity
10) Total Return on Investment
11) Sustainable Growth Rate
12) Distribution of Funds

Relevant comparative historical and current cost income statements, balance sheets, and funds statement information reported by Borg-Warner Corporation for 1980 are summarized in Tables 1, 2, and 3 respectively.

Current Cost to Historical Cost Income

The ratio of current cost to historical cost net income (Exhibit 1) is a primary measure of the effect of inflation on a company or business unit: The lower the ratio, the higher the effect of inflation.

Exhibit 1: Current Cost to Historical Cost Income

Formula:

$$\frac{\text{Net Income After Taxes—Current Cost}}{\text{Net Income After Taxes—Historical Cost}}$$

Example:

$$\frac{76}{126} = 60.3\%$$

Current cost net income is almost always depressed by inflation because cost of sales increases as a result of the higher costs of replacing inventories and equipment. Companies that value their inventories on a FIFO basis are more seriously affected than those that value their inventories on a LIFO basis because LIFO provides a partial surrogate for current cost. Business entities with substantial physical assets[3] or older physical assets are ordinarily more affected by inflation

---

2. AT & T 1980 Annual Report, p. 44.

3. Defined as inventories, property, plant and equipment, and other non-monetary assets subject to current cost adjustments.

Table 1

Comparative Condensed Income Statement

	(Millions of Dollars) Historical Cost (As Reported)	Current Cost	Difference
Sales	$2,673	$2,673	0
Cost of sales	2,134	2,148	14
Depreciation	64	100	36
Other items—net	373	373	0
Total costs and expenses	$2,571	$2,621	50
Income before income taxes	102	52	(50)
Provision for income taxes	47	47	0
Income from consolidated operations	55	5	(50)
Income from nonconsolidated operations	71	71	0
Net income*	126	76	(50)
Holding gains			
Inventories	0	29	29
Property, plant and equipment	0	29	28
Total	0	57	57

*Compares with $156 million (historical cost) and $127 million (current cost) net income in 1979. (See Annual Report.)

than entities with few assets or new assets. Because income taxes are based on historical costs rather than on current costs, the provision for income taxes leverages the effect of increased current costs on net income.

Income Growth

Differences in growth or declines in net income (Exhibit 2) can be caused by variations in specific prices, changes in the level or mix of physical assets, or changes in accounting policy. Current cost increases in excess of historical cost increases, or current cost decreases below historical cost decreases, often indicate that the business entity is modernizing its physical assets, disposing of unneeded physical assets, more conservatively valuing (e.g., LIFO vs. FIFO) its inventories, or is accelerating its depreciation rates (e.g., if tax law is revised).

Exhibit 2: Income Growth

Formula:

$$\frac{\text{Net Income Current Year}}{\text{Net Income Previous Year}} - 100$$

Historical cost example:

$$\frac{126}{156} - 100 = (19.2\%)$$

Current cost example:

$$\frac{76}{127} - 100 = (40.2\%)$$

Table 2

Comparative Condensed Balance Sheet

| | (Millions of Dollars) | | |
	Historical Cost (As Reported)	Current Cost	Difference
Assets			
Monetary Assets			
Cash and marketable securities	$ 46	$ 46	0
Receivables	342	342	0
Other assets	68	80	12
Total monetary assets	$ 456	$ 468	12
Physical Assets			
Inventories	320	520	200
Property, plant and equipment	607	861	254
Total physical assets	927	1,381	454
Investments and advances	519	519	0
Total assets	$1,902	$2,368	$466
Liabilities and Shareholders' Equity			
Monetary Liabilities			
Current liabilities	$ 432	$ 432	0
Long-term debt	165	165	0
Deferred liabilities	130	130	0
Total monetary liabilities	727	727	0
Minority interests	21	21	0
Shareholders' equity	1,154	1,620	466
Total liabilities and equity	$1,902	$2,368	$466

Margin on Sales

Margins are depressed by decreases in current cost net income in comparison to historical cost net income (Exhibit 3). Companies or business entities with healthy profit margins are less vulnerable to decreases in current cost net income than businesses with thin profit margins. Thus, the economics of inflation suggest that investments in higher profit margin businesses are more attractive than those in businesses with lower profit margins.

Exhibit 3: Margin on Sales

Formula:

$$\frac{\text{Net Income After Taxes}}{\text{Sales}}$$

Historical cost example:

$$\frac{126}{2,673} = 4.7\%$$

Current cost sample:

$$\frac{76}{2,673} = 2.8\%$$

Table 3

Comparative Condensed Funds Statement

	Historical Cost (As Reported)	Current Cost	Difference
		(Millions of Dollars)	
Net income	$126	$ 76	(50)
Depreciation	64	100	36
Other non fund credits—net	(30)	(30)	0
Funds from continuing operations	160	146	(14)
Funds provided by changes in assets and liabilities	69	83	14
Net funds provided by operations	229	229	0
Net funds provided by financing	11	11	0
Total sources of funds	240	240	0
Dividends paid	50	50	0
Funds available for growth and investment	190	190	0
Investments—net	185	185	0
Net increase in cash and marketable securities	5	5	0

Effective Tax Rate

The effective income tax rate (Exhibit 4) is almost always increased by inflation because income taxes (the numerator) are of a monetary nature not affected by inflation, and income before income taxes (the denominator) is almost always reduced by inflation.

The effective income tax rate is clearly the most widely referred to application of current costs. In fact, 18 of the 30 companies that constitute the Dow Jones Industrial Average called attention to the effective income tax rate based on current cost in their 1980 annual reports. Managements point out that the difference between the rate based on historical cost and the rate based on current cost in effect represents a tax on capital.

Exhibit 4: Effective Income Tax Rate

Formula

$$\frac{\text{Provision For Income Taxes}}{\text{Income Before Income Taxes}}$$

Historical cost example:

$$\frac{47}{102} = 46.1\%$$

Current cost example:

$$\frac{47}{52} = 90.4\%*$$

*The calculation used as an example includes the effect of liquidation of LIFO inventories.

Dividend Payout Ratio

The dividend payout ratio (Exhibit 5) represents the proportion of earning (net income) that a company distributed to its stockholders. This ratio is also almost always increased by inflation because dividends paid are not affected by inflation, and net income is reduced.

Companies almost exclusively refer to this ratio on a historical cost basis, and they seldom refer to it on a current cost basis. Unlike references to the effective tax rate, there is little incentive to suggest that dividends might be paid out of capital.

Exhibit 5: Dividend Payout Ratio

Formula:

$$\frac{\text{Dividends Paid}}{\text{Net Income}}$$

Historical cost example:

$$\frac{50}{126} = 39.7\%$$

Current cost sample:

$$\frac{50}{76} = 65.8\%$$

Operating Return on Investment

The operating rate of return (Exhibit 6) indicates the return on shareholders' equity that is being realized by operations. This return is almost always cut by inflation because net income is reduced, and shareholders' equity is increased.

Year-end equity is used in the example to illustrate the arithmetic involved. However, average equity, or beginning-of-the-year equity, may be more appropriate denominators upon which to compute the return.

Exhibit 6: Operating Return on Investment

Condensed formula:

$$\frac{\text{Net Income}}{\text{Shareholders' Equity}}$$

Component formula:

$$\frac{\text{Net Income}}{\text{Sales}} \times \frac{\text{Sales}}{\text{Shareholders' Equity}}$$

Historical cost example:

$$\frac{126}{1,154} = 10.9\%$$

Current cost example:

$$\frac{76}{1,620} = 4.7\%$$

Holding Gain Returns

Holding gains on physical assets (Exhibit 7), such as inventories, property, plant and equipment, and other non-monetary assets, occur because inflation increases the replacement cost of such assets. While such gains may be "realizable," they are not "realized" and thus do not apply to historical costs. It should also be noted that holding gains are shown without giving effect to income taxes.

In many companies and business units, holding gains offset the decline in the operating return caused by inflation. Some companies are realizing holding gains by divesting themselves of certain assets. For example, American Can announced that it is seeking to sell its forest products business which, in effect, may permit this company to realize a portion of its holding gains.

The measurement of holding gains quantifies the reality that it is better to invest in physical assets that produce higher holding gains than in physical assets that produce lower holding gains. This reality is not reflected in historical cost accounting until the asset is sold.

Exhibit 7: Holding Gain Returns on Physical Assets

Formula:

$$\frac{\text{Holding Gains}}{\text{Physical Assets}}$$

Current cost example:

$$\frac{57}{1,381} = 4.1\%$$

Physical Asset Ratio

The physical asset ratio (Exhibit 8) quantifies the proportion of total assets that are subject to current cost adjustments, e.g., higher cost of sales and depreciation, reduced current cost net income, and holding gains. The type of business that a company is engaged in usually determines the magnitude of the physical asset ratio that is reported and the effect of inflation on that company. Business entities with relatively few physical assets, such as financial service companies, are less affected by inflation than companies with substantial physical assets. Capital-intensive business entities, such as steel, chemical, and paper companies, generally have a high proportion of physical assets to total assets and are substantially affected by inflation.

Differences between the historical cost and current cost ratios provide an indication of the extent to which physical assets may be undervalued on a historical cost basis. Large differences suggest a greater undervaluation.

Exhibit 8: Physical Asset Ratio

Formula:

$$\frac{\text{Physical Assets}}{\text{Total Assets}}$$

Historical cost example:

$$\frac{927}{1,902} = 48.7\%$$

Current cost example:

$$\frac{1,381}{2,368} = 58.3\%$$

Total Assets to Equity

Total assets to shareholders' equity (Exhibit 9) is a measure of the extent to which assets are financed, and holding gains are leveraged, by monetary liabilities. In a sense, this ratio is a current cost substitute for the gain or loss on the net monetary assets held concept that is part of constant dollar accounting. A high ratio generally signifies that the company is employing substantial debt or other monetary liabilities. A low ratio indicates that substantial portions of the company's capital have been provided by equity.

Calculations based on current costs will always be lower than those based on historical costs, because holding gains are included in both the numerator and the denominator when current costs are used.

Inflation provides an incentive to increase the asset to equity ratio to the extent feasible without impairing liquidity in order to maximize the benefits to shareholders from holding physical assets.

Exhibit 9: Total Assets to Equity

Formula:

$$\frac{\text{Total Assets}}{\text{Shareholders' Equity}}$$

Historical cost example:

$$\frac{1,902}{1,154} = 1.6$$

Current cost example:

$$\frac{2,368}{1,620} = 1.5$$

Total Return on Investment

Total return on investment (Exhibit 10) combines the Operating Return on Investment, Holding Gain Return on Physical Assets, Physical Asset Ratio, and Total Assets to Shareholders' Equity measurements that have been previously described. It is a measure of the overall "real" return on shareholders' equity in nominal dollars. While income taxes on holding gains are not reflected in this equation, we suggest that the return calculated in the manner shown provides a better indication of economic performance than the return on investments calculated on a historical basis. The critical implication here is that it is of prime importance to manage holding gains and elements of the balance sheet as well as operating returns in periods of changing prices.

Exhibit 10: Total Return on Investment

Condensed formula:

$$\frac{\text{Net Income} + \text{Holding Gains}}{\text{Shareholders' Equity}}$$

Component formula:

$$\frac{\text{Net Income}}{\text{Shareholders' Equity}} + \frac{\text{Holding Gains}}{\text{Physical Assets}} \times$$

$$\frac{\text{Physical Assets}}{\text{Total Assets}} \times \frac{\text{Total Assets}}{\text{Shareholders' Equity}}$$

Historical cost example:
(Same as Operating Return)

$$\frac{126}{1,154} = 10.9\%$$

Current cost example:

$$\frac{76 + 57}{1,620} = 8.2\%$$

Sustainable Growth Rate

The sustainable growth rate (Exhibit 11) is an old Dupont formula that is often used for strategic planning. It measures the rate of growth that can be sustained by the net income retained in the business. Growth in excess of the sustainable growth rate must, in the long run, be externally financed or financed with higher net income.

The sustainable growth rate decreases as a result of applying the current cost information to the formula. This drop dramatically illustrates the underlying capital formation problem caused by inflation that many companies face. The numerator of the equation is reduced because dividends are subtracted from current cost income, and the denominator increases because shareholders' equity reflects current replacement costs.

Exhibit 11: Sustainable Growth Rate

Condensed formula:

$$\frac{\text{Net Income} - \text{Dividends Paid}}{\text{Shareholders' Equity}}$$

Expanded formula:

$$\frac{\text{Sales}}{\text{Total Assets}} \times \frac{\text{Net Income}}{\text{Sales}} \times \frac{\text{Assets}}{\text{Debt}} \times$$

$$\frac{\text{Debt}}{\text{Equity}} \times \% \text{ Net Income Retained}$$

Historical cost example:

$$\frac{126 - 50}{1{,}154} = 6.6\%$$

Current cost example:

$$\frac{76 - 50}{1{,}620} = 1.6\%$$

Distribution of Funds

The following formula for the analysis of the distribution of funds (Exhibit 12) provides a measure of the funds available for growth after allowing for the replacement of the property and plant and equipment, but before giving consideration to additional external financing. It is a simplified variation of the distributable funds concept that has been proposed by Alfred Rappaport[4] and others. It is also a funds statement-oriented substitute for an income-statement-oriented sustainable growth rate concept that was previously described.

The application of the measurement again illus-

4. Alfred Rappaport, "Measuring Company Growth Capacity During Inflation," *Harvard Business Review,* January–February 1979, pp. 91–100.

trates the capital formation bind that many companies face. While all physical assets do not have to be replaced in kind each year, and technological improvements may reduce the cost of replacing some assets, other assets will have to be replaced sooner or later; and new machinery and equipment needed to achieve productivity improvements must also be financed.

Exhibit 12: Distribution of Funds

Formula:

Funds Available for Growth
= Funds from Continuing Operations
 − Depreciation
 − Dividends Paid

Historical cost example:

$$160 - 64 - 50 = 46$$

Current cost example:

$$146 - 100 - 50 = (4)$$

Conclusion

Even though current cost information is inherently imprecise and generally limited to the effect of changing prices on inventories and property, and plant and equipment, such information can be usefully applied in conjunction with historical cost information at the corporate and business-unit levels to assist with making intelligent strategic planning, financing, and investment decisions in an inflationary environment. Current cost information is available in many large companies, and many of the financial formulas used are familiar to most preparers and users of financial statements. What is new, however, is applying these formulas to current cost information and comparing the results of this calculation with historical cost measurements in order to make better decisions to combat inflation.

Chapter Twenty-Two

Manufacturing Accounting: Cost Elements and Reporting

Reviewing the Chapter

1. **Management accounting** aids the decision-making process by providing management with pertinent financial information. The types of information that management seeks are (a) product costing information, (b) planning and control information, and (c) special reports and analyses to support management's decisions.

2. Merchandising companies purchase goods in finished form and resell them. Manufacturing companies, on the other hand, produce the goods that they sell. To find product costs and inventory valuation, the merchandiser just uses the purchase cost figures. The manufacturer, however, must add together the costs of production.

3. Manufacturers use **cost accounting systems** to determine the costs of their manufactured products. Accurate cost data is necessary for producing reliable financial statements. Thus the manufacturing company must accumulate the costs of materials, labor, and overhead for its products. The cost of goods that are sold appears in the income statement as cost of goods sold. The ending inventory accounts in the balance sheet contain period-end costs of materials, work in process, and finished goods, which are a manufacturing company's three kinds of inventory.

4. Materials are the substances used in manufacturing a product. Work in process consists of the costs attached to all goods that have been begun but are unfinished. Finished goods are goods that are ready for sale.

5. Manufacturing costs are classified as direct materials, direct labor, or factory overhead (indirect manufacturing costs).

6. A **direct cost** is any cost that can be conveniently and economically traced to a specific product or cost objective. An **indirect cost** is one that cannot.

7. **Direct materials** are materials that can be conveniently and economically traced to specific products. Direct materials used in producing a desk are legs, drawers, and a desk top. However, the cost of nails, glue, and screws used to build the desk are too insignificant to assign as part of its direct materials cost. These materials are termed **indirect materials**, and their costs are classified with other indirect costs as factory overhead.

8. To ensure an efficient system of materials purchases, certain documents should be used. A **purchase requisition (purchase request)** is used by a production department to request that the company purchase certain materials. The materials are purchased when the purchasing department sends the supplier a **purchase order**. When the ordered goods are received, a **receiving report** is prepared, indicating the quantity and condition of the goods. When materials are needed for production, a **materials requisition** form is prepared and presented to the storeroom clerk.

9. **Direct labor** costs are all labor costs that can be conveniently and economically traced to specific products. Wages for machine operators are an example of a direct labor cost. On the other hand, wages for maintenance workers are termed **indirect labor**, and are classified as factory overhead.

10. **Time cards** are used to keep accurate track of the number of hours worked by employees. **Job cards**, on the other hand, record labor hours per job and help verify the time recorded on the time cards.

11. **Gross payroll** equals all wages and salaries earned by the employees, and is used in figuring manufacturing costs. **Net payroll** is the amount paid to the employees after all payroll deductions have been subtracted from the gross payroll. Labor-related costs that arise from direct labor costs and can be conveniently traced to such costs should be accounted for as direct labor. Otherwise, they are considered part of factory overhead. One example of a labor-related cost is employee fringe benefits such as vacations, sick pay, and pension plans. Another is employer payroll taxes such as unemployment taxes and the employer's share of social security.

12. **Factory overhead** is all manufacturing costs that are not classified as direct materials or direct labor. It is also called manufacturing overhead, factory burden, or indirect manufacturing costs. Examples of factory overhead are depreciation, insurance, utilities, and all indirect labor and materials associated with the manufacturing operation.

13. Manufacturing costs may be classified as variable, fixed, or semivariable depending on the way the cost changes with changes in production. **Variable manufacturing costs** go up or down in direct proportion to the number of units produced. Examples are direct materials and direct labor. Costs such as insurance, rent, and supervisory salaries that do not vary with units produced are called **fixed manufacturing costs**. Semivariable costs, such as those for telephone use, are part fixed and part variable.

14. **Product costs** are made up of the three cost elements—direct materials, direct labor, and factory overhead—that are included in the cost of a product. A product cost becomes an expense in the year in which the associated product is sold. **Period costs (expenses)** do not benefit future periods. So they are classified as expenses in the period incurred. In a narrow view, any costs that cannot be inventoried, such as selling and administrative costs, are considered period costs.

15. Under the **periodic inventory method**, manufacturing costs are recorded in the general ledger but are not assigned to specific inventory items. At the end of the accounting period the beginning inventory balances are updated, and then only by taking a physical inventory. Interim inventory balances cannot be known without a physical count.

16. Under the **perpetual inventory method**, manufacturing costs are recorded in the general ledger and are assigned to inventory accounts as production takes place. Therefore, inventory account balances are continually being updated, and they can be determined at any point in time without a physical count. However, a physical count should be taken periodically to verify the account balances.

17. The manufacturer's inventories are **materials, work in process**, and **finished goods**. The Materials Inventory balance represents costs connected to all purchased but unused materials. The Work in Process Inventory balance contains costs attached to partially completed products. The Finished Goods Inventory balance represents the cost of goods completed but not yet sold.

18. Product costing and inventory valuation rely on a structured flow of manufacturing costs. **Manufacturing cost flow** begins when materials are purchased and other manufacturing costs are incurred. Once incurred, these costs are classified as direct materials, direct labor, or factory overhead, and are transferred into the Work in Process Inventory account. When the goods are complete, their cost is assigned to a Finished Goods Inventory account. Finally, costs connected to goods sold are transferred to the Cost of Goods Sold account.

19. The manufacturer's income statement is much like the merchandiser's. The two differences are that the manufacturer uses the heading Cost of Goods Manufactured instead of Merchandise Purchases, and Finished Goods Inventory instead of Merchandise Inventory.

20. The manufacturer prepares a **statement of cost of goods manufactured** so that cost of goods sold can be computed in the income statement. Three steps are involved in preparing this statement, as follows:
   a. First, the cost of materials used must be found. Arbitrary numbers will be used to aid understanding.

Materials Inventory, beginning of period	$100
Add materials purchased	350
Cost of materials available for use	$450
Less Materials Inventory, end of period	200
Cost of materials used	$250

b. Second, **total manufacturing costs** must be figured.

Cost of materials used (computed in section a)	$ 250
Add direct labor costs	900
Add factory overhead costs	750
Total manufacturing costs	$1,900

c. Third, **cost of goods manufactured** must be computed.

Total manufacturing costs (computed in section b)	$1,900
Add Work in Process Inventory, beginning of period	400
Total cost of work in process during the period	$2,300
Less Work in Process Inventory, end of period	700
Cost of goods manufactured	$1,600

21. When the figure for cost of goods manufactured has been found, it can be transferred to the cost of goods sold section of the income statement, as follows:

Finished Goods Inventory, beginning of period	$1,250
Add cost of goods manufactured (computed in section c)	1,600
Total cost of finished goods available for sale	$2,850
Less Finished Goods Inventory, end of period	300
Cost of goods sold	$2,550

22. The objective of the statement of cost of goods manufactured is to translate manufacturing cost data into usable information for inventory valuation, profit measurement, and external reporting. However, a cost accumulation system is first needed for day-to-day activities.

(Note: The rest of this review is not covered in the text. You will find a full discussion in the Work Sheet Analysis for this chapter in the Working Papers.)

23. The year-end work sheets for a manufacturer are the same as those for a merchandiser, except that two columns are included for the statement of cost of goods manufactured. These two columns contain amounts for all items appearing in that statement. When a periodic inventory system is used, Materials and Work in Process must be debited for their beginning balances (amounts in Adjusted Trial Balance column) and credited for their ending balances as determined by a physical inventory. When the columns are totaled, a credit entitled Cost of Goods Manufactured to Income Statement must be added to balance the columns. The corresponding debit goes to the Income Statement column.

24. A manufacturer using the periodic inventory system prepares the closing entries that follow. (a) Close all manufacturing accounts to Manufacturing Summary. (b) Close the beginning balances in Materials Inventory and Work in Process Inventory to Manufacturing Summary and establish ending balances in these inventory accounts. (c) Close Manufacturing Summary and all revenues and nonmanufacturing expenses to Income Summary. (d) Close beginning Finished Goods Inventory to Income Summary and establish ending Finished Goods Inventory. (e) Close Income Summary to Retained Earnings.

Testing Your Knowledge

Matching

Match each term with its definition by writing the appropriate letter in the blank.

____ 1. Manufacturing company

____ 2. Time card

____ 3. Factory overhead

____ 4. Direct materials

____ 5. Indirect materials

____ 6. Direct labor

____ 7. Indirect labor

____ 8. Variable manufacturing costs

____ 9. Fixed manufacturing costs

____ 10. Product cost

____ 11. Period cost (expense)

____ 12. Management accounting

____ 13. Periodic inventory method

____ 14. Perpetual inventory method

____ 15. Cost of goods manufactured

____ 16. Total manufacturing costs

____ 17. Manufacturing Summary (For this term, see the Work Sheet Analysis for this chapter in the Working Papers.)

____ 18. Materials Inventory

____ 19. Work in Process Inventory

____ 20. Finished Goods Inventory

a. The account showing costs connected to goods completed but not yet sold

b. Materials that cannot be conveniently and economically traced to specific products

c. Materials that can be conveniently and economically traced to specific products

d. The account showing costs connected to all purchased but unused materials

e. The account showing costs connected to partially completed products

f. All indirect manufacturing costs

g. A producer of goods

h. Wages, salaries, and related costs that cannot be conveniently and economically traced to specific products

i. Total costs charged to completed units during the period

j. The account that summarizes cost of goods manufactured during the closing procedure

k. A cost that will not benefit any future period and is expensed in the period incurred

l. The field involved in providing pertinent financial information for decision making

m. Wages, salaries, and related costs that can be conveniently and economically traced to specific products

n. A record of the number of hours worked by an employee

o. The system that updates inventory account balances only when a physical count is taken

p. Costs that vary proportionately with units produced

q. Costs that do not vary with units produced

r. The system that keeps a continuous record of inventory account balances

s. A cost that is assigned to a specific job

t. Total costs charged to production during the period

Completion

Use the lines provided to complete each item.

1. Manufacturers have three types of inventory. Name them.

   _____

   _____

   _____

2. What are the three chief components of manufacturing costs?

   _____

   _____

   _____

3. When is a cost considered to be a direct cost?

   _____

   _____

   _____

4. What three types of information does management receive from the management accountant?

   _____

   _____

   _____

5. Show how cost of materials used is computed.

      _____

   + _____

   = _____

   − _____

   = _____

6. Show how total manufacturing costs are computed.

      _____

   + _____

   + _____

   = _____

7. Show how cost of goods manufactured is computed.

      _____

   + _____

   = _____

   − _____

   = _____

8. Show how cost of goods sold is computed for the manufacturer.

      _____

   + _____

   = _____

   − _____

   = _____

True-False

Circle T if the statement is true, F if it is false.

T F 1. A merchandiser's goods that are for sale are called finished goods.

T F 2. A product cost should not appear in the income statement until the period in which the product is sold.

T F 3. The Work in Process account does not contain any period costs (expenses).

T F 4. Direct labor data for a particular job can be found on a time card.

T F 5. Factory burden is another term for factory overhead.

T F 6. Factory rent is considered a fixed manufacturing cost.

T F 7. An inventoriable cost is one that can be associated with a specific product.

T F 8. Direct labor is an example of a variable manufacturing cost.

T F 9. The function of the management accountant is to make the important decisions for the company.

T F 10. Under the periodic inventory method, the trial balance will show beginning-of-period figures for its inventory accounts.

T F 11. Under the perpetual inventory method, material purchases are debited to a separate Purchases account.

T F 12. The statement of cost of goods manufactured must be prepared after the income statement.

T F 13. For the manufacturer to compute cost of goods sold under a periodic inventory system, the beginning finished goods amount must be known.

T F 14. Cost of goods manufactured minus total manufacturing costs equals the change in Work in Process during the period.

T F 15. Cost of goods manufactured must be computed before total manufacturing costs.

T F 16. Cost of materials used must be computed before cost of goods manufactured.

T F 17. Under a periodic inventory system, all three inventory accounts of a manufacturer are debited for their beginning balances in the Cost of Goods Manufactured column of the work sheet.

T F 18. Advertising is included in the computation of cost of goods sold.

T F 19. All beginning inventory accounts are closed with credits.

(For this question and the next, see the Work Sheet Analysis for this chapter in the Working Papers.)

T F 20. Manufacturing Summary is closed with a debit.

Multiple-Choice

Circle the letter of the best answer.

1. Which of the following is considered a direct product cost?
   a. The cost of glue used in making a bookcase
   b. The janitor's salary
   c. The cost of legs used in making a chair
   d. The cost of rags used in cleaning a machine

2. Documents relating to materials must be processed in a specific order. Which of the following lists those documents in their proper order?
   a. Materials requisition, purchase requisition, purchase order, receiving report
   b. Purchase order, purchase requisition, receiving report, materials requisition
   c. Purchase requisition, purchase order, receiving report, materials requisition
   d. Receiving report, purchase order, materials requisition, purchase requisition

3. Which of the following would probably be considered a period cost?
   a. Salaries paid to the salespeople
   b. Wages paid to an assembly-line worker
   c. Freight in
   d. Materials used in the manufacture of a product

4. A document sent to the vendor to buy goods is a
   a. purchase requisition.
   b. materials requisition.
   c. receiving report.
   d. purchase order.

5. Before materials can be issued into production, which form should be presented to the storeroom clerk?
   a. Materials requisition
   b. Purchase requisition
   c. Job card
   d. Purchase order

6. Which of the following is a variable cost?
   a. Rent
   b. Insurance
   c. Electricity
   d. Property taxes

7. Which of the following is computed last?
   a. Total manufacturing costs
   b. Cost of goods sold
   c. Cost of materials used
   d. Cost of goods manufactured

8. Which of the following is least likely to appear in the manufacturer's income statement?
   a. Total manufacturing costs
   b. Cost of goods sold
   c. Cost of goods manufactured
   d. Finished goods inventory, beginning of period

(For this and the remaining multiple-choice questions, see the Work Sheet Analysis in the Working Papers.)

9. Which of the following accounts is included in a separate closing entry from the others?
   a. Indirect Labor
   b. Work in Process Inventory, beginning of period
   c. Materials Inventory, end of period
   d. Direct Labor

10. The Adjusted Trial Balance column of a manufacturer's work sheet will *not* include
   a. Finished Goods Inventory, beginning of period.
   b. Materials Purchases.
   c. Cost of Goods Manufactured.
   d. Materials Inventory, beginning of period.

11. The Income Statement column of a manufacturer's work sheet will *not* include
   a. Work in Process Inventory, end of period.
   b. Net Income.
   c. Cost of Goods Manufactured.
   d. Finished Goods Inventory, end of period.

12. Which of the following is closed to Manufacturing Summary?
   a. Finished Goods Inventory, end of period
   b. Depreciation Expense, Machinery
   c. Income Summary
   d. Finished Goods Inventory, beginning of period

Applying Your Knowledge

Exercises

1. Corbin Corporation has provided the following data for 19xx:

Cost of Goods Manufactured	$450,000
Finished Goods, Jan. 1	75,000
Finished Goods, Dec. 31	80,000
Materials, Jan. 1	92,000
Materials, Dec. 31	70,000
Work in Process, Jan. 1	55,000
Work in Process, Dec. 31	64,000

   In the space provided, compute Cost of Goods Sold.

2. Given the following accounting data, complete the statement of cost of goods manufactured for Spencer Company in the form provided.

Depreciation, Factory Building and Equipment	$ 31,800
Direct Labor	142,900
Factory Insurance	2,300
Factory Utilities Expense	26,000
Finished Goods Inventory, Jan. 1	82,400
Finished Goods Inventory, Dec. 31	71,000
General and Administrative Expenses	163,000
Indirect Labor	42,800
Net Sales	855,100
Other Factory Costs	12,600
Materials Inventory, Jan. 1	8,700
Materials Inventory, Dec. 31	32,600
Materials Purchased	168,300
Selling Expenses	88,500
Work in Process Inventory, Jan. 1	34,200
Work in Process Inventory, Dec. 31	28,700

3. Classify each of the following costs as direct materials, direct labor, or factory overhead by using the letters DM, DL, or OH.

___ a. Sandpaper
___ b. Worker who assembles the product
___ c. Worker who cleans and sets up machinery
___ d. Steel plates used in production
___ e. Glue and nails
___ f. Worker who sands product before painting
___ g. Wheels attached to product
___ h. Depreciation of machinery
___ i. Paint used to touch up finished product
___ j. Overtime for factory worker (½ time of 1½ time rate)

Spencer Company Statement of Cost of Goods Manufactured For the Year Ended December 31, 19xx		

Crossword Puzzle
For Chapters 21 and 22

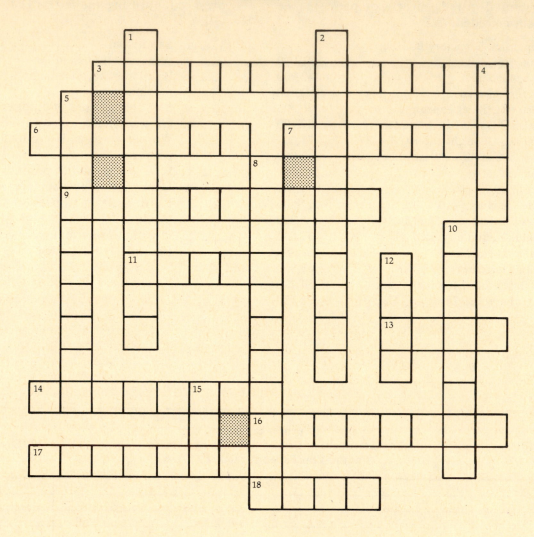

ACROSS

3. Document sent to a supplier (2 words)
6. Certain labor document (2 words)
7. With 4-Down, a measure of liquidity
9. Volatility of the price of stock (2 words)
11. _____ analysis, a variation of horizontal analysis
13. Measure of 9-Across
14. Inventory method
16. Indirect manufacturing costs
17. Price/_____ ratio
18. _____ card (labor document)

DOWN

1. Measure of liquidity (2 words)
2. Purchase request
4. See 7-Across
5. Statement showing percentage relationships (hyphenated)
8. Expenditure that can be traced to goods (2 words)
10. Analysis resulting in 5-Down
12. _____ to equity ratio
15. _____ and Bradstreet

Measuring Operating Performance Through Cost Accounting

Cost accounting is more than just a traditional means of valuing cost-of-goods-sold and inventory. Today's sophisticated cost accounting systems can help you monitor the effectiveness and efficiency of operating functions in your business.

Business executives are constantly advised of the need for timely and accurate management information. They are told that a new or updated computer system is needed, or that more sophisticated planning or control procedures must be put in place, or even that significant organizational and reporting relationship changes must be made. In short, most of the advice they receive is directed at technical solutions to their current or anticipated business problems.

Certainly, taking the proper technical approach is essential. However, such advice often does not show *how to measure* the benefits that should result from technical changes. This is particularly true of operational or manufacturing information systems.

Cost accounting can be used to measure the improvements brought about by technical changes so that business executives can make more effective use of their operational information systems. In order to take full advantage of this feature of modern cost systems, executives should first understand the role of cost accounting as a management tool.

We shall look briefly at the traditional uses of cost accounting and then contrast that with the experience of two companies utilizing more progressive applications of costing. Both were well managed but were facing increasingly difficult business environments; they profited by enhancing their ability to measure and monitor the uses and effects of technical improvements.

Finally, we shall define the position of cost accounting in the hierarchy of operational information and explain, in specific terms, the form and content of measurement information that a modern cost system should provide. Sophisticated cost accounting, as we have analyzed it, is indispensible for evaluating technical changes and getting the most out of your operational systems.

Source: Article by Edward L. Krommer and William T. Muir. *Price Waterhouse Review* (1983, No. 1). Reprinted by permission.

The Need for Cost Systems

Historical Uses of Cost Systems Traditionally, cost accounting has been associated with the accumulation of historical data on material, labor, and related overhead costs for valuing inventory and cost-of-goods-sold. The data is generally collected on a lot, job order, or process basis and the techniques used to analyze it include the identification of many variance factors and historical cost trends (unadjusted for inflationary impact or changes in production processes). The variances that are developed are usually financial and rarely show operational productivity trends.

In nonmanufacturing industries, cost accounting is often thought of as a special purpose analytical tool, not an ongoing process. Cost data usually is expressed in terms of expense items, such as salesmen's commissions, advertising copy, and research and development. These accounts generally reflect only the actual expenses measured against a budget. If any analysis is performed, it may measure average cost per sales call, cost per copy column inch, or the actual cost for various special projects. It does not address the impact of inflation or changes in the operational side of the business.

Cost accounting often has been left to the accountants as a historical record-keeping system. It generally has not been an integrated and dynamic part of a management control and measurement process.

Modern Uses of Cost Systems Cost accounting should be the primary barometer of the effectiveness and efficiency of the various operating functions of a company. It should help meet the objective of optimizing resource utilization. If used properly, cost accounting is a company's primary operational management information system.

In one sense, cost accounting is the process of connecting the incurrence of costs (that is, labor, material, and equipment) with the recognition of total labor, material, and overhead costs at the end of the general accounting period. The incurrence and recognition of these costs are linked through entries from the payroll, accounts payable, and other accounting feeder systems. This linkage is a basic feature of an effective cost system, but it is one that is often overlooked or not totally achieved. This failure is not one of form but of substance.

In addition to this linkage, a cost system should provide timely, accurate, and complete information about the critical success factors of the company's business. To do this, the purpose of the cost system must be clearly and precisely defined. Special industry factors such as material yield for a chemical process, set-up costs for a customer or small lot machining operation, equipment utilization for a heavily capitalized and automated company, or quality control within a food packing firm should be carefully addressed. These factors then have to be supplemented with considerations of cause and effect variances, such as engineering changes, method changes, labor rates, nonstandard labor costs, alternate sourcing, nonstandard lot sizes, variable crew sizing, and alternate processes. Industry specifics, together with generally accepted variance analyses adjusted for the impact of inflation, provide a basis for management awareness and action.

Because these elements constantly fluctuate, a dynamic and integrated information approach is required. Daily, weekly, and monthly summaries of key data are vital to control a business. Reliable, integrated, and controlled operational systems for inventory, production, and project management planning and control must be in place. Indeed, to consider a cost accounting system as something separate and apart from manufacturing and financial systems completely misrepresents what a cost system is.

Structure of a Cost System

Integration with Support Systems The functions of cost accounting are analogous to threading simultaneously the eyes of several needles. The needles represent the various manufacturing support systems (that is, production and distribution) and the accounting feeder system (that is, accounts payable, payroll, and financial reporting). A cost accounting system depends on substantial, timely, and accurate information from these other systems to achieve its objectives. To perform the cost accounting function separately and apart from these important "support" and "feeder" systems is not only redundant, but also invites a significant loss of data integrity.

A critical element in the development and implementation of a cost system is minimizing and eliminating, wherever possible, redundant transaction processing steps. This begins with inventory record keeping. The use of perpetual inventory records for manufacturing purposes and a different set for accounting purposes should be avoided. The general ledger inventory control accounts should be supported by the manufacturing inventory control system. All transactions which affect the perpetual inventory on-hand records should have a corresponding dollar cost impact on the general ledger inventory accounts. Timing differences must be segregated and physical adjustments to the perpetual records must affect the general ledger.

This isolated example demonstrates a concept that should be applied throughout a cost system. The substance and timing of production efficiency information in the manufacturing system should correspond to financial efficiency information in the cost system. Therefore, reporting efficiencies against current manufacturing standards in the cost system is vital. If the company maintains frozen yearly standards for valuation purposes, then a method variance must be developed to maintain the integrity of the financial statements.

Another example is the way complete units are reported by the production department against an open work-in-process lot as contrasted to the stockroom receipt of completed production. Often the adjustment of work-in-process or inventory dollar transfers to stock is based on reported production. This results in timing differences and possible errors if appropriate recognition is not given to the stockroom receipt transaction. To prevent this, an integrated approach will identify any difference between reported production and stockroom receipt quantities.

Performance Reporting Statistical analysis is a key feature of a responsive cost system. Management has traditionally been interested in key ratios and indices for monitoring and controlling its business. However, the cost system usually has not provided this important data. Unfortunately, various nonintegrated and makeshift special reporting systems have been established to do this. A consistent basis for reporting is often absent and meaningful overall reporting is hampered.

An extensive performance reporting system is mandatory for a cost accounting system to truly measure the efficiency and effectiveness of an organization's overall management of its resources. Labor utilization, equipment used, the ratio of indirect to direct workers, the level of rework labor, material yields, unplanned scrap, manufacturing schedule adherence, and inventory levels are key measurements which the cost system must make.

The manufacturing function is not the only one that requires statistical reporting. Pertinent indices and ratios for research and development, marketing, finance, personnel, and other functional areas should be included in the system. Productivity improvement opportunities and overall control of costs are equally important in these overhead expense areas. This includes such items as the average number of sales calls per salesman, the amount of proposals and contracts per salesman, and the total regular accounts and lost accounts per salesman. Ratios and goals should be established for each organizational unit in the company and actual performance must be monitored. Consideration should also be given to incorporating comparable industry data.

How Two Companies Benefited

We can now look at how two companies applied these lessons to their planning procedures and received immediate benefits.

Case 1: Measuring the Cost Impact of Change Profitable Company, Inc., processes a variety of consumer products and markets them through food, drug, and discount outlets. Anyone who looked at it two years ago might well have said it was a solid company. It had paid a dividend to its shareholders for many years. Management had established a material management system that was timely and accurate. The company had effective planning and control procedures—its external auditors loved it. The structure of its organization was well conceived and documented, with a clear definition of responsibility and authority.

Unfortunately, many problems lurked beneath this veneer of excellent management information and controls. Profit percentages relative to sales were maintained by constant price increases, but data indicated consumer resistance. A high level of customer service was needed in Profitable's industry, but inventory levels supporting this objective were extremely expensive to maintain. Compounding these problems, consumers were demanding changes in container size and structure, and historical product mixes were continually being altered.

In short, Profitable's business environment was one of constant change that the company's management could not anticipate. This prevented competent action. Because the effectiveness of the planning and control systems could not be measured, management could only wait until a change occurred and then react to it.

This inability to plan for change was directly related to the kind of information that management received, particularly from its cost system. Profitable had an excellent consumer demand forecasting process—rare for most companies. Management could rapidly detect changes in consumer buying habits, but this information was used only to modify the production schedule to fit changing demand. No attempt was made to determine (1) the impact of the change in the schedule on production and distribution costs or (2) whether an operational change to satisfy the revised schedule was cost-effective.

Profitable, like some corporations, had not done a good job of integrating the revenue and the cost sides of the profit/loss equation. Therefore, the cost impact of changes in revenue mix or trends were not determined in time to allow production processes to be effectively controlled. Productivity and resource utilization measurements were not developed from the cost system, financial reporting system, or demand forecasting processes.

Fortunately, this was corrected before disaster struck. Armed with a knowledge of the modern concepts of cost accounting, management undertook a detailed study of its information requirements and of the best way to measure the effectiveness of its decisions. As a result, Profitable decided to incorporate resource utilization reporting into its cost accounting process. A mechanism was developed and then integrated with the information captured and processed for the cost accounting system. Several steps were involved:

☐ Establishing performance criteria (that is, standards, measures, and ratios).
☐ Determining performance standards.
☐ Developing product-specific routings and department-specific capacity measures.
☐ Improving the methods used to capture actual data.
☐ Structuring and formatting output reports so that the operational activity could be monitored frequently.

Implementing this reporting process was not easy. Middle management personnel had always had their performance evaluated against their budget, which had been based on the prior year's results adjusted for inflation. No one ever considered measuring results based on resource utilization (defined as the units of production inputs adjusted for seasonal and volume fluctuations) against usage standards that had been established on the basis of machine, labor, or scheduled capacities. Because managment practices had to be changed, there was a significant lapse between the completion of detailed specifications for the measuring processes and their successful and total implementation.

Substantial profits have resulted from this management-oriented cost system. Direct production and warehousing labor costs have been reduced by about 20%. Of course, the resource reporting system did not by itself produce this result. The major reason for the labor cost reduction was the development of labor standards and the adherence to them by middle management. However, the information base that supports the resource reporting system brought to management's attention the resource excesses in the plant warehouse.

Other benefits that have resulted from the system are improved scheduling efficiency and a better understanding of the causes of the substantial operating variances that were reported by the old cost system. It is now possible for Profitable's management to reconcile operating cost variances isolated by the cost accounting system with efficiency levels that are based upon established performance standards. This is done by reporting performance against current standards and against annual standards to identify both efficiency and method change variances.

Equipment utilization is closely monitored to identify productive and nonproductive time and the effect of set-ups on product costs. Significant costs, such as material yield, scrap, and rework, are specially reported under the resource management system. In all of these areas, key indices and ratios are given for the current period and trends are computed showing progress over time.

Case 2: Identifying True Costs International Manufacturer, Inc., is in some respects quite similar to Profitable. It is a well managed, growing, and highly respected company. International sells products which compete directly and successfully with the Japanese.

International's industry, however, is very different from Profitable's. Its product line consists of many large and different items. They are produced in plants around the world. But, like Profitable, International saw trouble ahead because of changing product mix and demand patterns. Management was disturbed that its inflation-adjusted financial performance was not as good as the company's historical accounting system would lead one to believe.

To correct these problems, International's management initiated a critical examination of its cost accounting approach, including a study of its information systems and its product pricing methods and results. This study showed:

☐ Growing sales but diminishing inflation-adjusted profits.
☐ Changing manufacturing techniques but overhead allocation formulas that were unchanged for 20 years.

☐ An inability to analyze the substantial variance problems that were revealed by the company's financial reporting system.
☐ An absence of comprehensive product line profitability information.

These led to the inescapable conclusion that International's cost systems were inadequate.

International, like Profitable, is known for excellence in material planning. Its raw material planning and control systems are state-of-the-art, its data processing support is first-rate, and its products' reputation for quality is without peer. Material control, however, was not enough to reverse the problems disclosed by the management study.

International had not implemented order-specific or department-specific work-in-process control. Its shop floor data capture methods did not include department-to-department transfers or an ability to obtain yield loss information. Its labor costs—and, of more concern, the related direct and indirect overhead costs—were rough estimates based on historical data rather than performance standards.

To resolve the problem of monitoring operating efficiency and to better establish selling prices that related to production costs, management elected to restructure its cost accounting system. The system was redesigned to:

☐ Develop a cost profile for each operating unit so that the sources of cost (direct labor, direct material, and manufacturing and support overhead) could be more precisely established.
☐ Improve shop floor control procedures and associated data capture so that nonstandard activities during the work-in-process cycle could be isolated and analyzed.
☐ Provide a basis of overhead allocation related to the manufacturing process instead of an unrelated method such as a formula based on direct labor dollars.
☐ Provide a basis for the support of the company's LIFO computations (and incidentally retain IRS approval).
☐ Determine the company's overall product line profitability by considering both direct and indirect costs and expenses.

The system's implementation is still in progress. However, benefits have already been derived from the preparation of each operating unit's cost profiles. Management now knows what critical success factors are needed to monitor and control the manufacturing process. Also, management now is committed to attaining real, inflation-adjusted growth for the company. This has made International's employees aware of the need for product quality and personal efficiency.

When an improved shop floor data capture system (which is tightly coupled to, but not part of, the improved cost system project) is implemented, additional cost information benefits are anticipated because management will be able to:

☐ Prepare and analyze meaningful performance variances on both a department and job order basis.

☐ Accurately cost, and thus price, individual products rather than aggregated product families.

☐ Make meaningful make/buy decisions—confident that the cost in both cases can be accurately estimated.

The Importance of Cost Accounting

To gain the most benefit from sophisticated cost accounting systems, management should keep in mind two significant principles:

1. Cost accounting should provide more than just cost-of-goods-sold and inventory valuation information. *It also should provide information measuring the utilization of resources and the impact of anticipated changes to those resources.*
2. Cost accounting is not an isolated system. It is the proper merging of financial, administrative, and operational planning and control systems. *The data produced from any cost accounting process is only as comprehensive, timely, or accurate as the information given it by the operational and administrative support feeder system.*

Chapter Twenty-Three

Product Costing: The Job Order System

Reviewing the Chapter

1. The main reason for having a cost accounting system is to find the **unit cost** of manufacturing a company's products. Unit cost information aids a business in (a) determining a proper selling price, (b) forecasting and controlling operations and costs, (c) determining ending inventory balances, and (d) determining Cost of Goods Sold.

2. The two basic approaches to cost accounting systems are job order costing and process costing. The kind of production process a company has will dictate which of the two approaches it uses.

3. A **job order cost accounting system** is used in companies that manufacture one-of-a-kind or special-order products such as ships, wedding invitations, or bridges. In a job order cost system, the following conditions exist: (a) All manufacturing costs are assigned to and accumulated for specific jobs. (b) Emphasis is placed on job completion periods rather than on weekly or monthly time periods. (c) One Work in Process Inventory account is used. Its balance is supported by the job order cost sheets of jobs still in production.

4. A **process cost accounting system** is used when a large number of similar products are being manufactured. Companies producing paint, automobiles, or breakfast cereal would probably use some form of a process costing system. The following conditions exist in a process cost system: (a) Manufacturing costs are accumulated by department with little concern for specific job orders. (b) Emphasis is placed on a weekly or monthly time period rather than on the completion period of a specific order. (c) A Work in Process Inventory account is used for each department in the manufacturing process.

5. Product costing may be accomplished only when the costing method being used specifies the types of manufacturing costs to be included in the analysis. The most common product costing methods are based on **absorption costing**, in which direct materials, direct labor, variable factory overhead, and fixed factory overhead are assigned to their products. Job order costing generally uses absorption costing.

6. **Predetermined overhead rates** are useful for product costing, price determination, and inventory valuation. The rate is determined at the beginning of the accounting period by dividing total estimated overhead for the period by some logical basis. The most common bases used are (a) estimated direct labor hours, (b) estimated direct labor dollars, (c) estimated machine hours, and (d) estimated units produced. After the rate has been determined, it is multiplied by the actual amount of the basis (hours, dollars, et cetera) for each job or product to obtain the overhead that should be applied.

7. If estimated figures for overhead costs and the basis equal the actual amounts for the period, then total overhead applied to jobs will equal actual overhead incurred during that period. Because estimates and actual amounts will seldom be equal, there will usually be an under- or over-application of overhead. When actual overhead is more than applied overhead, overhead has been **underapplied**. When the reverse is true, overhead has been **overapplied**. The only way to assure that actual overhead will equal applied overhead is to wait until the end of the year to apply the year's actual overhead to the jobs worked on during the year. However, this is not done because interim cost figures are usually necessary, and a small under- or overapplication of overhead must therefore be tolerated.

8. At the end of the period, an adjustment must be made for the difference between actual and applied overhead.
   a. If the difference is small or if all items worked on during the period have been sold, the entire amount can be added to or subtracted from Cost of Goods Sold. When overhead has been underapplied, Cost of Goods Sold and Factory Overhead Applied are debited and Factory Overhead Control is credited. The entry is the same when overhead has been overapplied, except that Cost of Goods Sold is credited.
   b. Another method is used when the difference is large or when the costs of the items worked on during the period are still in Work in Process and Finished Goods, as well as Cost of Goods Sold, at the end of the period. In such a case, the difference should be divided among these three accounts proportionately.

9. Product costing is very important for income statement and balance sheet purposes. Only those manufacturing costs assigned to units sold should be reported in the income statement (as cost of goods sold). The manufacturing costs assigned to goods in ending inventory should appear on the balance sheet, and should be transferred to the income statement only in the period in which the goods are sold.

10. In a job order cost system, there is a specific procedure for recording materials, labor, and factory overhead. Basically, a perpetual inventory system is used. Costs flow through the Work in Process and Finished Goods Inventory accounts to Cost of Goods Sold. The costs are connected with specific jobs by means of **job order cost cards**. One job card is maintained for each job to accumulate its cost. The cost cards for all uncompleted jobs make up the Work in Process **subsidiary ledger** (detailed records to support the **control account**).

11. The journal entries in a job order cost system reflect the actual flow of costs during production. Note from the following analysis that costs are transferred into an account with a debit, and out of an account with a credit.
   a. The purchase of materials is recorded by debiting Materials Inventory Control and crediting Cash or Accounts Payable.
   b. When materials or supplies are issued into production, Work in Process Inventory Control is debited for the direct materials portion, Factory Overhead Control is debited for the indirect materials portion, and Materials Inventory Control is credited.
   c. The factory payroll and actual overhead costs are recorded by debiting Factory Payroll and Factory Overhead Control, respectively, and crediting Cash or some other appropriate account.

d. To distribute the payroll to the production accounts, Work in Process Inventory Control is debited for the direct labor portion, Factory Overhead Control is debited for the indirect labor portion, and Factory Payroll is credited for the gross payroll.

e. Factory overhead is applied to specific jobs by debiting Work in Process Inventory Control and crediting Factory Overhead Applied.

f. Upon the completion of a specific job, Finished Goods Inventory Control is debited, and Work in Process Inventory Control is credited.

g. When the finished goods are sold, two entries must be made. First, the sale is recorded by debiting Cash or Accounts Receivable and crediting Sales for the total sales price. Second, Cost of Goods Sold is debited and Finished Goods Inventory Control is credited for the cost attached to the goods sold.

h. At the end of the period, an adjustment must be made for under- or overapplied overhead.

12. The first step in computing unit costs in a job order cost system is to total all manufacturing costs accumulated on a particular job order cost card. Then, this amount is divided by the number of units produced for that job to find the unit cost. Finally, the unit cost is entered on the job order cost card and used for inventory valuation.

(Note: The rest of this review is not covered in the text. You will find a full discussion in the Work Sheet Analysis for this chapter in the Working Papers.)

13. When a perpetual inventory system is used, the work sheet of a manufacturer will differ from the work sheet prepared when a periodic inventory system is used (as discussed in the Work Sheet Analysis for Chapter 22). First of all, Cost of Goods Manufactured columns are not provided. Second, adjustments are not made to eliminate beginning inventories and to establish ending inventories because the inventory accounts are always current under a perpetual system. Third, a balancing figure labeled Cost of Goods Manufactured to Income Statement is not used.

14. A manufacturer's closing entries are much simpler under a perpetual inventory system than under a periodic system. The only accounts that need closing are Sales, Cost of Goods Sold, operating expenses, and miscellaneous nonoperating items.

Testing Your Knowledge

Matching

Match each term with its definition by writing the appropriate letter in the blank.

____ 1. Absorption costing

____ 2. Overapplied overhead

____ 3. Underapplied overhead

____ 4. Process cost system

____ 5. Job order cost system

____ 6. Job order cost cards

____ 7. Control account

____ 8. Subsidiary ledger

a. The result when actual overhead exceeds applied overhead

b. The accounting method used by a manufacturer of one-of-a-kind or special-order products

c. The product costing method that includes all manufacturing costs

d. Records of the accumulation of job costs

e. The result when applied overhead exceeds actual overhead

f. The accounting method used by a manufacturer of a large number of similar products

g. Individual accounting records that support the corresponding control account

h. A ledger account that represents the accumulation of several related individual account balances

Completion

Use the lines provided to complete each item.

1. If estimated overhead costs equal actual overhead costs for the period, could an underapplication of overhead occur? Explain.

_____

_____

2. What are the three components of Work in Process Inventory?

_____

_____

3. What two methods are used to adjust for under- or overapplied overhead?

_____

_____

_____

_____

4. List three products for which a job order cost system should be used.

_____

_____

_____

Circle T if the statement is true, F if it is false.

T F **1.** If the predetermined overhead rate is based on direct labor hours, and actual direct labor hours equal estimated direct labor hours for the period, then overhead will be neither underapplied nor overapplied in all cases.

T F **2.** A small underapplication of overhead should be charged to cost of goods sold.

T F **3.** A large under- or overapplication of overhead should be divided among Materials, Work in Process, and Finished Goods Inventories.

T F **4.** A large toy manufacturer would probably use a process cost system.

T F **5.** A job order cost system uses a Work in Process Inventory account for each department.

T F **6.** Indirect manufacturing costs bypass Work in Process Inventory and are charged directly to Finished Goods Inventory.

T F **7.** If a company determines a job's selling price by taking 120 percent of its computed cost, then the company will not make the desired profit when overhead has been underapplied.

T F **8.** The subsidiary ledger for Work in Process Inventory consists of job order cost cards for uncompleted jobs.

T F **9.** As soon as work begins on a job, its sale should be recorded.

T F **10.** The factory payroll is distributed to production with a debit to Work in Process Inventory (for direct labor), a credit to Factory Overhead Control (for indirect labor), and a credit to Factory Payroll.

T F **11.** When overhead costs are applied to specific jobs, Work in Process Inventory is debited and Factory Overhead Applied is credited.

T F **12.** When goods are shipped to the customer, Cost of Goods Sold should be debited and Work in Process Inventory credited.

T F **13.** A manufacturer of custom-made clothing would probably use a job order cost system.

T F **14.** A job order cost system normally uses a periodic inventory system.

T F **15.** The cost information needed in computing product unit cost may be found on the job order cost cards.

Multiple-Choice

Circle the letter of the best answer.

1. Which of the following represents an over-application of overhead?
   a. Estimated overhead exceeds actual overhead
   b. Actual overhead exceeds estimated overhead
   c. Applied overhead exceeds estimated overhead
   d. Applied overhead exceeds actual overhead

2. A job order cost system would most likely be used for the manufacturer of which of the following?
   a. Paper clips
   b. Gasoline
   c. Supersonic jets
   d. Electric typewriters

3. When overhead is underapplied, and many of the goods worked on during the period are still in work in process and finished goods inventories, then
   a. net income is overstated before the adjustment is made.
   b. cost of goods sold is understated before the adjustment is made.
   c. the entire underapplication should be charged to cost of goods sold.
   d. ending inventory is understated before the adjustment is made.

4. Which of the following does not require a debit to Factory Overhead Control in a job order cost system?
   a. Indirect material
   b. Applied overhead
   c. Depreciation expense
   d. Indirect labor

5. Factory Payroll is recorded as a
   a. debit when paid.
   b. debit when distributed to production.
   c. credit when paid.
   d. none of the above.

6. Absorption costing
   a. includes direct materials, direct labor, and variable factory overhead only.
   b. includes direct materials and direct labor only.
   c. may not be used with a job order cost system.
   d. includes direct materials, direct labor, variable factory overhead, and fixed factory overhead.

Applying Your Knowledge

Exercises

1. Parkinson Manufacturing Company estimates that overhead costs for 19xx will be $720,000. It also estimates that 450,000 direct labor hours will be worked during the year, with all workers receiving $4 per hour.
   a. What is the predetermined overhead rate, assuming that the application base is direct labor hours? $ _____

   b. What is the predetermined overhead rate, assuming that the basis is direct labor dollars? $ _____

   c. If a job required 150 direct labor hours, how much overhead cost should be applied to the job, assuming a direct labor hour basis? $ _____

2. The King-Size Shoe Company manufactures shoes of unusual lengths and widths on special order. For each of the following sets of facts, prepare the journal entry in the journal provided on the next page. Assume that the company uses a job order cost system.

Dec. 23 Purchased (on credit) materials costing $2,950.
   26 Issued materials costing $850 into production. Of this amount $50 was for indirect materials.
   26 Paid the following bills:

Utilities	$350
Rent	$700
Telephone	$150

   27 The week's gross payroll of $1,500 was distributed to production accounts. Of this amount, 80 percent represents direct labor. (Do not prepare the entries when the payroll is *paid*.)
   27 The week's overhead costs are applied to production based upon direct labor dollars. Estimated overhead for the year is $165,000, and estimated direct labor dollars are $55,000.

29 Goods costing $3,900 were completed.
30 Finished goods costing $2,000 were shipped to a customer. The selling price was 70 percent greater than the cost, and payment for the goods is expected next month.

31 Applied overhead for the year was $150,000, and actual overhead was $130,000. The difference is divided among Work in Process Inventory Control, Finished Goods Inventory Control, and Cost of Goods Sold in proportion to their respective ending balances of $30,000, $10,000, and $160,000.

		General Journal		
Date		Description	Debit	Credit

The Rebirth of Cost Accounting

Recent developments suggest it might be a good idea for practicing accountants to study up on cost accounting.

Prior to World War II, there was a general presumption that the purpose of cost accounting was to measure the direct costs plus a fair share of the indirect costs of a product or service. The measurement of direct costs was relatively easy; the difficult task was to allocate an appropriate part of the indirect costs. Although techniques for doing this were developed in the 19th century, they were not widely used in practice until the second and third decades of the 20th century.

In the 1930s, college courses in cost accounting did actually deal with cost accounting; that is, they focused on measuring the full cost of products or other cost objectives. In the 1940s, however, three developments occurred that cast doubt on the necessity, or even the desirability, of making cost accounting allocations. As a result, the teaching of cost accounting has decreased to the point where it is not much of an exaggeration to say that cost accounting—as a subject concerned with the measurement of full costs—has practically died.

Direct Costing

The first of these developments was the invention, or more properly the reinvention, of the technique called direct costing. In his original article on this subject in 1936, Jonathan N. Harris showed that, in certain circumstances, data on the allocated full cost of a product could lead to erroneous conclusions about the true profitability of a business.[1] He therefore proposed that the allocation of indirect costs to products be eliminated. At first, not much attention was paid to this proposal, but by the late 1940s it had become quite popular. In 1947, *Accounting Research Bulletin No. 29* tried to stem the tide by stating that "... the exclusion of all overheads from inventory

costs does not constitute an accepted accounting procedure." This had some dampening effect on the acceptance of direct costing, but a great many people regarded this statement as a reflection of the views of old-fashioned accountants who did not appreciate the wave of the future. Its spirit, and sometimes its letter, was increasingly disregarded, even in published financial statements.

Direct costing has great appeal to students. If one accepts the concept, it is unnecessary to learn the techniques of overhead allocation—the creation of overhead pools, methods of charging costs out of these pools to cost centers, methods of estimating volume, and the advantages and disadvantages of various kinds of overhead rates. These are complicated topics, and if they can be avoided, the student's life is much easier.

Direct costing appeals to teachers for a similar reason. If a student wants to know why one method of allocation is better than another in a given situation, it is easy to avoid a thoughtful answer simply by saying, "All cost allocations are arbitrary, so don't worry about whether one method is better than another."

Manangerial Economics and Operations Research

The second development was the growth of managerial economics, and the related disciplines of operations research and management sciences. The development was stimulated by the successful use of operations research in World War II. A flood of articles in journals such as *The Journal of the Operations Research Society* and *Management Science,* described its possibilities, and most textbooks on economics quickly picked it up. The message of these new disciplines to cost accounting is indicated by the following quotation from Joel Dean's *Managerial Economics,* published in 1951, and one of the most influential early books:

"When an executive asks the cost of a product, the answer he gets is a historical, fully allocated, average unit cost. There are *comparatively few* executive decisions for which this kind of cost

Source: Article by Robert N. Anthony. Reprinted by permission from the October 1975 issue of *Management Accounting.*

1. Jonathan N. Harris, "What Did We Earn Last Month?" *NACA Bulletin,* January 15, 1936.

is relevant, although it *occasionally* approaches the relevant concept."[2] (Emphasis added.)

In other words, full costs are rarely useful, so there is no point in learning how to measure them. The economists, the operations researchers, and the management scientists therefore downgraded allocated costs, and emphasized instead opportunity, differential, incremental, and marginal costs.

Although operations research started out by solving important practical problems, by the 1950s its literature tended to focus on the development of elaborate formulas requiring data nonexistent in the real world. Although the models were complicated and elegant, they were, unfortunately, not complicated enough to describe the actual situation with sufficient accuracy so that reliable conclusions could be drawn. Classroom teaching thus became increasingly divorced from reality; relevant costs were simply assumed to exist, and the problem of finding these costs in real world situations was addressed superficially, if at all.

Also, the techniques became increasingly impractical to businessmen. One critic remarked that the trouble with management scientists is that they forget the maxim: "Anything not worth doing at all is not worth doing well."

Responsibility Accounting

The third development was the growth of responsibility accounting. Here the original paper was published by Arthur Andersen & Company in 1940.[3] Responsibility accounting proposes that since costs can be controlled only by human beings, the proper way to collect costs is in terms of responsibility centers, that is, organization units headed by responsible supervisors. Since allocated costs, by definition, cannot be related to personal responsibility, responsibility accounting does not deal with allocated costs.

Responsibility accounting is a powerful concept and a sound concept. It led to great improvements in the management control process. But it also was another blow against cost accounting: Why worry about how to allocate costs if allocated costs cannot be used for control?

Consequences of These Developments

These three movements—direct costing, managerial economics, and responsibility accounting—had the

effect of killing cost accounting as a respectable subject in many colleges and universities. There continued to be many courses and many texts with the word "cost" somewhere in the title, but in the full title great efforts were made to signal that the emphasis was no longer on finding the cost of something. Instead, courses and books carried such titles as Cost Administration, Cost Behavior, Accounting for Managerial Analysis, Managerial Costing, Cost Planning and Control, Accounting Data for Management's Decisions, Information Systems, and on and on. A course in just plain cost accounting—how to find the cost of something—became rare, especially in the most influential schools.

In these so-called modern texts, the authors do have a chapter or two on cost allocation, but there is a clear implication that this material is included primarily as a bow toward a quaint, outdated tradition, rather than as a topic that should be taken seriously. No attempt is made to go thoroughly into the concepts appropriate for allocating costs. The word "arbitrary" is used frequently and disparagingly to describe allocated costs, and in the discussion of the use of cost data, there are so many warnings against the use of allocated costs that students must wonder why even one chapter on cost allocations is included.[4]

In short, cost accounting—full costing or absorption costing—faded away. It didn't die out entirely, but it became to be regarded as a low-grade subject, not to be emphasized in good schools, not a fit subject for serious research or for scholarly articles.

There are, however, good reasons to believe that the period of sneering at cost accounting is coming to a close, and that its real importance will be generally recognized again. These reasons can be grouped into two categories. First, there are challenges to the rationale of those who have played down the importance of cost accounting. Second, there are a number of developments that focus renewed attention on the subject.

The Rationale

Managerial economists advance the case that selling prices should not be based on full cost, and that the

---

2. Joel Dean, *Managerial Economics*, Prentice-Hall, Inc., New York, N.Y., 1951, p. 315.
3. Arthur Andersen & Company, *Responsibility Accounting*, Chicago, Ill., 1940.

4. It is also of interest that not one of the two dozen continuing education courses offered by the National Association of Accountants in 1973-4 discusses full cost. On the two Certificate of Management Accounting examinations offered to date, less than 10 percent of the coverage (as indicated by time allowances) has been on topics even indirectly related to the measurement of full costs. Estimated from data presented by Jack L. Krogstad and John K. Harris in "The CMA Examination: A Content Analysis," *Management Accounting*, October 1974.

calculation of product costs as a basis of setting selling prices is therefore a waste of time. Indeed, economists have succeeded so well in selling college students on this point that a teacher of cost accounting today has a real problem generating respect for the subject if his students have previously had a course in economics. Although most elementary economics texts still approach cost accounting with this attitude, some economists are beginning to realize that in many situations the selling price of a product has some relationship to its cost.

Professor Wassily Leontief, a Nobel prize winner in economics, said recently, "The whole idea of price formation through free competition [by which he meant the price theory taught in economics courses] is ridiculous."[5] Perhaps if economists spent less time reading esoteric articles on theory written by other economists and more time observing what goes on in the real world, they would come to agree with Professor Leontief. It should be obvious that a great many selling prices are based on cost calculations. This is so for all regulated prices—public utility rates, airplane fares, railroad and truck freight rates, and telephone rates. It is so for most important construction projects—buildings, roads, bridges, dams and so on. It is so for $40 billion of contracts that are let annually by the Department of Defense and approximately an equal amount of cost contracts let by other government agencies. It is so for about $50 billion of hospital and related health care charges. And it is likewise so for the majority of commercial products.

Of course, in pricing commercial products the task is a lot more complex than simply adding up the cost and tacking on a specified profit margin. Nevertheless, the calculation of cost is an important input to the pricing process for the great majority of companies that can in fact set a price (as contrasted with those who are forced for competitive reasons to use a price that some other company has set).

A second development is that operations researchers seem to be descending from Cloud Nine and dealing with real-world problems again. Indeed, the revolt against unrealistic theory has become so strong that new professional journals have been started in protest against the theoreticians. When real-world problems are tackled, real costs are needed.

A still further development is the growing recognition that differential costs and responsibility costs do not take the place of full costs. Yes, we do need differential costs for operations research and for many other problems. And yes, we do need responsibility

accounting in order to control the activity of responsibility centers. But we need these cost constructions in addition to full costs. If operations researchers were a little more modest, they would realize that although it is perfectly appropriate that they request costs constructed in a certain way for their problems, it is equally appropriate that costs be constructed in some other way for someone else's problem.

Recent Developments

There are several recent developments that emphasize the importance of cost accounting:

Price Control. The Price Commission and its successor, the Cost of Living Council, used the basic principle that increases in selling prices are justified only when there have been corresponding increases in cost. By "cost," they meant full cost. The price controllers required good evidence of such cost increases, and some companies found their systems inadequate to provide convincing support for price increases to which they felt they were entitled. From summaries of Cost of Living Council decisions picked at random, here are some examples: A requested increase in cigarette prices was cut by a third, celanese fibers by 18 percent, glass containers by 26 percent, gypsum products by 37 percent, all because of deficiencies in methods of computing costs.[6] Indeed, most of the denials of requested price increases were made for this reason. By contrast, companies that had good cost systems could generally support their requested price increases without question.

Although price control is not with us right now, the lessons learned from this experience remain.

Segment Reporting. The SEC is pushing hard to require segment reporting of both revenue and earnings, a push industry has been generally resisting. Companies generally argue that there exist so many different practices for allocating common costs to individual profit centers, divisions, or other segments that the figures are not comparable from one company to another. The SEC does not seem to be much impressed by this argument, and it seems likely that segment reporting will become mandatory. This will focus attention on the most appropriate way of allocating common costs to segments, which is a problem in cost accounting.

The Federal Trade Commission also is starting to collect cost data by individual product lines. Although there is strong opposition to the specific approach it

---

5. *Harbus News,* April 11, 1974, p. 5.

6. Cost of Living Council, Decision List 73–47, December 12, 1973.

has taken, the need for reliable cost data by industry is generally recognized. Even the Financial Executives Institute, which is a leading critic of the FTC plan, recognizes this need in principle.[7]

The Cost Accounting Standards Board. The CASB has so far issued nine standards, four of which are substantive; two are on the capitalization and depreciation of fixed assets, one is on the allocation of home office costs to segments, one is on standard costs, and one is on accounting for compensated personal absences. It has, however, some 15 other topics in various stages of consideration covering practically all the controversial areas of cost accounting.[8] Although the law that created the CASB gave it authority only for costs used in defense contracting, a number of other government agencies have already agreed to use CASB standards for their own cost contracts. If these standards are sound, it seems likely they will become generally adopted. They are a far cry from the cost accounting of a few decades ago, which essentially permitted a company to define direct costs and to allocate indirect costs in any way it wished.

Consider Standard 403 on allocation of home office costs to segments, as an example. It is a sensible standard, and spells out principles with more care than is found in almost any text. If a company is thinking about this problem, it is reasonable to expect that they will at least look at 403, and since it is at least as good as any alternative, it is reasonable to expect that many companies will adopt the method described.

IRS Regulations on Methods of Inventory Valuation. These regulations, which take effect in 1975, make it clear that the only acceptable method of measuring inventory costs is on a full-absorption basis.[9] Direct costing is out; prime costs are out. Full costs must include direct production costs and a fair share of most indirect production costs and expenses. The regulations spell out in considerable detail which items of indirect cost must be included in inventory for income tax purposes (whether or not the company includes them in inventory for financial statement purposes); which items must be included for tax purposes if the company also includes them for financial statement purposes; which items may be treated differently for tax and book purposes at the company's options; and which items must be excluded altogether from inven-

tory valuation. This detail is considerably greater than most people thought it would be. Companies must, in the future, give careful attention to their cost accounting systems so as to insure they are in conformance with these regulations. The regulation does not, incidentally, prescribe methods of allocating indirect costs to products.

Banking. Commercial banks cannot pay interest on demand deposits. So, to induce companies to leave money on deposit, they provide a number of services, ranging from advice to outright clerical operations such as collection of accounts receivable. In recent years they have come to realize that some customers get services costing more than the revenue derived from the money they have deposited. This has led to an interest in finding the cost of each service the bank provides, and in some cases in making changes for this service based on cost. In 1960 few banks did cost accounting; today most do.

Health Care. After the passage of Medicare and Medicaid legislation in 1965, hospitals and other health providers discovered they had to keep accurate records of costs in order to obtain reimbursement. Although Blue Cross had for years made payments based supposedly on cost, they would accept as valid any "number" the hospital submitted. By contrast, the Medicare and Medicaid people demand reliable cost information, including a well worked-out allocation of indirect costs. As reimbursement shifts to a prospective rate basis, which seems likely, costs will become even more important because these rates will be based on budgets supported by historical costs, and health providers will be reimbursed only on the basis of their approved budgets.

Revenue Sharing. The Federal government has started to channel some of its revenues back to the states and municipalities. The amounts are likely to increase. The Federal government has a natural interest in finding out how this money is spent. This involves auditing, but reliable audits cannot be made unless there is a good cost accounting system. Thus, state and municipal accounting systems, now generally poor, are likely to improve.

Benefit/Cost Analysis. There is a growing realization that a program should not be undertaken unless its benefits exceed its cost, and there is a corresponding increase in the application of benefit/cost analysis. The cost side of such an analysis requires reliable cost data, and the analysts legitimately require that such data be developed in areas where it does not now exist.

7. Committee on Corporate Reporting, Financial Executives Institute, letter to Federal Trade Commission, January 28, 1974.
8. Cost Accounting Standards Board, *Progress Report,* 1974.
9. Internal Revenue Service, Regulation 1.471.11.

Pricing Philosophy. There is a change in the philosophy about the proper role of business in our society which cannot be documented as accurately as the points made above, but which does nonetheless have an influence on pricing practices, and hence on cost accounting systems. Economics texts still teach that the overriding objective of a business is to maximize profits. A number of business leaders are currently questioning that this is, or should be, the dominant business objective. The public and Congress—as the representative of the public—are becoming increasingly vocal about this matter; talk about price gouging is a case in point. The alternative to profit maximization, and an alternative consistent with what society thinks the proper role of business is, is a reasonable profit. The achievement of such an objective requires the careful measurement of product costs, and the application of the concept that the price of each product should recover its cost, including a fair share of common costs, plus a reasonable profit.

The Future

For these reasons, cost accounting is about to experience a rebirth. In colleges and universities, it will again become a respectable subject. This means a renewed interest in cost accounting courses as well as a new interest in research.[10]

___

10. It is a strange fact, incidentally, that the National Association of Accountants, which once was called the National Association of Cost Accountants, has in recent years sponsored little, if any, research on the cost allocation process, which is the central problem in cost accounting. NAA has here an opportunity to take the lead in nurturing the rebirth.

This renewed interest should also have an impact on business. To many cost accountants wrestling with real-word problems, its rebirth should help them adapt their practices to the new requirements. With the computer and with the much better understanding of the nature of business we now have, significant improvements in techniques of cost allocation are possible. Methods of assigning more items of cost directly to cost objectives will be developed. Better transfer prices will be constructed. Plant-wide overhead rates increasingly will be replaced by a variety of allocations more closely measuring benefits received or the causes of cost incurrence.

Conclusion

Recent developments suggest it might be a good idea for practicing accountants to study up on cost accounting. That is, on both the basic concepts and the techniques of allocation appropriate in various circumstances, particularly on new techniques that have emerged in recent years. For teachers, they suggest the time has come to think about developing new courses in straight cost accounting, emphasizing the concepts and techniques of cost measurement without the distractions of performance measurement or relevant cost analysis. And for the businessman, they suggest the practicality and the importance of measuring full cost, and of understanding the significance of these measurements.

Chapter Twenty-Four

Product Costing: The Process Cost Accounting System

Reviewing the Chapter

1. A process cost system is used mainly by companies that produce large quantities of identical products and have a continuous product flow. The objectives of such a system are to determine (a) product unit costs and (b) ending balances for Work in Process and Finished Goods Inventories. Whereas job order costing is concerned with the cost of a particular batch or job, process costing deals with production cost over a certain period of time.

2. Before a product is completed, it usually must go through several departments. For example, a bookcase might go through cutting, assembling, and staining departments. In a process cost system, a separate Work in Process Inventory account is maintained for each department. Each Work in Process Inventory account contains costs of materials (if any), direct labor, and manufacturing overhead for that department plus any costs that have been transferred in from the previous department.

3. The process costing analysis revolves around (a) the schedule of equivalent production, (b) the unit cost analysis schedule, and (c) the cost summary schedule.

4. The unit cost for materials, direct labor, and factory overhead make up the product unit cost for a department.
   a. The unit cost for materials is found by dividing total material costs by the equivalent units for materials.
   b. The unit cost for direct labor and overhead equals direct labor and overhead costs (also called **conversion costs**) divided by equivalent units for direct labor and factory overhead.

5. **Equivalent production** (also called **equivalent units**) produced equals the sum of (a) the number of units started and completed during the period, (b) the number of units in ending Work in Process Inventory times their percentage of completion as of the end of the period, and (c) the number of units in beginning Work in Process Inventory times (100 percent minus their percentage of completion as of the beginning of the period). Equivalent unit figures for both raw materials and conversion costs must be computed in the **schedule of equivalent production**. Because production flows in a first-in, first-out manner in operations utilizing a process cost system, a **FIFO product and cost flow** is frequently assumed for product costing.

6. The purposes of a **unit cost analysis schedule** are to (a) add all costs charged to the Work in Process Inventory account of each department and (b) compute the cost per equivalent unit for both materials and conversion costs. The schedule is divided into a "total cost analysis" part and a "computation of equivalent unit costs" part.

   a. The total cost analysis consists of beginning inventory costs plus current period costs for both materials and conversion costs. The result is total costs to be accounted for.

   b. Equivalent unit costs equal the current period's materials and conversion costs divided by equivalent units for materials and conversion costs from the schedule of equivalent production.

7. The **cost summary schedule** distributes total costs accumulated during the period to units in ending Work in Process Inventory and to units completed and transferred out of the department. Data for the cost summary schedule are taken from the schedule of equivalent production and the unit cost analysis schedule. When figures for ending Work in Process Inventory and cost of goods transferred out of the department are determined, they are totaled and compared with "total costs to be accounted for" in the unit cost analysis schedule. If the figures do not agree, then there has been an error in arithmetic.

   a. Ending Work in Process Inventory is arrived at as follows: (1) Multiply equivalent units for materials in ending Work in Process Inventory by the unit cost as computed in the unit cost analysis schedule. (2) Multiply equivalent units for conversion costs in ending Work in Process Inventory by the unit cost as computed in the unit cost analysis schedule. (3) Add the two amounts together.

   b. The cost of goods transferred out of the department is arrived at as follows: (1) Multiply units started and completed by the total unit cost as computed in the unit cost analysis schedule. (2) Determine the cost connected to units in beginning inventory (same as ending inventory of preceding period). (3) Figure the costs necessary to complete the units in beginning inventory by using unit cost and equivalent unit figures. (4) Add the amounts together.

8. Once the figure for cost of goods transferred out of the department has been found, it can be journalized to record the transfer of goods to the next department. Then Work in Process Inventory (next department) is debited and Work in Process Inventory (this department) is credited. When goods are completed, the debit is instead to Finished Goods Inventory.

9. Product cost information is important not just for inventory pricing. It also helps companies set selling prices. Cost-based pricing is only a starting point, however. Other factors are usually considered before the selling price is finally established.

Testing Your Knowledge

Matching

Match each term with its definition by writing the appropriate letter in the blank.

____ 1. Process cost system

____ 2. Schedule of equivalent production

____ 3. Unit cost analysis schedule

____ 4. Cost summary schedule

____ 5. Equivalent units

____ 6. Conversion costs

a. The schedule used to distribute costs during the period to ending Work in Process Inventory and transferred units

b. Direct labor plus overhead

c. The schedule in which equivalent unit production is figured

d. The accounting method used when large quantities of identical products are being produced

e. Whole units produced, taking into consideration partially completed units

f. The schedule that computes a cost-per-unit figure

Completion

Use the lines provided to complete each item.

1. What three schedules are prepared in a process cost system? List them in their order of preparation.

_____

_____

_____

2. Show the computation for equivalent units.

_____

+ _____

+ _____

= equivalent units

3. What two items are computed in the cost summary schedule?

_____

_____

4. Show the computation for cost of goods transferred out of the department.

_____

+ _____

+ _____

= cost of goods transferred out of the department

True-False

Circle T if the statement is true, F if it is false. For all questions, assume a process cost system.

T F 1. Because process costing is used where large quantities of identical items are being produced, only one Work in Process Inventory account is ever needed.

T F 2. Factory overhead must be applied to production for the period.

T F 3. The finished units of one department become in effect the materials input of the next department.

T F 4. Product unit cost is made up of cost elements used in all departments.

T F 5. Equivalent units produced equal the number of units that were started and completed during the period.

T F 6. Conversion costs equal direct labor plus factory overhead.

T F 7. A separate unit cost figure is normally computed for direct labor and for factory overhead in the unit cost analysis schedule.

T F 8. In computing equivalent production, beginning inventory is multiplied by the percentage completed as of the beginning of the period.

T F 9. In the schedule of equivalent production, "units to be accounted for" must equal equivalent units for materials plus equivalent units for conversion costs.

T F 10. The unit cost analysis schedule must be prepared before the cost summary schedule.

T F 11. Ending Work in Process Inventory is determined by multiplying total units by total cost per unit.

T F 12. When goods are completed in Department 1 and are transferred to Department 2, Finished Goods Inventory is debited and Work in Process (Department 1) is credited.

T F 13. Units completed minus units in beginning inventory equals units started and completed (assuming that all units in beginning inventory have been completed).

T F 14. When cost per equivalent unit is computed in the unit cost analysis schedule, the costs associated with the beginning inventory are ignored under a FIFO cost flow assumption.

T F 15. The computational check for total costs to be accounted for is made in the unit cost analysis schedule.

T F 16. In most manufacturing operations that use a process cost system, production flows in a LIFO manner.

Multiple-Choice

Circle the letter of the best answer.

1. A certain department started and completed 10,000 units during the period. Beginning inventory of 5,000 units was 60 percent complete for conversion costs, and ending inventory of 7,000 units was 30 percent complete for conversion costs. What is equivalent production for conversion costs for the period?
   a. 4,000 units
   b. 14,100 units
   c. 15,000 units
   d. 15,100 units

2. Which of the following is not a schedule prepared under a process cost system?
   a. Cost summary schedule
   b. Schedule of equivalent production
   c. Schedule of conversion costs
   d. Unit cost analysis schedule

3. Which of the following is not a component of cost of goods transferred out of the department in the cost summary schedule?
   a. Costs necessary to complete units in beginning inventory
   b. Costs attached to units in beginning inventory
   c. Costs of units started and completed
   d. Costs necessary to complete units in ending inventory

4. On which of the following schedules will no unit costs appear?
   a. Schedule of equivalent production
   b. Unit cost analysis schedule
   c. Cost summary schedule
   d. None of the above

5. A certain department began the period with 5,000 units that were 80 percent complete, started and completed 12,000 units, and ended with 2,000 units that were 30 percent complete. Equivalent units produced would equal
   a. 13,600.
   b. 14,400.
   c. 16,600.
   d. 19,000.

6. Conversion costs represent the sum of
   a. materials and direct labor.
   b. direct labor and factory overhead.
   c. factory overhead and materials.
   d. materials, direct labor, and factory overhead.

7. The cost of ending Work in Process Inventory is computed in the
   a. schedule of equivalent production.
   b. cost summary schedule.
   c. unit cost analysis schedule.
   d. income statement.

8. The cost of goods transferred to Finished Goods Inventory is computed in the
   a. schedule of equivalent production.
   b. cost summary schedule.
   c. unit cost analysis schedule.
   d. balance sheet.

Applying Your Knowledge

Exercise

1. Data for Department 1 of the Morris Manufacturing Company for the month of May are as follows:

Beginning Work in Process Inventory
Units = 2,000
Materials = 100% complete
Conversion costs = 30% complete
Materials costs = $12,000
Conversion costs = $3,000

Ending Work in Process Inventory
Materials = 100% complete
Conversion costs = 30% complete

Operations for the month of May
Units started = 24,000
Materials costs = $114,000
Conversion costs = $30,750
Units completed and transferred to the next department = 19,000

Assuming a FIFO cost flow, complete the three schedules that follow.

		Morris Manufacturing Company Schedule of Equivalent Production For the Month Ended May 31, 19xx		
Units—Stage of Completion	Units to Be Accounted For	Equivalent Units		
		Materials	Conversion Costs	

Morris Manufacturing Company
Unit Cost Analysis Schedule
For the Month Ended May 31, 19xx

Total Cost Analysis

Computation of Equivalent Unit Costs

	Cost of Goods Transferred To Next Department	Cost of Ending Work in Process Inventory
Beginning Inventory		
Units Started and Completed		
Ending Inventory		
Computational Check		

Morris Manufacturing Company
Cost Summary Schedule
For the Month Ended May 31, 19xx

Crossword Puzzle
For Chapters 23 and 24

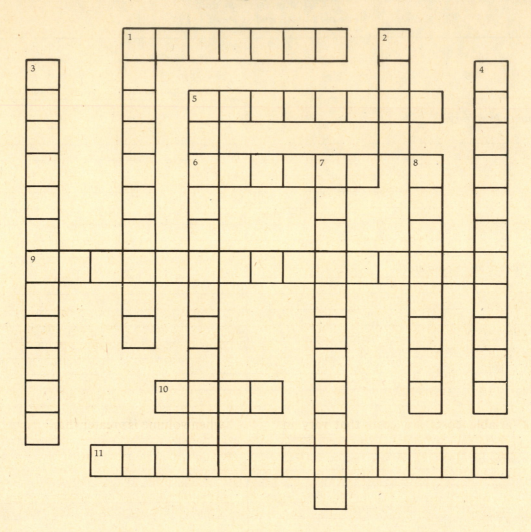

ACROSS

1. Account supported by subsidiary records
5. Outlay per manufactured item (2 words)
6. Cost that can be traced to a specific job or product
9. Productive output of 4-Down (2 words)
10. Product and cost flow assumption
11. _____ overhead rate

DOWN

1. Direct labor and factory overhead costs
2. See 8-Down
3. Accounting system for batches of products (3 words)
4. Accounting system for homogeneous units (2 words)
5. Misallocated overhead
7. Schedule used in 4-Down (2 words)
8. With 2-Down, denominator in computing 11-Across

Chapter Twenty-Five

Basic Cost Planning and Control Tools

Reviewing the Chapter

1. **Cost behavior** refers to how costs change in relation to volume (units of output). Understanding cost behavior is useful in predicting future costs and in analyzing past cost performance. Normally, a cost can be classified as either variable or fixed.
   a. **Variable costs** are costs that vary in direct proportion to volume. On a per-unit basis, variable costs remain constant as volume changes.
   b. **Fixed costs** are costs that remain constant within the relevant range of activity. The **relevant range** is the volume range within which actual operations are likely to occur. On a per-unit basis, fixed costs decrease as volume increases.

2. A **semivariable cost** acts like both a variable and a fixed cost. Telephone expense, for example, includes a fixed monthly service charge plus variable charges for long-distance calls.

3. **Mixed costs** are a combination of fixed and variable costs charged to the same general ledger account.

4. **Theoretical (ideal) capacity** is the maximum productive output possible over a given period of time. **Practical capacity** is theoretical capacity reduced by normal and anticipated work stoppages. **Normal capacity** is the average annual operating capacity needed to satisfy expected sales demand. It realistically measures what *will* be produced rather than what *can* be produced. **Excess capacity** refers to extra machinery and equipment available when regular facilities are being repaired or when volume is greater than expected.

5. **Cost-volume-profit (C-V-P) analysis** is used to measure **net** income at different activity levels and to measure the performance of a department within a company. In the formula used, sales revenues equal

   variable costs + fixed costs + net income

   a. The **break-even point** is the point at which sales revenues equal the sum of all variable and fixed costs. The break-even point in *units* is computed as follows:

   $$\frac{\text{fixed costs}}{\text{selling price} - \text{variable cost per unit}}$$

   The break-even point in *dollars* is computed as follows:

   break-even units × selling price per unit

   b. In graph form, the break-even point is at the point where the total revenue line crosses the total cost line. The area below the break-even point represents a loss. The area above represents a profit.

c. The **contribution margin** equals sales minus total variable costs. The contribution margin per unit equals selling price minus variable cost per unit. The break-even point in units equals fixed costs divided by contribution margin per unit. To find the units that must be sold for a certain net income, fixed costs plus the target net income are divided by the contribution margin per unit.

6. Many manufacturing costs apply to more than one segment of a corporation. A system of **cost allocation** or **assignment** must be used to assign the costs to the segments in a logical manner.
   a. A **cost center** is any segment of a business for which costs are accumulated.
   b. A **cost objective** is anything (such as a department or a product) that receives an assigned cost.

7. A **direct cost** is any cost that can be conveniently and economically traced to a specific product or cost objective. An **indirect cost** is one that cannot.

8. A **supporting service function** assists the production departments. Its costs must be allocated to the production departments in a logical manner. Examples of supporting service departments are a repair and maintenance department, a production scheduling department, and an inspection department.

9. Joint products (such as petroleum or beef) are produced from a common input or raw material. They cannot be identified as separate items throughout much of the production process. It is not until the **split-off point** that separate products emerge. A **joint cost** is a cost that relates to a joint product. Joint costs are allocated to the specific products by either the **physical volume method** or the **relative sales value method**.

10. A **responsibility accounting system** (also called **activity accounting** or **profitability accounting**) reports accounting information according to specific areas of managerial responsibility within a company. Under this system each area of responsibility files a report. The report lists only cost and revenue items that are **controllable** (can be influenced) by the area's management. Emphasis is on reports that communicate operating results throughout the company's organizational hierarchy.

11. To minimize costs and maximize profits, the origin of all controllable cost and revenue items must be determined, and the manager responsible for each item must be identified. In this way, at least one manager is held accountable for each item in the company's performance reports. The result is more efficient operations and faster location of trouble spots.

Testing Your Knowledge

Matching

Match each term with its definition by writing the appropriate letter in the blank.

_____ 1. Cost behavior

_____ 2. Variable costs

_____ 3. Fixed costs

_____ 4. Relevant range

_____ 5. Semivariable costs

_____ 6. Responsibility accounting system

_____ 7. Ideal (theoretical) capacity

_____ 8. Practical capacity

_____ 9. Normal capacity

_____ 10. Cost-volume-profit analysis

_____ 11. Break-even point

_____ 12. Contribution margin

_____ 13. Cost center

_____ 14. Cost objective

_____ 15. Split-off point

_____ 16. Joint cost

a. The operating level needed to satisfy expected sales demand

b. Where a joint product becomes several products

c. The maximum productive output possible over a given period of time

d. The sales volume at which overall net income is zero

e. Anything that receives an assigned cost

f. How costs change in relation to volume

g. A reporting system that holds each manager accountable for certain costs and revenues

h. Sales minus total variable cost

i. A business segment for which costs are accumulated

j. The volume range within which actual operations are likely to occur

k. A method of determining net income at different levels of volume

l. Costs that vary in direct proportion to volume

m. Costs that remain constant within the relevant range of volume

n. Ideal capacity minus normal work stoppages

o. A cost that is common to two or more products

p. Costs with both fixed and variable elements

Completion

Use the lines provided to complete each item.

1. The break-even formula is

_____

2. Three examples of semivariable costs are

_____

_____

_____

True-False

Circle T if the statement is true, F if it is false.

T F **1.** On a per-unit basis, variable costs remain constant with changes in volume.

T F **2.** On a graph, fixed costs can be represented by a straight, horizontal line.

T F **3.** A fixed cost may change when it is outside the relevant range.

T F **4.** Factory insurance is an example of a variable cost.

T F **5.** The most realistic plant capacity measure is practical capacity.

T F **6.** At the break-even point, sales equal variable costs.

T F **7.** At the break-even point, the contribution margin equals fixed costs.

T F **8.** The break-even point in dollars can be determined by multiplying break-even units by the selling price.

T F **9.** Property taxes are an example of a fixed cost.

T F **10.** Responsibility accounting deals mainly with internal users of accounting information.

T F **11.** As accounting information travels upward under a responsibility accounting system, the accounting data will probably be more detailed for a given department or division.

T F **12.** Joint costs include all costs incurred before and after the split-off point.

T F **13.** Cutting costs by 10 percent is an example of a cost objective.

T F **14.** It is easier to assign a division's costs to its departments than it is to do the reverse.

Multiple-Choice

Circle the letter of the best answer.

1. Taxi fares with a certain base price plus a mileage charge would be an example of a
   a. fixed cost.
   b. variable cost.
   c. semivariable cost.
   d. standard cost.

2. When fixed cost is $10,000, variable cost is $8 per unit, and selling price is $10 per unit, the break-even point is
   a. 1,000 units.
   b. 1,250 units.
   c. 5,000 units.
   d. 10,000 units.

3. When volume equals zero units,
   a. fixed cost equals $0.
   b. variable cost equals $0.
   c. total cost equals $0.
   d. net income equals $0.

4. At the break-even point,
   a. contribution margin equals fixed cost.
   b. sales equal variable cost.
   c. total cost equals contribution margin.
   d. net income equals total cost

5. In graph form, the break-even point is at the intersection of the
   a. total revenue and variable cost lines.
   b. total cost line and vertical axis.
   c. variable cost and fixed cost lines.
   d. total cost and total revenue lines.

6. The operating capacity that is required to satisfy anticipated sales demand is
   a. normal capacity.
   b. ideal capacity.
   c. practical capacity.
   d. theoretical capacity.

7. Which of the following is *not* true about a responsibility accounting system?
   a. It is a basis for judging management performance.
   b. It is helpful in pinpointing inefficiency.
   c. It consists of a series of reports.
   d. It holds management equally responsible for all costs.

8. Which of the following is *not* an example of a supporting service department?
   a. Building and grounds department
   b. Health center
   c. Factory cafeteria
   d. Assembling department

9. The physical volume method
   a. results in a more realistic gross profit percentage than the relative sales method.
   b. ignores revenue per unit of volume.
   c. is applied to costs incurred after the split-off point.
   d. allocates joint costs in proportion to the revenue that each product can generate.

Applying Your Knowledge

Exercises

1. Leisure Manufacturing Company is planning to introduce a new line of bowling balls. Annual fixed costs are estimated to be $80,000. Each ball will be sold to the retailer for $13, and requires $9 of variable costs.
   a. The break-even point in units is
      _____ .
   b. The break-even point in dollars is
      $ _____ .
   c. If 12,000 balls are sold per year, the overall profit or loss will be
      $ _____ .
   d. The number of balls that must be sold for an annual profit of $50,000 is
      _____ .

2. Before a certain process reaches the split-off point, $36,000 has been expended. After the split-off point, three separate products are manufactured:

   24,000 units of X, which will sell at $.50
   8,000 units of Y, which will sell at $1.00
   16,000 units of Z, which will sell at $5.00

   Compute the portion of the $36,000 joint cost that should be allocated to each of the products, using the physical volume method and relative sales value method.

Physical Volume Method	*Relative Sales Value Method*
X = $ _____	X = $ _____
Y = $ _____	Y = $ _____
Z = $ _____	Z = $ _____

3. Raymer Manufacturing Company has four production departments that share a maintenance department. Maintenance department costs are allocated to the production departments on the basis of their square footage:

   Dept. 1—2,500 sq. ft.
   Dept. 2—4,000 sq. ft.
   Dept. 3—2,000 sq. ft.
   Dept. 4—1,500 sq. ft.

   How much of November's $50,000 maintenance department cost should be allocated to

   Dept. 1? $ _____

   Dept. 2? $ _____

   Dept. 3? $ _____

   Dept. 4? $ _____

The Controller

Inflation gives him more clout with management.

To U.S. business today, tough financial controls have suddenly become synonymous with not merely success but survival, and the corporate controller has moved from the backroom right to center stage. At companies that once stressed growth and expansion beyond all else, the job of measuring the costs of doing business—and cutting them—gets the highest priority today. Elaborate budgets have been devised and are being strictly enforced. New investments must promise bigger returns than ever before—which is one reason why the pace of capital spending is so sluggish—and old projects that fall below expectations are being lopped off. Corporate debt, taken on in gigantic amounts in the past to finance growth, is being paid down rapidly, and companies are loath to take on heavy loads of new debt.

Indeed, in a dramatic turnabout from the strategies of the late 1960s and early 1970s, corporations today are far more interested in improving profit margins than in building up market share or new business. And if that raises serious questions about the future growth of U.S. business and the economy, it nonetheless is the way corporations believe they must go. "Sheer economic pressure has dictated that we have to get more out of things already in place—that is, people, bricks, and mortar," says Robert E. Northam, controller of J.C. Penney Co.

Nowhere is this new management focus—some observers call it an obsession—more palpable than in the recent rise of the controller (derived from the French *compte,* for "account"). Only 10 years ago, most controllers were relegated to obscurity, to adding the debits and credits and reporting what had already happened. In the past few years, however, former controllers have ascended to the top of such mammoth companies as General Motors Corp., FMC Corp., Fruehauf Corp., and Pfizer Inc. Controllers are now getting involved with the operating side of the company, where they give advice and influence production, marketing, and investment decisions as well as corporate planning. Moreover, many controllers who have not made it to the top have won ready access to top management. "Ten years ago, the controller never got

Source: Reprinted from the August 15, 1977 issue of *Business Week* by special permission, © 1977 by McGraw-Hill, Inc.

into the boss's office," says Chairman and President Robert T. Campion of Lear Siegler Inc., the diversified manufacturer with $700 million in sales last year. "Now he's part of the management team. He's not just keeping score—he's playing the game."

Why the Emphasis Shifted

Executive recruiters also attest to the growing importance of the controller. Most major placement firms say that requests for controllers have risen more than for any other corporate function. Compensation for controllers has risen 25% to 30% faster than inflation in the past five years, and it now often tops the going salary for treasurers. In fact, the demand for chief executive officers with a controller background has increased sharply and "is even bigger than that for controllers," claims Thomas J. Neff, vice-president of Spencer Stuart Management Consultants in New York.

As the controller's job has changed, so have the tools of the trade. In the old days, the controller simply worked up the profit-and-loss statement and the balance sheet. Today the job involves elaborate monitoring and cross-checking of scads of financial data from profits and expenses to return on investment and the cost of capital. Instead of the adding machine and ledger books, the controller works with increasingly complex, sophisticated computer programs that keep him in almost daily touch with almost every facet of the business.

The reasons behind the new emphasis on corporate controls are clear. In the early 1950s, production efficiency received most of top management's attention. Later in that decade, the marketing people took

How the Controller's Office Has Grown

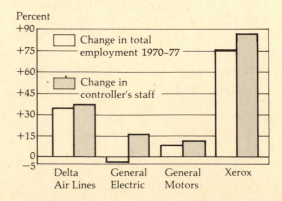

over, and advertising and market research flourished. By the late 1960s, with capital plentiful and corporations increasingly diversified, the financial men who could make deals and raise new money rose to the top. Corporations borrowed to the hilt to keep up their all-important growth rates and make acquisitions.

By 1973, of course, that bubble had burst, and defensive-minded corporations called on the controllers to get the business back on track. In fact, Lear Siegler's Campion credits the rapid rise of the controller directly to the economic tremors of the early 1970s. When inflation hit double-digit rates in 1973, the costs of doing business—not the least of which was the interest rate on all that debt—soared. And when the economy dived into its worst post war recession a year later, corporations saw their profits drop 30% and 40%, sometimes more.

Even so sophisticated a company as General Electric Co., with a history of superior financial controls, found itself somewhat at sea in the economy of three and four years ago: business slowing, costs getting out of control, and profits under intense pressure. "The financial crisis of 1974, and the double-digit inflation, brought the controller's job into the limelight," says Alva O. Way, GE's financial vice-president. "The general managers of each of our businesses needed that fellow just to understand what was going on."

Nor has the economic recovery since 1974 inspired much confidence. For one thing, when executives began looking back over the wreckage of the mid-1970s, they discovered that 1973 and 1974 had not been their only bad years. Costs of goods sold and of interest had been rising rapidly as a percentage of sales since the mid-1960s. And many of the grand expansion plans of the booming 1960s simply did not pan out. By 1976, profit margins had been falling almost continuously for 10 years, slipping to 5.3% of sales from their 1966 average level of 7%.

In such an environment, the turn to tougher financial controls may be inevitable. But it also raises concern among economists, and some businessmen themselves, that corporations are tightening the reins too much and seeking quick returns at the expense of longer-term payoffs. Whereas new investment in the 1960s got out of hand, businessmen's reluctance today to put up new plants and take on new ventures accounts for a good deal of the current softness in plant and equipment spending. "In watching expenses, you can let opportunities slip away," says Charles H. Davison, deputy chairman of Peat, Marwick, Mitchell & Co., the Big Eight accounting firm.

There is deep concern that some companies are overstressing mechanistic control and slighting not only capital spending but also critical research and development—truly borrowing from the future to get by today. "What I worry about is that pressure to keep up current earnings and dividend payouts will hurt development programs," says Professor Joseph L. Bower of the Harvard Business School.

Indeed, at some companies there is already something of a retreat from tight controls. The dethroning of Arthur R. Taylor as president of CBS Inc. is said to have resulted in part from his emphasis on placing tight controls on a business that depends far more on creative energy: Similarly, observers say the trouble that Franklin M. Jarman had at Genesco Inc., the apparel and retail store conglomerate, had a lot to do with his insistence on controls that straitjacketed operations. Jarman was ousted as Genesco's chief executive last January. Even J.C. Penney, well-known as a tightly managed company, is relaxing some of its controls because they have occasionally taken more of the employees' time than they are worth. "We are very aggressively trying to back off unneccessary controls," says Penney's Northam.

As Controls Tighten Up

Nevertheless, most companies—beset by costs that will not quit rising and by the demands of investors for higher returns and better ratios of debt to equity—are still tightening financial controls. And the procedures they are now setting up will affect the way these companies do business for years to come. Such companies as General Motors Corp., Gould Inc., and R.J. Reynolds Industries have boosted their controller staffs by 10% or more in recent years. As a result of tighter controls, H.J. Heinz Co. has been able to pare down inventories by $74 million and short-term debt by $77 million, according to David A. Lattanzio, the company's controller. And its return on equity has improved to 13.4% from 9.6% in 1966. But Heinz will continue to tighten controls until they raise the return still further, says Lattanzio. Clearly, many managements are happy with their tighter approach and will not abandon it soon. "We're doing the same level of business on substantially less assets," says Joseph F. Alibrandi, president of Whittaker Corp., the West Coast conglomerate.

The changing duties of Lear Siegler's controller, David J. Louks, are probably representative of the evolving role of the controller today. Louks, a certified public accountant, started with Lear Siegler as corporate controller in 1963, when the company's sales were around $200 million. "I was the company's historian, its record-keeper," he says. In 1963, he had one assistant. Today, he has an assistant controller, four senior accountants, and an internal audit staff of

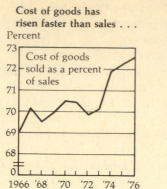

Cost of goods has risen faster than sales . . .

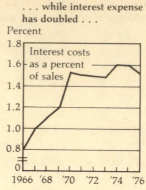

. . . while interest expense has doubled . . .

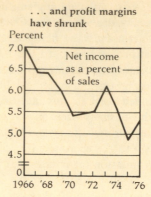

. . . and profit margins have shrunk

Average of companies listed in Standard & Poor's 400
Data: Investors Management Sciences

seven. "Maybe I talked to the president once every two weeks 10 years ago," says Louks. Now he has daily contact with senior management, and, he notes, "I attend occasional board meetings."

Whereas once Louks merely recorded the results of divisions, today he and his staff must evaluate business forecasts of each division on a quarterly basis. And his internal audit staff has more clout. "We have regular opportunities to make recommendations at the operational level," he says. "Undoubtedly, this chafes line managers," he admits. "But they're learning that controls are here to stay."

One of Louk's most controversial actions as controller came when his staff discovered that overdue receivables at one division were unusually high. Louks recommended that the division manager beef up his reserve for bad debts, which would have damaged his division's profits. The manager resisted, and Louks took the decision higher. Top management forced the division manager to follow Louk's recommendation.

In the past five years, Louks claims that controls have enormously improved the company's profitability. Profit margins have tripled since 1972 to nearly 4%. Return on equity is also way up from 4% to 14.1%. And the company has nearly halved its debt-equity ratio to about 0.5, while boosting working capital by some $33 million to $166 million.

A Role in Decision-Making

Case histories similar to that of Louks are being repeated from company to company across the country. Heinz's Lattanzio says that his duties have expanded in much the same way. He was appointed the company's controller four years ago, after seven years at a public accounting firm. "At that time, my main concern was with the publication of financial statements and compliance with Securities & Exchange Commission and accounting rules," he says. "Now we are more involved in decision-making." Lattanzio's big project these days is how to control inventory and capital spending. But he is also required to appraise marketing programs, analyze acquisition opportunities, and control the company's foreign exchange holdings.

In addition, controllers these days are more often reporting directly to headquarters, often going over the heads of divisional operating managers. The goal is to get critical, unbiased information to top management right away. A few years ago, American Can Co. reorganized its controller function for this purpose (page 90). Now each divisional controller reports directly to the chief controller at company headquarters in Greenwich, Conn. Litton Industries has also recently made the divisional controller directly responsible to corporate headquarters.

Corporations have also been trying to make all of their managers—financial and nonfinancial—more familiar with, and more receptive to controls. For example, in 1974, GE initiated courses on "managing in inflation" and "cash effectiveness," that eventually will reach 9,000 people throughout the company.

Probably the main reason that the controller is getting the ear of top management these days is that he or she is virtually the only person familiar with all the working parts of the company. The controller is more or less "the seeing-eye dog," says Charles T. Horngren, professor of accounting at Stanford University's business school. "Often a chief executive or division manager won't go to anything important without that controller," Robert B. Hoffman, financial vice-president of Chicago based FMC Corp., puts it very plainly. "The role of the controller," he says, "is to reduce a company's business to common denominators that everyone in the corporation can understand."

For Hoffman, those measures include return on

equity, working capital, and a fairly complicated series of measures of the risk and volatility of various ventures. Hoffman has developed a set of parameters to describe all the various businesses his company is in, which range from chemicals to construction equipment and food-processing machinery. He ranks the divisions according to whether they are cash-heavy, in need of new investment, holding their own, or ripe for divestment. "As business grows," he says, "the corporate management becomes more and more remote and needs these common denominators even more."

More Detailed Budgets

As the controller's function gets increasingly complex, the budget still remains undoubtedly his chief concern. But whereas budgets once included only sales and expense figures, controllers now demand not only details of expenses but also sales prices, volume projections by product, working capital, and even an analysis of risk factors. Such an analysis often involves a subjective analysis of how likely it is that a sales goal will be met.

Budgets are also getting more frequent attention. At J.C. Penney, there are now monthly updates of its regular annual and quarterly budgets. "If you're going to succeed, you can't wait for quarters to pass by," says Controller Northam. Gould Inc. demands a weekly budget, due every Friday night, from each of its division managers. The budget contains 12 pieces of information, including daily sales order backlog, and working capital. Controller Gerald E. Schultz explains: "We feel that by being on top and planning, we can go out and make things happen rather than wait for them to happen."

While the budgets are becoming more complex, management is also tightening up on monitoring and enforcing them. At FMC, division managers must submit a report in the middle of each month on whether they can meet a number of different goals, including inventory and working capital levels, set out in the yearly budget. And the managers must follow that report up with another at the end of the month reporting on the actual results. "When the corporation is off 10¢ a share," says Hoffman, "we can pinpoint exactly where it has come from. We try to use anticipatory controllership."

International Telephone & Telegraph Corp., probably the pioneer in modern financial controls, has raised so-called anticipatory controllership to a very sophisticated level. Not only does the multinational giant ($15 billion in sales worldwide in 1976) calculate all the costs of the labor and materials that go into each of its products. It has also devised an index that is designed to signal a warning as soon as costs start to rise. ITT management then consults the index monthly for help in setting prices.

Return on Investment

Hand in hand with controlling expenses, corporations are also watching their return on investment more closely these days. Many have markedly raised their ROI targets for new investments. Penney, for example, settled for a 10% return on investment 10 years ago but now demands 20% because of inflation and higher cost of capital.

Moreover, corporations are quicker these days to find out what is wrong when returns fall below expectations. FMC's Hoffman has taken harsh action when divisions or product lines fell below their return-on-investment criteria. In five years, FMC has pruned some 20 divisions or major product lines.

Hanes Corp., which had never adopted firm ROI targets before, two years ago set a 12% target for return on assets for each of its three divisions. That led to the shutdown of two plants whose rates of return did not measure up. Hanes, an apparel manufacturer with $372 million in sales last year, believes it will achieve its 12% in each of the divisions next year. "The discipline of looking at the return on assets makes you face up to problems," admits John B. McKinnon, the company's financial vice-president.

Today's corporate controller uses his increasingly sophisticated tools to seek out problems that need correcting. One of the most common uses is in culling products that have low profit margins. For example, Mark Controls Corp., a valve manufacturer in Evanston, Ill., installed a cost-accounting system that enabled it to cost out each of its 15,000 products.

The result of this approach was that Mark dropped about 15% of its product line. Companies as diverse as Studebaker-Worthington, a conglomerate; Gable Industries, a building supplies company; and APL Corp., a maker of packaging materials, have pruned operations for similar reasons.

Controllers, often with the help of enlarged crews of internal auditors, have also been turning their attention to reducing inventories and receivables. Abbott Laboratories, for example, was able to hold its inventory growth down to 3.8% last year, while sales grew 15%. One successful tactic was to tie a bonus system for managers to inventory targets. Phillips & Jacobs Inc., the graphics division of Tasty Baking Co., sliced a full 30% off its inventory over the past three years by identifying slow-moving film products and setting up a system that helps the company shift them among branches more efficiently.

Cutting the fat out of receivables has become common at many companies. Corporations are also improving their management of cash and foreign currency with increasing help from the controller. The controller is even getting involved with acquisitions these days. When Fisher Scientific Co. bought the Lederle Laboratories Div. of American Cyanamid Co. this June, it depended largely on background work supplied by its controller, Michael J. Foglia. "From the first, Foglia analyzed the financial status of Lederle, the size of the marketplace, share of market, and so on," says John D. Herrington, vice-president and treasurer of Fisher. "He had to set up all the charts of accounts and accounting procedures we'll use there. Ten years ago, when we bought a company, the financial department wasn't even asked to look at it."

Swinging More Weight

So far at least, the emphasis on controls has apparently paid off. In the past 18 months profit margins and return on equity have increased significantly for most corporations. The economic recovery, of course, helped. But companies such as FMC, Lear Siegler, Heinz, and Mark Controls, where financial controls have been emphasized, have been strengthened markedly.

Indeed, for that reason, the controller's office may have become a place to be for the rising young executive. Job recruiters note that such well-known controller training grounds as Xerox, GM, Ford, ITT, and General Electric are often raided by other corporations for new personnel. And, says one rising executive who is working in his company's budgeting office: "A couple of years ago, I would never have wanted to spend time in the controller's department. But I see now that this job gives me high visibility and frequent access to the chief executive."

The debate over whether corporate controls are going too far, however, is heating up as the current economic recovery grows older while corporate investment remains disappointingly soft. Critics claim that the experiences of Taylor at CBS and Jarman at Genesco should serve as a warning that too much emphasis on controls can lead to serious problems. The trimming back on controls by some companies is alerting other companies to the need to review and refine their system as they review and refine any other parts of the business. Jarman's tight budgets, says one source close to the operation, made it difficult for divisions that were running over budget in June to order new merchandise for the fall season. A delay of only a few weeks resulted in the loss of precious selling time at the height of the season.

Penney's control tightness cannot compare to Genesco's. But one of several procedures that have been scotched lately was a daily cash monitoring system in some of Penney's stores. Management found that the procedure was simply taking too much employee time. Perhaps more important, says Controller Northam, it caused morale problems. So Penney now monitors the cash weekly instead of daily.

Similar problems are cropping up in many places. One big New York commercial bank recently set up an ad hoc committee to determine whether important bank services were being neglected in complying with stringent control procedures. Elsewhere, complaints from employees about excessive paperwork and minute scrutiny of the smallest expenses are common. Gillette Co., for example, refuses to allow its divisional controllers to bypass the local operating management. "When the controller reports directly to headquarters, there is the tendency of local management to treat them as spies," says Edward G. Melaugh, senior vice-president of finance.

Corporate critics also worry about top management's recent concern with quick returns on investment. "You've got to get better performance quicker to satisfy investors," says one controller. Such objectives often mean that corporations would rather take such short-term measures to shore up profits as raising prices or slashing budgets than marketing a product harder or starting up new ventures. It also means adding gingerly to capacity, if at all, rather than building a new plant.

Borrowing Future Trouble

Recently a Heinz affiliate found that it needed more warehouse space for frozen potatoes. Ten years ago, the company would have simply built the new facility without considering its potential impact on earnings, says Lattanzio. But this time Lattanzio opposed construction because the return from investing in a warehouse was not as great as that from investing the cash elsewhere. Heinz leased the space instead.

Because the controller gets involved in such decisions, he is going to remain a controversial figure inside the corporation. Nor will that controversy fade soon, because it will take years to judge all that the controllers are doing today. The problem, of course, is that while the savings can show up at once, potential side effects, such as lost opportunities, may not be apparent for many years. "If you cut back things like R&D," says Kenneth W. Reese, senior vice-president for finance at Tenneco Inc., "the results won't show up in earnings for five years—but they can be disastrous." Many managers are aware of such dangers. They also feel that in uncertain times, and with inflation likely to push up costs dramatically, they must not stretch their cash too thinly.

"The main thing is to be sure the decision is made with the facts," says Robert McAdams Jr., controller of Ampex Corp. "But if an idea doesn't meet our rate-of-return goals, there may be other reasons to pursue it. The risk factor is the key element that might have to be determined by gut feel."

In short, while overzealous controllers and overrigid controls may indeed be smothering some companies, that need not necessarily be the case. "You can go back to fundamentals and still be very entrepreneurial," declares Way of General Electric. Nor is there evidence that GE's controls have inhibited either its growth or its investment in the future. "There is no inherent reason," says J. Fred Weston, who is professor of finance at the UCLA business school, "why the controller can't cause companies to be more flexible, faster to react, better at seizing opportunities."

Chapter Twenty-Six

Budgetary Control: The Planning Function

Reviewing the Chapter

1. The principles of effective budgeting are (a) long-range objectives and goals principles, (b) short-range goals and strategies principles, (c) human responsibilities and interaction principles, (d) budget housekeeping principles, and (e) follow-up principles.

   a. Before annual operating budgets can be developed, top management must communicate their long-range goals for the company to those who will prepare the budgets. The expected quality of products or services, company growth, and profit expectations are three examples of long-range goals.

   b. The short-range yearly operating budget turns the long-range goals into detailed plans for the coming year. The budget director is responsible for developing the annual budget and its timetable.

   c. The budget director should bring all levels of management into the budgeting process. This effort leads to **participative budgeting**. Budget implementation tends to be less effective if top management simply dictates its goals to lower-level management or displays little support for the participants' input.

   d. Budgets should be based on realistic, not inflated, goals, and deadlines for their development should always be met. In addition, they should be flexible enough to deal with changes in revenues and expenses during the period.

   e. Finally, follow-up principles are part of budgetary control. The budget should be checked at all times to assure that operations are going as planned. Performance reports should be prepared for each operating segment so that problem areas can be identified, analyzed, and handled in the next period's budget.

2. Budgetary control means planning future company activities and controlling operations to help achieve those plans. The planning function should consist of projecting a long-term plan covering five to ten years and a short-term plan covering one year at a time. Long-term plans are general in nature and must be translated by management into specific goals for the year. Short-term plans, which are expressed in a **period budget**, consist of a forecast of operations as well as specific planned activities for segments of the company.

3. Responsibility accounting, together with the concepts of cost allocation and cost accumulation, are cost accounting tools that are very helpful in preparing the period budget (one-year budget).

   a. When a responsibility accounting system is used, budget preparation begins with the communication of annual sales and production plans from top management to the various managerial levels. This information then allows the segment managers to develop detailed operating budgets for their areas of responsibility. Finally, these managers submit the detailed budgets to the budget director, who puts together the operating budget for the entire company.

b. When unit sales have been forecast, cost-volume-profit analysis can be used to determine associated costs and to predict net income for the period.

4. The **master budget** is a combined set of departmental or functional period budgets that have been consolidated into forecasted financial statements for the whole company. Preparation of the master budget consists of preparing (a) detailed operating or period budgets, (b) the forecasted income statement, (c) the cash budget, and (d) the forecasted balance sheet.

5. The detailed period budgets mentioned above normally include the budgets for (a) sales (in units), (b) production (in units), (c) selling expenses, (d) direct materials purchases, (e) direct materials usage, (f) labor hour requirements, (g) labor dollars, (h) factory overhead, (i) general and administrative expenses, and (j) capital expenditure. These budgets are closely related and must be prepared in a certain order (for instance, the sales budget must always be prepared first). At this point, a thorough review of Figure 26-2 of the text is recommended.

6. Budget implementation will be successful if there is (a) proper communication of budget targets to all key operating personnel and (b) support and encouragement from top management.

7. A **cash flow forecast (cash budget)** is a period projection of beginning cash, cash receipts, cash disbursements, and ending cash. It is a summary of all planned cash transactions found in the detailed period budgets and in the forecasted income statement. For example, cash receipts may be predicted mainly from the sales budget. The main objectives of a cash budget are to (a) show the projected ending cash balance and (b) allow management to anticipate periods of high or low cash availability. An expected period of low cash availability, for example, would alert management that short-term borrowing may be necessary. Care must be taken to include only cash inflows and outflows that are likely during the period.

8. The budgeting principles for profit-oriented businesses also apply, for the most part, to not-for-profit and public-sector organizations. However, the budgeting process for such organizations results in planned changes in fund balances instead of in profits or losses. Generally, expenditures are restricted to funds available from appropriations, dues, or donations. Significant cost overruns must usually receive legislative or board approval.

Testing Your Knowledge

Matching

Match each term with its definition by writing the appropriate letter in the blank.

_____ 1. Budgetary control

_____ 2. Period budget

_____ 3. Participative budgeting

_____ 4. Master budget

_____ 5. Cash budget

_____ 6. Sales budget

_____ 7. Budget director

_____ 8. Production budget

a. The basis for all other operating budgets

b. A combined set of departmental or functional period budgets that have been consolidated into forecasted financial statements for the whole company

c. The planning of and control over future company activities

d. The basis for the materials, labor, and overhead budgets

e. The involvement of all levels of management in the budgeting process

f. The person in charge of the budgeting process

g. The budget prepared after all period budgets and the forecasted income statement

h. Yearly operating plans for a segment of the business

Completion

Use the lines provided to complete each item.

1. List the five groups of effective budgeting principles.

_____

_____

_____

_____

2. Which budgets are prepared immediately after the production budget?

_____

_____

_____

_____

True-False

Circle T if the statement is true, F if it is false.

T F 1. Budgetary control refers only to the control of operations.

T F 2. A long-term plan is called a master budget.

T F 3. A period budget refers to planned activities for a segment of the business only.

T F 4. A projection of sales must be made before the production budget can be devised.

T F 5. The main objective of governmental organizations is to earn a profit.

T F 6. Monitoring the budget is considered a follow-up principle of effective budgeting.

T F 7. Depreciation expense would be listed as a cash disbursement in the cash budget.

T F 8. Establishing long-range objectives and goals should go before establishing short-range ones.

T F 9. Participative budgeting is of little value to a not-for-profit organization.

T F 10. Total sales for a period would be included in that period's cash budget as part of cash receipts.

T F 11. The direct materials usage budget must be prepared before the direct materials purchases budget.

T F 12. Cost-volume-profit analysis is very helpful in budget preparation.

Multiple-Choice

Circle the letter of the best answer.

1. The first step involved in preparing a master budget is preparing
   a. a forecasted income statement.
   b. a general operating budget.
   c. a forecasted balance sheet.
   d. detailed period budgets.

2. Which of the following components of the master budget must be prepared before the others?
   a. Direct labor dollars budget
   b. Cost of goods sold forecast
   c. Production budget
   d. Direct materials purchases budget

3. The period budget should begin with a forecast of
   a. overhead.
   b. production.
   c. sales.
   d. direct labor.

4. The cash budget is prepared
   a. before all period budgets are prepared.
   b. after the forecasted income statement but before the forecasted balance sheet.
   c. as the last step in the master budget.
   d. only if the company has doubts about its debt-paying ability.

5. Integrating realism and flexibility into budget preparation is a
   a. human responsibilities and interaction principle.
   b. follow-up principle.
   c. short-range goals and strategies principle.
   d. budget housekeeping principle.

6. Which of the following budgets would not be a source of cash disbursements in the cash budget?
   a. Sales budget
   b. Capital expenditure budget
   c. Selling expense budget
   d. Direct labor dollars budget.

7. Budget preparation
   a. should be done entirely by independent professionals hired by the company.
   b. should involve all levels of management.
   c. should be done entirely by the budget director.
   d. should be done entirely by top management.

8. The following budget information is provided for Schramm Company:

Quarter	1	2	3
Sales in units	20,000	25,000	23,000
Production in units	23,000	24,000	21,000

Each finished unit requires three pounds of material. The inventory of material at the end of each quarter should equal 10 percent of the following quarter's production needs. How many pounds of material should be purchased for the second quarter?
   a. 71,100 lb
   b. 72,000 lb
   c. 74,400 lb
   d. 75,000 lb

Applying Your Knowledge

Exercises

1. E & J produces and sells a single product. Expected sales for the next four months are:

April	10,000 units
May	12,000
June	15,000
July	9,000

The company needs a *production budget* for the second quarter. Experience indicates that end-of-month finished goods inventory must equal 10 percent of the following month's sales in units. At the end of March, 1,000 units were on hand. Compute production needs for the second quarter.

E & J Company
Production Budget
For the Quarter Ended June 30, 19xx

---

2. Rensch Enterprises needs a cash budget for the month of June. The following information is available:

a. The cash balance on June 1 is $7,000.

b. Sales for May and June are $80,000 and $60,000, respectively. Cash collections on sales are 30 percent in the month of the sale, 65 percent in the following month, and 5 percent uncollectible.

c. General and administrative expenses are budgeted at $24,000 for June. Depreciation represents $2,000 of this amount.

d. Inventory purchases will total $30,000 in June, and totaled $40,000 in May. Half of inventory purchases are always paid for in the month of the purchase. The remainder are paid for in the following month.

e. Office furniture costing $3,000 will be purchased for cash in June, and selling expenses (exclusive of $2,000 in depreciation) are budgeted at $14,000.

f. The company must maintain a minimum ending cash balance of $4,000, and can borrow from the bank in multiples of $100. All loans are repaid after 60 days.

In the space provided, prepare a cash budget for Rensch Enterprises for the month of June.

Rensch Enterprises
Cash Budget
For the Month Ending June 30, 19xx

Crossword Puzzle
For Chapters 25 and 26

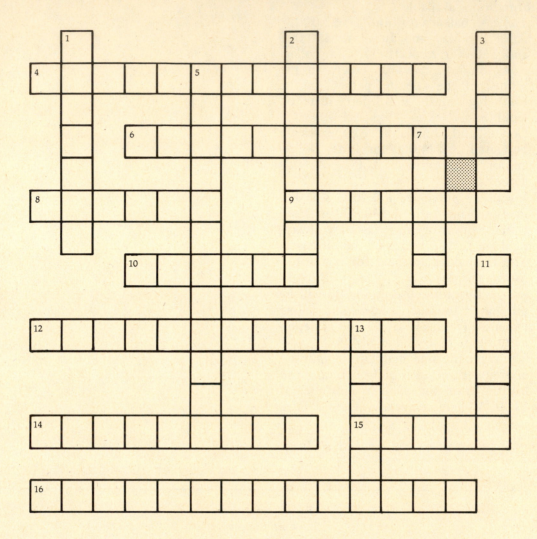

ACROSS

4. Budgeting that involves many people
6. _____ margin
8. With 9-Across, overall plan for operations
9. See 8-Across
10. Physical _____ method
12. Probable activity level (2 words)
14. Point of no profit (hyphenated)
15. Cost with fixed and variable components
16. Accounting system that assigns costs to managers

DOWN

1. Plant and equipment budget
2. Cost that changes with activity level
3. Cost that relates to several products
5. Cost that can be influenced
7. Maximum productive capacity
11. Yearly budget
13. Productive capacity for anticipated sales demand

The Controller's Role in Corporate Planning

The implementation of the strategic planning process is a natural extension of the control aspect inherent in the controller's function.

The scope of the modern controller's responsibilities is expanding in more and more companies to encompass coordinating the planning activities associated with the annual planning cycle. Strategic planning is becoming recognized as the most effective way to manage as we move into the turbulent 80s. Strategic planning is a conceptual exercise that establishes a framework for strategic management decisions that will affect the future of the company.

The controller is uniquely positioned to capitalize on this opportunity to expand his horizons considerably. In major corporations the controllers who have been able to administer effectively the strategic and operating planning cycles have gone on to participate in management of some of the new businesses that evolved out of the strategic planning process. In addition, the controller involved in planning is positioned to assess the financial viability of embryonic strategies in terms of their long-term financial requirements thanks to his intimate knowledge of the financial structure of the organization.

Strategic planning is an iterative integrated managerial accounting exercise. It is financially fine tuning the organization by establishing a discipline of constantly measuring performance against the short-term annual budget, as well as the strategic milestones and their related capital expenditures that are built into the operating plan, which evolves out of the strategic plan. Let's explore how the controller gets involved.

The Start of Real Planning

The greatest contribution the controller can make to the planning process is in providing financial education to line managers.

In most companies strategic planning gets started by the chief executive officer getting bit by the "planning bug." This can happen in a variety of ways: the CEO can read about it in a magazine, can be introduced to it by one of his peers at lunch or the club,

Source: Article by Robert M. Donnelly. Reprinted by permission from the September 1981 issue of *Management Accounting.*

can attend a seminar on strategic planning, or can simply decide that if other companies have used it, successfully maybe his company should try it, too. In any case, the first step in the process is to identify an administrator, or coordinator, of the planning process. Because planning concepts have to be financially quantified before any decision can be made, and if implemented then have to be controlled—who is better qualified to do both than the controller? In addition, the controller manages the budgeting and is the keeper of all of the historical management information critical to starting the strategic planning process.

It almost becomes a natural extension of the controller's duties for him to become the administrator of the planning cycle. In order to do this the controller has to be one of the first members of the management team to familiarize himself with the fundamentals of strategic planning. In most cases, the controller assumes the position of being the right hand of the CEO in the implementation of the strategic planning exercise. It is a natural extension of the control aspect inherent in the controller's function.

Strategic planning starts with the introduction of the concept to senior management, or those who report directly to the CEO, which would include the controller. At that introductory session it should be made clear to those present that the controller will be available for consultation on the process, with the financial support to analyze strategies, and will function as the coordinator of the exercise.

The formalized strategic planning process starts at some agreed upon time shortly after the initial presentation, and usually begins with the management team getting back together for about two days, when each member of the team presents his individual perceptions of the internal and external strengths and weaknesses of the business.

As this kind of presentation unfolds, it usually becomes obvious that there is a divergence of perceptions as to the overall strengths and weaknesses of the organization. Sometimes these perceptions differ from the CEO's. But strategic planning's basic thrust is to bring the management team together by enabling team members to identify with the same problems and opportunities to work toward the same common goals and objectives.

Out of this first formal planning session should come either a dictated set of strengths and weaknesses by the chief executive officer, or the management team's concensus of the same. In any case, the assignment for the team at the end of this first session is to take the agreed-upon strengths and weaknesses and develop strategies which will emphasize the organization's strengths and improve, or overcome, its weaknesses. The assignments are then given to each member of the mamagement team as they relate to his or her expertise and area of responsibility. The controller should plan to give financial guidance to each respective manager.

The second formal session should take place after a reasonable period of time is allowed to get all the work done (which in most cases is about a month to six weeks), and should be at least a two-day session during which all of the proposed strategies are thoroughly discussed by the management team. Out of this discussion will come tentative viable strategies, some that will be discarded as unachievable, and others as modified "group" strategies.

This session's function is to produce a set of achievable strategies that the group agrees can be accomplished with existing resources and that appear to be economically attractive. Then the respective managers must "price-out" these strategies with the help of the controller's staff. In other words, analyze: how much will the strategy cost? Who will be accountable for getting it done? How long will it take? And what will be the projected results of implementing these plans?

This second session analysis necessitates involvement of subordinate management and is usually a longer process because of the level of detail required in planning the best possible moves. And, as a result, this detailed preliminary analysis may result in some strategies being scrapped.

The third session is spent reviewing the second session's analytical results. And the number of strategies to be reviewed will determine the length of the third session—usually not more than two days because not too many strategies survive to this phase. The surviving strategies coming out of the third meeting will constitute the basis for developing the mission statement of the company and the strategic planning document.

The last phase consists in putting the strategic plan document together and writing a cohesive narrative of the combination of strategies. This document is then communicated to management and becomes the basis for developing operating plans and budgets.

It is now up to the management team to implement the strategic plan, measure its performance, and periodically update the plan and organization as business conditions warrant. Strategic planning sets the parameters for a company's long-term growth by identifying opportunities and setting in motion a series of chronological planning activities to exploit them. The process constitutes setting futuristic goals and objectives and working back in time to plan for the specific subsets of the overall plan. These subsets are generally referred to as operating plans and are usually three-year periods of time.

Contained in the first year of the operating plan is the budget or the month-by-month tasks that must be accomplished to make the operating plan a reality.

The strategic plan identifies opportunities in a prioritized fashion, with the most important heading the chronological order of action plans or strategies to be implemented. Those deemed lower priority strategies have a longer implementation schedule and may, or may not, be dependent on the success or failure of higher priority action plans. The strategic plan encompasses all of these strategies and is based on the assumption that the total plan is achievable.

The operating plan is developed from the most important action plans and coordinated by the controller. It is important to understand that the life of a strategy can range from a few months to several years. The operating plan contains all of the strategies for the first three years of the strategic plan and their respective time-phased capital expenditures.

Some strategies may begin and end in the budget year, start at the beginning of the budget year and end in one of the operating plan years, or begin and conclude in the operating plan years.

The development of the operating plan initiates the detailed planning process of fitting the plan's conceptual framework into a more specific set of action objectives with timetables. This is where the controller's real involvement as an administrator and financial planning consultant begins. The process is begun by laying out the chronological order of strategies and their respective time frames.

Operating Plan

Once the operating plan has been developed, it can be folded into the budgeting activity and the preparation of the overall operating plan. To reemphasize: the operating plan provides the control mechanism to measure progress against strategic milestones. In addition, this process allows for the identification of capital expenditures for the planning period so that prudent financing can be arranged. Arraying these strategies guarantees the opportunity for human resources planning and development of organizational structures in advance of implementation.

After these jobs have been done, the budget year then becomes the most detailed month-by-month set of goals and objectives crucial to an effective operating plan and, finally, the strategic plan. As this process becomes the managerial discipline it should be, one operating plan flows into the next, and the whole exercise becomes a tremendously valuable managerial activity.

Operating plan strategies should be evaluated on a quarterly basis. Because of their independency and the significance of the capital expenditures associated with each action plan, it is critical that the performance of each strategy be carefully synchronized with the overall operating plan. The interaction of the budget with the operating plan determines the future impact of the present business conditions. This kind of futuristic barometer is an integral part of sound business planning.

Moreover, budget and operating plan interaction produces a continuing demand for contingency planning. Good budgets are developed on a range of potential business situations of pitfalls and opportunities. Well-done budgets contain scenarios ranging from the most optimistic to pessimistic forecasts, and project financial results. In turn, these potential situations each have an impact on planned strategies, and management should be made aware of them by the controller. Figure 1 illustrates the interaction of strategic planning with operating plans and budgets.

The Controller as Planning Coordinator

The major problem controllers have in taking on the responsibility of planning coordinator is that it represents a major change in "image." Controllers are thought of as bean counters, accountants, and are generally considered to be dealing with the past (historical data). Planning is futuristic. In addition, controllers keep talking that funny language which no one else in the company really understands, and if we can't understand what the controller is trying to tell us about the financial results now, how are we ever going to understand planning?

Unfortunately, in many companies the controller is misunderstood because he does not take the time to educate the rest of the management team about the financial ramifications of different business decisions. However, planning is a great opportunity for the controller to overcome that image problem because planning has to be explained. The process of planning requires other managers to become more financially oriented because all plans have to eventually be financially quantified. This exercise has to involve the controller and in the process the controller and the manager should work together as a team.

So the best way for the controller to start out as

Figure 1
Interaction of Strategic Planning with Operating Plans and Budgets

Strategic Plan
Flexible
Iterative
Sensitive
Conceptual

Mission
Why are we in business?
Where are we going?
What objectives do we think we can realistically accomplish and when?
Markets, products, competitive posture
Resource requirements/technology
Ethics, social responsibility, environmental
Human resources

Operating Plan
Specific strategies
Performance tracking
Capital requirements
Acquisitions/divestitures

Expansion of current business
Performance incentives
Opinion survey
Management development
New business ventures
Technological innovations

Budget
Month by month
Quantified goals and objectives

Projected P&L
Departmental operating expense budgets
Specific strategy time tables
Responsibility assignments
Monthly reports to management (budget vs. actual)
Quarterly reviews
Capital requirements
Organizational structure

Telescoping

1980s   One year   Three years   Five years

the planning coordinator is to have a planning orientation session to explain the purpose of the exercise. This orientation session has to be attended by the CEO and the CEO *must* support the process.

The second major problem controllers have as planning coordinator is the schedule and getting everyone to adhere to the schedule. Unfortunately, again, in too many companies, controllers send out "budgeting" schedules in the form of a schedule stapled to a bunch of forms with a note that says, "Please fill these forms out and get them back to me according to the attached schedule." This approach will get an equally impersonal response in the form of haphazardly completed forms, or no forms at all. This scenario creates part of that image problem because everyone mentally concludes: here comes those damn forms again and the controller will be bugging me if I don't do something.

The right way to solicit cooperation in the planning process is to explain to managers why it is important to get their best input, how to fill out the forms, and to offer to be helpful and available for consultation. When the controller takes on the responsibility of planning coordinator it becomes a natural extension of the budgeting exercise into a more conceptual and futuristic process. Scheduling is an integral part of planning. The controller has to be the enforcer and work with management to help it meet the planning schedule.

The third problem controllers have when they first take on the responsibility of planning coordinator is that they have to summarize all of the respective managers' plans into the overall company plan. This summary also requires evaluation, which means that the controller has to become familiar with all aspects of the business. In reality this is a great opportunity for the controller but also represents a delicate political needle to thread. The controller is faced with making an evaluation of an operating manager's plan and comparing all of those plans to the financial criteria necessary for the overall profitable growth and stability of the company.

Perhaps the greatest contribution that the controller can make to the planning process is providing financial education to line managers so that they have a better appreciation for how their actions impact the company. This learning experience also contributes to the team concept of good planning and the controller acts as the facilitator in this educational process.

The next key phase of team planning is management reporting, which also falls under the controller's responsibility. Most controllers produce the standard financial statements and each month there is an agonizing management meeting where the controller "goes over" the financial results line-by-line.

Unless the management team has a financial background this process literally leaves them cold, unsure as to what actually happened as a result of their individual actions last month. Good planning creates a slightly different way of looking at results by concentrating on trends and the analysis of the impact of those trends in the future. A planning technique that is particularly effective is looking at *key performance indicators* every month (Table 1).

Key performance indicators are those volume-related six or seven factors that drive the business—those most significant results that impact everything else in the business and act as barometers for the future. The controller is the keeper of this data and is responsible for producing the key performance indicators' report. When constructed properly, this report will summarize all of the pertinent information the management team really needs to react to short-team problems and opportunities. More important, the constant use of key performance indicators focuses management's attention on the interactions of all aspects of the business, and each component clearly has an interrelation-

---

Table 1
Key Performance Indicators

	Jan	Feb	Mar	Apr	May	Jun	Jul	Aug	Sep
Sales reps productivity									
Average revenue product									
Months-on-hand (inv.)									
Days-of-sales outstanding									
Mean time between product failure									
Absenteeism									
New accounts									

Table 2
Typical Set of Instructions

Interoffice Memo

TO: Divisional CEO's, General Managers, (etc.)

FROM: Corporate CEO

RE: Annual Operating Plan Schedule and Guidelines

This package includes the forms to be completed for our annual operating plan exercise. You are also expected to develop a narrative on your respective operations that addresses:
- Summary & Highlights (this year vs. next)
- Key Problems & Opportunities
- Marketing Summary with Product Line Profit & Loss discussions
- Strategies: (by strategy)

  Description of the strategy.

  Why it is necessary.

  Who will be responsible for it.

  How long will it take to implement.

  How much will it cost.

  What is the expected return on the investment.
- Asset Management, including strategies in the capital spending projection.
- Organization, with manpower comparisons.

We would also like to know of all of your planning assumptions with as much rationale as possible. Please discuss this with your budget coordinator if you have any questions. For planning purposes use the following overall guidelines:

Compensation: Exempt—Cost of living 7% across the board

Meritorious 10% avg. by department

Nonexempt—Cost of living 7% across the board

Meritorious 9% avg. by department

Inflation factors: Materials and utilities 15%

All other expenses   10%

Financial Returns: On capital expenditures (investments) 15%

Profit on sales   10%

In addition, we expect to receive projections for your respective businesses as follows:

Sales by product	September 30
Standard cost by product	October 31
Expenses	November 30

Your complete operating plan is due in my office by the end of the first week in December. We will begin operating plan review meetings in the second week in December, and you should be prepared for at least a three-hour meeting on your plan. The schedule of these review meetings will be sent to you later this year. As in the past you should plan to make a presentation of this year's plan highlighting the key performance indicators and your contingency plans for greater than or less than plan performance.

After your respective operating plan has been approved, you should also be prepared to discuss individual compensation plans to accomplish the goals and objectives set forth in the operating plan.

ship with the others. So the controller should blend the concept of key performance indicators into the introduction and explanation of planning. These indicators represent trends that have a significant impact on future planning.

Another important problem for controllers when they first take over the planning responsibility is that they, themselves, often are unfamiliar with planning. If, in turn, they don't have the right level of authority to implement their new-found responsibility it becomes an even greater challenge.

In the case where the controller is unfamiliar with planning there are two quick solutions, attend a seminar and get some good books on planning. A third alternative might be to visit other controllers who are involved in planning to get their advice.

Even with this knowledge, however, the only way the controller can be effective is to have the authority to command a response to the planning guidelines, schedules, and forms. The controller should clearly control the process.

The Coordination Process

The planning cycle begins with the controller developing the planning guidelines in a memoranda format for signature by the CEO (Table 2). The guidelines should include: an overall statement of the inherent responsibility of managers to plan and budget, the corporate planning assumptions, financial return expectations for individual businesses, the planning timetable, and forms with explanations on how to complete them. The next step should be a brief meeting to go over the memo with all respective operating unit managers and their planning coordinators (usually divisional budget analysts) to resolve any questions about the schedule, assumptions, or how to complete the forms.

Then the controller becomes both the counselor and the policeman. The forms are collected when due and the controller begins to array all the data from the respective business units and compares them for reasonableness and growth, or decline, from historic patterns. This comparative data analysis process is best done by the controller and his group so that it can present the overall corporate consolidated planning results.

The controller's group also should be responsible for scheduling the planning review meetings between the business unit manager team and the corporate management group, which should include the controllers and respective divisional budget analysts. Minutes of those meetings are usually kept by the controller.

Once the plan has been approved, it has to be seasonalized, calendarized, or spread-by-month. The controller then begins the second phase of becoming the planning coordinator by producing the monthly management reports to commence the *control* phase of the process.

Controlling the Strategic Plan

Monthly management reports should contain:

☐ A one-page narrative on the nature of the business (Table 3).
☐ The Key Performance Report.
☐ Several Charts or Graphs of the Most Important Indicators.
☐ The Financial Statements.

This format allows for a fairly thorough discussion of operations so that when the financial statements are reached they represent the results of the business trends discussed in the narrative, portrayed by the key performance indicators, and illustrated on the charts and graphs. The controller should present this report to management, attend the management meeting, and follow up on any "action items" for the next meeting.

The next step in the process is the First Quarter Review. The First Quarter Review is a mini-budgeting activity that requires the controller to develop a quarterly review memo and forms with instructions. The controller has to monitor the quarterly data collection process, prepare the presentation, and attend the quarterly review meeting.

Monthly management reports are developed for the next three months. The First Half Review is similar to the First Quarter Review with comparisons of the first six months actual to the same six months of last year, and the six months budget. The last six months of last year, the budget, and a projection of the balance of the year make up the review package. A nine-month review is not required because you are back in the planning cycle for the next operating plan.

Developing, Monitoring, Updating

The Quarterly and First Half Reviews also require the controller to develop reports on capital expenditures and progress against the strategic milestones represented by those expenditures. The progress, or lack thereof, of strategies can cause a realignment of strategic priorities, which is usually decided at these quarterly review meetings. The controller is responsible for monitoring these changes and incorporating these decisions in the upcoming annual planning process.

So the role of the controller as coordinator of the planning process encompasses: developing the initial plan, monitoring progress against that plan, and updating the plan based upon management's ability to make the plan happen.

Table 3
Monthly Management Report

ABC Division
Management Report for the Month of _____
($000's)

Actual sales for _____ of $X were 97% of plan, but 105% of _____ last year. Especially good performance was accomplished with our new line of Y products. On a year-to-date basis, we are 95% of plan and 101% of last year.

Cost for _____ were on budget, which brings year-to-date cost to 98% of plan. Slow-moving inventories are being analyzed and special promotions are being planned to dispose of those products by the end of the quarter.

Expenses for _____ were 4% over budget primarily due to accelerating promotions for Y products that were budgeted for later periods. This brings year-to-date expenses to 101% of budget. Total full year expenses are expected to be only 95% of budget as a result of planned reductions in travel and sales meetings in the second half.

Profits for _____ were 5% below budget, which brings year-to-date performance to 97% of plan. Full year profitability is still expected to come in on budget.

Total manpower for _____ is still six below plan, two in production and four in the field sales force. Active recruiting is under way.

Collection of receivables is slightly behind plan, but this has been identified as a timing problem and not a collection issue. About $X of inventory has been determined to be obsolete and will be written off in the next accounting period.

Chapter Twenty-Seven

Cost Control Using Standard Costing

Reviewing the Chapter

1. **Standard costs** are predetermined costs that are expressed as a cost per unit of finished product. They are used in preparing operating budgets, in identifying production areas that need better cost control, and in simplifying cost accounting procedures for inventories and product costing. In general, standard cost figures are maintained for all manufacturing accounts and are compared with the actual cost figures at the end of the period. Any large variances, whether favorable or unfavorable, should then be analyzed.

2. The standard cost per unit of output is the result of the following standard amounts:
   a. **Standard direct materials cost = direct materials price standard X direct materials quantity standard.**
   b. **Standard direct labor cost = direct labor time standard X direct labor rate standard.**
   c. **Standard factory overhead cost = (standard variable overhead rate + standard fixed overhead rate) X application basis.**

3. Under a standard cost system, the journal entries are similar to those discussed in prior chapters for a manufacturer's inventory system. However, direct materials, direct labor, and factory overhead are entered into Work in Process Inventory at standard (not actual) cost.

4. **A flexible budget** is a summary of expected costs for various levels of production. For each level of production, budgeted fixed and variable costs and their totals are presented. Also presented is the budgeted variable cost per unit, which of course is the same for all levels of output. Once prepared, the flexible budget is used to determine the flexible budget formula. This formula can then be applied to any level of output to figure its budgeted total cost. The budgeted total cost can be compared with actual costs to measure the performance of individuals and departments.

5. Variances are differences between actual operating results and budgeted (standard) results. Once variances have been measured, corrective measures can be taken for those areas that are operating inefficiently.

6. **Management by exception** locates and analyzes only those areas of unusually good or bad performance. It uses variance analysis to a great degree.

7. Variances between standard and actual costs are usually determined for direct materials, direct labor, and factory overhead. When standard costs exceed actual costs, the variance is favorable (F). When the reverse is true, the variance is unfavorable (U).

8. The total direct materials cost variance consists of the direct materials price variance plus the direct materials quantity variance.
   a. The **direct materials price variance** equals the difference between actual price and standard price, times actual quantity of material purchased.
   b. The **direct materials quantity variance** equals the difference between quantity of material used and standard quantity, times standard price.

9. The total direct labor cost variance consists of the direct labor rate variance plus the direct labor efficiency variance.
   a. The **direct labor rate variance** equals the difference between the actual labor rate and the standard labor rate, times actual hours worked.
   b. The **direct labor efficiency variance** equals the difference between actual hours worked and standard hours allowed, times the standard labor rate.

10. The total factory overhead variance consists of controllable overhead variance plus overhead volume variance.
    a. The **controllable overhead variance** equals actual overhead costs minus budgeted factory overhead for the level of production achieved.
    b. The **overhead volume variance** equals budgeted factory overhead for the level of production achieved minus factory overhead applied using the standard overhead rate.

11. As was already stated, cost data are journalized at standard cost under a standard cost system. However, when variances exist, they should also be recorded in the accounts—as a debit when unfavorable and a credit when favorable. A separate account should be maintained for each of the six variances described above. At this point, a thorough review of the textbook entries involving variances is recommended.

12. At the end of the accounting period, the variances are closed into Cost of Goods Sold if their balances are small or if most or all of the goods produced during the period were sold. Otherwise, the net variance balance is divided among Work In Process Inventory, Finished Goods Inventory, and Cost of Goods Sold based on their relative ending balances.

13. Performance reports should contain only those cost items controllable by the manager receiving the report. They should show actual costs, budgeted costs, and variances.

14. Public-sector organizations (such as the federal government or a state university) receive only those funds that are appropriated. Revenues for not-for-profit organizations (such as a charitable group or a professional organization) are limited to dues or contributions. Clearly, then, both kinds of organizations must maintain effective cost control. In general, the basis for cost control is the budget, which is approved by the legislature or governing body. Accordingly, any significant increase in cost (over budget) must be formally requested and approved.

Testing Your Knowledge

Matching

Match each term with its definition by writing the appropriate letter in the blank.

____ 1. Standard costs

____ 2. Management by exception

____ 3. Favorable variance

____ 4. Unfavorable variance

____ 5. Direct materials price variance

____ 6. Direct materials quantity variance

____ 7. Direct labor rate variance

____ 8. Direct labor efficiency variance

____ 9. Controllable overhead variance

____ 10. Overhead volume variance

____ 11. Performance report

____ 12. Flexible budget

a. The difference between the standard labor rate and the actual labor rate, times actual hours worked

b. Locating and analyzing only those areas of unusual performance

c. Actual costs exceeding standard costs

d. Predetermined costs that are expressed as a cost per unit of finished product

e. Actual overhead costs minus budgeted factory overhead for the level of production achieved

f. Expected costs for various levels of anticipated production

g. The difference between actual price and standard price, times actual quantity of material purchased

h. A written comparison between actual costs and budgeted costs for a segment of the business

i. The difference between quantity of material used and standard quantity, times standard price

j. The difference between actual hours worked and standard hours allowed, times standard labor rate

k. Standard costs exceeding actual costs

l. Budgeted factory overhead for the level of production achieved minus factory overhead applied using the standard overhead rate

Completion

Use the lines provided to complete each item.

1. The six standards used to compute total standard unit cost are

_____

_____

_____

_____

2. A favorable direct materials quantity variance would exist when

_____

_____

3. An unfavorable direct labor rate variance would exist when

_____

_____

Circle T if the statement is true, F if it is false.

T F 1. One application basis used in computing standard costs is actual direct labor hours.

T F 2. Time and motion studies of workers are used in establishing direct labor rate standards.

T F 3. Under a standard cost system, all costs that flow through the inventory accounts are at standard.

T F 4. Computing variances is an essential part of the planning function of budgetary control.

T F 5. Management by exception uses the data provided by variances.

T F 6. It is impossible to have unfavorable direct materials price and direct materials quantity variances and have a favorable total direct materials cost variance.

T F 7. The flexible budget includes both budgeted fixed costs and budgeted variable costs for each level of anticipated activity.

T F 8. The purchasing agent should be held responsible for direct materials price variances.

T F 9. Labor rate variances are normally the responsibility of the production supervisor.

T F 10. An overhead volume variance will exist only if more or less than normal capacity is used.

T F 11. To compute the controllable overhead variance, the actual level of production must be known.

T F 12. Computing the total direct labor cost variance is more important than computing the direct labor rate and direct labor efficiency variances.

T F 13. For a public-sector organization, spending is normally limited to the amount appropriated by the governing body.

T F 14. Under a standard cost system, variances would not be recorded in the entry to record the transfer of completed units to Finished Goods Inventory.

Multiple-Choice

Circle the letter of the best answer.

1. An unfavorable direct labor efficiency variance would probably occur when
   a. the workers are overpaid.
   b. most workers are inexperienced.
   c. the workers are underpaid.
   d. most workers are experienced.

2. A performance report does not include data for
   a. total direct labor cost variance.
   b. actual costs.
   c. overhead volume variance.
   d. budgeted costs.

3. When there is a favorable direct materials price variance,
   a. the purchasing agent has purchased direct materials at below the standard price.
   b. The production department has used a smaller quantity of direct materials than is standard.
   c. the purchasing agent has purchased more direct material than is needed.
   d. the production department has done a good job at cutting its overhead costs.

4. Management by exception uses which accounting tool to a great extent?
   a. C-V-P analysis
   b. Financial statement analysis
   c. A work sheet
   d. Variance analysis

5. Which of the following items would follow the computation of variances?
   a. Performance reports
   b. The master budget
   c. The period budget
   d. Budget implementation

6. Workers' wages are all that is needed to compute the
   a. direct labor time standard.
   b. direct labor rate standard.
   c. standard direct labor cost.
   d. direct labor cost variance.

7. When recording direct labor costs under a standard cost system,
   a. Work in Process Inventory is debited for actual direct labor costs.
   b. Factory Payroll is credited for standard direct labor costs.
   c. A favorable direct labor efficiency variance would be credited.
   d. Factory Payroll is debited for standard direct labor costs.

8. When recording the purchase of materials under a standard cost system,
   a. Materials Inventory is debited for actual quantity purchased times standard cost.
   b. Accounts Payable is credited for actual quantity purchased times standard cost.
   c. a direct materials quantity variance might be recorded.
   d. an unfavorable direct materials price variance would be credited.

Exercises

1. Kranmar Company employs a standard cost system in the manufacture of expensive hand-painted dishes. The standards for the current year are:

   Direct materials price standards

Porcelain	$.80/lb
Red paint	$1.00/tube
Blue paint	$1.00/tube

   Direct materials quanity standards

Porcelain	½ lb/dish
Red paint	1 tube/20 dishes
Blue paint	1 tube/50 dishes

   Direct labor time standards

Molding department	.03 hour/dish
Painting department	.05 hour/dish

   Director labor rate standards

Molding department	$4.00/hour
Painting department	$6.00/hour

   Standard factory overhead rates

Standard variable overhead rate	$3.00/direct labor hour
Standard fixed overhead rate	$2.00/direct labor hour

   Compute the standard manufacturing cost per dish for direct materials, direct labor, and overhead.

Porcelain	$_____
Red paint	_____
Blue paint	_____
Molding department wages	_____
Painting department wages	_____
Variable overhead	_____
Fixed overhead	_____
Standard cost of one dish	$_____

2. Los Feliz Company expects fixed overhead to total $50,000 for 19xx. In addition, variable costs per unit are expected to be: direct labor, $4.50; direct materials, $1.25; and variable overhead, $2.75. Using these data, prepare a flexible budget for a 10,000-unit, 15,000-unit, and 20,000-unit volume. In addition, determine the flexible budget formula.

Los Feliz Company
Flexible Budget
For the Year Ended December 31, 19xx

---

3. The Larsen Sporting Goods Company uses a standard cost system for producing 10-pound steel dumbbells. The standard cost for steel is $.60 per pound, and each dumbbell should require .3 standard direct labor hours at a standard rate of $4.50 per hour. The standard variable overhead rate is $2.30 per direct labor hour, and normal capacity was set at a monthly level of 19,000 hours of direct labor. Fixed overhead cost of $3,800 was budgeted for March. During the month of March, 65,000 dumbbells were actually produced, using 657,000 pounds of steel. During the period, 657,000 pounds of steel were also purchased and the cost of the steel was $381,060. Direct labor hours numbered 22,100 at an expense of $100,555. Total overhead expenses came to $57,000. Using the data above, compute the following variances for the month of March. Indicate whether each variance is favorable or unfavorable by writing F or U after each amount.

a. Direct materials price variance = $_____

b. Direct materials quantity variance = $_____

c. Direct labor rate variance = $_____

d. Direct labor efficiency variance = $_____

e. Controllable overhead variance = $_____

f. Overhead volume variance = $_____

Chapter Twenty-Eight

Capital Budgeting and Other Management Decisions

Reviewing the Chapter

1. One important function of the management accountant is to provide management with relevant decision-making information. **Relevant decision information** refers to future cost, revenue, or resource usage data that will be different for the alternative courses of action under study.

2. The management decision cycle is made up of (a) discovering the problem or need, (b) identifying the alternative courses of action, (c) analyzing the effects of each alternative on operations, (d) selecting the best alternative, and (e) judging the success of the decision.

3. Variable costing and incremental analysis are the two most common decision tools used by the accountant.
   a. **Variable costing** (also called direct costing) uses only direct materials, direct labor, and variable factory overhead in product costing. Fixed factory overhead is considered a period cost (expense). Variable costing is very useful for internal management decision making but is not acceptable for tax or financial reporting. Under variable costing, the income statement discloses the contribution margin, a very useful figure for decision analysis. Absorption costing includes one more product cost that variable costing does not—fixed factory overhead. Therefore, unit cost will vary with volume under absorption costing, whereas it will not under variable costing.
   b. **Incremental analysis** is a decision-making tool that compares only cost and revenue data that differ among alternatives. According to this method, the alternative that results in the highest increase in net income or cost savings is the best alternative.

4. When management needs quantitative information, the accountant can usually present the data in a contribution reporting or incremental analysis format. However, when special qualitative information is desired, the accountant must prepare a special report that is structured to facilitate specific decision-making needs.

5. Deciding when and how much to spend on capital facilities, such as buildings or equipment, is referred to as the **capital expenditure decision. Capital budgeting** is the process of (a) identifying the need for a facility, (b) analyzing different courses of action, (c) preparing the reports for management, (d) choosing the best alternative, and (e) rationing capital expenditure funds among competing resource needs. Because it is probably the largest and most complicated decision analysis

facing management, it requires the aid of all functional areas of the business.

6. The evaluation part of capital budgeting may be accomplished by using the accounting rate of return method, the payback method, or the present value method.

7. Most companies have established a minimum rate of return, below which an expenditure request is automatically refused. The most common measures used for the minimum rate are the cost of capital, the corporate return on investment, the industry average return on investment, or the bank interest rate. The cost of capital is the cost of financing the company's activities. In many cases, a company will use an **average cost of capital** measure based on (a) **cost of debt**, (b) **cost of preferred stock**, (c) **cost of equity capital**, and (d) **cost of retained earnings.**

8. The **accounting rate of return** equals

$$\frac{\text{project's average annual after-tax net income}}{\text{average investment cost}}$$

The average investment cost equals

$$\frac{\text{total investment + salvage value}}{2}$$

If this method is used, management should think seriously about the investment if the rate of return is higher than the minimum desired rate.

9. The **payback method** is a tool for finding the minimum length of time it would take to recover an initial investment. When a choice must be made between investment alternatives, the one with the shortest payback period is best under this method. The payback period is found by dividing the cost of the investment by the annual net cash inflow.

10. The basis for the **present value method** is that cash flows from different time periods have different values when measured in current dollars. For example, a dollar that will be received one year from now is worth somewhat less than a dollar received today. The method is applied by first discounting all cash flows to the present. (The discount multiplier is based on the minimum desired rate of return and the discount period.)

Then, if the **discounted cash flow** exceeds the cost of the asset, the expenditure is justified.

11. Management is continually faced with the **make or buy decision** about parts that go into product assembly. Probably the best method to employ is incremental analysis, in which only the relevant costs are compared. All other things being equal, the alternative resulting in the lowest incremental cost is the one that should be chosen.

12. Management often must decide whether to accept or reject special product orders. In such **special order decisions**, both incremental analysis and contribution reporting can be used. In either case, the goal is to compare data assuming acceptance with data assuming rejection.

13. **Sales mix analysis** is used to find the most profitable combination of product sales when the company is producing more than one product. Generally, the strategy is first to figure the contribution margin for each product. Then, the ratio of contribution margin to capital equipment should be figured for each to see if some products are more profitable than others. If extra demand exists for more profitable products, then production should be shifted to those products.

14. All capital expenditure analysis should include the effect of income taxes. A company's tax liability will increase as a result of revenues and gains on the sale of assets. The tax liability will decrease as a result of cash and noncash expenses and losses on the sale of assets. An example of a noncash expense is depreciation. It provides a cash benefit, however, by reducing the amount of taxes to be paid. One important way to keep taxes as low as possible is through careful timing of business transactions. If a company is nearing the top of its tax bracket late in its fiscal year, it may put off an income-producing transaction until the next year. Or it may time the selling of assets in a way that reduces taxes. The capital-gains tax and other aspects of the tax law offer preferential treatment for certain transactions. It is always good management to consider such possibilities.

Testing Your Knowledge

Matching

Match each term with its definition by writing the appropriate letter in the blank.

---- 1. Variable costing (direct costing)

---- 2. Incremental analysis

---- 3. Capital budgeting

---- 4. Average cost of capital

---- 5. Accounting rate of return method

---- 6. Payback method

---- 7. Present value method

---- 8. Sales mix analysis

---- 9. Capital expenditure decision

a. The capital budgeting method that determines the minimum length of time it would take to recover the initial investment in an asset

b. The assignment of direct materials, direct labor, and variable factory overhead costs to products

c. The process of identifying the need for a facility, analyzing different actions, preparing reports, choosing the best alternative, and rationing available funds among competing needs

d. Determining the most profitable combination of product sales

e. The cost of financing the company's activities

f. The capital budgeting method that divides a proposed project's net income by the average investment cost

g. The capital budgeting method that discounts all net cash inflows to the present

h. The comparison of cost and revenue data that differ among alternatives

i. Determining when and how much to spend on capital facilities

Completion

Use the lines provided to complete each item.

1. The five steps in the management decision cycle are

_____

_____

_____

_____

_____

2. The five steps involved in capital budgeting are

_____

_____

_____

_____

_____

3. Four rate of return measures that are frequently used by businesses are

_____

_____

_____

4. Three methods frequently used to evaluate capital expenditure proposals are

_____

_____

_____

5. Distinguish between relevant and irrelevant information.

_____

_____

_____

True-False

Circle T if the statement is true, F if it is false.

T F 1. Absorption costing is not acceptable for financial reporting purposes.

T F 2. Ending inventory is valued higher under variable costing than it is under absorption costing.

T F 3. Under absorption costing, fixed factory overhead is considered a period cost.

T F 4. When the contribution margin is less than fixed costs, a net loss has occurred.

T F 5. When incremental analysis is used, the main concern is with each alternative's net income projection.

T F 6. Capital budgeting involves the various methods of obtaining cash for business operations.

T F 7. The simplest method to apply in evaluating a capital investment proposal is the present value method.

T F 8. The time value of money is ignored in both the rate of return and the payback methods.

T F 9. The payback period is the maximum length of time it should take to recover the cost of an investment.

T F 10. The payback period equals the cost of the capital investment divided by the annual net cash inflow.

T F 11. Under the present value method, there is no need for a minimum desired ratio of return.

T F 12. Under the present value method, a negative net present value means that the project proposal should probably be rejected.

T F 13. Incremental analysis is very useful for make or buy decisions.

T F 14. For special order analysis, costs that vary because of this special decision are the only relevant costs.

T F 15. When a sales mix analysis is being performed, the product with the highest contribution margin per scarce resource is always the one that is most beneficial to the company.

Multiple-Choice

Circle the letter of the best answer.

1. Under the accounting rate of return method, which of the following data is irrelevant?
   a. Salvage value of asset
   b. Annual net cash inflow
   c. Cost of asset
   d. Project's average annual after-tax net income

2. Which of the following is not a measure of cost of capital?
   a. Cost of sales
   b. Cost of retained earnings
   c. Cost of debt
   d. Cost of equity capital

3. When volume increases,
   a. the unit cost increases under variable costing.
   b. the unit cost decreases under variable costing.
   c. the unit cost increases under absorption costing.
   d. the unit cost decreases under absorption costing.

4. Probably the best method to use in deciding to make or buy a part for a product is
   a. direct costing.
   b. the payback method.
   c. incremental analysis.
   d. the present value method.

5. The contribution approach would probably not be used
   a. when deciding whether to discontinue a particular product line.
   b. when performing sales mix analysis.
   c. when deciding which of two machines to purchase.
   d. when deciding whether to accept a special product order.

6. Products A, B, and C have contribution margins of $3, $5, and $4 per unit, respectively. Granada Company intends to manufacture one of the products, and expects sales to be $30,000 regardless of which product they manufacture. Which product will result in the highest net income for Granada, assuming that the same machinery and workers would be used to produce each?
   a. A
   b. B
   c. C
   d. More information is needed.

7. Which of the following costs is a product cost under absorption costing but not under variable costing?
   a. Variable factory overhead
   b. Fixed factory overhead
   c. Direct materials
   d. Direct labor

8. When using the present value method, which of the following net cash inflows will result in the highest amount when discounted to the present period (19x1) at a 10 percent discount rate? (Use the tables in Appendix B of the text.)
   a. $755 from 19x1
   b. $815 from 19x2
   c. $880 from 19x3
   d. $1,000 from 19x4

Applying Your Knowledge

Exercises

1. A company must decide whether to purchase machine Q for $10,000 or machine R for $17,000. Machine Q will require the use of two operators, each of whom earns $8,000 per year. It will require maintenance of $300 per year, but will save the company $50 per year in electricity over the machine currently in use. Machine R will require only one operator at $8,000 per year. It will require maintenance of $500 per year, but will cost $80 per year more for electricity over the machine currently in use. In addition, each machine will generate the same amount of revenue. Prepare an incremental analysis to determine which machine to purchase.

2. A company is considering the purchase of a machine to produce plastic chin protectors used in hockey. The machine costs $70,000 and would have a 5-year life (no salvage value). The machine is expected to produce $8,000 per year in net income (after depreciation and taxes). Assume that all income is taxed at 50 percent, that the company uses straight-line depreciation, and that the minimum payback period is 3 years.

a. Using the payback approach, determine whether or not the company should invest in the machine. Show all work.

b. Determine the accounting rate of return.

3. A machine that costs $20,000 will produce a net cash inflow of $5,000 in the first year of operations and $6,000 in the remaining 4 years of use. Present value information for the 16 percent rate of return is as follows.

Present value of 1 due in 1 year = .862
Present value of 1 due in 2 years = .743
Present value of 1 due in 3 years = .641
Present value of 1 due in 4 years = .552
Present value of 1 due in 5 years = .476

Using the present value method, determine whether the company should purchase the machine.

Crossword Puzzle
For Chapters 27 and 28

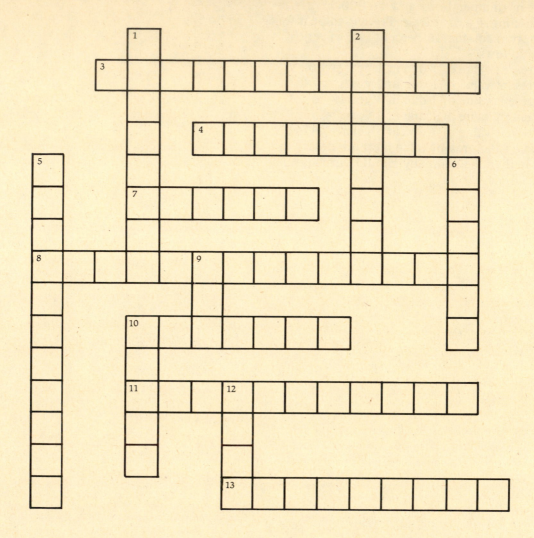

ACROSS

3. Measure of yield on investment (3 words)
4. Standard cost minus actual cost
7. With 9-Down, special management decision (2 words)
8. Cost forecast for different activity levels (2 words)
10. Method to evaluate capital investment
11. Analysis focusing on relevant information
13. Management by _____

DOWN

1. Analysis for combination of products (2 words)
2. Predetermined cost for a unit of product
5. Report comparing budget with actual
6. Average _____ capital (2 words)
9. See 7-Across
10. Direct materials variance
12. Direct labor variance

The Changing Role of the Financial Executive

"A high standard of integrity. Intelligence. Common sense. Hardworking (workaholic preferred). Appropriate academic background in accounting, economics or finance—MBA or its equivalent. Highest level of technical competence."

That might have been the typical job description ten years ago for those seeking careers or advancement in the financial arena. It's a job description that hadn't changed much since 1960—or 1950—or even the years prior to that. And those who met the specifications and won those positions knew what to expect. Like the hiring guidelines, the role of the financial executive within the corporation had remained relatively constant, relatively predictable, during the decades before 1970.

In 1981, with the financially-turbulent 1970's behind us, those tranquil, stable years have a dreamlike, unreal quality. Today, volatile economic conditions prevail worldwide. New and increasingly demanding regulations abound. Technological changes have accelerated the pace and increased the complexity of our executive decisions. And as a result, the role of the financial executive has undergone an unprecedented metamorphosis, becoming increasingly sophisticated, demanding and challenging.

In today's dynamic economic atmosphere, the basic skills and personal qualities traditionally required of financial executives have never been more necessary. But these alone will not suffice for today's financial professional. There are new dimensions to the classic job description—qualities like sophistication, vision, courage and creativity, and, above all, the ability to communicate effectively with others.

In short, technical competence, knowledge, intelligence and hard work are no longer the primary attributes of successful financial executives. As one chief financial officer put it: "The continuing challenge in our field is developing people who are by nature somewhat reserved and introverted into positions that call for dynamic human relations skills."

Source: Article by Edward W. Golden. Reprinted by permission from the October 1981 issue of *Financial Executive.*

Volatile Economic Conditions

Financial executives we speak to are virtually unanimous in their belief that volatile economic conditions worldwide, more than any other single factor, have catapulted the financial executive from the classic role of "historian" and "recordkeeper" to one of leadership—an individual of vision and courage with eyes not on the past, but on the future.

The instability and turbulence of the economy have placed new burdens of responsibility on the financial executive, while multiplying the challenges and opportunities, those in positions of authority agree.

"In earlier years, our responses to problems were somewhat rote," says Charles A. Walker, Jr., vice president and treasurer, Armstrong World Industries, Inc. "We looked to the past for solutions. If we'd solved a problem five years ago by floating a bond, we'd float a bond again. Today, we need to be more creative. What worked five years ago, or even six months ago, won't necessarily work today. Conditions are constantly changing, requiring bold, innovative solutions."

The meteoric rise of interest rates, the instability of the prime, an inflation rate that bounces up and down with schizophrenic energy: all are factors in the new complexity of the financial executive's world. "Ten years ago, emerging from the 1960's, we had a more predictable environment, a more controlled economy," says Kenneth V. Jaeggi, vice president and chief financial officer, Data General Corp. "Now predictability is almost moot; there no longer is a crystal ball. Every chief financial officer has become a mini-economist."

All these factors are exacerbated when placed in the context of an equally volatile international money market, a factor rarely considered by the typical financial executive ten years ago. Today, as the world grows smaller, more and more American companies are enmeshed in a system of international monetary interdependence, in which fluctuating currency rates and the demise in value of the U.S. dollar are increasingly critical.

All of this requires new skills and insights of the financial executive. "If the chief financial officer doesn't understand how financial exchange rates are determined, or get someone on his staff who does, he'll not be able to function in the international marketplace," one high-ranking financial officer said.

Vacillating money supplies and the increased cost of capital, both here and abroad, have placed added pressures on the financial executive, whose leadership is sought in meeting the short term and long term corporate objectives.

"In the area of financial planning, there are many more challenges and many more opportunities," says James R. Kendrick, senior vice president for finance, United Van Lines. "But you have to work much harder to find them."

One ramification of the need to seek out new sources of capital is the rush of acquisitions and mergers observable today on the corporate scene. When expansion or diversification is planned, it is often less costly to buy a new plant than to build one.

All of these "remedies," of course, impact directly on the role of the financial executive, necessitating wider business acumen, new competence and understanding of economic conditions, a broader knowledge and perspective.

Regulatory Pressures

Today's financial executive must meet the challenges of vision and creativity demanded by today's economy —but with no sacrifice of technical competence. In fact, more than ever before, that basic commodity is essential as finance departments struggle to comply with the plethora of government-(and industry-) imposed regulatory pressures.

The federal government is the major culprit in the proliferation of regulations impacting upon the financial executive. It's safe to say, for example, that there have been more changes in the tax law in the past ten years than in the previous fifty. And these tax-related regulations are minor responsibilities when compared to the financial implications of such "new" government programs as ERISA, programs that require a whole new set of fiduciary skills. "It's motherhood and apple pie," sighs one financial officer when ERISA is mentioned. "But it's also endless hours of work and one hell of a new responsibility."

Technological Changes

Today's rapidly-developing technology is both altering the methodology of the financial executive and accelerating the pace at which work is accomplished and financial decisions must be made. "The world is swimming a little faster," as one financial officer says. And another agrees: "If the financial executive ever

had a green eye shade, he doesn't have time to put it on anymore."

Computerization is a case in point. Today's financial executives are using computers to do what, ten years ago, was done by hand—or not at all—record keeping, statistical calculations, numerical computations.

Additionally, more sophisticated uses of computer technology are already routine for more and more finance departments. Modeling, termed by some "the wave of the future," is already standard practice for most major corporations, and more and more small companies are using time-shared equipment to ride that modeling wave.

Financial executives foresee the real technological breakthroughs still ahead, however, as computer programs are developed to accomplish the sophisticated financial analyses required routinely today—"the kind," says one financial officer, somewhat wistfully, "that's still being done today on the backs of envelopes."

To help cope with all these competing and compelling factors, today's financial executive is literally bombarded with facts and information—from interoffice memos to professional journals to daily and weekly business publications. Most regard the overwhelming array of "must" reading as a mixed bag of blessing and curse.

"There's a wealth of information coming in, but just getting through it is a Herculean task," says a weary financial officer. "To use it properly, you have to develop a technique for getting through it faster, learning to apply what's useful—and ruthlessly discarding the rest."

The Human Relations Dynamic

Today's financial executive has come to grips with the volatile conditions of our rapidly-changing environment—with economic turbulence, with burgeoning regulations, with complex new technology and accelerated pace. But mere mastery of the new demands of the financial executive's role is just half the battle.

The financial executive who will lead the pack into the uncharted 1980's is the one who can successfully communicate and interpret the financial realities to all of the individuals and groups with whom he or she must interact—with the chief executive officer, to colleagues in other departments, to customers and clients, to stockholders and their representatives.

"Ten years ago, technical competence was the most important asset you could bring to your job," says Jesse Simmons, vice president of finance and treasurer,

NBI, Inc. "Today, it's equally important to have the ability to work effectively with and through others."

The most important of those "others," in the eyes of most financial executives, is the CEO. And as the financial management aspect of a company's operations becomes more critical, the role of the financial executive is taking on added importance in the eyes of many chief executive officers. The financial executive's advice and recommendations are sought; his or her insights become crucial.

In this atmosphere, the financial executive, more than ever before, must not only have the ability to present ideas and make recommendations, but must be able to articulate those recommendations, to persuade and convince associates. "Today, you can't just take your information to the CEO and leave the decision there," says Armstrong's Walker. "You have to be a leader, to make those hard choices and then educate your associates in comprehending your position. If you succeed, your job will be all that much easier."

Likewise, the financial executive today generally finds more interaction between the finance area and other divisions of the company, those interviewed agree. "There's more involvement in every area of management," says Simmons. "And it's not just manufacturing, where there's a historic tie, but also sales and marketing, engineering, R & D. To be successful, the financial person has to be keenly aware of the goals and the problems of every other division, and be able to provide advice and counsel."

Here, too, the communications skills of the financial officer become critical. "You don't just drop your recommendations on someone's desk—there's a lot of packaging involved," says one high level financial officer.

The financial executive's advice is also in demand in dealing with customers and clients, to a greater extent than ever before. Some top level financial people report that an unprecedented amount of their time is now directed externally—dealing with sales people, helping customers with financing, overseeing leasing contracts, and the like.

Finally, stockholder relations and communications with Wall Street consume larger chunks of time, while challenging the communications abilities of financial executives. The active interest of investors in the financial management of the company is a recurring theme among finance people today. "Once stockholders were content to watch the parade," says Data General's Jaeggi. "Now they want to march in it."

This transfer from passive to active investor and the resulting trend toward more frequent and more open communication has direct impact for those in the financial area, which is responsible for assembling and providing that information. "Once it was just an annual report," says one financial executive. "There's definitely a trend toward keeping the stockholder well informed all through the year—and that can't help but create more work for us."

And the chief financial officer is the natural resource person for market analysts, who represent the company stockholders and who translate the company's financial position to investors and potential investors. "Security analysts come to call today armed with sophisticated analytical tools, and ask probing, perceptive questions," says Walker. "They can't be put off with generalizations. We have to be straightforward and provide satisfactory answers."

Concurrently, communications skills are the best tool for those who favor professional meetings and symposia as the means for keeping up with the state-of-the-art. And most financial executives favor talking with other finance people as the best means of exchanging information.

"There's no substitute for getting together with other finance people to exchange ideas on how to handle situations," says one financial executive. "Seminars can help, but only if they come at just the right time. You can't wait three months for a seminar if a problem needs a solution today."

In Summary

The dynamically-changing function of the financial executive has created a demand for a new type of individual to fill what has become the exciting focal point of the American business community.

Men and women with the dedication and determination to meet today's challenge will find the role of the financial executive more rewarding than ever before.

What will they find?

More Pressure. Today's emphasis on profits, on the bottom line, creates more pressure on the financial executive. "In the past, we could afford to make a mistake; it wasn't all that earth-shattering," says one high-level financial officer. "Today, the bottom line depends on how fast capital can be recouped. Much more depends on the judgement and the decisions of the chief financial officer."

Increased Visibility. The role of the finance person is perceived as more critical, both by the CEO and by colleagues in other top level management positions, all of whom must look to the financial executive for guidance and solutions to their economic problems.

More Mobility. The track to the top is wider than ever before for financial executives. Opportunities for advancement are available, not only for those who come up through the more traditional ranks of controllership, but also to those whose primary experience has been in a treasurer's role.

And while mobility from industry to industry is rare for most professionals, it is more common for financial executives, whose skills and insights are in demand today in virtually every industry.

Better Compensation. The toughest person to negotiate with is the individual who knows he or she is in short supply. And the financial executives who have the qualities required by the job today are indeed in short supply—and are commanding salaries and compensation packages concomitant with their qualifications.

More Opportunity. In more and more instances, the position of Chief Financial Officer is not the last step up on the corporate ladder. On the contrary, there is a perceivable trend toward the elevation of financial executives to positions of Chief Operating Officer or Chief Executive Officer.

In short, it's a bull market today for the qualified financial executive. Those who can accommodate the changing demands and meet the challenges of today are assured a bright tomorrow.

Specimen Financial Statements

The Coca-Cola Company

Source: Reprinted from the Coca-Cola Company *Annual Report 1982*. Used by permission.

BUSINESS OBJECTIVES AND STRATEGY

The core of the Company's strategy is a commitment to achieve growth in earnings at a rate in excess of inflation, in order to give shareholders an above average total return on their investment.

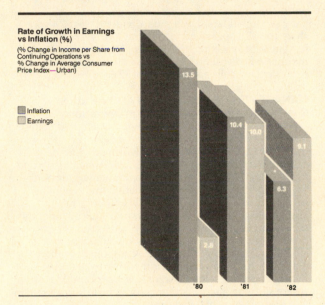

Rate of Growth in Earnings vs Inflation (%)
(% Change in Income per Share from Continuing Operations vs % Change in Average Consumer Price Index—Urban)

- Inflation
- Earnings

13.5
10.4 10.0
9.1
6.3
2.8

'80 '81 '82

To achieve this commitment, management focuses on the following areas:

Unit Sales Volume: A primary goal is to increase unit sales volume, at rates in excess of the respective industry rates. Within the main business of soft drinks, for example, unit growth of the worldwide soft drink industry was restrained by the worldwide economy in 1982; however, unit sales of the Company products increased. This performance helped the Company obtain its objective of increasing earnings at a rate in excess of inflation.

Profit Margins: While increasing unit volume in excess of industry rates is a key objective, the profit contribution per unit sold is also important. It is the Company's objective to maintain or improve "real" profits per unit (after adjusting for the effects of inflation). This objective is accomplished by maintaining tight controls over pricing policies and operating expenses.

At December 31, 1982, bottlers representing over 90% of the Company's soft drink volume in the United States had agreed to an amended bottler contract which gives the Company more pricing flexibility and results in additional marketing expenditures by the Company. In 1982, the Company raised prices in most of its major markets, including the United States, principally to cover the effects of inflation.

In 1980, the Company commenced the 50% use of high fructose corn syrup (HFCS), a form of sugar, in Coca-Cola. This action results in cost savings to the Company and its bottlers. In 1983, the Company authorized the increase to the 75% use of HFCS in fountain syrup.

By carefully managing expenses, the Company can improve its operating results. Management uses the percentage of expenses to gross profits as a primary tool for monitoring efficiency. In 1982 this percentage was 68.0% compared to 69.1% in 1981; this improvement represents an increase in operating income of approximately $30 million. The Company's success in controlling expenses has helped achieve earnings increases in difficult economic times.

Management of Resources: A key element of the Company's strategy is to concentrate its resources in consumer markets offering attractive returns and high growth potential.

In line with this strategy, the Company sold its Aqua-Chem and Tenco operations in 1981 and 1982, respectively, generating approximately $130 million in cash. In addition, the Company carefully manages its investment in the various components of working capital.

The pattern of investment spending shows the Company's emphasis on growth. Cumulative reinvestment in the soft drink business exceeded $1 billion for the last 4 years. The Company's Foods Division is making significant investments in TETRA-BRIK aseptic packaging equipment to support the expected growth in this area. Since 1977, the Company has invested more than $200 million in the wine business, including the initial acquisition cost of the Company's wineries. The Company is now the third largest domestic producer and marketer of wines. On June 21, 1982, the Company invested $692 million in cash and stock to purchase Columbia Pictures Industries, Inc., which gives the Company a leading position in the entertainment industry.

The above actions are part of the Company's strategy for increasing its return on assets.

Return on Assets (%)
(Income from Continuing Operations to Average Total Assets)

12.8 12.6 12.1

'80 '81 '82

Capital Structure: One of the Company's financial goals is to maintain a strong financial position as evidenced by its AAA bond rating from both Standard and Poor's and Moody's. Prudent amounts of long-term debt will continue to be used for attractive investment opportunities. Such debt is not expected to generally exceed 20-25% of total capital. This policy is aimed at increasing the return on shareholders' equity and the return to shareholders.

Long-Term Debt to Total Capital (%)

13.7
5.8 5.5
'80 '81 '82

Return on Shareholders' Equity (%)
(Income from Continuing Operations to Average Shareholders' Equity)

20.3 20.6 20.3
'80 '81 '82

Dividends: The Company has increased its dividend in each of the past 21 years. While management expects to continue its policy of paying regular cash dividends, management intends to gradually reduce the dividend payout ratio. This policy is designed to provide more funds for reinvestment in areas of the business offering attractive returns and to increase the total return to the Company's shareholders. The annual dividend was $2.48 per share and $2.32 per share in 1982 and 1981, respectively. At its March 1983 meeting, the Board of Directors increased the quarterly dividend to 67 cents, an increase of 8%, equivalent to a full year dividend of $2.68 in 1983.

MANAGEMENT'S DISCUSSION AND ANALYSIS
Change in Accounting for Foreign Operations

Effective January 1, 1982, the Company adopted Statement of Financial Accounting Standards No. 52, "Foreign Currency Translation" (SFAS 52), which provides new rules for the translation of foreign financial statements and for the classification of resulting adjustments. One objective of SFAS 52 is to provide information that generally reflects expected economic effects of exchange rate changes on a company's cash flows and equity. Under this translation method, most currency translation adjustments that do not affect cash flows are excluded from income and reported as a separate component of shareholders' equity. An exception is made for hyperinflationary countries, such as Argentina, Brazil and Mexico, where all exchange adjustments continue to be included in the determination of net income.

Adoption of the new rules required establishment of a foreign currency translation adjustment reducing shareholders' equity by $11.7 million as of January 1, 1982. In 1982, translation adjustments determined in accordance with the new rules further reduced shareholders' equity by $42.8 million. Translation adjustments are an inherent result of the process of translating financial statements of entities with a functional currency other than the U.S. dollar. Translation adjustments accumulated in shareholders' equity do not represent the effect on net income resulting from the adoption of SFAS 52.

Exchange gains of $27 million, determined in accordance with the new translation rules, are included in other income (net of other deductions) for 1982. Under the translation method used in prior years, the 1982 gains would have been approximately $10 million. Exchange adjustments were not material in 1981 or 1980.

The full effect of exchange rate changes on the Company's operations cannot be quantified because of many interrelated factors. A decline in exchange rates reduces revenues, costs and expenses and profits when foreign financial statements are translated into U.S. dollars. However, exchange rate changes may reflect changes in inflation rates and other local economic conditions that may also affect profitability. In some instances, the effects of exchange rate changes may be somewhat offset by changes in local currency selling prices, costs and expenses and the combination of these factors may affect sales volume and net income.

Management believes that, overall, declining exchange

rates had a negative effect on the Company's financial
results in 1982 and 1981, due to the effect of translating foreign earnings into U.S. dollars at generally lower exchange
rates than in the prior year.

Results of Operations

Revenues: Net operating revenues continued to
increase in 1982 as in 1981. Sales volume for the Company's
major product—soft drinks—increased in both years; however, revenues from soft drink sales were reduced by lower
exchange rates and sugar prices. Revenues for 1982
increased because of the purchase of Columbia Pictures
Industries, Inc., in June 1982. Columbia's operating
results, since the date of acquisition, are included in the
consolidated statement of income and accounted for
approximately 7.3% of revenues for 1982.

Soft drinks accounted for 72% and 80% of net operating
revenues in 1982 and 1981, respectively. Sales volume
increased approximately 3% in 1982 including a 5%
increase in the Company's non-U.S. operations. Unit ship-
ments of syrups and concentrates were even with 1981 levels in the U.S., but increased after adjusting for bottler
inventory effects. In 1981, worldwide sales volume
increased approximately 2%. Sugar prices were generally
lower during 1982 and 1981 as compared to the preceding
years. Changing sugar prices affect net operating revenues
in the United States and for Company-owned bottling
operations outside the United States. Foreign exchange
rates decreased in 1982 and 1981, tending to reduce the
U.S. dollar amount of reported foreign revenues.

Revenues for other products and services increased by
5.9% and 9.7% in 1982 and 1981, respectively. These
increases were caused primarily by increased volume for
citrus and wine products combined with modest price
increases.

Gross Profit: Gross profit as a percentage of net operating revenues was 45% in 1982, 44% in 1981, and 43% in
1980. Maintaining and improving gross profit margins
while holding down price increases is an integral part of
the Company's operating philosophy. During the past two
years, the Company has implemented programs which
enhance efficiency through close monitoring of inventories and production expenses. Other factors which
impact gross profit margins are the Company's innovative marketing techniques, flexible pricing policies,
and market acceptance and demand for the Company's
major products.

The price of Coca-Cola syrup sold to bottlers in the
United States is adjusted quarterly for changes in the price
of sugar. This procedure minimizes the effect on gross
profits of changing sugar prices.

Selling, Administrative and General Expenses: Selling expenses, including media advertising, were $1.43 bil-
lion in 1982, $1.37 billion in 1981, and $1.30 billion in 1980.
Expenditures for media advertising were $417 million in
1982, $414 million in 1981, and $395 million in 1980. These
increases are due to the introduction of new products,

promotions to maintain or increase market share for
major soft drink, wine and citrus products, and general
inflation. Expenditures in 1982 include amounts related to
the introduction and promotion of diet Coke. In 1982, an
additional $69 million of media spending was included in
film costs in accordance with film industry accounting
standards.

Administrative and general expenses increased 14.4%
and 9.9% in 1982 and 1981, respectively, primarily because
of inflation and expansion of the business. The 1982
increase includes expenses of Columbia since the date
of acquisition.

Total Selling Expenses ($ Millions)

▪ Media Advertising

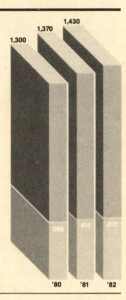

1,300   1,370   1,430

395   414   417

'80   '81   '82

Interest Income and Expense: Interest income was $106
million and $71 million in 1982 and 1981, respectively. The
increase in 1982 was caused primarily by higher invested
balances. The increase in 1981 of $31 million resulted from
higher invested balances and interest rates.

Interest expense was $75 million in 1982, compared to
$38 million in 1981. This increase was caused primarily by
increased borrowings resulting from the acquisitions of
Columbia Pictures and Associated Coca-Cola Bottling Co.,
Inc. In 1981, interest expense increased only slightly over
the prior year.

Other Income and Deductions: The increase in other
income (net) in 1982 is due primarily to net exchange gains
of $27 million. In 1982, the Company adopted Statement
of Financial Accounting Standards No. 52, "Foreign Currency Translation" (SFAS 52). See "Change in Accounting
for Foreign Operations."

The increase in other deductions (net) in 1981 was primarily due to net exchange losses as measured under the
previous accounting method. The financial statements for
1981 have not been restated for the adoption of SFAS 52.

Selected Financial Data

(In millions except per share data)

Year Ended December 31,	1982	1981	1980
	(a)		
Summary of operations			
Net operating revenues	**$6,249**	$5,889	$5,621
Cost of goods and services	**3,453**	3,308	3,198
Gross profit	**2,796**	2,581	2,423
Selling, administrative and general expenses	**1,902**	1,783	1,682
Operating income	**894**	798	741
Interest income—net	**32**	32	5
Other income (deductions)—net	**6**	(23)	(9)
Income from continuing operations before income taxes	**932**	807	737
Income taxes	**420**	360	331
Income from continuing operations	**$ 512**	$ 447	$ 406
Year-End Position			
Cash and marketable securities	**$ 311**	$ 393	$ 289
Property, plant and equipment—net	**1,539**	1,409	1,341
Total assets	**4,923**	3,565	3,406
Long-term debt	**462**	137	133
Total debt	**583**	232	228
Shareholders' equity	**2,779**	2,271	2,075
Total capital (b)	**3,362**	2,503	2,303
Per Share Data (d)			
Income from continuing operations	**$ 3.95**	$ 3.62	$ 3.29
Net income	**3.95**	3.90	3.42
Dividends	**2.48**	2.32	2.16
Financial Ratios			
Income from continuing operations to net operating revenues	**8.2%**	7.6%	7.2%
Income from continuing operations to average shareholders' equity	**20.3%**	20.6%	20.3%
Long-term debt to total capital	**13.7%**	5.5%	5.8%
Total debt to total capital	**17.3%**	9.3%	9.9%
Dividend payout	**62.8%**	59.5%	63.2%
Other Data			
Average shares outstanding (d)	**130**	124	124
Capital expenditures	**$ 382**	$ 330	$ 293
Depreciation	**149**	137	131

Notes:

(a) Includes the results of Columbia Pictures Industries, Inc. from June 21, 1982.

In 1982, the Company adopted Statement of Financial Accounting Standards No. 52, "Foreign Currency Translation." See Note 1 to the Consolidated Financial Statements.

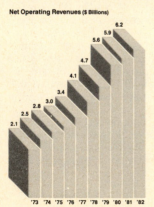

Net Operating Revenues ($ Billions)

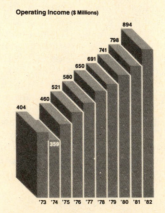

Operating Income ($ Millions)

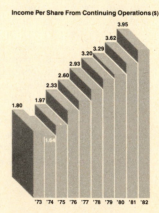

Income Per Share From Continuing Operations ($)

Specimen Financial Statements

1979	1978	1977	1976	1975	1974	1973
$4,689	$4,095	$3,394	$2,989	$2,834	$2,483	$2,124
2,583	2,253	1,876	1,648	1,669	1,496	1,118
2,106	1,842	1,518	1,341	1,165	987	1,006
1,415	1,192	938	820	705	628	602
691	650	580	521	460	359	404
25	28	23	23	16	15	14
(3)	(14)	(9)	(5)	(9)	3	(1)
713	664	594	539	467	377	417
318	303	273	251	224	175	195
$ 395	$ 361	$ 321	$ 288	$ 243	$ 202(c)	$ 222
$ 209	$ 369	$ 418	$ 403	$ 409	$ 260	$ 308
1,284	1,065	887	738	647	601	563
2,938	2,583	2,254	2,007	1,801	1,610	1,461
31	15	15	11	16	12	8
139	69	57	52	42	69	24
1,919	1,740	1,578	1,434	1,302	1,190	1,109
2,058	1,809	1,635	1,486	1,344	1,259	1,133
$ 3.20	$ 2.93	$ 2.60	$ 2.33	$ 1.97	$ 1.64(c)	$ 1.80
3.40	3.03	2.68	2.38	2.02	1.65(c)	1.82
1.96	1.74	1.54	1.325	1.15	1.04	.90
8.4%	8.8%	9.5%	9.6%	8.6%	8.1%	10.4%
21.6%	21.8%	21.3%	21.0%	19.5%	17.6%	21.1%
1.5%	.8%	.9%	.7%	1.2%	1.0%	.7%
6.8%	3.8%	3.5%	3.5%	3.1%	5.5%	2.1%
57.6%	57.4%	57.5%	55.7%	56.9%	63.0%	49.5%
124	124	123	123	123	123	123
$ 381	$ 306	$ 264	$ 191	$ 145	$ 154	$ 127
110	91	80	70	66	59	58

(b) Includes shareholders' equity and total debt.

(c) In 1974, the Company adopted the last-in, first-out (LIFO) accounting method for certain major categories of inventories. This accounting change had the effect of reducing net income in 1974 by $31.2 million ($.25 per share).

(d) Adjusted for a two-for-one stock split in 1977.

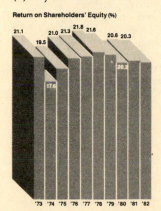

Return on Shareholders' Equity (%)

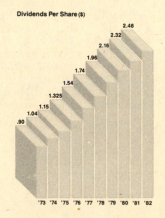

Dividends Per Share ($)

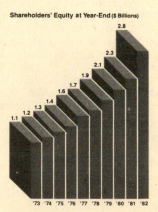

Shareholders' Equity at Year-End ($ Billions)

Discontinued Operations: The Company's subsidiary, Aqua-Chem, Inc., was sold in the third quarter of 1981, resulting in a net gain on the sale of approximately $29 million or 6% of net income. In addition, the Company sold its Tenco Division in February 1982, for approximately book value. Income from discontinued operations accounted for 1.2% of net income in 1981.

Industry Segments

The Company operates principally in the soft drink industry. Soft drinks include carbonated and non-carbonated beverages and fruit drinks.

In June 1982, the Company acquired Columbia Pictures Industries, Inc., which operates in the entertainment industry. On a pro forma combined basis, Columbia's revenues would have represented approximately 12.3% and 11.1% of the combined totals for 1982 and 1981, respectively.

Citrus, coffee, pasta, wine, and plastic products are included in other industries which represented approximately 20% of consolidated revenues in 1982, 1981, and 1980. Income from other industries represented 12% of income from industry segments in 1982, 1981, and 1980.

Income from industry segments excludes interest expense and also excludes income and expenses not attributable to the operations of any specific segment.

Financial Position

Liquidity and Capital Resources: The Company acquired Columbia Pictures Industries, Inc., during 1982 for consideration valued at approximately $692 million, consisting of 12.2 million shares of the Company's common stock and $333 million in cash. The cash portion was funded with available corporate cash and short-term borrowings. Most of the short-term borrowings have been or are in the process of being refinanced with long-term debt. At December 31, 1982, long-term debt was $462 million, compared to $137 million at December 31, 1981. Long-term debt as a percent of total capital was 14% and 5% at December 31, 1982 and 1981, respectively.

Working capital was $750 million at December 31, 1982, a $120 million increase over 1981. This increase was due primarily to the acquisition of Columbia, the issuance and planned issuance of $300 million principal amount of long-term debt and continued profitable operations. Cash and marketable securities were $261 million at December 31, 1982. Also included in other current assets at December 31, 1982, is the Company's remaining investment of $120 million in Associated Coca-Cola Bottling assets, a temporary investment accounted for under the cost method of accounting.

Working capital was $630 million at December 31, 1981, a $69 million increase over 1980. Cash and marketable securities were $340 million at December 31, 1981, $108 million

above 1980. Current debt was $95 million, unchanged from 1980. The increase in marketable securities and the decrease in accounts receivable and inventories were due primarily to the sale of Aqua-Chem, Inc., and management's efforts to improve control over working capital.

Capital Expenditures: In 1982, capital expenditures totaled $382 million (including property, plant and equipment of purchased companies), including $250 million in the soft drink industry, $54 million in the entertainment industry, and $78 million in other industries and operations. Capital expenditures were $330 million in 1981, approximately 75% of which related to the soft drink industry.

In both 1982 and 1981, most capital expenditures related to improved efficiency and plant expansion.

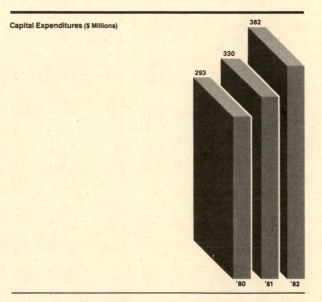

Capital Expenditures ($ Millions)

293   330   382
'80   '81   '82

Additional Information

For additional information concerning the Company's operations, cash flow, liquidity and capital sources, this analysis should be read in conjunction with the Letter to Shareholders and the information on pages 30 through 39 of this Annual Report. For information relating to the effects of inflation on the operations of the Company see pages 42 to 43, "Supplementary Information on the Effects of Changing Prices." Additional information concerning operations in different industries and different geographical areas is presented on pages 38 to 39.

Year Ended December 31,	1982	1981	1980
Net operating revenues	$6,249,718	$5,889,035	$5,620,749
Cost of goods and services	3,453,493	3,307,574	3,197,733
Gross Profit	2,796,225	2,581,461	2,423,016
Selling, administrative and general expenses	1,901,962	1,782,875	1,681,861
Operating Income	894,263	798,586	741,155
Interest income	106,177	70,632	40,099
Interest expense	74,561	38,349	35,102
Other income (deductions)—net	6,112	(23,615)	(9,425)
Income From Continuing Operations			
Before Income Taxes	931,991	807,254	736,727
Income taxes	419,759	360,184	330,409
Income From Continuing Operations	512,232	447,070	406,318
Discontinued operations:			
Income from discontinued operations			
(net of applicable income taxes of $7,271 in 1981,			
and $11,782 in 1980)	—	5,641	15,790
Gain on disposal of discontinued operations			
(net of applicable income taxes of $13,274)	—	29,071	—
Net Income	$ 512,232	$ 481,782	$ 422,108
Per Share:			
Continuing operations	$ 3.95	$ 3.62	$ 3.29
Discontinued operations	—	.28	.13
Net income	$ 3.95	$ 3.90	$ 3.42
Average Shares Outstanding	129,793	123,610	123,578

See Notes to Consolidated Financial Statements

Consolidated Balance Sheets

(In thousands except share data)

Assets	1982	1981
Current		
Cash	$ 177,530	$ 120,908
Marketable securities, at cost (approximates market)	83,381	218,634
Trade accounts receivable, less allowances of		
$21,336 in 1982 and $8,579 in 1981	751,775	483,491
Inventories and unamortized film costs	808,799	750,719
Prepaid expenses and other assets	255,080	62,494
Total Current Assets	2,076,565	1,636,246
Investments, Film Costs and Other Assets		
Investments, at cost	221,909	176,332
Unamortized film costs	211,460	—
Other assets	241,395	211,086
	674,764	387,418
Property, Plant and Equipment		
Land and improvements	126,201	96,468
Buildings	602,475	570,356
Machinery and equipment	1,383,668	1,271,065
Containers	333,472	306,243
	2,445,816	2,244,132
Less allowances for depreciation	907,250	834,676
	1,538,566	1,409,456
Goodwill and Other Intangible Assets	633,415	131,661
	$4,923,310	$3,564,781

Liabilities and Shareholders' Equity	1982	1981
Current		
Loans and notes payable	$ 70,561	$ 89,647
Current maturities of long-term debt	50,623	5,515
Accounts payable and accrued expenses	792,250	672,049
Participations and other entertainment obligations	154,803	—
Accrued taxes—including income taxes	258,574	239,114
Total Current Liabilities	1,326,811	1,006,325
Participations and Other Entertainment Obligations	190,408	—
Long-Term Debt	462,344	137,278
Deferred Income Taxes	165,093	150,406
Shareholders' Equity		
Common stock, no par value—		
Authorized—140,000,000 shares;		
Issued: 136,099,741 shares in 1982		
and 124,024,735 shares in 1981	68,427	62,389
Capital surplus	478,308	114,194
Retained earnings	2,300,217	2,109,542
Foreign currency translation adjustment	(54,486)	—
	2,792,466	2,286,125
Less treasury stock, at cost (359,338 shares		
in 1982; 401,338 shares in 1981)	13,812	15,353
	2,778,654	2,270,772
	$4,923,310	$3,564,781

See Notes to Consolidated Financial Statements

Specimen Financial Statements

Consolidated Statements of Shareholders' Equity

The Coca-Cola Company and Subsidiaries

(In thousands except per share data)

Three Years Ended December 31, 1982

	Number of Shares		Amount				
	Common Stock	Treasury Stock	Common Stock	Capital Surplus	Retained Earnings	Foreign Currency Translation	Treasury Stock
Balance January 1, 1980	123,960	401	$62,357	$112,333	$1,759,367	$ —	$(15,353)
Sales to employees exercising stock options and appreciation rights	30	—	15	711	—	—	—
Tax benefit from sale of option shares by employees	—	—	—	128	—	—	—
Net income	—	—	—	—	422,108	—	—
Dividends (per share—$2.16)	—	—	—	—	(266,928)	—	—
Balance December 31, 1980	123,990	401	62,372	113,172	1,914,547	—	(15,353)
Sales to employees exercising stock options and appreciation rights	35	—	17	841	—	—	—
Tax benefit from sale of option shares by employees	—	—	—	181	—	—	—
Net income	—	—	—	—	481,782	—	—
Dividends (per share—$2.32)	—	—	—	—	(286,787)	—	—
Balance December 31, 1981	124,025	401	62,389	114,194	2,109,542	—	(15,353)
Effect of restating asset and liability balances as of January 1, 1982 for adoption of SFAS No. 52 (net of income taxes of $2,316)	—	—	—	—	—	(11,657)	—
Sales to employees exercising stock options and appreciation rights	121	—	61	3,685	—	—	—
Tax benefit from sale of option shares by employees	—	—	—	814	—	—	—
Purchase of Columbia Pictures Industries, Inc.	11,954	—	5,977	359,579	—	—	—
Translation adjustments (net of income taxes of $11,188)	—	—	—	—	—	(42,829)	—
Treasury stock issued to officers	—	(42)	—	36	—	—	1,541
Net income	—	—	—	—	512,232	—	—
Dividends (per share—$2.48)	—	—	—	—	(321,557)	—	—
Balance December 31, 1982	136,100	359	$68,427	$478,308	$2,300,217	$(54,486)	$(13,812)

See Notes to Consolidated Financial Statements

Year Ended December 31,	1982	1981	1980
Source Of Working Capital			
From operations:			
Income from continuing operations	$ 512,232	$447,070	$ 406,318
Add charges not requiring outlay of working capital during the year:			
Depreciation	148,856	136,868	131,042
Amortization of noncurrent film costs	43,495	—	—
Deferred income taxes	50,807	23,692	31,500
Other (principally amortization of goodwill and container adjustments)	34,304	61,009	37,932
Total From Continuing Operations	789,694	668,639	606,792
Discontinued operations (excludes provisions for depreciation, amortization and deferred income taxes of $2,429 in 1981, and $4,521 in 1980)	—	37,141	20,311
Total From Operations	789,694	705,780	627,103
Common stock issued	370,152	1,090	854
Increase in long-term debt	249,392	4,057	99,415
Transfer of noncurrent film costs to current	93,909	—	—
Disposals of property, plant and equipment	44,467	71,788	77,053
Decrease in investments and other assets	21,836	—	—
Other	5,153	—	—
	1,574,603	782,715	804,425
Application Of Working Capital			
Cash dividends	321,557	286,787	266,928
Acquisitions of purchased companies excluding net current assets:			
Property, plant and equipment—net	56,739	9,814	5,885
Other assets net of other liabilities	89,693	103	(2,862)
Goodwill	516,115	10	10,455
Additions to property, plant and equipment	325,016	319,792	287,186
Additions to noncurrent film costs	95,804	—	—
Increase in investments and other assets	—	85,131	95,254
Foreign currency translation	21,693	—	—
Other	28,153	11,830	2,348
	1,454,770	713,467	665,194
Increase In Working Capital	$ 119,833	$ 69,248	$ 139,231
Increase (Decrease) In Working Capital By Component			
Cash	$ 56,622	$ (8,777)	$ 22,799
Marketable securities	(135,253)	117,233	59,716
Trade accounts receivable	268,284	(39,632)	88,044
Inventories and unamortized film costs	58,080	(59,516)	140,621
Prepaid expenses and other current assets	192,586	4,685	5,470
Loans and notes payable	19,086	(2,060)	16,229
Current maturities of long-term debt	(45,108)	2,013	(3,144)
Accounts payable and accrued expenses	(120,201)	60,974	(156,161)
Participations and other entertainment obligations	(154,803)	—	—
Accrued taxes—including income taxes	(19,460)	(5,672)	(34,343)
Increase In Working Capital	$ 119,833	$ 69,248	$ 139,231

See Notes to Consolidated Financial Statements

1. Accounting Policies. The major accounting policies and practices followed by the Company and its subsidiaries are as follows:

Consolidation

The consolidated financial statements include the accounts of the Company and its majority-owned subsidiaries. All significant inter-company accounts and transactions are eliminated in consolidation.

Inventories and Unamortized Film Costs

Inventories are valued at the lower of cost or market. The last-in, first-out (LIFO) method of inventory valuation is used for sugar and other sweeteners used in beverages in the United States, for certain major citrus concentrate and wine products, for substantially all inventories of United States bottling subsidiaries and for certain other operations. All other inventories are valued on the basis of average cost or first-in, first-out (FIFO) methods. The excess of current costs over LIFO stated values amounted to approximately $72 million and $76 million at December 31, 1982 and 1981, respectively.

Unamortized film costs include film production, print, pre-release and national advertising costs, and capitalized interest. The individual film forecast method is used to amortize these costs based on the revenues recognized in proportion to management's estimate of ultimate revenues to be received.

The costs of feature and television films are classified as current assets to the extent such costs are expected to be recovered through the respective primary markets. Other costs relating to film production are classified as noncurrent.

Revenues from theatrical exhibition of feature films are recognized on the dates of exhibition. Revenues from television licensing agreements are recognized when films are available for telecasting.

Property, Plant and Equipment

Property, plant and equipment is stated at cost, less allowance for depreciation, except that foreign subsidiaries carry bottles and shells in service at amounts (less than cost) which generally correspond with deposit prices obtained from customers. Approximately 89% of depreciation expense was determined by the straight-line method for 1982 and approximately 87% for both 1981 and 1980. Investment tax credits are accounted for by the flow-through method.

Goodwill and Other Intangible Assets

Goodwill and other intangible assets are stated on the basis of cost and, if purchased subsequent to October 31, 1970, are being amortized, principally on a straight-line basis, over the estimated future periods to be benefited (not exceeding 40 years). Accumulated amortization amounted to $26 million and $16 million at December 31, 1982 and 1981, respectively.

Capitalized Interest

Interest capitalized as part of the cost of acquisition, construction or production of major assets (including film costs)

was $14 million, $8 million and $6 million in 1982, 1981, and 1980, respectively.

Foreign Currency Translation

In the second quarter of 1982, the Company adopted Statement of Financial Accounting Standards No. 52, "Foreign Currency Translation" (SFAS 52), effective as of January 1, 1982, and restated the results for the first quarter. Exchange gains (gains and losses on foreign currency transactions and translation of balance sheet accounts of operations in hyperinflationary economies) included in income were $27 million for 1982. Under the translation rules used in prior years, such gains would have been approximately $10 million. The impact on 1981 and 1980 operating results is not material and such financial statements have not been restated.

An equity adjustment ($11.7 million) was recorded as of January 1, 1982, for the cumulative effect of SFAS 52 on prior years.

2. Inventories and Unamortized Film Costs. Inventories and unamortized film costs are comprised of the following (in thousands):

	December 31,	
	1982	1981
Finished goods	**$219,000**	$259,391
Work in process	**96,305**	92,464
Raw materials and supplies	**368,730**	398,864
Unamortized film costs (includes in process costs of $23,260)	**124,764**	—
	$808,799	$750,719
Noncurrent—Unamortized film costs		
Completed	**$113,527**	$ —
In process	**97,933**	—
	$211,460	$ —

3. Short-Term Borrowings and Credit Arrangements. Loans and notes payable include amounts payable to banks of $71 million and $61 million at December 31, 1982 and 1981, respectively.

Under line of credit arrangements for short-term debt with various financial institutions, the Company and its subsidiaries may borrow up to $768 million. These lines of credit are subject to normal banking terms and conditions. At December 31, 1982, the unused portion of the credit lines was $674 million. Some of the financial arrangements require compensating balances which are not material.

4. Accounts Payable and Accrued Expenses are composed of the following amounts (in thousands):

	December 31,	
	1982	1981
Trade accounts payable	**$647,061**	$565,697
Deposits on bottles and shells	**67,725**	67,489
Other	**77,464**	38,863
	$792,250	$672,049

5. Accrued Taxes are composed of the following amounts (in thousands):

	December 31,	
	1982	1981
Income taxes	**$190,790**	$175,753
Sales, payroll and miscellaneous taxes	**67,784**	63,361
	$258,574	$239,114

6. Long-Term Debt consists of the following amounts (in thousands):

	December 31,	
	1982	1981
9⁷/₈% notes due June 1, 1985	**$ 99,928**	$ 99,898
11³/₄% notes due October 1, 1989	**97,548**	—
10³/₈% notes due June 1, 1988	**23,200**	—
Short-term borrowings to be refinanced with long-term debt	**173,000**	—
Other	**119,291**	42,895
	512,967	142,793
Less current portion	**50,623**	5,515
	$462,344	$137,278

The 9⁷/₈% notes may not be redeemed before June 1, 1983. After that date, the notes may be redeemed at the option of the Company in whole or in part at 100% of their principal amount, plus accrued interest.

The 11³/₄% notes were issued in international markets and may not be redeemed prior to October 1, 1986, except under certain limited conditions. After that date, the notes may also be redeemed at the option of the Company in whole or in part at 101% of the principal amount during the succeeding twelve month period, and thereafter at 100% of the principal amount, together in each case with accrued interest.

The principal amount of the 10³/₈% notes is $100 million. The notes were issued in the international markets on a partly paid basis, whereby 25% of the issue price was received on December 1, 1982, and the remaining 75% will be received on June 1, 1983. These notes may not be redeemed prior to maturity, except under certain limited conditions.

At December 31, 1982, $173 million of short-term borrowings have been classified as long-term debt as management intends to repay such borrowings with proceeds from the remaining installment of the 10³/₈% notes, and from the proceeds of an additional $100 million of partly paid notes issued on February 2, 1983 (these notes have an annual coupon rate of 9⁷/₈%, require payment in installments of 30% on February 2, 1983, and 70% on August 1, 1983, and mature on August 1, 1992).

Other long-term debt consists of various mortgages and notes with maturity dates ranging from 1983 to 2010. Interest on a portion of this debt varies with the changes in the prime rate, and the weighted average interest rate applicable to the remainder is approximately 11.3%.

The above notes and other long-term debt instruments include various restrictions, none of which are presently significant to the Company.

Maturities of long-term debt for the five years succeeding December 31, 1982, are as follows (in thousands):

1983	$ 50,623
1984	12,822
1985	110,357
1986	8,856
1987	10,990

The Company is contingently liable for guarantees of indebtedness by its independent bottling companies and others in the approximate amount of $70 million at December 31, 1982.

7. Foreign Operations. The Company's identifiable assets and liabilities outside the United States and Puerto Rico are shown below (in thousands):

	December 31,	
	1982	1981
Current assets	**$ 776,095**	$ 751,835
Property, plant and equipment—net	**585,320**	567,179
Other assets	**77,003**	121,903
	1,438,418	1,440,917
Liabilities	**626,888**	637,015
Net assets	**$ 811,530**	$ 803,902

Appropriate United States and foreign income taxes have been provided for on earnings of subsidiary companies which are expected to be remitted to the parent company in the near future. Accumulated unremitted earnings of foreign subsidiaries which are expected to be required for use in the foreign operations amounted to approximately $63 million at December 31, 1982, exclusive of amounts which if remitted would result in little or no tax.

8. Stock Options. The Company's 1979 stock option plan provides for the granting of stock appreciation rights and stock options to certain officers and employees. Stock appreciation rights permit the holder, upon surrendering all or part of the related stock option, to receive cash, common stock, or a combination thereof, in an amount up to 100% of the difference between the market price and the option price. Included in options outstanding at December 31, 1982, are various options granted under a previous plan and other options granted not as a part of an option plan.

Further information relating to options is as follows:

	1982	1981	1980
Options out-standing at January 1	1,406,360	1,392,457	1,259,886
Options granted in the year	288,300	244,975	362,350
Options exercised in the year	(120,791)	(35,651)	(29,559)
Options cancelled in the year	(66,707)	(195,421)	(200,220)
Options out-standing at December 31	1,507,162	1,406,360	1,392,457
Options exercisable at December 31	781,906	755,598	728,067
Shares available at December 31 for options which may be granted	25,261	278,121	400,408
Option prices per share Exercised in the year	$22-$44	$22-$34	$19-$25
Unexercised at year-end	$25-$68	$22-$68	$19-$68

Not included above are options assumed in connection with the purchase of Columbia Pictures Industries, Inc. covering 504,997 shares of the Company's common stock. The value of these options in excess of the option price has been included in the acquisition cost. At December 31, 1982, options for 263,281 such shares were outstanding at an average option price of $31.

9. Pension Plans. The Company and its subsidiaries sponsor and/or contribute to various pension plans covering substantially all domestic employees and certain employees in foreign countries. Pension expense for continuing operations determined under various actuarial cost methods, principally the aggregate level cost method, amounted to approximately $37 million in 1982, $35 million in 1981, and $32 million in 1980. Amendments which resulted in improved benefits for retired employees increased 1982 pension expense by $1.2 million and increased the value of vested benefits by $12 million at January 1, 1982.

The actuarial present value of accumulated benefits, as estimated by consulting actuaries, and net assets available for benefits of Company and subsidiary-sponsored domestic plans are presented below (in thousands):

	January 1,	
	1982	1981
Actuarial present value of accumulated plan benefits:		
Vested	$178,343	$146,884
Nonvested	14,284	12,669
	$192,627	$159,553
Net assets available for benefits	$234,836	$193,268

The weighted average assumed rates of return used in determining the actuarial present value of accumulated plan benefits were approximately 10% for 1982 and 9% for 1981. Changes in the assumed rates of return reduced the actuarial present value of accumulated plan benefits by approximately $18 million and $19 million at January 1, 1982 and 1981, respectively.

The Company has various foreign pension plans which are not required to report to certain governmental agencies pursuant to the Employee Retirement Income Security Act (ERISA) and do not otherwise determine the actuarial present value of accumulated plan benefits or net assets available for benefits as calculated and disclosed above. For such plans, the value of the pension funds and balance sheet accruals exceeded the actuarially computed value of vested benefits as of January 1, 1982 and 1981, as estimated by consulting actuaries.

10. Income Taxes. The components of income before income taxes for both continuing and discontinued operations consisted of the following (in thousands):

	Year Ended December 31,		
	1982	1981	1980
United States	**$357,063**	$309,654	$251,807
Foreign	**574,928**	552,857	512,492
	$931,991	$862,511	$764,299

Income taxes for continuing and discontinued operations consisted of the following amounts (in thousands):

	Year Ended December 31,			
	United States	State & Local	Foreign	Total
1982				
Current	**$79,605**	**$22,638**	**$266,709**	**$368,952**
Deferred	**33,281**	**1,363**	**16,163**	**50,807**
1981				
Current	$86,589	$22,461	$248,292	$357,342
Deferred	15,574	1,646	6,167	23,387
1980				
Current	$63,636	$17,438	$228,013	$309,087
Deferred	25,518	2,390	5,196	33,104

Total tax expense differed from the amount computed by applying the statutory federal income tax rate to income before income taxes principally because of investment tax credits which had the effect of reducing the tax provision by approximately $24 million in 1982, $14 million in 1981 and $11 million in 1980.

Deferred taxes are provided principally for depreciation and film costs which are recognized in different years for financial statement and income tax purposes.

11. Acquisitions. On June 21, 1982, the Company acquired all of the outstanding capital stock of Columbia Pictures Industries, Inc. ("Columbia") in a purchase transaction. The purchase price, consisting of cash and common stock of the Company, is valued at approximately $692 million. The values assigned to assets acquired and liabilities assumed are based on studies conducted to determine their fair values. The excess cost over net fair value is being amortized over forty years using the straight-line method; amortization amounted to $6 million in 1982.

The pro forma consolidated results of operations of the Company, as if Columbia had been acquired as of January 1, 1981, are as follows (in thousands, except per share data):

	Year Ended December 31,	
	1982	1981
Net operating revenues	**$6,602,571**	$6,623,775
Income from continuing operations	**498,692**	456,452
Income from continuing operations per share	**3.67**	3.36

The pro forma results include adjustments to reflect interest expense on $333 million of the purchase price assumed to be financed with debt bearing interest at an annual rate of 11%, the amortization of the unallocated excess cost over net assets of Columbia, the income tax effects of pro forma adjustments and the issuance of 12.2 million shares of the Company's common stock.

The pro forma results for the twelve months ended December 31, 1981, have been further adjusted to reflect Columbia's repurchase in February, 1981, of 2.4 million shares of Columbia common stock from certain shareholders as if such repurchase had been consummated as of January 1, 1981. Accordingly, interest expense has been increased for amounts necessary to fund the cash portion of the purchase price, legal expenses incurred in litigation with such shareholders have been eliminated and income taxes have been adjusted.

In June 1982, the Company purchased Associated Coca-Cola Bottling Co., Inc. ("Associated") at a cost of approximately $419 million. Associated was acquired with the intent of selling its properties to other purchasers as part of the Company's strategy to assist in restructuring the bottler system. Accordingly, the acquisition has been accounted for as a temporary investment under the cost method of accounting. At December 31, 1982, approximately 70% of Associated's operating assets had been sold for cash equal to the allocated costs of such assets. A substantial portion of such assets were sold for $245 million to a corporation principally owned by a former director of the Company.

The remaining investment in Associated of $120 million at December 31, 1982 is included in other current assets.

In September 1982, the Company purchased Ronco Foods Company, a manufacturer and distributor of pasta products, for cash. This transaction had no significant effect on the Company's operating results.

12. Discontinued Operations. In 1981, the Company sold Aqua-Chem, Inc., a wholly-owned subsidiary which produced steam generators, industrial boilers and water treatment equipment. In February 1982, the Company sold its Tenco Division for approximately book value. Tenco was an operating unit which manufactured and distributed private label instant coffees and teas.

Net sales of discontinued operations were $240 million and $292 million in 1981 and 1980, respectively.

13. Industry Segments. The Company operates principally in the soft drink industry. Carbonated and noncarbonated beverages and Hi-C fruit drinks are classified as soft drinks. In June 1982, the Company acquired Columbia Pictures Industries, Inc., which operates in the entertainment industry. Citrus, coffee, wine and plastic products are included in other industries. Inter-segment transfers are not material. Information concerning operations in different industries is as follows (in thousands):

Year Ended December 31,	1982	1981	1980
Net operating revenues:*			
Soft drinks	$4,515,813	$4,683,467	$4,522,048
Entertainment	457,305	—	—
Other industries	1,276,600	1,205,568	1,098,701
Total	$6,249,718	$5,889,035	$5,620,749
Income from industry segments:*			
Soft drinks	$ 893,221	$ 803,748	$ 731,783
Entertainment	35,535	—	—
Other industries	127,196	113,759	101,138
Total	1,055,952	917,507	832,921
Other income, net of other deductions	(50,089)	(37,671)	(37,893)
General expenses	(73,872)	(72,582)	(58,301)
Income from continuing operations before income taxes	$ 931,991	$ 807,254	$ 736,727
Identifiable assets at year-end:*			
Soft drinks	$2,521,410	$2,472,533	$2,436,192
Entertainment	1,309,837	—	—
Other industries	615,872	578,588	529,184
Total	4,447,119	3,051,121	2,965,376
Corporate assets (principally marketable securities, investments and fixed assets)	476,191	452,693	289,202
Discontinued operations	—	60,967	151,380
Total	$4,923,310	$3,564,781	$3,405,958
Capital expenditures by industry segment including fixed assets of purchased companies:			
Soft drinks	$ 249,529	$ 251,539	$ 224,152
Entertainment	53,913	—	—
Other industries	53,686	58,422	40,924
Depreciation of fixed assets and amortization of intangible assets by industry segment:*			
Soft drinks	$ 118,404	$ 112,476	$ 108,126
Entertainment	8,296	—	—
Other industries	26,455	22,817	20,731

*Amounts for 1980 have been restated to reflect the sale of the Company's Aqua-Chem, Inc., subsidiary and Tenco Division.

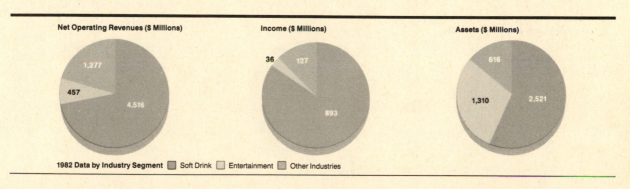

Net Operating Revenues ($ Millions)   Income ($ Millions)   Assets ($ Millions)

1982 Data by Industry Segment ▮ Soft Drink ▯ Entertainment ▮ Other Industries

14. Operations in Geographic Areas. Information about the Company's operations in different geographic areas is presented below (in thousands). Africa, which is not a significant geographic area as defined by SFAS 14, has been grouped with Europe in accordance with the Company's management organizational structure. Other insignificant geographic areas are combined as Canada and Pacific. Inter-company transfers between geographic areas are not material.

Year Ended December 31,	1982	1981	1980
Net operating revenues:*			
United States and Puerto Rico	$3,580,140	$3,238,673	$3,059,953
Latin America	516,336	608,110	560,164
Europe and Africa	1,155,564	1,096,257	1,170,294
Canada and Pacific	997,678	945,995	830,338
Total	$6,249,718	$5,889,035	$5,620,749
Income from geographic areas:*			
United States and Puerto Rico	$ 417,542	$ 337,522	$ 279,315
Latin America	174,742	179,739	148,055
Europe and Africa	276,279	248,802	278,707
Canada and Pacific	187,389	151,444	126,844
Total	1,055,952	917,507	832,921
Other income, net of other deductions	(50,089)	(37,671)	(37,893)
General expenses	(73,872)	(72,582)	(58,301)
Income from continuing operations before income taxes	$ 931,991	$ 807,254	$ 736,727
Identifiable assets at year-end:*			
United States and Puerto Rico	$3,008,701	$1,631,123	$1,604,490
Latin America	435,879	436,215	420,197
Europe and Africa	582,037	583,017	579,851
Canada and Pacific	420,502	400,766	360,838
Total	4,447,119	3,051,121	2,965,376
Corporate assets (principally marketable securities, investments and fixed assets)	476,191	452,693	289,202
Discontinued operations	—	60,967	151,380
Total	$4,923,310	$3,564,781	$3,405,958

*Amounts for 1980 have been restated to reflect the sale of the Company's Aqua-Chem, Inc., subsidiary and Tenco Division.

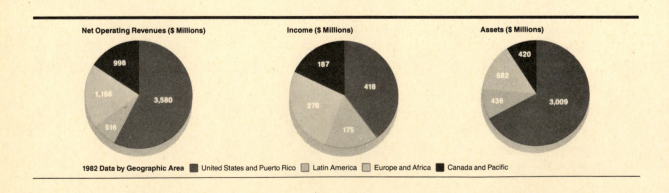

Net Operating Revenues ($ Millions)   **Income ($ Millions)**   **Assets ($ Millions)**

1982 Data by Geographic Area ■ United States and Puerto Rico ■ Latin America ■ Europe and Africa ■ Canada and Pacific

Board of Directors and Shareholders
The Coca-Cola Company
Atlanta, Georgia

We have examined the consolidated balance sheets of The Coca-Cola Company and subsidiaries as of December 31, 1982 and 1981, and the related consolidated statements of income, shareholders' equity and changes in financial position for each of the three years in the period ended December 31, 1982. Our examinations were made in accordance with generally accepted auditing standards and, accordingly, included such tests of the accounting records and such other auditing procedures as we considered necessary in the circumstances.

In our opinion, the financial statements referred to above present fairly the consolidated financial position of The Coca-Cola Company and subsidiaries at December 31, 1982 and 1981, and the consolidated results of their operations and the changes in their financial position for each of the three years in the period ended December 31, 1982, in conformity with generally accepted accounting principles consistently applied during the period except for the change in 1982, with which we concur, in the method of accounting for foreign currency translation as described in Note 1 to the consolidated financial statements.

Atlanta, Georgia
February 14, 1983

Ernst & Whinney

Report of Management

Management is responsible for the preparation and integrity of the consolidated financial statements appearing in this Annual Report. The financial statements were prepared in conformity with generally accepted accounting principles appropriate in the circumstances and, accordingly, include some amounts based on management's best judgments and estimates. Other financial information in this Annual Report is consistent with that in the financial statements.

Management is responsible for maintaining a system of internal accounting controls and procedures to provide reasonable assurance, at an appropriate cost/benefit relationship, that assets are safeguarded and that transactions are authorized, recorded and reported properly. The internal accounting control system is augmented by a program of internal audits and appropriate reviews by management, written policies and guidelines, careful selection and training of qualified personnel and a written Code of Business Conduct adopted by the Board of Directors, applicable to all employees of the Company and its subsidiaries. Management believes that the Company's internal accounting controls provide reasonable assurance that assets are safeguarded against material loss from unauthorized use or disposition and that the financial records are reliable for preparing financial statements and other data and maintaining accountability for assets.

The Audit Committee of the Board of Directors, composed solely of Directors who are not officers of the Company, meets with the independent accountants, management and internal auditors periodically to discuss internal accounting controls, auditing and financial reporting matters. The Committee reviews with the independent accountants the scope and results of the audit effort. The Committee also meets with the independent accountants without management present to ensure that the independent accountants have free access to the Committee.

The independent accountants, Ernst & Whinney, are recommended by the Audit Committee of the Board of Directors, selected by the Board of Directors and ratified by the shareholders. Ernst & Whinney are engaged to examine the financial statements of The Coca-Cola Company and subsidiaries and conduct such tests and related procedures as they deem necessary in conformity with generally accepted auditing standards. The opinion of the independent accountants, based upon their examination of the consolidated financial statements, is contained in this Annual Report.

Roberto C. Goizueta
Chairman, Board of Directors,
and Chief Executive Officer

Sam Ayoub
Senior Executive Vice President
and Chief Financial Officer

February 14, 1983

Quarterly Results of Operations
(In thousands except per share data)

	Net Operating Revenues		Gross Profit	
	1982	1981	**1982**	1981
First quarter	**$1,271,289**	$1,346,462	**$ 589,071**	$ 584,925
Second quarter	**1,567,851**	1,600,247	**727,885**	701,879
Third quarter	**1,745,157**	1,529,810	**747,365**	661,166
Fourth quarter	**1,665,421**	1,412,516	**731,904**	633,491
	$6,249,718	$5,889,035	**$2,796,225**	$2,581,461

	Income From Continuing Operations		Net Income	
	1982	1981	**1982**	1981
First quarter	**$ 107,616**	$ 97,633	**$ 107,616**	$ 100,097
Second quarter	**139,821**	126,992	**139,821**	128,876
Third quarter	**143,463**	116,219	**143,463**	146,581
Fourth quarter	**121,332**	106,226	**121,332**	106,228
	$ 512,232	$ 447,070	**$ 512,232**	$ 481,782

	Income Per Share From Continuing Operations		Net Income Per Share	
	1982	1981	**1982**	1981
First quarter	**$ .87**	$ .79	**$ .87**	$ .81
Second quarter	**1.13**	1.03	**1.13**	1.04
Third quarter	**1.06**	.94	**1.06**	1.19
Fourth quarter	**.89**	.86	**.89**	.86
	$ 3.95	$ 3.62	**$ 3.95**	$ 3.90

Net operating revenues and gross profit for the first three quarters of 1981 have been restated to reflect the sale of the Company's Aqua-Chem, Inc., subsidiary and Tenco Division.

General. The following unaudited disclosures were prepared in accordance with Statement Nos. 33 and 70 issued by the Financial Accounting Standards Board and are intended to quantify the impact of inflation on earnings and production facilities. The inflation-adjusted data is presented under the specific price changes method (current cost). Only those items most affected by inflation have been adjusted; i.e., inventories, property, plant and equipment, the related costs of goods and services sold and depreciation and amortization expense. Although the resulting measurements cannot be used as precise indicators of the effects of inflation, they do provide an indication of the effect of increases in specific prices of the Company's inventories and properties.

The adjustments for specific price changes involve a substantial number of judgments as well as the use of various estimating techniques employed to control the cost of accumulating the data. The data reported should not be thought of as precise measurements of the assets and expenses involved, or of the amount at which the assets could be sold. Rather, they represent reasonable approximations of the price changes that have occurred in the business environment in which the Company operates.

Inflation-adjusted data based on the constant dollar method is not presented because a significant part of the Company's operations is in foreign locations whose functional currency is not the U.S. dollar.

A brief explanation of the current cost method is presented below.

Current Cost. The current cost method attempts to measure the effect of increases in the specific prices of the Company's inventories and properties. It is intended to estimate what it would cost in 1982 dollars to replace the Company's inventories and existing properties.

Under this method, cost of goods sold valued on the average method is adjusted to reflect the current cost of inventories at the date of sale. That portion of cost of goods sold valued on the LIFO method approximates the current cost of inventory at the date of sale and generally remains unchanged from the amounts presented in the primary financial statements.

Current cost depreciation expense is based on the average current cost of properties in the year. The depreciation methods, salvage values and useful lives are the

Statement of Income Adjusted for Changing Prices
(In millions except per share data)

Year Ended December 31, 1982	As Reported in the Primary Statements	Adjusted for Changes in Specific Prices (Current Costs)
Net operating revenues	$6,249.7	$6,249.7
Cost of goods and services (excluding depreciation)	3,386.8	3,412.0
Depreciation and amortization	156.9	235.4
Other operating expenses	1,817.6	1,817.6
Net of other (income) and deductions	(43.6)	(41.3)
Income from continuing operations before income taxes	932.0	826.0
Income taxes	419.8	419.8
Income from continuing operations	$ 512.2	$ 406.2
Income per share from continuing operations	$ 3.95	$ 3.13
Effective income tax rate	45.0%	50.8%
Purchasing power gain from holding net monetary liabilities in the year		$ 17.7
Increase in specific prices of inventories and property, plant and equipment held in the year		$ 261.8
Less effect of increase in general price level		147.2
Increase in specific prices over increase in the general price level		$ 114.6
Estimated translation adjustment		$ (300.0)
Inventory and film costs	$1,020.3	$1,109.7
Property, plant and equipment—net	$1,538.5	$2,342.8

A significant part of the Company's operations are measured in functional currencies other than the U.S. dollar. Adjustments to reflect the effects of general inflation were determined on the translate-restate method using the U.S. CPI(U).

same as those used in the primary statements.

The current cost of finished products inventory was approximated by adjusting historical amounts to reflect current costs for material, labor and overhead expenses as well as current cost depreciation, where applicable. The current cost for inventories other than finished products was determined on the basis of price lists or appropriate supplier quotations and by other managerial estimates consistent with established purchasing and production procedures.

Since motion picture films are the result of a unique blending of the artistic talents of many individuals and are produced under widely varying circumstances, it is not feasible to develop the current cost of film inventories, particularly since the Company would rarely, if ever, attempt to duplicate an existing film property. As a result, film inventories have been valued based on studies conducted to determine their fair value in connection with the purchase price allocation process.

Direct supplier quotations, published price lists, engineering estimates, construction quotations, appraisals, published and internally developed indexes were the methods used to determine the current cost of property, plant and equipment.

Under current cost accounting, increases in specific prices (current cost) of inventories and properties held during the year are not included in income from continuing operations.

Income Taxes. Taxes on income included in the supplementary statement of income are the same as reported in the primary financial statements. In most countries, present tax laws do not allow deductions for the effects of inflation. Thus, taxes are levied on the Company at rates which, in real terms, exceed established statutory rates.

Purchasing Power Gain. During periods of inflation, monetary assets, such as cash, marketable securities and accounts receivable, lose purchasing power since they will buy fewer goods when the general price level increases. The holding of monetary liabilities, such as accounts payable, accruals and debt, results in a gain of purchasing power because cheaper dollars will be used to repay the obligations. The Company has benefited from a net monetary liability position in recent years, resulting in a net gain in purchasing power. This gain does not represent an increase in funds available for distribution to shareholders and does not necessarily imply that incurring more debt would be beneficial to the Company.

Increase in Specific Prices. Shown separately are the total changes in current costs for inventories and properties, that component of the total change due to general inflation and that component of the change attributable to fluctuations in exchange rates.

Five-Year Comparison of Selected Supplemental Financial Data Adjusted for Effects of Changing Prices (In Average 1982 Dollars)
(In millions except per share data)

Year Ended December 31,	1982	1981	1980	1979	1978
Net operating revenues	**$6,249.7**	$6,258.6	$6,595.5	$6,245.9	$6,069.6
Current cost information:					
Income from continuing operations	**406.2**	372.7	310.7	369.0	
Income per share from continuing operations	**3.13**	3.02	2.51	2.99	
Increase in specific prices over (under) increase in the general price level, including translation adjustments	**(185.4)**	(220.0)	25.9	213.8	
Net assets at year-end	**3,622.8**	3,334.2	3,733.3	3,768.4	
Purchasing power gain on net monetary items	**17.7**	26.0	50.6	27.6	
Cash dividends declared per share:					
As reported	**2.48**	2.32	2.16	1.96	1.74
Adjusted for general inflation	**2.48**	2.47	2.53	2.61	2.58
Market price per common share at year-end:					
Historical amount	**52.00**	34.75	33.375	34.50	43.875
Adjusted for general inflation	**52.00**	36.93	39.16	45.96	65.03
Average Consumer Price Index—Urban	**289.6**	272.5	246.8	217.4	195.4

Review of Financial Accounting Theory

This section will review some important accounting principles. Recall that Chapter 1 described accounting as an information system that measures, processes, and communicates economic information about an identifiable entity. This system helps users make informed decisions. Accounting is thus a link between economic activities and the decision maker. This is illustrated in Figure 1–2 in the textbook, and the diagram presented here (Figure A) expands on it. This diagram will serve as the focal point for a review of financial accounting theory.

Figure A
The Role of Financial Accounting

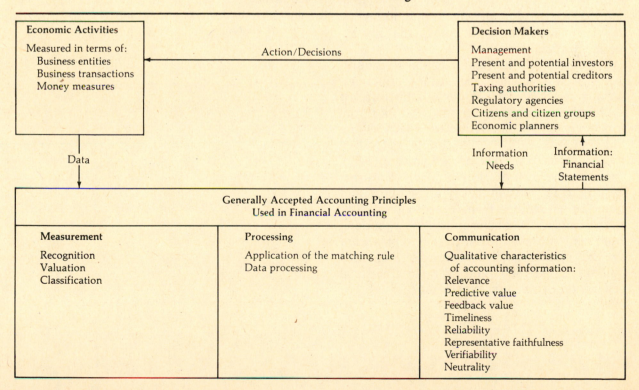

Economic Activities		Decision Makers

Measured in terms of:
  Business entities
  Business transactions
  Money measures
	← Action/Decisions	Management
		Present and potential investors
		Present and potential creditors
		Taxing authorities
		Regulatory agencies
		Citizens and citizen groups
		Economic planners

Data → → Information Needs → Information: Financial Statements

Generally Accepted Accounting Principles Used in Financial Accounting

Measurement	Processing	Communication
Recognition Valuation Classification	Application of the matching rule Data processing	Qualitative characteristics of accounting information: Relevance Predictive value Feedback value Timeliness Reliability Representative faithfulness Verifiability Neutrality

The goal of financial accounting is to give a fair picture of the real world as a basis for action by decision makers. Of course the information that the accountant communicates is not perfect and cannot be, but it does increase the probability that the decision maker will reach the right decision. This end is accomplished in several ways.

Generally Accepted Accounting Principles (GAAP)

Chapter 1 described generally accepted accounting principles (GAAP) as the conventions, rules, and procedures necessary to define accounting practice at a given point in time. These principles are not natural laws, such as the laws of motion in physics, but represent practices that developed because of their usefulness. Historically, accounting principles evolved from changes in business practices and in the economic, social, and legal environment. Because of their usefulness or practical value to a large number of businesses, they were said to have *authoritative support*. The words *generally accepted* in the GAAP name imply widespread support from the business community. More recently, however, authoritative support has increasingly come from official and unofficial pronouncements of many accounting, business, and government organizations.

As pointed out in Chapter 1, many accounting groups influence accounting principles. Among them are the American Institute of Certified Public Accountants (AICPA), the American Accounting Association (AAA), the National Association of Accountants (NAA), and the Financial Executives Institute (FEI). Each of these organizations publishes a journal relating to accounting theory and practice and issues other studies from time to time. The international side of accounting is becoming more and more important. It is represented by the International Accounting Standards Committee (IASC) and the International Federation of Accountants (IFAC).

These organizations (especially the AAA and AICPA) have tried to formulate broad statements of accounting theory. However, the practice of accounting has remained fragmented and inconsistent. A major cause of this problem is that the most influential (authoritative) bodies approach accounting on an issue-by-issue, topic-by-topic basis. These bodies (summarized in Table A) are the Financial Accounting Standards Board (FASB) and its predecessors, the Accounting Principles Board (APB) and the Committee on Accounting Research, and the Securities and Exchange Commission (SEC). To understand the basis for their approach, we should briefly look at the authority and procedures of the FASB.

Financial Accounting Standards Board

The FASB was established on June 30, 1972, as a replacement for the Accounting Principles Board. It is an independent nongovernmental body whose purpose is to develop and issue standards of financial accounting. Its establishment was the result of a recommendation by an AICPA study group, headed by former SEC commissioner Frances M. Wheat. This group examined the organization of the Accounting Principles Board and pinpointed changes that were necessary to get better results faster.

Table A
Authoritative Accounting Pronouncements

Type of Pronouncement	Issuing Body (Dates Active)	Description
Accounting Research Bulletins (ARBs)	AICPA Committee on Accounting Procedures (1939–1959)	Issued 51 ARBs dealing with many specific topics. ARB 43, issued in 1953, was a codification of the first 42 ARBs. This committee was replaced by the APB.
APB Opinions (APBs)	AICPA Accounting Principles Board (1959–1972)	Issued 31 APBs similar in scope to the ARBs. This board was replaced by the FASB.
Statements of Financial Accounting Standards (SFASs)	Financial Accounting Standards Board (1972–)	More than 80 SFASs issued to date. Similar in scope to ARBs and APBs. Usually amend or supersede existing pronouncements or establish GAAP in new areas.
FASB Interpretations	Financial Accounting Standards Board (1972–)	More than 50 issued to date. Purpose is to interpret existing pronouncements and usually deal with a very narrow area in comparison to SFACs.
Accounting Series Releases	Securities and Exchange Commission (1934–)	More than 300 ASRs issued to date. ASRs are codified in Regulation S–X. In recent years, emphasis on disclosure issues such as disclosure of replacement costs.

The seven-member FASB replaced the eighteen-member APB. All members of the APB served part time, without pay, and were members of the AICPA. They were allowed to continue their affiliations with their firms or institutions. One criticism of the APB was that it was not independent of the AICPA and, in particular, the large accounting firms. The FASB, therefore, was organized so as to remove this potential conflict of interest and to include other parties who have an interest in financial statements. Only four of the members of the FASB are required to be CPAs. The other three members may be business executives, financial analysts, accounting educators, or others. All members must resign from their firm or institution and serve full time, and they receive pay. The FASB is governed by a nine-member Financial Accounting Foundation and advised by a Financial Accounting Standards Advisory Council. An illustration of how the FASB develops a financial accounting standard is given in the accompanying diagram (Figure B).

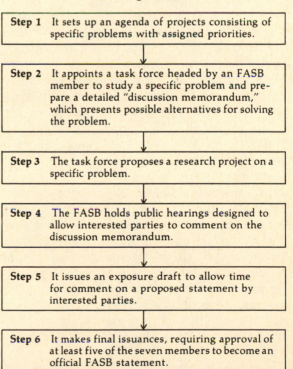

Figure B
How Does the FASB Develop a Financial Accounting Standard?

Step 1 It sets up an agenda of projects consisting of specific problems with assigned priorities.

Step 2 It appoints a task force headed by an FASB member to study a specific problem and prepare a detailed "discussion memorandum," which presents possible alternatives for solving the problem.

Step 3 The task force proposes a research project on a specific problem.

Step 4 The FASB holds public hearings designed to allow interested parties to comment on the discussion memorandum.

Step 5 It issues an exposure draft to allow time for comment on a proposed statement by interested parties.

Step 6 It makes final issuances, requiring approval of at least five of the seven members to become an official FASB statement.

The thrust of all these developments is to counter criticism of the accounting profession. Criticism of the FASB has continued, however, especially from certain members of the U.S. Congress. These legislators have proposed that the Securities and Exchange Commission, which has been active in accounting matters, become more active in dictating accounting principles. For companies reporting to the SEC—that is, most large companies and many smaller ones—the SEC presently has the power to dictate accounting principles through its Accounting Series Releases. In most matters, though, it has left decisions up to the FASB and its predecessors. The AICPA, FASB, and other accounting bodies are trying to make changes that will prevent congressional action. So there will likely be more changes in the way in which accounting principles are issued in the near future.

Financial Statements

The decision makers served by financial accounting are a diverse group. Some of them can demand special information. For instance, management can ask for a special analysis, taxing authorities require tax returns, and regulatory agencies need special reports. However, to meet the needs of most decision makers, the FASB in its *Statement of Financial Accounting Concepts No. 1* has identified three objectives for financial reporting: a) to furnish information that is useful for investment and credit decisions; b) to provide information useful in assessing cash flow prospects; and c) to provide information about business resources, claims to resources, and changes in them. To meet these goals, accountants have developed four general-purpose financial statements—the balance sheet, the income statement, the statement of owner's equity, and the statement of changes in financial position. Financial accounting is concerned with the content of these statements. The content is determined by generally accepted accounting principles related to the measurement of business or economic activities, the application of the matching rule, and communication in accordance with the standards for information.

The FASB has classified the content of financial statements in *Statement of Financial Accounting Concepts No. 3*. There are ten interrelated elements or building blocks that go into financial statements:

1. **Assets** Probable future economic benefits obtained or controlled by a particular entity as a result of past transactions or events.
2. **Liabilities** Probable future sacrifices of economic benefits arising from present obligations of a particular entity to transfer assets or provide services to other entities in the future as a result of past transactions or events.
3. **Equity** The residual interest in the assets of an entity that remains after deducting its liabilities. In a business enterprise, the equity is the ownership interest.
4. **Investments by Owners** Increases in net assets of a particular enterprise resulting from transfers to it from other entities of something of value to obtain or increase ownership interests (or equity) in it. Assets are most commonly received as investments by owners, but that which is received may also include services or satisfaction or conversion of liabilities of the enterprise.
5. **Distributions to Owners** Decreases in net assets of a particular enterprise resulting from transferring assets, rendering services, or incurring liabilities by the enterprise to owners. Distributions to owners decrease ownership interests (or equity) in an enterprise.
6. **Comprehensive Income** The change in equity (net assets) of an entity during a period from transactions and other events and circumstances from nonowner sources. It includes all changes in equity during a period except those resulting from investments by owners and distributions to owners.
7. **Revenues** Inflows or other enhancements of assets of an entity, or settlements of its liabilities (or a combination of both) during a period from delivering or producing goods, rendering services, or other activities that constitute the entity's ongoing major or central operations.
8. **Expenses** Outflows or other using up of assets or incurrences of liabilities (or a combination of both) during a period from delivering or producing services, or

carrying out other activities that constitute the entity's ongoing major or central operations.

9. **Gains** Increases in equity (net assets) from peripheral or incidental transactions of an entity and from all other transactions and other events and circumstances affecting the entity during a period except those that result from revenues or investments by owners.

10. **Losses** Decreases in equity (net assets) from peripheral or incidental transactions of an entity and from all other transactions and other events and circumstances affecting the entity during a period except those that result from expenses or distributions to owners.

Economic Activities

In a study of the many kinds of business activities in our society, the question of what to measure is not an easy one. This problem is solved in accounting by focusing on three attributes of economic activity:

1. **Specific business entity** A business is treated as an entity that is separate and distinct from its owners, creditors, and other businesses. The types of business entities are sole proprietorships, partnerships, and corporations.
2. **Business transactions** Economic events that affect the financial position of the business entity are measured.
3. **Money measures** The basic measuring unit for accounting measures is the monetary unit.

In other words, accounting measures business transactions of specific business entities in terms of money.

Measurement

Deciding on the objects to be measured does not solve all the problems of accounting measurement. Also to be answered are the questions of when to measure, what value to place on the measure, and how to classify the measurement. In the most general terms, these questions are answered as follows:

1. **Recognition** Revenues are recognized when sales are made, goods are delivered, or services performed. Expenses are recognized when they are used to produce revenue.
2. **Valuation** Most accounting measures are valued at historical cost.
3. **Classification** Transaction components are classified in accordance with a chart of accounts.

In this course, these questions have been answered in a straightforward way to introduce you to the basic nature of accounting. However, they are by no means settled issues in the accounting profession, nor have they been solved to the satisfaction of all accountants. For instance, in FASB Statement No. 33, the FASB has mandated experimentation in the valuation area by requiring certain large companies to provide supplementary information based on constant dollar accounting and current cost accounting.

Processing

One part of processing is keeping up a system of accounts and data processing, as described in text Chapters 6 and 7. Another part is the application of the matching rule. The matching rule is necessary in measuring the progress of a business from one point in time to another. It is perhaps the single most important concept in financial accounting because most decision makers need to know how well they have succeeded in meeting their income objectives. The matching rule, as stated in Chapter 4, is as follows: "Revenues must be assigned to the accounting period in which the goods were sold or the services performed, and expenses must be assigned to the accounting period in which they were used to produce revenue." However, to apply this rule properly, two additional concepts are needed:

1. **Periodicity assumption** Measurements identified with short periods of time are based on estimates and are necessarily tentative.
2. **Continuity (going-concern) assumption** Without evidence to the contrary, the business entity must be assumed to continue to operate for an indefinite period of time.

Much of this course was devoted to the application of the matching rule to various aspects of accounting. For instance, the matching rule was applied to adjusting entries (Chapter 4); to merchandising concerns (Chapter 6); to accounting for estimated uncollectible accounts and other receivables problems (Chapter 10); to inventory accounting (Chapter 11); to depreciation, depletion, and amortization of long-term assets (Chapters 13 and 14); to current liabilities (Chapter 12); and to long-term liabilities (Chapter 18).

Communication

Successful communication involves a meeting of the minds between the accountant and the decision maker. The accountant must understand the needs of the decision maker, and the decision maker must understand the financial statements prepared by the accountant. For this understanding to occur, accounting information, according to *Statement of Financial Accounting Concepts No. 2* of the Financial Accounting Standards Board, must possess certain qualitative characteristics, which might also be thought of as standards of information. These characteristics, which were described in more detail in Chapter 9, are as follows:

1. **Relevance** The information provided must bear on the economic decision.
2. **Predictive value** The information provided must be useful in making predictions.
3. **Feedback value** The information provided must tell something about the accuracy of earlier expectations.
4. **Timeliness** The information must be received in time to make a difference.

5. **Reliability** The information must have representative faithfulness, verifiability, and neutrality.
6. **Representative faithfulness** The information must correspond with what it purports to represent.
7. **Verifiability** The information must be capable of being confirmed or duplicated by independent parties.
8. **Neutrality** The information provided should not be geared toward a particular interest.

Communication is also aided by certain conventions that accountants follow in preparing the financial statements. These conventions are:

1. **Comparability and consistency** The information is presented in such a way that the decision maker can recognize similarities, differences, and trends. In addition, a particular accounting procedure, once adopted, is not changed from period to period.
2. **Materiality** Items or events that would affect a decision maker's actions are reflected in the financial statements.
3. **Conservatism** When faced with major uncertainties as to which accounting procedure is to be used, the one that is least likely to overstate assets and income is chosen.
4. **Full disclosure** All information relevant to the decision maker's use of the financial statement is presented.
5. **Cost/Benefit** The cost of providing information should not be more than the benefits it gives the decision maker.

Answers

Chapter 1

Matching

1. m	**6.** d	**11.** i	**16.** a
2. c	**7.** g	**12.** k	**17.** j
3. q	**8.** o	**13.** b	
4. h	**9.** p	**14.** f	
5. l	**10.** n	**15.** e	

Completion

1. Management accounting, public accounting, nonprofit accounting, accounting instruction
2. Set a goal, consider alternatives, make the decision, take action, evaluate the results
3. Bookkeeping deals only with the mechanical and repetitive record-keeping process. Accounting involves bookkeeping as well as the design of an accounting system, its use, and the analysis of its output.
4. Auditing, tax services, management advisory services
5. Management, financially interested outsiders, government and citizen groups
6. To earn a satisfactory profit to hold investor capital; to maintain sufficient funds to pay debts as they fall due

True-False

1. T
2. F A corporation is managed by its board of directors.
3. F Internal auditing is a function of management accounting.
4. F The auditor's opinion indicates whether a company's financial statements are accurate and fair, not whether the company is a good investment.
5. T
6. T

7. T
8. F The attest function is carried out by an auditor.
9. F The FASB is an independent body.
10. T
11. F Accounting has changed enormously in recent years.
12. T
13. T
14. T

Multiple-Choice

1. b	**3.** d	**5.** b	**7.** d
2. c	**4.** a	**6.** c	**8.** a

Exercises

1. a. Potential investors need all recent financial statements to assess the future profitability of a company and thus whether they should invest in it.
   b. The principal goal of the SEC is to protect the public. Insisting that Lindlay make its statements public as well as examining the statements for propriety will certainly aid the public in making decisions regarding Lindlay.
   c. The bank will have difficulty in determining Lindlay's ability to repay the loan if it does not have access to Lindlay's most recent financial statements.
   d. Present stockholders will wish to see the statements in order to decide whether to sell, maintain, or increase their investment.
   e. Management will want to see the statements because the statements should help them pinpoint the weaknesses that caused the year's loss.

Chapter 2

Matching

1. h	6. c	11. j
2. m	7. l	12. e
3. b	8. i	13. d
4. k	9. a	
5. f	10. g	

Completion

1. a. Balance sheet
   b. Income statement
   c. Statement of Changes in Financial Position
   d. Statement of Owner's Equity
2. Alpha Company
   Income Statement
   For the Year Ended June 30, 19xx
3. All of the following are acceptable forms of the balance sheet equation:
   assets = liabilities + owner's equity
   assets – liabilities = owner's equity
   assets – owner's equity = liabilities

a. Shows financial position at point in time
b. Measures net income during a certain period
c. Discloses financing and investing activities during the period
d. Shows how owner's capital changed during the period.

True-False

1. T
2. F Balance sheets do not include revenues and expenses.
3. T
4. T
5. T
6. F Assets *minus* liabilities equals owner's equity.
7. F The balance sheet equation must always be in balance.
8. T
9. T
10. F Cash will increase, but Accounts Receivable will decrease.
11. T
12. F It indicates that they have one or more *debtors*.
13. T
14. F The measurement stage refers to the recording of business transactions.
15. F Withdrawals appear as a deduction in the statement of owner's equity.

Multiple-Choice

1. d	3. d	5. d	7. a
2. a	4. b	6. c	8. d

Exercises

1. $35,000

2.

Acme TV Repair
Balance Sheet
December 31, 19xx

Assets

Cash	$ 950
Accounts Receivable	1,500
Equipment	850
Land	1,000
Building	10,000
Truck	4,500
	$18,800

Liabilities

Accounts Payable	$ 1,300

Owner's Equity

Roger Sands, Capital	17,500
	$18,800

3.

Trans-action	Assets				Liabilities	Owner's Equity
	Cash	Accounts Receiv.	Supplies and Equipment	Trucks	Accounts Payable	Pat Sanet, Capital
a	+$20,000					+$20,000
b	–650		+650			
c				+5,200	+5,200	
d	+525					+525
e	–2,600				–2,600	
f		+150				+150
g	–250					–250
h	+150	–150				
i		+20	–20			
j	–1,000					–1,000
Balance, at end of month	$16,175	$20	$630	$5,200	$2,600	$19,425

SOLUTION TO CROSSWORD PUZZLE

(Chapters 1 and 2)

```
 C   W I T H D R A W A L S
 A P B           U       
 A         P     D     C 
 A S S E T S   C R E D I T O R
       E   O     T     R 
 B A L A N C E   F   A I C P A
 O   I     I       N     O 
 K   A C C O U N T I N G   R 
 K   B     A       T A X T 
 K   I   E B             T 
 E   L I Q U I D I T Y   M I S
 E   I   U   L           O 
 P   T   I   I           N 
 E   Y   T E N T I T Y     
 R       Y   Y             
```

Chapter 3

Matching

1. k	**6.** g	**11.** j	**16.** h
2. f	**7.** a	**12.** r	**17.** c
3. q	**8.** m	**13.** e	**18.** i
4. o	**9.** l	**14.** n	
5. b	**10.** d	**15.** p	

Completion

1. Journalize transactions, post journal entries to the ledger accounts, prepare a trial balance
2. **a.** July 14
   b. $150
   c. Cash and Accounts Receivable
3. Two examples are the purchase of any asset for cash and collection on an account receivable.
4. One example is the payment of an account payable.

True-False

1. F A sale should be recorded when it takes place.
2. T
3. T
4. F The credit side of an account does not imply anything favorable or unfavorable.
5. F Only those accounts with zero balances will have equal debits and credits.
6. F One quickly determines cash on hand by referring to the ledger.
7. T
8. F Notes Payable is the proper account title; the liability is evidenced by the existence of a promissory note.
9. T
10. T
11. F It is possible to have all increases or all decreases in a journal entry.
12. F Both the debit and the credit of the entry would be missing. Therefore the trial balance would be incomplete, but it would nevertheless be in balance.
13. F Journal entries are made before they are posted to the ledger.
14. F Liabilities and owner's equity accounts are indented only when credited.
15. T
16. T
17. T

Multiple-Choice

1. c	**4.** d	**6.** b	**8.** b
2. d	**5.** c	**7.** a	**9.** a
3. c			

Exercises

1.

		General Journal		
Date		Description	Debit	Credit
May	2	Cash	28,000	
		Joe Romano, Capital		28,000
		To record the owner's original investment		
	3	Prepaid Rent	900	
		Cash		900
		Paid 3 months' rent in advance		
	5	Printing Press	10,000	
		Photographic Equipment	3,000	
		Cash		2,000
		Accounts Payable		11,000
		Purchased a press and equipment from Irvin Press, Inc.		
	8	No Entry		
	9	Cash	1,200	
		Unearned Revenue		1,200
		Received payment in advance from Doherty's Department Store for brochures to be printed		
	11	Printing Supplies	800	
		Notes Payable		800
		Purchased paper from Pulp Supply Co.		
	14	Cash	250	
		Accounts Receivable	250	
		Revenue from Services		500
		Completed job for Sullivan Shoes		
	14	Salaries Expense	200	
		Cash		200
		Paid the pressman his weekly salary		
	15	Accounts Payable	1,000	
		Cash		1,000
		Payment on account owed to Irwin Press, Inc.		
	18	Cash	250	
		Accounts Receivable		250
		Sullivan Shoes paid its debt in full		
	20	Joe Romano, Withdrawals	700	
		Cash		700
		Mr. Romano withdrew $700 for personal uses		
	24	Utilities Expense	45	
		Accounts Payable		45
		To record electric bill		
	30	Accounts Payable	45	
		Cash		45
		To record payment of electric bill		

2. **a.** $1,750 debit balance
   b. $1,000 credit balance
   c. $14,600 debit balance

3.

General Journal					Page 7
Date		Description	Post. Ref.	Debit	Credit
Apr.	3	Cash	11	1,000	
		Revenue from Services	41		1,000
		Received payment from Malden Company			
	5	Accounts Payable	21	300	
		Cash	11		300
		Paid Douglas Supply Company for supplies			
		purchased on March 31 on credit			

Cash							Account No. 11
Date		Item	Post. Ref.	Debit	Credit	Balance Debit	Balance Credit
Apr.	3		7	1,000		1,000	
	5		7		300	700	

Accounts Payable							Account No. 21
Date		Item	Post. Ref.	Debit	Credit	Balance* Debit	Balance* Credit
Apr.	5		7	300		300	

Revenue from Services							Account No. 41
Date		Item	Post. Ref.	Debit	Credit	Balance Debit	Balance Credit
Apr.	3		7		1,000		1,000

*Previous postings have been omitted, resulting in an improbable debit balance in Accounts Payable.

Chapter 4

Matching

1. i	6. q	11. a	16. j
2. d	7. f	12. h	17. b
3. n	8. k	13. m	18. g
4. r	9. e	14. p	19. t
5. c	10. o	15. l	20. s

Completion

1. Dividing recorded expenses among two or more accounting periods; dividing recorded revenues among two or more accounting periods; recording unrecorded expenses; recording unrecorded revenues.
2. The matching rule means that revenues should be recorded in the period in which they are earned, and that all expenses related to those revenues should also be recorded in that period.
3. Depreciation is the allocation of the cost of a long-lived asset to the periods benefitting from the asset.
4. Prepaid expenses are expenses paid for in advance; they are initially recorded as assets. Unearned revenues represent payment received in advance of providing goods or services; it is initially recorded as a liability.

True-False

1. T
2. T
3. F A calendar year lasts specifically from January 1 to December 31.
4. T
5. F Under accrual accounting, the timing of cash exchanges is irrelevant in recording revenues and expenses.
6. F Adjusting entries are made before the financial statements are prepared.
7. T
8. F It would be debited for the amount available during the period less ending inventory.
9. F Accumulated Depreciation (a contra account) will have a credit balance, even though it appears on the left side of the balance sheet.
10. T
11. F Unearned Revenues is a liability account.
12. F The credit is to Accounts Payable.
13. T
14. F If payment has not yet been received, the debit is to Accounts Receivable.
15. T
16. T
17. T

Multiple-Choice

1. c	3. b	5. c	7. a
2. b	4. a	6. d	8. d

Exercises

1.

Gotham Bus Company
Balance Sheet
December 31, 19x3

Assets

Cash		$ 5,000
Accounts Receivable		3,000
Company Vehicles	$24,000	
Less Accumulated		
Depreciation	9,000	15,000
Total Assets		$23,000

2. a. $970
b. $1,750
c. $450

3.

		General Journal		
Date*		**Description**	**Debit**	**Credit**
a.		Supplies Expense	125	
		Supplies		125
		To record supplies consumed during the period		
b.		Wages Expense	2,000	
		Wages payable		2,000
		To record accrued wages		
c.		Unearned Revenues	600	
		Revenues from Services		600
		To record earned revenues		
d.		Depreciation Expense, Building	4,500	
		Accumulated Depreciation, Building		4,500
		To record depreciation on building		
e.		Advertising Expense	2,000	
		Prepaid Advertising		2,000
		To record advertising used up during the year		
f.		Insurance Expense	250	
		Prepaid Insurance		250
		To record insurance expired during the year		
g.		Accounts Receivable	2,200	
		Revenues from Services		2,200
		To record revenues earned for which payment has not been received		
h.		Interest Expense	52	
		Interest Payable		52
		To record accrued interest on notes payable		

*In reality, all of the adjusting entries would be dated December 31.

SOLUTION TO CROSSWORD PUZZLE

(Chapters 3 and 4)

```
 C O N T R A     I N C O M E
 O       E     W         X
 S   D E F E R R A L   L P
 T       G     R     I
     L E D G E R   E     R
 J   M       S E R V I C E
 O   A   V     A     R
 U   T R I A L B A L A N C E
 R   C   L   C     U D
 N   H   U   C   D E B I T
 A   I   S A L A R Y   S T
 L A N D   T   U     N
 I   G   I   A   N   O
 Z     D O U B L E E N T R Y
 E A R N   N     T   E
```

Chapter 5

Matching

1. d	4. b	7. c	9. e
2. g	5. h	8. a	
3. i	6. f		

Completion

1. Revenue accounts, expense accounts, Income Summary, owner's withdrawals account
2. Trial Balance, Adjustments, Adjusted Trial Balance, Income Statement, Balance Sheet
3. Assets, liabilities, and the owner's capital accounts will appear. Revenue and expense accounts, Income Summary, and the owner's withdrawals account will not appear.
4. The steps should be numbered as follows: 3, 6, 1, 4, 2, 5.

True-False

1. T
2. T
3. T
4. T
5. F Income Summary does not appear in any statement.
6. F Only nominal accounts are closed.
7. T
8. T
9. F When there is a net loss, Income Summary will be credited.
10. F It will not include the owner's withdrawals account, because it will have a zero balance.
11. F The work sheet is never published.
12. F The key letter is in the *Adjustments* column to relate debits and credits of the same entry.
13. T

Multiple-Choice

1. c	3. c	5. a	7. c
2. d	4. a	6. b	8. b

Exercises

1.

		General Journal		
Date		Description	Debit	Credit
July	31	Revenues from Services	4,700	
		Income Summary		4,700
		To close revenue accounts		
	31	Income Summary	700	
		Rent Expense		500
		Telephone Expense		50
		Utilities Expense		150
		To close the expense accounts		
	31	Income Summary	4,000	
		Eleanor Barrett, Capital		4,000
		To close Income Summary account		
	31	Eleanor Barrett, Capital	2,500	
		Eleanor Barrett, Withdrawals		2,500
		To close the withdrawals account		

2.

Barrett's Fix-it Shop
Statement of Owner's Equity
For the Month Ended July 31, 19xx

Eleanor Barrett, Capital, July 1, 19xx	$3,000
Add net income for July	4,000
Subtotal	$7,000
Less withdrawals during July	2,500
Eleanor Barrett, Capital, July 31, 19xx	$4,500

3.

Steve's Outdoor Maintenance Service
Work Sheet
For the Year Ended December 31, 19xx

Account Name	Trial Balance Debit	Trial Balance Credit	Adjustments Debit	Adjustments Credit	Adjusted Trial Balance Debit	Adjusted Trial Balance Credit	Income Statement Debit	Income Statement Credit	Balance Sheet Debit	Balance Sheet Credit
Cash	2,560				2,560				2,560	
Accounts Receivable	880		(e) 50		930				930	
Prepaid Rent	750			(a) 550	200				200	
Lawn Supplies	250			(c) 150	100				100	
Lawn Equipment	10,000				10,000				10,000	
Accum. Deprec. Lawn Equip.		2,000		(b) 1,500		3,500				3,500
Accounts Payable		630				630				630
Unearned Landscaping Fees		300	(f) 120			180				180
Steve Charles, Capital		6,000				6,000				6,000
Steve Charles, Withdrawals	6,050				6,050				6,050	
Grass-Cutting Fees		15,000		(e) 50		15,050		15,050		
Wages Expense	3,300		(d) 280		3,580		3,580			
Gasoline Expense	140				140		140			
	23,930	23,930								
Rent Expense			(a) 550		550		550			
Depreciation Expense			(b) 1,500		1,500		1,500			
Lawn Supplies Expense			(c) 150		150		150			
Landscaping Fees Earned				(f) 120		120		120		
Wages Payable				(d) 280		280				280
			2,650	2,650	25,760	25,760	5,920	15,170	19,840	10,590
Net Income							9,250			9,250
							15,170	15,170	19,840	19,840

4.

		General Journal		
Date		Description	Debit	Credit
Dec.	*1*	Cash	20,000	
		Notes Payable		20,000
		To record 90-day bank note		
	31	Interest Expense	200	
		Interest Payable		200
		To record accrued interest on note		
	31	Income Summary	200	
		Interest Expense		200
		To close interest on note		
Jan.	*1*	Interest Payable	200	
		Interest Expense		200
		To reverse adjusting entry for interest		
Mar.	*1*	Notes Payable	20,000	
		Interest Expense	600	
		Cash		20,600
		To record payment of note plus interest		

Chapter 6

Matching

1. c	5. l	9. i	13. a
2. h	6. k	10. d	14. f
3. j	7. b	11. m	15. p
4. e	8. g	12. o	16. n

Completion

1. Revenues from sales (net sales)
   - Cost of goods sold
   = Gross margin from sales
   - Operating expenses
   = Net income
2. Merchandise inventory, beginning
   + Net purchases
   = Cost of goods available for sale
   - Merchandise inventory, ending
   = Cost of goods sold
3. (Gross) purchases
   - Purchases returns and allowances
   - Purchases discounts
   = Subtotal
   + Freight in
   = Net purchases

4. Gross sales
   - Sales returns and allowances
   - Sales discounts
   = Revenues from sales (net sales)
5. Income Summary is debited and Merchandise Inventory credited for the beginning balance. Merchandise Inventory is debited and Income Summary credited for the ending balance. Both entries are treated as adjusting entries, independent of the closing entries.

True-False

1. F It will result in an understated net income.
2. F It means that payment is due 10 days after the end of the month.
3. T
4. F The dealer is more likely to use the perpetual inventory method.
5. T
6. T
7. T
8. T
9. T
10. T
11. T
12. F It is closed with a debit.
13. F It normally has a debit balance.
14. F It requires a debit to Office Supplies, because it is not merchandise.
15. T
16. T
17. F Both are done at the end of the period.

Multiple-Choice

1. d	3. d	5. b	7. c
2. c	4. c	6. d	

Exercises

1.

		General Journal		
Date		Description	Debit	Credit
May	*1*	Purchases	500	
		Accounts Payable		500
		Purchased merchandise on credit, terms 2/10, n/60		
	3	Accounts Receivable	500	
		Sales		500
		Sold merchandise on credit, terms 2/10, 1/20, n/30		
	4	Freight In	42	
		Cash		42
		Paid for freight charges		
	5	Office Supplies	100	
		Accounts Payable		100
		Purchased office supplies on credit		
	6	Accounts Payable	20	
		Office Supplies		20
		Returned office supplies of May 5 purchase		
	7	Accounts Payable	50	
		Purchases Returns and Allowances		50
		Returned merchandise from May 1 purchase		
	9	Accounts Receivable	225	
		Sales		225
		Sold merchandise on credit, terms 2/10, 1/15, n/30		
	10	Accounts Payable	450	
		Purchases Discounts		9
		Cash		441
		Paid for purchase of May 1		
	14	Sales Returns and Allowances	25	
		Accounts Receivable		25
		The customer of May 9 returned merchandise		
	22	Cash	198	
		Sales Discounts	2	
		Accounts Receivable		200
		The customer of May 9 paid		
	26	Cash	500	
		Accounts Receivable		500
		The customer of May 3 paid for merchandise		

2.

		General Journal		
Date		Description	Debit	Credit
Dec.	31	Sales	100,000	
		Merchandise Inventory	8,000	
		Purchases Discounts	500	
		Purchases Returns and Allowances	500	
		Income Summary		109,000
		To close out nominal accounts with credit balances, and to establish the ending inventory		
	31	Income Summary	81,500	
		Advertising Expense		5,000
		Freight In		2,000
		Freight Out		4,000
		Merchandise Inventory		10,000
		Rent Expense		3,000
		Sales Returns and Allowances		200
		Sales Discounts		300
		Wages Expense		7,000
		Purchases		50,000
		To close nominal accounts with debit balances, and to close out beginning inventory		
	31	Income Summary	27,500	
		Arthur Jefferson, Capital		27,500
		To close out the income summary account		
	31	Arthur Jefferson, Capital	12,000	
		Arthur Jefferson, Withdrawals		12,000
		To close out withdrawals account		

3.

Jefferson Merchandising Corporation			
Partial Income Statement			
For the Year 19xx			
Gross Sales			$100,000
Less:			
Sales Discounts		$300	
Sales Returns and Allowances		200	500
Net Sales			$ 99,500
Less Cost of Goods Sold			
Merchandise Inventory, Jan. 1		$10,000	
Purchases	$50,000		
Less:			
Purchases Discounts	500		
Purchases Returns and Allowances	500		
	$49,000		
Add Freight In	2,000		
Net Purchases		51,000	
Cost of Goods Available for Sale		$61,000	
Less Merchandise Inventory, Dec. 31		8,000	
Cost of Goods Sold			53,000
Gross Margin on Sales			$46,500

Mammoth Mart
Work Sheet
For the Month Ended March 31, 19xx

Account Name	Trial Balance Debit	Trial Balance Credit	Adjustments Debit	Adjustments Credit	Adjusted Trial Balance Debit	Adjusted Trial Balance Credit	Income Statement Debit	Income Statement Credit	Balance Sheet Debit	Balance Sheet Credit
Cash	1,000				1,000				1,000	
Accounts Receivable	700				700				700	
Merchandise Inventory	400				400		400	620	620	
Prepaid Rent	750			(a) 250	500				500	
Equipment	4,200				4,200				4,200	
Accounts Payable		900				900				900
Marion Valdez, Capital		4,200				4,200				4,200
Sales		9,800				9,800		9,800		
Sales Discounts	300				300		300			
Purchases	3,700				3,700		3,700			
Purchases Returns and Allowances		150				150		150		
Freight In	400				400		400			
Salaries Expense	3,000		(b) 500		3,500		3,500			
Advertising Expense	600				600		600			
Rent Expense			(a) 250		250		250			
Salaries Payable				(b) 500		500				500
Depreciation Expense			(c) 375		375		375			
Accumulated Depreciation, Equipment				(c) 375		375				375
	15,050	15,050	1,125	1,125	15,925	15,925	9,525	10,570	7,020	5,975
Net Income							1,045			1,045
							10,570	10,570	7,020	7,020

SOLUTION TO CROSSWORD PUZZLE

(Chapters 5 and 6)

```
      G       D               W
      R       I               O
 I    O   S       R E V E R S I N G
 N    S   C               K
 C O S T O F G O O D S S O L D
 O    M   U           H
 M    A   N           E           C
 E    R   T   P E R P E T U A L   L
 S    G       E       T           O
 U    I   P U R C H A S E S       S
 M    N       I                   I
 M        C R O S S F O O T       N
 A    N   D                       G
 D E S T I N A T I O N
 R    T   C
 Y
```

Across:
5 REVERSING
6 COST OF GOODS SOLD
8 PERPETUAL
9 PURCHASES
10 CROSSFOOT
12 DESTINATION

Down:
1 GROSS
2 DISCOUNT
3 WORKSHEET
4 INCOME SUMMARY
7 CLOSING
8 PERIODIC

Chapter 7

Matching

1. f	5. n	9. i	12. k
2. b	6. d	10. m	13. g
3. l	7. c	11. e	14. a
4. j	8. h		

Completion

1.

Special-Purpose Journal	Type of Transaction
Purchases journal	Purchase of merchandise on credit
Sales journal	Sale of merchandise on credit
Cash receipts journal	Any collection of cash
Cash payments journal	Any disbursement of cash

2. As each Other Accounts item is recorded in the special-purpose journal, it is immediately posted to its ledger account. The total for "other" items at the end of the month actually represents *several* items, all of which have already been posted.

3. A controlling account is found in the general ledger, and keeps only a running total of all related subsidiary accounts. A subsidiary account keeps the balance for an individual customer or creditor, and is found in the subsidiary ledger.

4. a. *Cost/benefit principle*—The benefits must match or exceed the costs.
   b. *Control principle*—There must be good internal control.
   c. *Compatibility principle*—It must be a workable system.
   d. *Flexibility principle*—It must be able to accommodate changes.

5. Hardware, software, personnel, and configuration.

6. A double-posting may be found in the general journal and indicates that an account (such as Accounts Receivable or Accounts Payable) has been posted to both the controlling account in the general ledger and the supporting account in the subsidiary ledger.

True-False

1. T
2. F It should be recorded in the general journal (the single-column journal is only for the purchase of *merchandise* on credit).
3. F Posting to subsidiary accounts should be done daily.
4. F No column totals in the general journal should be posted.
5. T
6. F It should have been posted to the accounts *receivable* subsidiary ledger.
7. F It should have only one posting.
8. F Cash sales should be recorded in the cash receipts journal.
9. T
10. T
11. T
12. T
13. F It is an important part of a computer's hardware.
14. T

Multiple-Choice

1. b	**4.** d	**6.** a	**8.** b
2. c	**5.** c	**7.** d	**9.** c
3. c			

Exercises

1. a. J   **d.** CP   **g.** J   **j.** CP
   b. CR   **e.** S   **h.** J   **k.** CR
   c. P   **f.** CP   **i.** J

2.

				Credits			Debits	
Date	Account Credited	Post. Ref.	Other Accts.	Accts. Receiv.	Sales	Sales Disc.	Cash
Feb. 3	Frank Simpson	✓		500		10	490
9	Equipment	135	8,000				8,000
14	Miriam Riley, Capital	311	10,000				10,000
23	Stanley Hall	✓		150			150
28	Sales				25,000		25,000
			18,000	650	25,000	10	43,640
			(✓)	(114)	(411)	(412)	(111)

3. a. Cash payments journal.

  b. The "other accounts" total should have a check (not an account number) below it to signify that it is not posted at the end of the month.

  c. May 1 Paid Vincennes Supply Co. for $800 of supplies previously purchased. Paid within the discount period, receiving a $16 discount.

      May 7 Purchased for cash $2,000 of office equipment from Jeppson Business Supply.

      May 13 Paid for ad placed in the *Daily World*.

      May 19 Paid Olsen Motors for $420 of items previously purchased. Did not pay within the discount period.

  d. 1. The amounts in the Accounts Payable column were posted to the accounts payable subsidiary accounts (Vincennes Supply and Olsen Motors).

    2. The amounts in the Other Accounts column were posted to the general ledger accounts (Office Equipment and Advertising Expense).

    3. The 315 is an error, as already explained. The other numbers refer to the postings of column totals to the general ledger accounts.

Chapter 8

Matching

1. f	**5.** h	**9.** o	**13.** e
2. d	**6.** b	**10.** a	**14.** c
3. n	**7.** l	**11.** g	**15.** i
4. j	**8.** k	**12.** m	

Completion

1. To safeguard a company's assets, to check the accuracy and reliability of its accounting data, to promote operational efficiency, and to encourage adherence to prescribed managerial policies.
2. Separation of duties, sound accounting system, sound personnel policies, reliable personnel, regular internal review.
3. Purchase order, purchase requisition, receiving report, invoice
4. Bank service charge, a customer's NSF check, an error in recording a check (only if underrecorded)

True-False

1. F It increases the probability of accuracy but will not guarantee it.
2. F The reverse is true.
3. T
4. F It is a revenue account when it has a credit balance, an expense account when it has a debit balance.
5. T
6. F This procedure could easily lead to theft.
7. F The supplier is sent a purchase *order*.
8. T
9. T
10. F No entries are made for the outstanding checks.
11. F All purchases may be recorded in the voucher register.
12. T
13. F It is placed in the file in order of the date that payment is due.
14. F It will begin with September 30 balances.
15. F Rotating employees is good internal control because it might uncover theft.

Multiple-Choice

1. d	**3.** c	**5.** a	**7.** a
2. b	**4.** c	**6.** d	

Exercises

1. 1. d	**3.** b	**5.** a	
2. c	**4.** d	**6.** d	

2. $87.50

3.

		General Journal		
Date		Description	Debit	Credit
a.		Petty Cash	75	
		Vouchers Payable		75
		Established petty cash fund, voucher no. 200 (voucher register)		
b.		Purchases	350	
		Vouchers Payable		350
		Purchased merchandise, voucher no. 201 (voucher register)		
c.		Vouchers Payable	75	
		Cash		75
		Paid voucher no. 200 with check no. 601 (check register)		
d.		Vouchers Payable	350	
		Cash		350
		Paid voucher no. 201 with check no. 602 (check register)		
e.		Cab Fare Expense	12	
		Postage Expense	34	
		Miscellaneous Expense	7	
		Cash Over or Short	2	
		Vouchers Payable		55
		To record petty cash expenditures and to replenish fund, voucher no. 202 (voucher register)		
f.		Vouchers Payable	55	
		Cash		55
		Paid voucher no. 202 with check no. 603 (check register)		

SOLUTION TO CROSSWORD PUZZLE

(Chapters 7 and 8)

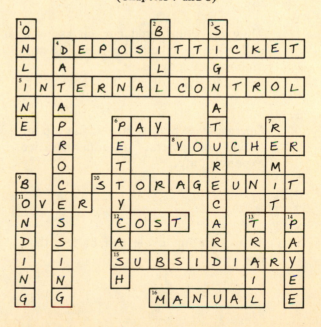

Chapter 9

Matching

1. e	**6.** o	**11.** n	**16.** q
2. m	**7.** d	**12.** p	**17.** k
3. h	**8.** l	**13.** c	**18.** a
4. b	**9.** i	**14.** r	
5. j	**10.** g	**15.** f	

Completion

1.

Business Organization	*Name for Owner's Equity Section*
Sole proprietorship	Owner's Equity
Partnership	Partners' Equity
Corporation	Stockholders' Equity

2. *Profit margin*—Shows net income in relation to sales.

   Return on assets—Shows net income in relation to total assets.

   Return on equity—Shows net income in relation to owners' investment.

   Debt to equity ratio—Shows the proportion of a business financed by creditors versus owners.

3. *Working capital*—Shows current assets minus current liabilities.

   Current ratio—Shows current assets divided by current liabilities.

4. *Consistency and comparability*—Applying the same accounting procedures from one period to the next

   Materiality—The relative importance of an item or event

   Cost/benefit—The cost of providing additional accounting information should not exceed the benefits gained from it.

   Conservatism—Choosing the accounting procedure that will be least likely to overstate assets and income

   Full disclosure—Showing all relevant information in the financial statements or in the footnotes

True-False

1. F They are considered current assets if collection is expected within the normal operating cycle.
2. F Retained Earnings is not a cash account.
3. T
4. F Operating expenses are made up of selling and general and administrative expenses only.
5. T
6. T
7. T
8. T
9. F The operating cycle can be less than one year.
10. F Net worth is merely another term for owner's equity, and does not necessarily equal net asset worth.
11. T
12. F The net income figures will be the same, though they are arrived at differently.
13. T
14. F Working capital equals current assets *minus* current liabilities.
15. T
16. F *Verifiability* is what is being defined.

Multiple-Choice

1. c	4. d	7. c	10. d
2. c	5. a	8. c	
3. b	6. a	9. c	

Exercises

1.
1. d	5. a	9. f	13. x	
2. e	6. c	10. e	14. a	
3. c	7. a	11. d	15. e	
4. g	8. b	12. a		

2.
a. $40,000		d. 12.5%
b. 3:1		e. 16 2/3%
c. 10%		

3. a.

Confrey Company
Income Statement (Multistep)
For the Year Ended December 31, 19xx

Net Sales	$200,000
Less Cost of Goods Sold	150,000
Gross Profit from Sales	$ 50,000
Less Operating Expenses	30,000
Income from Operations	$ 20,000
Add Interest Revenues	2,000
Income before Taxes	$ 22,000
Less Income Tax Expense	5,000
Net Income	$ 17,000
Earnings per Share	$4.86/share

b.

Confrey Company
Income Statement (Single-Step)
For the Year Ended December 31, 19xx

Revenues		
Net Sales	$200,000	
Interest Revenues	2,000	$202,000
Expenses		
Cost of Goods Sold	$150,000	
Operating Expenses	30,000	
Income Tax Expense	5,000	185,000
Net Income		$ 17,000
Earnings per Share		$4.86/share

Chapter 10

Matching

1. j	**5.** p	**9.** i	**13.** b
2. g	**6.** e	**10.** k	**14.** h
3. f	**7.** a	**11.** c	**15.** d
4. m	**8.** l	**12.** o	**16.** n

Completion

1. Percentage of net sales method, accounts receivable aging method, direct charge-off method.
2. It means that the original payee who discounts a note receivable must make good on the note if the maker does not pay at maturity.
3. There would be a debit balance when more accounts are written off (in dollar amounts) than have been provided for in the adjusting entries for estimated uncollectible accounts.

True-False

1. T
2. F It does follow the matching principle.
3. F The balance must be taken into account.
4. T
5. T
6. T
7. F The computation is .05 × 700 × 90/360.
8. T
9. F The payee must make good if the maker defaults.
10. F It is due on February 12.
11. T
12. F Total assets will remain the same.
13. T
14. F The debit is to Allowance for Uncollectible Accounts.
15. T
16. T

Multiple-Choice

1. d	**4.** a	**7.** a	**10.** c
2. b	**5.** d	**8.** b	
3. c	**6.** c	**9.** c	

Exercises

1. **a.** $16.00
   b. $910.00
   c. $43.17
   d. $4.00

2.

		General Journal		
Date		Description	Debit	Credit
Dec.	31	Interest Receivable	75	
		Interest Earned		75
		To record accrued interest on Notes Receivable		
	31	Uncollectible Accounts Expense	24,000	
		Allowance for Uncollectible Accounts		24,000
		To record estimated bad debts		
Jan.	3	Notes Receivable, Kohn	10,000	
		Accounts Receivable, Kohn		10,000
		Ms. Kohn substituted a 30-day, 6% note for her debt		
	8	Allowance for Uncollectible Accounts	1,000	
		Accounts Receivable, O'Brien		1,000
		To write off Mr. O'Brien's account		
	14	Accounts Receivable, Master Card	4,000	
		Sales		4,000
		To record credit card sales for the first two weeks in January		
	18	Cash	10,020	
		Notes Receivable, Kohn		10,000
		Interest Earned		20
		To record discount of Kohn's note		
	24	Cash	3,800	
		Credit Card Discount Expense	200	
		Accounts Receivable, Master Card		4,000
		Received check from Master Card		
	25	Accounts Receivable, O'Brien	600	
		Allowance for Uncollectible Accounts		600
		To reinstate O'Brien's account		
	28	Cash	200	
		Accounts Receivable, O'Brien		200
		Received $200 from O'Brien		
Feb.	2	Accounts Receivable, Kohn	10,060	
		Cash		10,060
		To record payment on Kohn's dishonored note (maturity value plus protest fee)		

SOLUTION TO CROSSWORD PUZZLE

(Chapters 9 and 10)

Crossword solution grid:

- 1 A
- 2 C Y
- 3 C U R R E N T R A T I O R
- 4 D I S C O U N T
- 5 H A R E S
- 6 S C O P E
- 7 C O N S L R
- 8 R E T U R N O N A S S E T S
- 9 N O T E
- 10 P R O T E S T F E E
- 11 E A R R I
- 12 I N T E R N
- 13 A G I T A T E D
- 14 D U R A T I O N
- 15 P R
- 16 L A N D
- 17 S I N G L E S T E P M
- 18 C A S H

Chapter 11

Matching

1. b   4. g   7. f   10. k
2. h   5. j   8. i   11. e
3. d   6. a   9. c

Completion

1. First-in, first-out; last-in, first-out; specific identification; average-cost
2. Item-by-item, by major category, total inventory
3. Gross profit method, retail method
4. The periodic system does not keep detailed records of its inventory, whereas the perpetual system does. Under the periodic system, physical inventory is taken at the end of each period. A physical inventory is not absolutely necessary under perpetual inventory (though it should be done).

True-False

1. T
2. T
3. T
4. T
5. F They belong in the buyer's ending inventory if the buyer has title to the goods.
6. T
7. F Not necessarily. The actual flow of goods is not known, though a flow of costs is assumed.
8. F It will result in the highest income.
9. F Items sold are recorded only at retail.
10. F Cost of goods sold is estimated by subtracting the gross margin percentage of sales from total sales.
11. T
12. F Average cost will result in a higher net income.
13. F Subsidiary files are kept under the perpetual method.

Multiple-Choice

1. b   3. c   5. b   7. d
2. a   4. c   6. a

Exercises

1. a. $6,600; $8,800
   b. $7,200; $8,200
   c. $6,820; $8,580

2. $26,400

3. $30,000

4.

Date	Purchased			Sold			Balance		
	Units	Cost	Total	Units	Cost	Total	Units	Cost	Total
May 1							100	10.00	1,000.00
4	60	12.00	720.00				100	10.00	
							60	12.00	1,720.00
8				50	12.00	600.00	100	10.00	
							10	12.00	1,120.00
17	70	11.00	770.00				100	10.00	
							10	12.00	
							70	11.00	1,890.00
25				70	11.00				
				10	12.00				
				20	10.00	1,090.00	80	10.00	800.00

5.

General Journal				
Date		Description	Debit	Credit
May	17	Merchandise Inventory	770	
		Accounts Payable		770
		To record purchase of inventory		
	25	Cash	2,000	
		Sales		2,000
		To record cash sales		
	25	Cost of Goods Sold	1,090	
		Merchandise Inventory		1,090
		To record cost of merchandise sold		

Chapter 12

Matching

1. b	**6.** j	**11.** f	**16.** d
2. l	**7.** h	**12.** n	**17.** p
3. g	**8.** c	**13.** a	
4. e	**9.** k	**14.** m	
5. o	**10.** i	**15.** q	

Completion

1. Definitely determinable liabilities, estimated liabilities
2. Some examples of contingent liabilities are pending lawsuits, tax disputes, discounted notes receivable, the guarantee of another company's debt, and failure to follow pollution regulations.
3. Income taxes payable, estimated warranty expense, vacation pay. (There are others.)
4. Some examples of definitely determinable liabilities are trade accounts payable, short-term notes payable, dividends payable, sales tax payable, excise tax payable, current portion of long-term debt, accrued liabilities, payroll liabilities, and deferred revenues.
5. FICA taxes, federal income taxes, state income taxes
6. FICA taxes, federal unemployment taxes, state unemployment taxes

True-False

1. F A deferred revenue is a liability on the balance sheet representing an obligation to deliver goods or services.
2. T
3. T
4. T
5. F Sales tax is a definitely determinable liability.
6. F A warranty is an estimated liability.
7. T
8. T
9. F FUTA is assessed against employers only.
10. T
11. F The account is associated with notes whose interest is included in the face amount.
12. T
13. T
14. F An estimate should be recorded for Product Warranty Expense in year 1, the year of the sale.
15. T

Multiple-Choice

1. c	**3.** a	**5.** b	**7.** d
2. d	**4.** d	**6.** c	**8.** a

Exercises

1.

		General Journal		
Date		Description	Debit	Credit
Dec.	31	Product Warranty Expense	525	
		Estimated Product Warranty Liability		525
		To record estimated warranty expense for washing machines		
Apr.	9	Estimated Product Warranty Liability	48	
		Parts, Wages Payable, etc.		48
		To record the repair of a washing machine		

2.

		General Journal		
Date		Description	Debit	Credit
May	11	Office Salaries Expense	260.00	
		FICA Taxes Payable		18.20
		Union Dues Payable		5.00
		State Income Taxes Payable		8.00
		Federal Income Taxes Payable		52.00
		Salaries Payable		176.80
		To record payroll liabilities and salaries expense for Frank Nelson		
	11	Payroll Taxes Expense	27.04	
		FICA Taxes Payable		18.20
		Federal Unemployment Taxes Payable		1.82
		State Unemployment Taxes Payable		7.02
		To record payroll taxes on Nelson's earnings		

SOLUTION TO CROSSWORD PUZZLE

(Chapters 11 and 12)

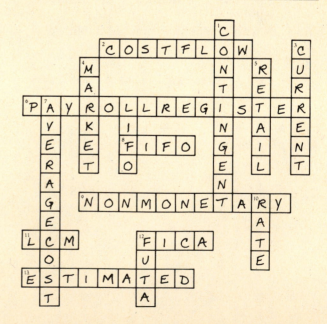

Chapter 13

Matching

1. e	5. l	9. d	13. m
2. f	6. i	10. j	14. c
3. n	7. a	11. b	15. k
4. g	8. h	12. o	

Completion

1. Depreciation Expense is an annual charge that appears in the income statement. Accumulated Depreciation is the sum of all past charges to depreciation expense, and is a contra account to the corresponding asset on the balance sheet.
2. Amortization, depreciation, depletion
3. When cash received equals the carrying value of the asset sold
4. Physical deterioration, obsolescence
5. Cost of oil well. Estimated residual value of oil well. Estimated barrels to be removed over life of well. Actual barrels removed and sold during that year.

True-False

1. T
2. T
3. T
4. F Depreciation is a process of allocation, not valuation.
5. F The wearing out of a machine is irrelevant in computing depreciation.
6. T
7. T
8. T
9. F Depreciation expense will be $1,000 in the second year also.
10. T
11. T
12. F A gain or loss should not be recorded under the income tax method.
13. F Accumulated Depreciation, Machinery would be debited, not credited.
14. T
15. F It will result in more net income.
16. F The production method most resembles the depletion computation.
17. F The carrying value will never reach zero under this method.
18. F The details should be included in the subsidiary ledger, not in the controlling account.
19. T

Multiple-Choice

1. c	3. d	5. c	7. b
2. a	4. d	6. b	8. b

Exercises

1. | | *Depreciation Expense* | *Accumulated Depreciation* | *Carrying Value* |
    |---|---|---|---|
    | a. | $4,800 | $ 9,600 | $16,400 |
    | b. | $6,400 | $14,400 | $11,600 |
    | c. | $6,240 | $16,640 | $ 9,360 |

2. $2,250 $\left(\dfrac{\$35,000 - \$5,000}{100,000 \text{ toys}} \times 7,500 \text{ toys} \right)$

3.

	General Journal			
Date		**Description**	**Debit**	**Credit**
Oct. 12		Machinery (new)	23,000	
		Accumulated Depreciation, Machinery	17,000	
		Loss on Trade-in of Machinery	500	
		Cash		15,500
		Machinery (old)		25,000
		To record trade-in of machine, following		
		APB Opinion No. 29		
12		Machinery (new)	23,500	
		Accumulated Depreciation, Machinery	17,000	
		Cash		15,500
		Machinery (old)		25,000
		To record trade-in of machine following		
		income tax rulings		

*Under this method, losses are recognized but gains are not. For income tax purposes, neither gains nor losses are recognized.

4.

	General Journal			
Date		**Description**	**Debit**	**Credit**
Dec. 31		Coal Inventory	10,000	
		Depletion Expense	30,000	
		Accumulated Depletion, Coal Mine		40,000
		To record depletion of coal mine for 19xx		

Chapter 14

Matching

1. f	5. n	9. h	13. c
2. i	6. d	10. a	14. m
3. l	7. e	11. g	
4. b	8. j	12. k	

True-False

1. F A *trademark* is a name or symbol that may be used only by its owner.
2. T
3. F Accounts payable is a monetary item.
4. T
5. F Research and development should be charged as expense in the year incurred.
6. T
7. T
8. F It is an example of a capital expenditure.

9. F The carrying value will increase because Accumulated Depreciation is debited (decreases).
10. F The two principal types of price changes are changes in specific price levels and changes in general price levels.
11. T
12. T
13. F They must present both.

Multiple-Choice

1. c	3. d	5. a
2. b	4. d	6. a

Exercises

1. Goodwill = $112,500 ($9,000 ÷ 8%)

2. a. C   d. C   f. R   h. C
   b. R   e. C   g. C   i. R
   c. R

3. a. Loss
   b. $26,000

Completion

1. A capital expenditure is recorded as an asset and charged to expense over the years in which it benefits the company. A revenue expenditure benefits the current period only, and is immediately charged to expense.
2. Cash, all receivables, all payables.

SOLUTION TO CROSSWORD PUZZLE

(Chapters 13 and 14)

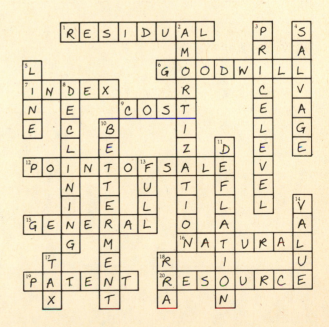

Chapter 15

Matching

1. e	**4.** b	**7.** f	**10.** l
2. k	**5.** c	**8.** i	**11.** d
3. j	**6.** h	**9.** a	**12.** g

Completion

1. Withdrawal of a partner, bankruptcy of a partner, incapacity of a partner, death of a partner, admission of a new partner, retirement of a partner, expiration of partnership agreement
2. Selling partnership assets, paying off partnership liabilities, distributing the remaining assets to the partners
3. Ease of formation and dissolution, ability to pool capital and individual talents, avoidance of the corporation's tax burden, freedom and flexibility of its partners' actions
4. Limited life, mutual agency, unlimited liability, capital limitation, difficulty of transferring ownership interest

True-False

1. F A partnership does not have to be in writing to be legal.
2. T
3. T
4. F Losses would also be shared in a 3:2 ratio.
5. F A net loss occurs only when expenses exceed revenues for the period.
6. T
7. T
8. F D's capital account is credited for $20,000.
9. F The original partners' capital accounts are increased in their stated ratio.
10. F The original partners' accounts will decrease in their stated ratio.
11. T
12. F The partners would be paid according to their capital balances.
13. T
14. F The remaining partners absorb the deficit, but do not contribute personal assets.

Multiple-Choice

1. b	**3.** c	**5.** c	**7.** d
2. c	**4.** a	**6.** c	

Exercises

1. **a.** A = \$14,500 (10,000 + 3,000 + 1,500)
     B = \$13,000 (10,000 + 2,000 + 1,000)
     C = \$13,000 (10,000 + 2,500 + 500)

   b. A = \$7,000 (10,000 + 3,000 − 6,000)
     B = \$8,000 (10,000 + 2,000 − 4,000)
     C = \$10,500 (10,000 + 2,500 − 2,000)

   c. A = (\$8,000) (10,000 + 3,000 − 21,000)
     B = (\$2,000) (10,000 + 2,000 − 14,000)
     C = \$5,500 (10,000 + 2,500 − 7,000)

2. D = \$0 (7,000 − 10,000 + 3,000 deficit absorbed by other partners)
   E = \$7,200 (15,000 − 6,000 − 1,800)
   F = \$14,800 (20,000 − 4,000 − 1,200)

3.

	General Journal		
Date	Description	Debit	Credit
a.	Cash	12,000	
	G, Capital	800	
	H, Capital	800	
	I, Capital	400	
	J, Capital		14,000
	To record purchase of one-third interest by J		
b.	Cash	15,000	
	J, Capital		15,000
	To record purchase of one-third interest by J		
c.	Cash	21,000	
	G, Capital		1,600
	H, Capital		1,600
	I, Capital		800
	J, Capital		17,000
	To record purchase of one-third interest by J		

Chapter 16

Matching

1. f	5. j	9. g	13. d
2. o	6. l	10. a	14. h
3. i	7. e	11. p	15. b
4. k	8. m	12. n	16. c

Completion

1. Separate legal entity, limited liability, ease of capital generation, ease of transfer of ownership, lack of mutual agency, continuous existence, centralized authority and responsibility, professional management
2. Government regulation, double taxation, limited liability, separation of ownership and control
3. Contributed capital, retained earnings
4. a. *Cumulative*—Unpaid back dividends are carried over to the next year.
   b. *Noncumulative*—Unpaid dividends of one year are not carried over to the next year.
   c. *Participating*—Its holders are entitled to more than the annual fixed amount, in certain cases.
   d. *Convertible*—The preferred stock may be exchanged for a set number of common stock shares.
   e. *Callable*—The corporation may buy back the stock at a specified price.

True-False

1. T
2. T
3. T
4. F Organization costs are normally amortized over the early years of a corporation's life.
5. T
6. T
7. F It may.
8. T
9. F Par value has no necessary relation to market value (worth).
10. F Stockholders' equity remains the same when cash is received.
11. T
12. F No stockholders are ever guaranteed dividends.
13. F Common stock is considered the residual equity of a corporation.
14. T
15. T
16. F A contributed capital account should be credited.

Multiple-Choice

1. d	4. a	6. c	8. d
2. a	5. b	7. b	9. b
3. c			

Exercises

1. Preferred stockholders receive $18,000 (1,000 × $100 × 6% × 3 years). Common stockholders receive $33,000 ($51,000 − $18,000).

2. Preferred = ($100,000 par × 6%) + 2/3 (42,000 remainder*) = $34,000.
Common = ($50,000 par × 6%) + 1/3 ($42,000 remainder*) = $17,000.

*Remainder = $51,000 minus 6% (that is, $9,000) given to preferred and common. Remainder is shared based on relative total par value outstanding.

3.

General Journal				
Date		Description	Debit	Credit
May	1	Subscriptions Receivable, Common	70,000	
		Common Stock Subscribed		50,000
		Paid-in Capital in Excess of Par Value		20,000
		Accepted subscriptions for 1,000 shares of $50 par-value common stock at $70 per share		
	1	Cash	14,000	
		Subscriptions Receivable, Common		14,000
		Collected 20% down payment on stock subscriptions		
June	3	Cash	28,000	
		Subscriptions Receivable, Common		28,000
		Collected 40% installment on stock subscriptions		
	18	Cash	28,000	
		Subscriptions Receivable, Common		28,000
		Collected remaining 40% on stock subscriptions		
	18	Common Stock Subscribed	50,000	
		Common Stock		50,000
		Issued 1,000 shares of $50 par-value common stock		

4.

Total stockholders' equity		$680,000
Less:		
Par value of outstanding preferred stock	$200,000	
Dividends in arrears	28,000	
Equity allocated to preferred shareholders		228,000
Equity pertaining to common shareholders		$452,000

Book value per share:
Preferred stock = $228,000/4,000 shares = $57 per share
Common stock = $452,000/30,000 shares = $15.07 per share

SOLUTION TO CROSSWORD PUZZLE

(Chapters 15 and 16)

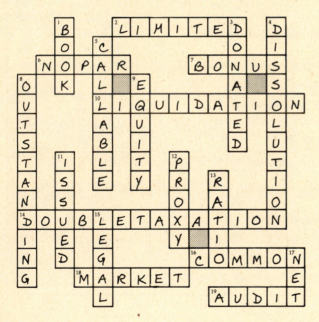

Chapter 17

Matching

1. j	6. b	11. p	16. h
2. c	7. n	12. d	17. g
3. r	8. f	13. o	18. q
4. e	9. i	14. a	
5. m	10. l	15. k	

Completion

1. Net loss from operations, cash dividend declaration, stock dividend declaration, certain prior period adjustments, and certain treasury stock transactions.
2. A stock split changes par or stated value, whereas a stock dividend does not. A stock dividend transfers retained earnings to contributed capital, whereas a stock split does not.
3. It must be unusual in nature. It must occur infrequently.
4. Treasury stock is stock that has been both issued and repurchased by the corporation. Unissued stock has never been issued.

True-False

1. T
2. F Appropriated Retained Earnings is not a cash account.
3. F Total assets and total liabilities decrease.
4. F Each stockholder owns the same percentage as before.
5. T
6. F Its main purpose is to increase marketability by causing a decrease in the market price. The decrease in par value is more a by-product of a stock split.
7. T
8. F Paid-in Capital, Treasury Stock Transactions should be recorded for the excess of issue price over cost.
9. F Treasury stock is listed in the Stockholders' Equity section, as a deduction.
10. F It does not because it is not an unusual and infrequently occurring event.
11. F Extraordinary items should appear on the income statement.
12. T
13. F It is classified as part of contributed capital.
14. T
15. F The net of taxes amount is less than $20,000.
16. F They must be held for more than twelve months to be classified as long-term capital assets.

Multiple-Choice

1. a	4. c	6. b	8. c
2. c	5. d	7. a	9. b
3. d			

Exercises

1.

		General Journal		
Date		Description	Debit	Credit
Sept.	*1*	Cash	1,200,000	
		Common Stock		1,000,000
		Paid-in Capital in Excess of Par Value		200,000
		To record issue of common stock		
Dec.	*31*	Income Summary	800,000	
		Retained Earnings		800,000
		To close out net income for the 4-month period		
Jan.	*10*	Dividends	25,000	
		Cash Dividends Payable		25,000
		To record declaration of cash dividend		
	31	No entry		
Feb.	*20*	Cash Dividend Payable	25,000	
		Cash		25,000
		To record payment of cash dividend		
Mar.	*7*	Retained Earnings	65,000	
		Common Stock Distributable		50,000
		Paid-in Capital in Excess of Par Value		15,000
		To record declaration of stock dividend		
	30	No entry		
Apr.	*13*	Common Stock Distributable	50,000	
		Common Stock		50,000
		To record distribution of stock dividend		

2.

		General Journal		
Date		Description	Debit	Credit
Jan.	2	All 50,000 shares of Quigley's stock have been split, 2 for 1, resulting in the reduction in par value to $5 per share and in the issuance of 50,000 additional shares of stock.		
	12	Treasuring Stock, Common	300,000	
		Cash		300,000
		To record purchase of treasury stock		
	18	Retained Earnings	70,000	
		Retained Earnings Appropriated for Purchase of Building		70,000
		To record the appropriation of retained earnings		
	19	Dividends Declared	95,000	
		Cash Dividends Payable		95,000
		To record declaration of cash dividend		
	30	Cash	130,000	
		Treasury Stock, Common		120,000
		Paid-in Capital, Treasury Stock Transactions		10,000
		To record reissue of treasury stock		
	31	Cash Dividends Payable	95,000	
		Cash		95,000
		To record payment of cash dividend		

3.

	Primary	Fully Diluted
Net income	$360,000	$360,000
Less dividend on preferred stock	60,000	–
Income applicable to common stock	$300,000	$360,000
Common stock for primary earnings per share	100,000	
Common stock for fully diluted EPS:		
Common stock		100,000
Dilutive securities (30,000 × 2)		60,000
		160,000
Earnings per share	$3.00	$2.25

4.

Net operating income before taxes		$100,000
Less income tax expense		40,000
Income before extra-ordinary item		60,000
Extraordinary lightning loss	$30,000	
Less applicable tax	(12,000)	18,000
Net income (loss)		$ 42,000

Chapter 18

Matching

1. i	**6.** t	**11.** e	**16.** s
2. d	**7.** j	**12.** m	**17.** n
3. q	**8.** f	**13.** l	**18.** h
4. a	**9.** c	**14.** b	**19.** k
5. o	**10.** r	**15.** g	**20.** p

Completion

1. A debenture is an unsecured bond, whereas an indenture is the contract between the bondholder and the corporation.
2. A premium would probably be received when the bond's interest rate is higher than the market rate for similar bonds at the time of the issue.
3. Interest = principal $\times$ rate $\times$ time.

True-False

1. T
2. T
3. F Bond interest must be paid on each interest date. It is not something that the board of directors declares.
4. T
5. F It will be less than cash recorded.
6. T
7. F Bond Interest Expense is credited.
8. T
9. F The trustee will have a larger sinking fund to invest in year 5 than in year 2, resulting in a larger increase in year 5.
10. T
11. T
12. F The premium amortized will increase in amount each year.
13. F They are classified as long-term investments.
14. T
15. T
16. T

Multiple-Choice

1. d	**3.** a	**5.** c	**7.** b
2. c	**4.** d	**6.** b	**8.** c

Exercises

1. a. $9,000 ($600,000 − $591,000)
   b. $21,000 ($600,000 $\times$ 7% $\times$ ½)
   c. $21,450 $\left(\$21,000 + \dfrac{\$9,000}{20}\right)$
   d. $593,700 ($600,000 − $6,300)

2. **a.** $550,000 ($500,000 × 110%)

   b. $17,500 ($500,000 × 7% × ½)

   c. $16,500 ($550,000 × 6% × ½)

   d. $1,000 ($17,500 − $16,500)

   e. $549,000 ($550,000 − $1,000)

3.

Interest payments ($600,000 × 8% × 10)	$480,000
Premium on bonds payable ($600,000 × 6%)	36,000
Total interest costs	$444,000 ($44,400/year)

4.

	General Journal		
Date	Description	Debit	Credit
19x1	Income Tax Expense	24,000	
	Deferred Income Taxes	8,000	
	Current Income Taxes Payable		32,000
	To record income taxes for 19x1		
19x2	Income Tax Expense	12,000	
	Deferred Income Taxes		4,000
	Current Income Taxes Payable		8,000
	To record income taxes for 19x2		
19x3	Income Tax Expense	28,000	
	Deferred Income Taxes		4,000
	Current Income Taxes Payable		24,000
	To record income taxes for 19x3		

SOLUTION TO CROSSWORD PUZZLE

(Chapters 17 and 18)

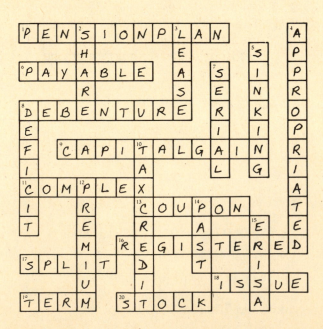

Chapter 19

Matching

1. d   3. g   5. a   7. h
2. b   4. e   6. f   8. c

Completion

1. Net income, sale of a noncurrent asset, long-term borrowing, issuance of capital stock
2. Net loss, purchase of a noncurrent asset, declaration of cash dividends, purchase or retirement of stock, retirement or reclassification of a long-term debt
3. The conversion of a convertible security into common stock. The issuance of common stock or bonds in exchange for a long-term asset. (There are other possibilities.)
4. Any two of the following examples would be a correct answer: depreciation of a plant asset, amortization of an intangible asset, depletion of a natural resource

True-False

1. F Working capital would stay the same.
2. T
3. T
4. T
5. T
6. F Depreciation expense is what must be added back.
7. F It is a use of working capital when declared, not when paid.
8. F It decreases working capital.
9. F It utilizes a comparative balance sheet.
10. F There are several other circumstances which would result in a $10,000 increase, such as the sale of land and the subsequent purchase of land for $10,000 more.
11. T
12. F The Dividends Payable account would not appear in the work sheet.
13. F It must accompany the statement to conform with generally accepted accounting principles.
14. F It is possible that it may result in an increase in working capital when items such as depreciation are added back.
15. T

Multiple-Choice

1. c   4. b   7. d   10. b
2. d   5. c   8. a
3. b   6. c   9. d

Exercises

1.

Dexter Corporation
Comparative Balance Sheets
As of December 31, 19x1, and December 31, 19x2

	19x2	19x1	Increase (Decrease) in Working Capital
Assets			
Cash	$ 2,000	$16,000	$(14,000)
Short-term Investments	0	10,000	(10,000)
Accounts Receivable	8,000	2,000	6,000
Inventory	32,000	8,000	24,000
Buildings	60,100	24,000	
Accumulated Depreciation, Buildings	(13,200)	(9,000)	
Total Assets	$88,900	$51,000	
Liabilities and Stockholders' Equity			
Notes Payable	$10,000	$ 1,600	$ (8,400)
Accounts Payable	6,400	9,400	3,000
Bonds Payable	24,000	0	
Common Stock	40,000	30,000	
Retained Earnings	8,500	10,000	
Total Liabilities and Stockholders' Equity	$88,900	$51,000	
Increase (Decrease) in Working Capital			$ 600

2.

Lewis Corporation
Statement of Changes in Financial Position
For the Year Ended December 31, 19x1

Sources of Working Capital		
Operations		
Net Income		$200,000
Add Expenses Not Requiring Outlay of Working Capital in the Current Period:		
Depreciation Expense		10,000
Working Capital Provided from Operations		210,000
Other Sources of Working Capital		
Proceeds from Sale of Machinery	13,500	
Issuance of Common Stock	7,000	20,500
Total Sources of Working Capital		230,500
Uses of Working Capital		
Purchase of Land	80,000	
Declaration of Dividend	100,000	
Purchase of Office Equipment	7,000	
Reclassification of Bonds Payable	10,000	
Total Uses of Working Capital		197,000
Increase (Decrease) in Working Capital		$ 33,500

Chapter 20

Matching

1. e	5. n	9. d	13. o
2. k	6. l	10. j	14. c
3. b	7. i	11. a	15. g
4. h	8. f	12. p	16. m

Completion

1.

Classification	Method
Noninfluential and noncontrolling	Cost
Influential but noncontrolling	Equity
Controlling	Equity (also, consolidate)

2. When the exchange rate changes between the transaction date and the payment date, and foreign currency changes hands, the domestic company would record an exchange gain or loss.
3. Under the cost method, Dividend Income is recorded when dividends are received. Under the equity method, the investment account is credited (decreased).
4. When the cost exceeds the book value of the net assets purchased, any excess that is not assigned to specific assets and liabilities should be recorded as goodwill.
5. Intercompany items are eliminated to avoid misleading consolidated financial statements. For example, if intercompany receivables and payables were (incorrectly) included in consolidated financial statements, that portion would represent the amount that the combined companies owed themselves.

True-False

1. T
2. F The investor would do that under the equity method.
3. F Over 50 percent is the requirement for consolidated financial statements.
4. T
5. F The subsidiary's earnings from the date of acquisition only are included.
6. T
7. F A minority interest should be reported in the stockholders' equity section.
8. T
9. T
10. T
11. F Purchases of goods and services from outsiders should not be eliminated.
12. T
13. T
14. T
15. F Although these two organizations have members from many countries, their pronouncements have yet to gain worldwide acceptance.
16. T
17. T
18. F The reverse is true.

Multiple-Choice

1. a	3. d	5. b	7. d
2. b	4. a	6. b	8. d

Exercises

1.

Accounts Debited	Amount	Accounts Credited	Amount
Common Stock (Carter)	$60,000	Investment in Carter Corporation	$165,000
Retained Earnings (Carter)	90,000	Minority Interest	30,000
Building	10,000		
Goodwill	35,000		

2.

		General Journal		
Date		Description	Debit	Credit
		Cash	12,000	
		Dividend Income		12,000
		To record cash dividend from Airdrome*		
		Cash	15,000	
		Investment in Wilkins Company		15,000
		To record cash dividend from Wilkins		
		Investment in Wilkins Company	19,500	
		Income, Wilkins Company Investment		19,500
		To recognize 30 percent of income		
		reported by Wilkins Company		

*Airdrome earnings of $110,000 are irrelevant since Fairfax is using the cost method to account for the investment.

3.

		General Journal		
Date		Description	Debit	Credit
		Accounts Receivable, Mexican Company	5,000	
		Sales		5,000
		To record sale of merchandise		
		Cash	4,500	
		Exchange Gain or Loss	500	
		Accounts Receivable, Mexican Company		5,000
		To record receipt of payment		

4.

		General Journal		
Date		Description	Debit	Credit
Mar.	*1*	Investment in Bonds	9,600.00	
		Accrued Interest Receivable	140.00	
		Cash		9,740.00
		To record purchase of bonds.		
July	*1*	Cash	420.00	
		Investment in Bonds ($288 – 280)	8.00	
		Accrued Interest Receivable		140.00
		Interest Earned ($9600 × 9% × 4/12)		288.00
		To record semiannual interest and amortization of discount.		
Dec.	*31*	Accrued Interest Receivable	420.00	
		Investment in Bonds	12.36	
		Interest Earned		432.36
		To record accrued interest and amortization of discount.		
Jan.	*1*	Cash	420.00	
		Accrued Interest Receivable		420.00
		To record receipt of interest.		
Mar.	*1*	Investment in Bonds*	4.31	
		Interest Earned		4.31
		To amortize 2 months' interest.		
	1	Cash ($9500 – 200 + 140)	9,440.00	
		Loss on Sale of Investments	124.67	
		Investment in Bonds		9,424.67
		Interest Earned		140.00
		To record sale of bonds.		
		*$9,620.36 × 9% × 1/6 = $144.31		
		10,000 × 8.4% × 1/6 = 140.00		
		$ 4.31		

SOLUTION TO CROSSWORD PUZZLE

(Chapters 19 and 20)

```
 ¹W  O  R  K  I  N  ²G  C  A  P  I  T  A  L
                      O
    ³M  I  N  O  R  I  T  Y           ⁴C
 ⁵H           N              ⁶E     ⁷U  ⁸E
 ⁹E  X  C  H ¹⁰A  N  G  E     L        R  Q
 L           L     P        I        R  U
 D           L     U        M        E  I
          ¹¹C      B        I        N  T
 ¹²P      A        L        N        C  Y
    ¹³S  U  B  S  I  D  I  A  R  Y
 A      H         C        T
 R      F              ¹⁴I  F  A ¹⁵C
¹⁶I  N  F  L  U  E  N  C  E     O     O
 T      O                 O     S
 W         ¹⁷F  U  N  D  S     T
```

Chapter 21

Matching

1. g	5. j	8. i	11. m
2. b	6. f	9. k	12. a
3. l	7. h	10. d	13. c
4. e			

Completion

1. Profit margin, asset turnover, return on assets, return on equity, earnings per share
2. Horizontal analysis presents absolute and percentage changes in specific financial statement items from one year to the next. Vertical analysis, on the other hand, presents the percentage relationship of individual items on the statement to a total within the statement.
3. Rule-of-thumb measures, analysis of past performance of the company, comparison with industry norms.
4. The risk of total loss is far less with several investments than with one investment because only a rare set of economic circumstances could cause several different investments to suffer large losses all at once.

True-False

1. T
2. F Common-size financial statements show relationships between items in terms of percentages, not dollars.
3. F The current ratio will increase.
4. T
5. F It equals the cost of goods sold divided by average inventory.
6. F The reverse is true, because the price/ earnings ratio depends upon the earnings per share amount.
7. F Interest is not added back.
8. T
9. F The higher the debt to equity ratio, the greater the risk.
10. F Receivable turnover measures how many times, on the average, the receivables were converted into cash during the period.
11. T
12. T
13. F It is a market test ratio.
14. F Sales would be labeled 100 percent.
15. T
16. T
17. T

Multiple-Choice

1. b	4. a	7. b	10. b
2. d	5. a	8. d	
3. c	6. c	9. c	

Exercises

1.

	19x1	19x2	Increase (or Decrease) Amount	Increase (or Decrease) Percentage
Sales	$200,000	$250,000	$50,000	25%
Cost of goods sold	120,000	144,000	24,000	20%
Gross margin	$ 80,000	$106,000	26,000	32.5%
Operating expenses	50,000	62,000	12,000	24%
Income before income taxes	$ 30,000	$ 44,000	14,000	46.7%
Income taxes	8,000	16,000	8,000	100%
Net income	$ 22,000	$ 28,000	6,000	27.3%

2. **a.** 2.0 ($500,000/$250,000)

   b. 1.3 $\left(\dfrac{\$500,000 - \$180,000}{\$250,000} \right)$

   c. $5 ($106,000/21,200)

   d. 1.9 times ($350,000/$180,000)

   e. 12.0% ($106,000/$880,000)

   f. 22.1% ($106,000/$480,000)

   g. 6.0 ($600,000/$100,000)

   h. 60.8 days (365/6.0)

   i. 17.7% ($106,000/$600,000)

   j. .68 ($600,000/$880,000)

   k. 8 times ($40/$5)

Chapter 22

Matching

1. g	6. m	11. k	16. t
2. n	7. h	12. l	17. j
3. f	8. p	13. o	18. d
4. c	9. q	14. r	19. e
5. b	10. s	15. i	20. a

Completion

1. Materials inventory, work in process inventory, finished goods inventory
2. Direct materials, direct labor, factor overhead
3. A cost is considered direct when it can be conveniently and economically traced to a specific product or other cost objective.
4. Product costing information, planning and control information, special reports and analyses
5. Materials inventory, beginning of period
   + Materials purchased
   = Cost of materials available for use
   − Materials inventory, end of period
   = Cost of materials used
6. Cost of materials used
   + Direct labor costs
   + Factory overhead costs
   = Total manufacturing costs

7. Total manufacturing costs
   + Work in process, beginning of period
   = Total cost of work in process during the period
   − Work in process, end of period
   = Cost of goods manufactured
8. Finished goods inventory, beginning of period
   + Cost of goods manufactured
   = Total cost of finished goods available for sale
   − Finished goods inventory, end of period
   = Cost of goods sold

True-False

1. F They are termed *inventory*.
2. T
3. T
4. F Direct labor data for a particular job can be found on a job card.
5. T
6. T
7. T
8. T
9. F The management accountant provides management with information needed for management to make the decisions.
10. T
11. F Materials Inventory is debited.

12. F It must be prepared before the income statement can be prepared.
13. T
14. T
15. F The reverse is true.
16. T
17. F Neither beginning nor ending Finished Goods Inventory will appear in either column.
18. F Advertising is an operating expense, and therefore is not included in the cost of goods sold computation.
19. T
20. F It is closed out with a credit.

Multiple-Choice

1. c	**4.** d	**7.** b	**10.** c
2. c	**5.** a	**8.** a	**11.** a
3. a	**6.** c	**9.** c	**12.** b

Exercises

1.

Finished goods, Jan. 1	$ 75,000
Add cost of goods manufactured	450,000
Cost of goods available for sale	$525,000
Less finished goods, Dec. 31	80,000
Cost of goods sold	$445,000

2.

Spencer Company
Statement of Cost of Goods Manufactured
For the Year Ended December 31, 19xx

Materials used		
Materials inventory, Jan. 1	$ 8,700	
Add materials purchased	168,300	
Cost of materials available for use	$177,000	
Less materials inventory, Dec. 31	32,600	
Cost of materials used		$144,400
Direct labor		142,900
Factory overhead costs		
Depreciation, factory building and equipment	$ 31,800	
Factory insurance	2,300	
Factory utilities expense	26,000	
Indirect labor	42,800	
Other factory costs	12,600	115,500
Total manufacturing costs		$402,800
Add work in process inventory, Jan. 1		34,200
Total cost of work in process during the year		$437,000
Less work in process inventory, Dec. 31		28,700
Cost of goods manufactured		$408,300

3.

a. OH	d. DM	g. DM	i. OH
b. DL	e. OH	h. OH	j. OH
c. OH	f. DL		

SOLUTION TO CROSSWORD PUZZLE

(Chapters 21 and 22)

Crossword puzzle solution grid:

Across:
- 3. PURCHASE ORDER
- 6. JOB CARD
- 7. CURRENT
- 9. MARKET RISK
- 11. TREND
- 13. BETA
- 14. PERIODIC
- 16. OVERHEAD
- 17. EARNINGS
- 18. TIME

Down letters shown in grid:
- 1. Q — QUICK
- 2. R Q — (REQ...)
- 4. R A T I O
- 5. C I —
- 6. M O N S I Z / OMONSIZ
- B K A T I O N — (BREAKTION)
- 8. P R O D U C T
- R I S I T I O N — (REQUISITION)
- 10. V E R T I C A L
- 12. D E R T — (DEBT)

Chapter 23

Matching

1. c   **3.** a   **5.** b   **7.** h
2. e   **4.** f   **6.** d   **8.** g

Completion

1. An underapplication could still occur if the **actual** overhead exceeds the **applied** overhead.
2. Direct materials, direct labor, and applied factory overhead.
3. Close a small difference to Cost of Goods Sold. Divide a large difference among Cost of Goods Sold, Finished Goods Inventory, and Work in Process Inventory.
4. Products such as railroad cars, bridges, wedding invitations, or any other unique or special-order products suggest the use of a job order cost system.

True-False

1. F This can be true only when, in addition, estimated overhead costs equal actual overhead costs for the period.
2. T
3. F It should be divided among Work in Process, Finished Goods, and Cost of Goods Sold.
4. T
5. F A process cost system uses a Work in Process Inventory account for each department.
6. F Indirect costs are charged to Work in Process Inventory through applied overhead.
7. T
8. T
9. F A sale should be recorded when the goods are shipped.
10. F Factory Overhead Control is debited.
11. T
12. F The credit is to Finished Goods Inventory.
13. T
14. F It uses a perpetual inventory system.
15. T

Multiple-Choice

1. d   **3.** d   **5.** a
2. c   **4.** b   **6.** d

Exercises

1. **a.** $1.60/direct labor hour
   b. $.40/direct labor dollar
   c. $240

2.

		General Journal		
Date		Description	Debit	Credit
Dec.	23	Materials Inventory Control	2,950	
		Accounts Payable		2,950
		To record purchase of materials		
	26	Work in Process Inventory Control	800	
		Factory Overhead Control	50	
		Materials Inventory		850
		Issued materials and supplies into production		
	26	Factory Overhead Control	1,200	
		Cash		1,200
		Paid telephone, rent, and utilities bills		
	27	Work in Process Inventory Control	1,200	
		Factory Overhead Control	300	
		Factory Payroll		1,500
		To distribute the factory payroll		
	27	Work in Process Inventory Control	3,600	
		Factory Overhead Applied		3,600
		To apply overhead for the week		
		($3 per direct labor dollar X $1,200 direct labor dollars)		
	29	Finished Goods Inventory Control	3,900	
		Work in Process Inventory Control		3,900
		To record completion of goods		
	30	Cost of Goods Sold	2,000	
		Finished Goods Inventory Control		2,000
		To record the shipment of goods		
	30	Accounts Receivable	3,400	
		Sales		3,400
		To record the sale of goods		
	31	Factory Overhead Applied	150,000	
		Work in Process Inventory Control		3,000
		Finished Goods Inventory Control		1,000
		Cost of Goods Sold		16,000
		Factory Overhead Control		130,000
		To divide overapplication of factory overhead for the year among the accounts		

Chapter 24

Matching

1. d	**3.** f	**5.** e
2. c	**4.** a	**6.** b

Completion

1. Schedule of equivalent production, unit cost analysis schedule, cost summary schedule
2. Units started and completed
   + Units in ending inventory × percentage of completion
   + Units in beginning inventory × (100% − percentage of completion)
   = Equivalent units

3. Cost of goods transferred out of the department and cost of ending Work in Process Inventory
4. Costs attached to units in beginning inventory
   + Costs necessary to complete units in beginning inventory
   + Costs of units started and completed during the period
   = Cost of goods transferred out of the department

True-False

1. F A Work in Process Inventory account is maintained for each department or operation.
2. T
3. T
4. T
5. F Units started and completed are only part of the computation.
6. T
7. F A combined (conversion cost) unit cost figure is computed for direct labor and factory overhead.
8. F Beginning inventory is multiplied by 100 percent minus the percentage of completion in computing equivalent production.

9. F There is much overlap between the last two quantities.
10. T
11. F Equivalent units for materials and conversion costs must be multiplied by their respective unit costs.
12. F Work in Process (Department 2) is debited and Work in Process (Department 1) is credited.
13. T
14. T
15. F It is made in the cost summary schedule.
16. F Production generally flows in a FIFO manner in manufacturing operations when a process cost system is used.

Multiple-Choice

1. b	**3.** d	**5.** a	**7.** b
2. c	**4.** a	**6.** b	**8.** b

Exercises

1.

Morris Manufacturing Company
Schedule of Equivalent Production
For the Month Ended May 31, 19xx

Units—Stage of Completion	Units to Be Accounted For	Equivalent Units	
		Materials	Conversion Costs
Beginning inventory	2,000		
(Materials—100% complete)		0	
(Conversion costs—30% complete)			1,400
Units started and completed	17,000	17,000	17,000
Ending inventory	7,000		
(Materials—100% complete)		7,000	
(Conversion costs—30% complete)			2,100
	26,000	24,000	20,500

2.

Morris Manufacturing Company
Unit Cost Analysis Schedule
For the Month Ended May 31, 19xx

Total Cost Analysis

	Costs from Beginning Inventory	Costs from Current Period	Total Costs to Be Accounted For
Materials	$ 12,000	$114,000	$126,000
Conversion costs	3,000	30,750	33,750
Totals	$ 15,000	$144,750	$159,750

Computation of Equivalent Unit Cost

	Current Period Cost	Equivalent Units	Cost per Equivalent Unit
Materials	$114,000	24,000	$4.75
Conversion costs	30,750	20,500	1.50
Totals	$144,750		$6.25

3.

Morris Manufacturing Company
Cost Summary Schedule
For the Month Ended May 31, 19xx

	Cost of Goods Transferred to Next Department	Cost of Ending Work in Process Inventory
Beginning inventory		
Costs from preceding period	$ 15,000	
Costs to complete this period		
Materials: $0		
Conversion costs: 1,400 units × $1.50	2,100	
Units started and completed		
17,000 units × $6.25	106,250	
Ending Inventory		
Materials: 7,000 units × $4.75		$ 33,250
Conversion costs: 2,100 units × $1.50		3,150
Totals	$123,350	$ 36,400
Computational check		
Costs to next department		$123,350
Costs to ending Work in Process Inventory		36,400
Total costs to be accounted for (unit cost analysis schedule)		$159,750

SOLUTION TO CROSSWORD PUZZLE

(Chapters 23 and 24)

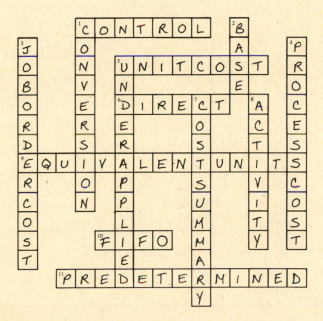

Chapter 25

Matching

1. f	5. p	9. a	13. i
2. l	6. g	10. k	14. e
3. m	7. c	11. d	15. b
4. j	8. n	12. h	16. o

Completion

1. Sales = variable costs + fixed costs
2. Any cost that has both fixed and variable elements, such as telephone expense, electricity expense, water expense, most utilities

True-False

1. T
2. T
3. T
4. F It is a fixed cost because it does not change with volume.
5. F Normal capacity is the most realistic.
6. F Sales = variable costs plus fixed costs, at the break-even point.
7. T
8. T
9. T
10. T
11. F The accounting data will probably be less detailed as they travel upward.
12. F They include only costs incurred before the split-off point.
13. F A cost objective is anything that receives an assigned cost.
14. F The reverse is true.

Multiple-Choice

1. c	4. a	6. a	8. d
2. c	5. d	7. d	9. b
3. b			

Exercises

1. a. 20,000 units
   b. $260,000
   c. $32,000 loss
   d. 32,500 units

2.

Physical Volume Method	Relative Sales Value Method
X = $18,000	X = $ 4,320
Y = $ 6,000	Y = $ 2,880
Z = $12,000	Z = $28,800

3. Dept. 1—$12,500
   Dept. 2—$20,000
   Dept. 3—$10,000
   Dept. 4—$ 7,500

Chapter 26

Matching

1. c	**3.** e	**5.** g	**7.** f
2. h	**4.** b	**6.** a	**8.** d

Completion

1. Long-range objectives and goals principles
   Short-range goals and strategies principles
   Human responsibilities and interaction principles
   Budget housekeeping principles
   Follow-up principles

2. Direct materials usage budget
   Direct materials purchases budget
   Labor hour requirements budget
   Direct labor dollars budget
   Factory overhead budget

True-False

1. F It refers to planning and control of operations.
2. F A master budget is a comprehensive budget, usually for a one-year period.
3. T
4. T
5. F Their main objective is to serve the purpose for which they were created.
6. T
7. F Depreciation expense does not represent a cash outflow and therefore would not be present in the cash budget.
8. T
9. F Even not-for-profit organizations must obtain input from all levels to budget effectively.
10. F Only cash collected from sales (including prior months' sales) would be included as cash receipts.
11. T
12. T

Multiple-Choice

1. d	**3.** c	**5.** d	**7.** b
2. c	**4.** b	**6.** a	**8.** a

Exercises

1.

E & J Company
Production Budget
For the Quarter Ended June 30, 19xx

	April	May	June
Beginning inventory	1,000 units	1,200 units	1,500 units
Add production in units	10,200	12,300	14,400
Units available for sale	11,200	13,500	15,900
Less units sold	10,000	12,000	15,000
Ending inventory	1,200 units	1,500 units	900 units

2.

Rensch Enterprises
Cash Budget
For the Month Ending June 30, 19xx

Cash receipts		
Sales—May	$52,000	
Sales—June	18,000	
Proceeds from loan*	1,000	
Total receipts		$71,000
Cash disbursements		
General and administrative expenses	22,000	
Inventory purchases—May	20,000	
Inventory purchases—June	15,000	
Purchase of office furniture	3,000	
Selling expenses	14,000	
Total disbursements		74,000
Cash increase (decrease)		(3,000)
Cash balance, June 1		7,000
Cash balance, June 30		$ 4,000

*Amount must be derived.

SOLUTION TO CROSSWORD PUZZLE

(Chapters 25 and 26)

```
 ¹C           ²V           ³J
⁴P A R T I ⁵C I P A T I V E   J O I N T
 P       O       R           O
     ⁶C O N T R I B U T I ⁷O N   I
 I       T       A       D   ▨   T
⁸M A S T E R   ⁹B U D G E T
 I       O       L       A
     ¹⁰V O L U M E       L   ¹¹P
 A       L                   E
¹²R E L E V A N T R A ¹³N G E   R
         B           O       I
         L           R       O
¹⁴B R E A K E V E N ¹⁵M I X E D
                     A
¹⁶R E S P O N S I B I L I T Y
```

Chapter 27

Matching

1. d	4. c	7. a	10. l
2. b	5. g	8. j	11. h
3. k	6. i	9. e	12. f

Completion

1. Direct materials price standard, direct materials quantity standard, direct labor time standard, direct labor rate standard, standard variable overhead rate, standard fixed overhead rate

2. A smaller quantity of direct materials is used than was expected for a particular level of volume.
3. A higher wage is paid than is standard for an employee doing a particular job.

True-False

1. F The application basis must be in terms of standard measures.
2. F They are used in establishing direct labor time standards.
3. T
4. F It is a part of the control function.
5. T
6. T
7. T
8. T
9. F They are the responsibility of the personnel department.
10. T
11. T
12. F The individual variances provide more information than the total variance.
13. T
14. T

Multiple-Choice

1. b	3. a	5. a	7. c
2. c	4. d	6. b	8. a

Exercises

1.

Porcelain	$ .40
Red paint	.05
Blue paint	.02
Molding department wages	.12
Painting department wages	.30
Variable overhead (.08 hr. × $3/hr.)	.24
Fixed overhead (.08 hr. × $2/hr.)	.16
Standard cost of one dish	$1.29

2.

Los Feliz Company
Flexible Budget
For the Year Ended December 31, 19xx

Cost Item	Unit Levels of Activity			Variable Cost per Unit
	10,000	15,000	20,000	
Direct labor	$ 45,000	$ 67,500	$ 90,000	$4.50
Direct materials	12,500	18,750	25,000	1.25
Variable overhead	27,500	41,250	55,000	2.75
	85,000	127,500	170,000	$8.50
Fixed overhead	50,000	50,000	50,000	
Total costs	$135,000	$177,500	$220,000	

Flexible budget formula: ($8.50 × units produced) + $50,000

3. a. $13,140 \text{ F} = \left(\$.60 - \dfrac{\$381,060}{657,000}\right) \times 657,000$

b. $4,200 \text{ U} = (657,000 - 650,000) \times \$.60$

c. $1,105 \text{ U} = \left(\dfrac{\$100,555}{22,100} - \$4.50\right) \times 22,100$

d. $11,700 \text{ U} = [22,100 - (65,000 \times .3)] \times \$4.50$

e. $8,350 \text{ U} = \$57,000 - [3,800 + (19,500 \times \$2.30)]$

f. $100 \text{ F} = [\$3,800 + (19,500 \times \$2.30)] - \left[19,500 \times \left(\$2.30 + \dfrac{\$3,800}{19,000}\right)\right]$

Chapter 28

Matching

1. b	4. e	6. a	8. d
2. h	5. f	7. g	9. i
3. c			

Completion

1. Discovering the problem or need, identifying the alternative courses of action, analyzing the effects of each alternative on operations, selecting the best alternative, judging the success of the decision
2. Identifying the need for a facility, evaluating different courses of action, preparing the reports for management, choosing the best alternative, rationing available capital expenditure funds among competing resource needs
3. Cost of capital, corporate return on investment, industry average return on investment, bank interest rate
4. Accounting rate of return method, payback method, present value method
5. Information is relevant when it differs among future alternative courses of action; information is irrelevant when it does not.

True-False

1. F It is acceptable for financial reporting purposes, but variable costing is not.
2. F The reverse is true.
3. F Fixed factory overhead is a product cost under absorption costing.
4. T
5. F The main concern is with the differences in costs and revenues.
6. F Capital budgeting does not deal with obtaining cash; it involves the purchase of plant facilities.
7. F The present value method is one of the more difficult methods to apply.
8. T
9. F The payback period is the *minimum* length of time to recover cost.
10. T
11. F The desired rate of return must be known.
12. T
13. T
14. T
15. F The most beneficial product is the one with the highest contribution margin in relation to capital equipment.

Multiple-Choice

1. b	3. d	5. c	7. b
2. a	4. c	6. d	8. a

1.

	Machine Q	Machine R	Difference (Q – R)
Cost of machine	$10,000	$17,000	($7,000)
Direct labor	16,000	8,000	8,000
Maintenance	300	500	(200)
Electricity savings	(50)	80	(130)
Totals	$26,250	$25,580	$ 670

Machine R should be purchased because of the lower incremental cost ($25,580).

2. a. Payback period = $\dfrac{\$70,000}{\$8,000 + \$14,000}$ = 3.2 years

(The $14,000 in the denominator is depreciation.) Since the minimum payback period is 3 years, the company should not invest in the machine.

b. Accounting rate of return = $\dfrac{\$8,000}{\$70,000}$ = 11.4%

3.

Year	Net Cash Inflow		Present Value Multiplier		Present Value
1	$5,000	X	.862	=	$ 4,310
2	6,000	X	.743	=	4,458
3	6,000	X	.641	=	3,846
4	6,000	X	.552	=	3,312
5	6,000	X	.476	=	2,856
Total					$18,782

The company should not purchase the machine, because the present value of future net cash inflows is less than the cost of the machine.

SOLUTION TO CROSSWORD PUZZLE

(Chapters 27 and 28)

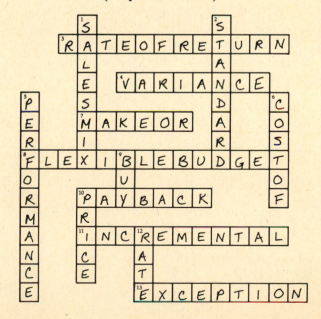